樋口大輔

I'm not only bad at talking but also bad at writing. When I began drawing manga, I realized that I needed to write, too. You never know what can become useful in life. So, while you're young, try and challenge yourself with different things and learn as much as you can. As I write this message, I'm picking up a survival manual...
  – Daisuke Higuchi

Daisuke Higuchi's manga career began in 1992 when the artist was honored with third prize in the 43rd Osamu Tezuka Award. In that same year, Higuchi debuted as creator of a romantic action story titled **Itaru**. In 1998, **Weekly Shonen Jump** began serializing **Whistle!** Higuchi's realistic soccer manga became an instant hit with readers and eventually inspired an anime series, debuting on Japanese TV in May of 2002. The artist is currently working on a yet-to-be-published new series.

**WHISTLE!**
VOL. 4: RE-START

**The SHONEN JUMP Manga Edition**

STORY AND ART BY
DAISUKE HIGUCHI

English Adaptation/Marv Wolfman
Translation/Naomi Kokubo
Touch-up Art & Lettering/Jim Keefe
Cover, Graphics & Layout/Sean Lee
Editor/Eric Searleman

Editor in Chief, Books/Alvin Lu
Editor in Chief, Magazines/Marc Weidenbaum
VP of Publishing Licensing/Rika Inouye
VP of Sales/Gonzalo Ferreyra
Sr. VP of Marketing/Liza Coppola
Publisher/Hyoe Narita

Printed in the U.S.A.

Published by VIZ Media, LLC
P.O. Box 77010
San Francisco, CA 94107

SHONEN JUMP Manga Edition
10 9 8 7 6 5 4 3 2
First printing, February 2005
Second printing, August 2007

www.viz.com

THE WORLD'S
MOST POPULAR MANGA

www.shonenjump.com

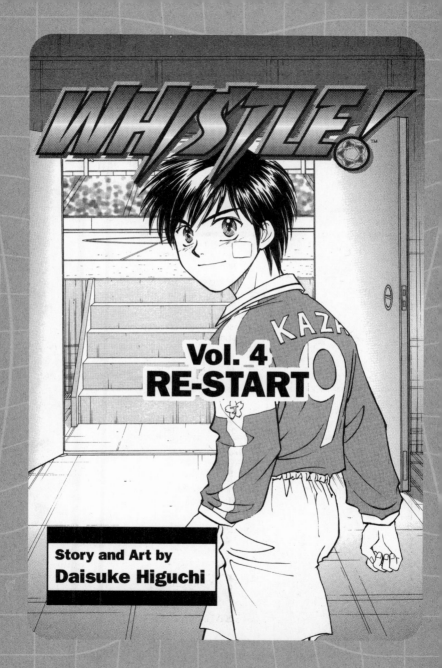

# WHISTLE!

## Vol. 4
## RE-START

**Story and Art by**
**Daisuke Higuchi**

# CHARACTERS

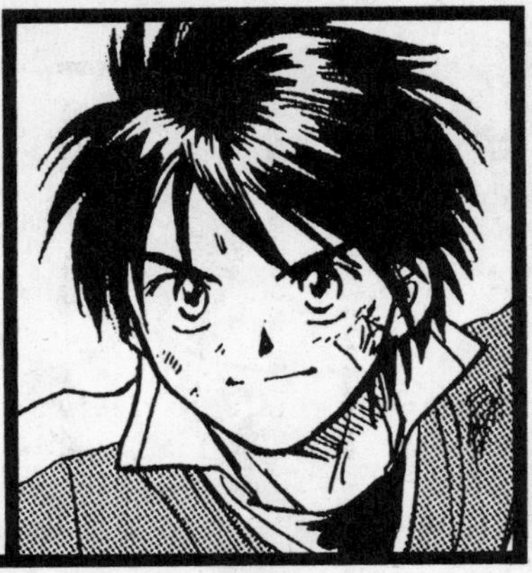

SHŌ KAZAMATSURI

- JOSUI JUNIOR HIGH SOCCER TEAM FORWARD

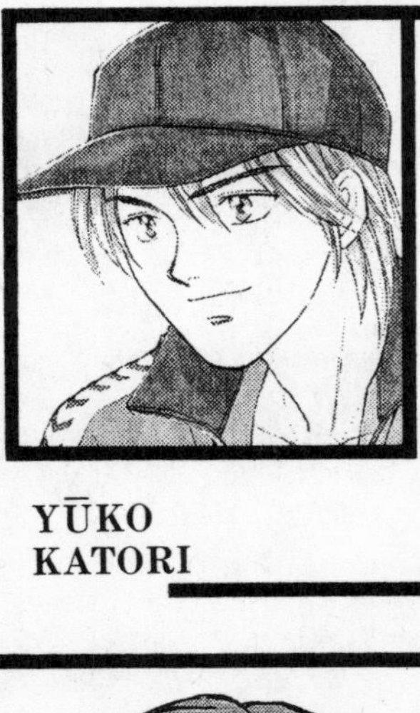

KŌ KAZAMATSURI

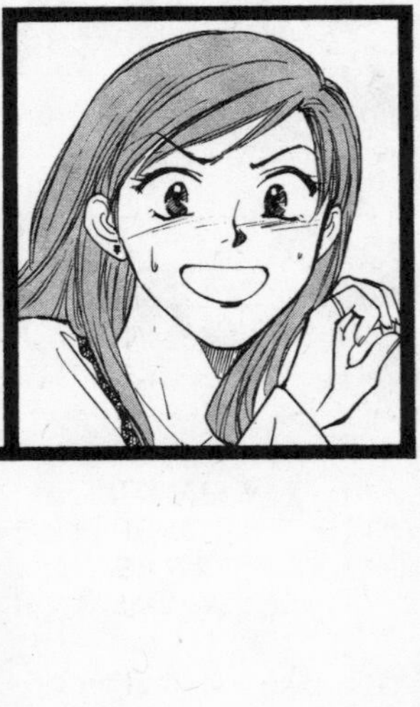

YŪKO KATORI

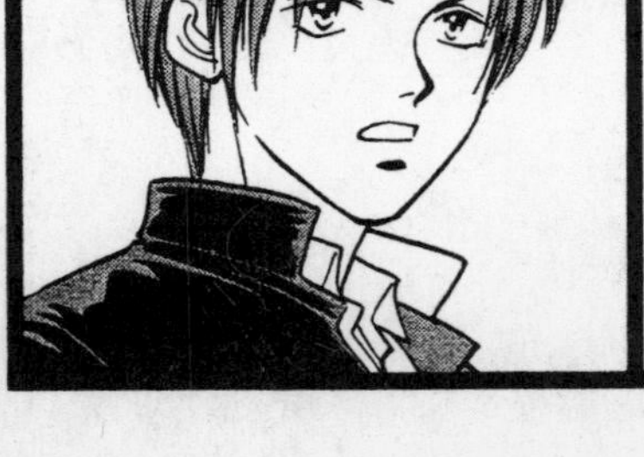

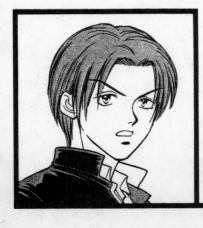

TATSUYA MIZUNO

- JOSUI JUNIOR HIGH SOCCER TEAM MIDDLE FIELDER

## KATSURŌ SHIBUSAWA

**MUSASHINOMORI SOCCER TEAM**

**FAMOUS GOAL KEEPER**

## SEIJI FUJISHIRO

**MUSASHINOMORI SOCCER TEAM**

**ACE STRIKER**

## SHIGEKI SATŌ

**JOSUI JUNIOR HIGH SOCCER TEAM**

**TEMPORARY GOAL KEEPER**

NOT WANTING TO GIVE UP HIS DREAM OF PLAYING SOCCER, SHŌ KAZAMATSURI, A SUBSTITUTE PLAYER AT MUSASHINOMORI, A SCHOOL KNOWN FOR ITS EXCELLENT SOCCER TEAM, TRANSFERS TO JOSUI JUNIOR HIGH.

HAVING RESOLVED THE TEAM'S BAD FEELINGS TOWARDS THEIR BEST PLAYER, TATSUYA, THE TEAM'S BOND IS DEEPENED AS JOSUI ENDEAVORS TO MAKE IT TO THE TOKYO CHAMPIONSHIP.

THE FIRST MATCH IS AGAINST THE VERY POWERFUL MUSASHINOMORI TEAM. JOSUI ENTERS THE SECOND HALF TWO POINTS BEHIND. DESPITE THEIR STRUGGLE AGAINST THE GUARDIAN DEITY, KATSURŌ SHIBUSAWA, THE TEAM'S DESIRE FOR VICTORY SUCCESSFULLY LEADS THEM TO SCORE ONE POINT. FURTHERMORE, RIGHT BEFORE THE MATCH IS OVER, SHIGEKI'S MIDDLE SHOT, DEFLECTED BY SHŌ'S HEAD, MIRACULOUSLY SCORES A GOAL, TYING THE MATCH!!

**STORY**

# WHISTLE!

**Vol. 4
RE-START**

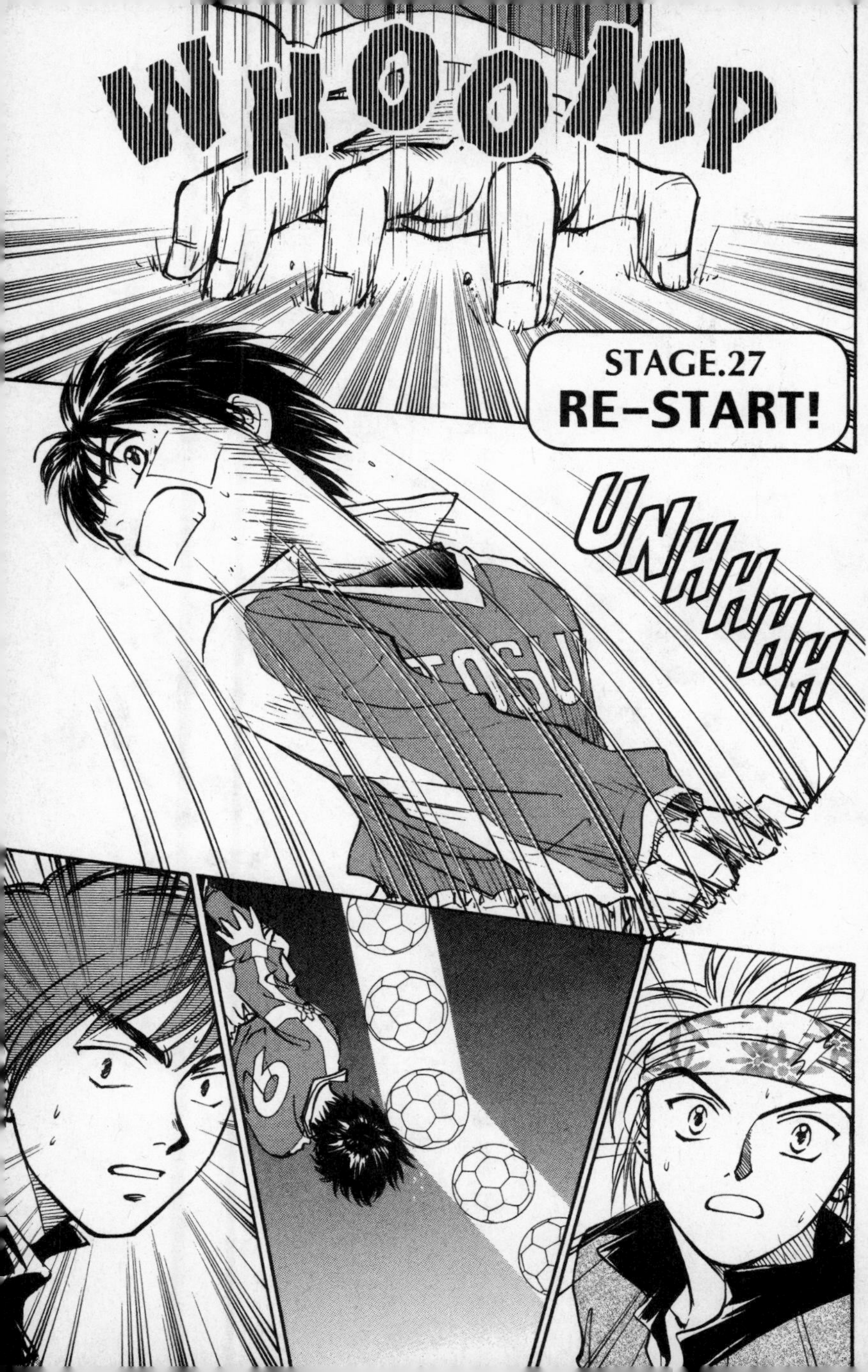
WHOOMP
STAGE.27
RE-START!
UNHHHH

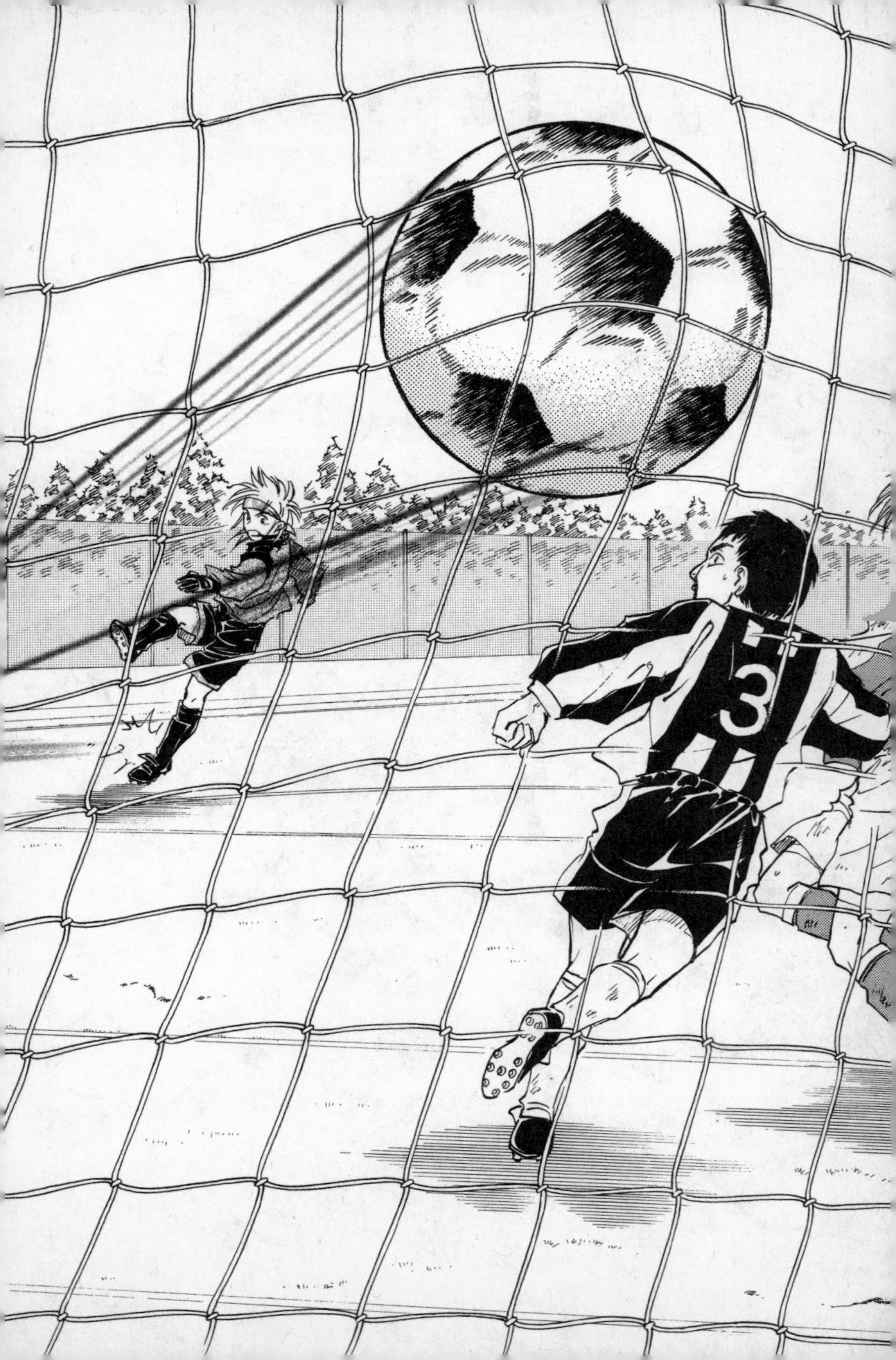

# STAGE.27 RE-START!

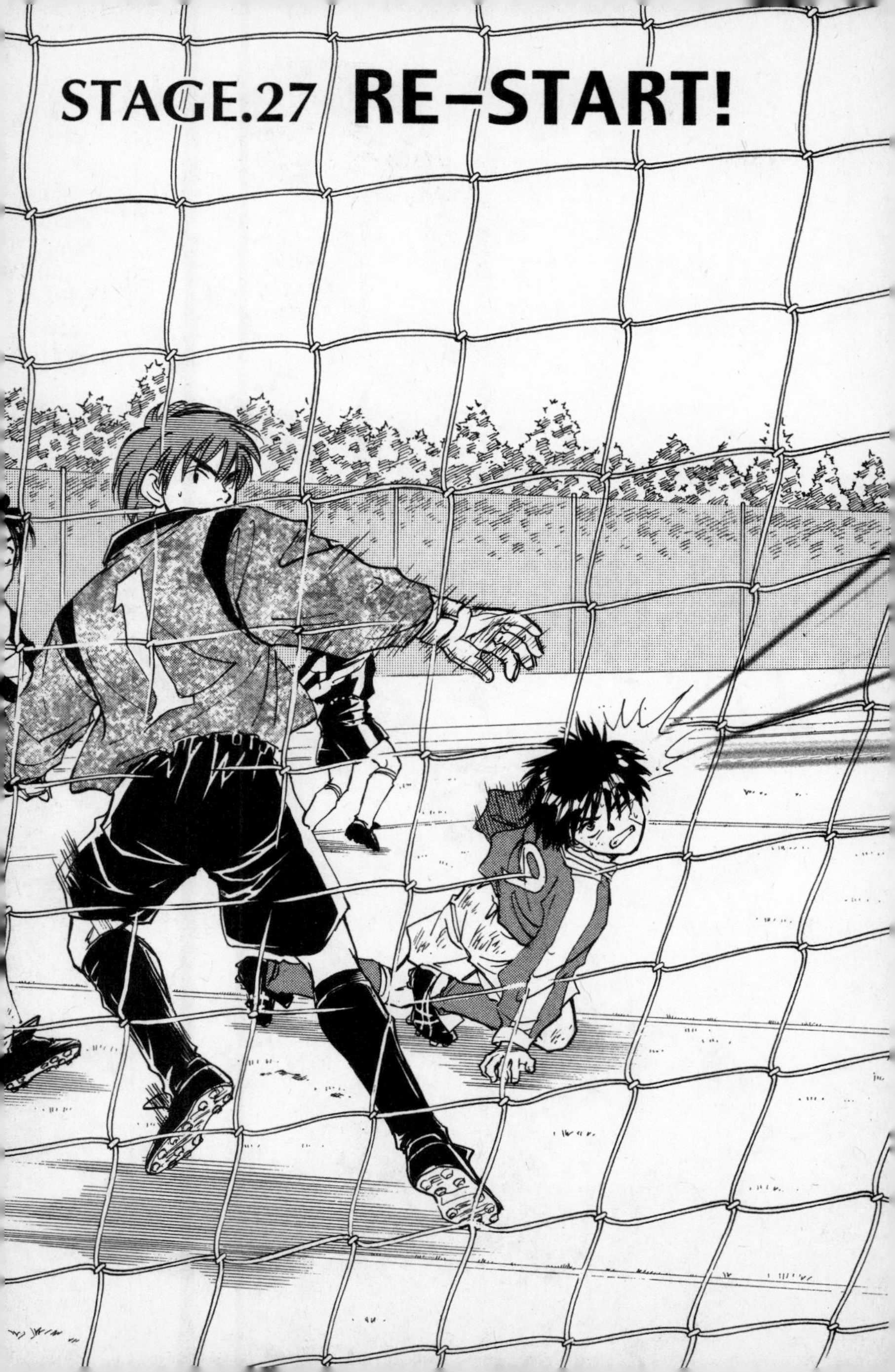

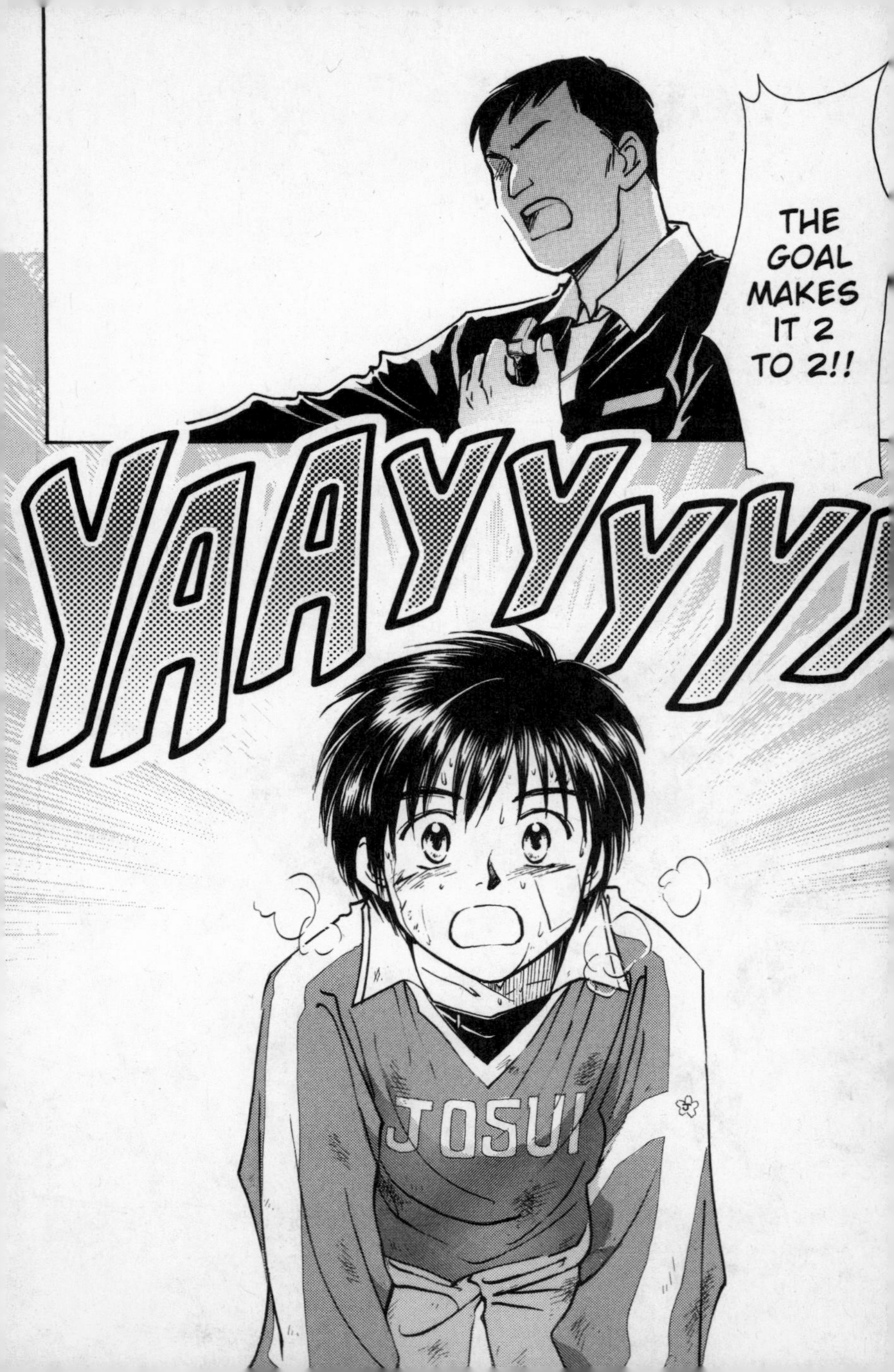
THE GOAL MAKES IT 2 TO 2!!
YAAYYYY
JOSUI

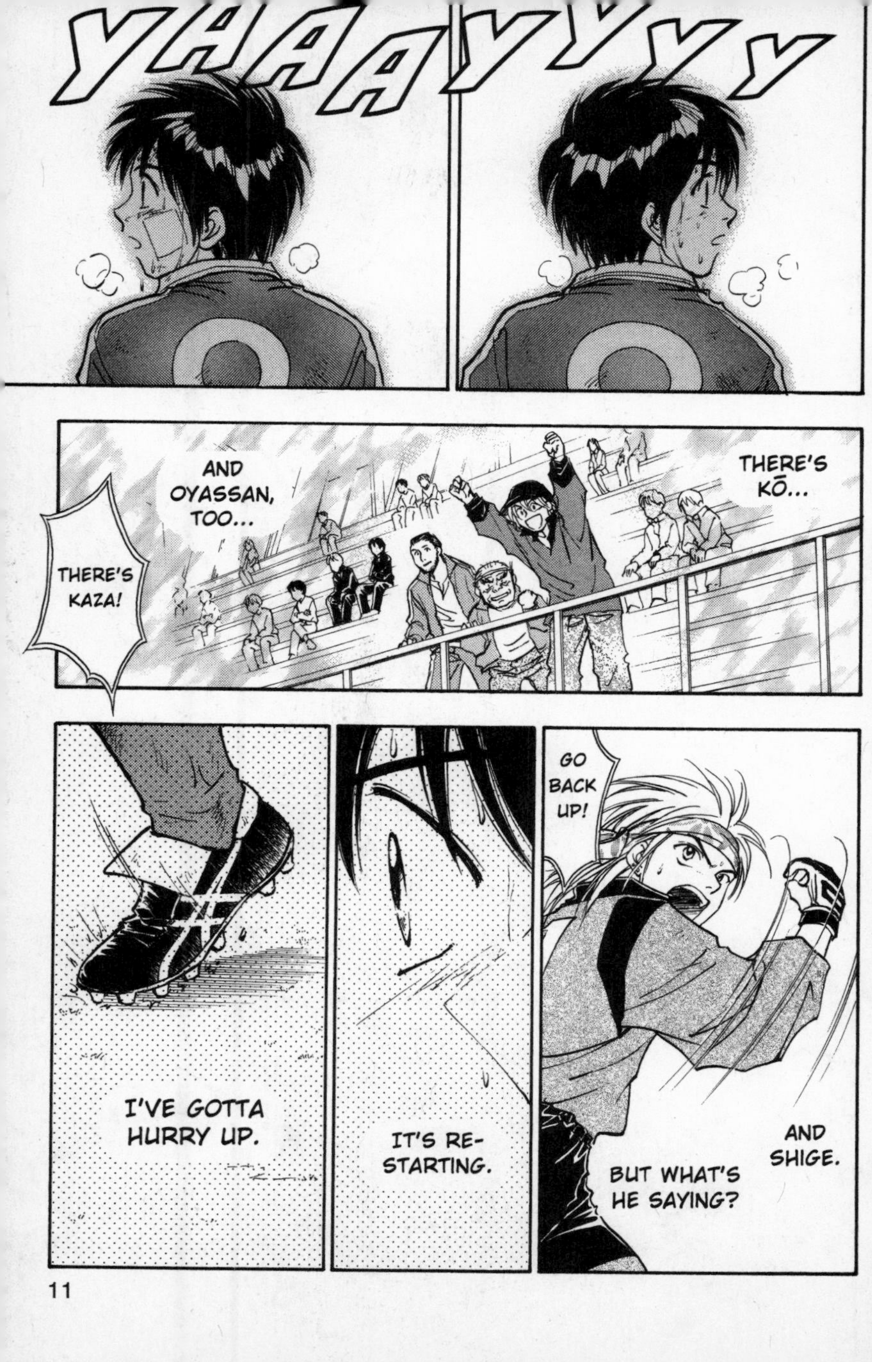
YAAAYYYY
THERE'S KŌ...
AND OYASSAN, TOO...
THERE'S KAZA!
GO BACK UP!
AND SHIGE.
BUT WHAT'S HE SAYING?
IT'S RE-STARTING.
I'VE GOTTA HURRY UP.

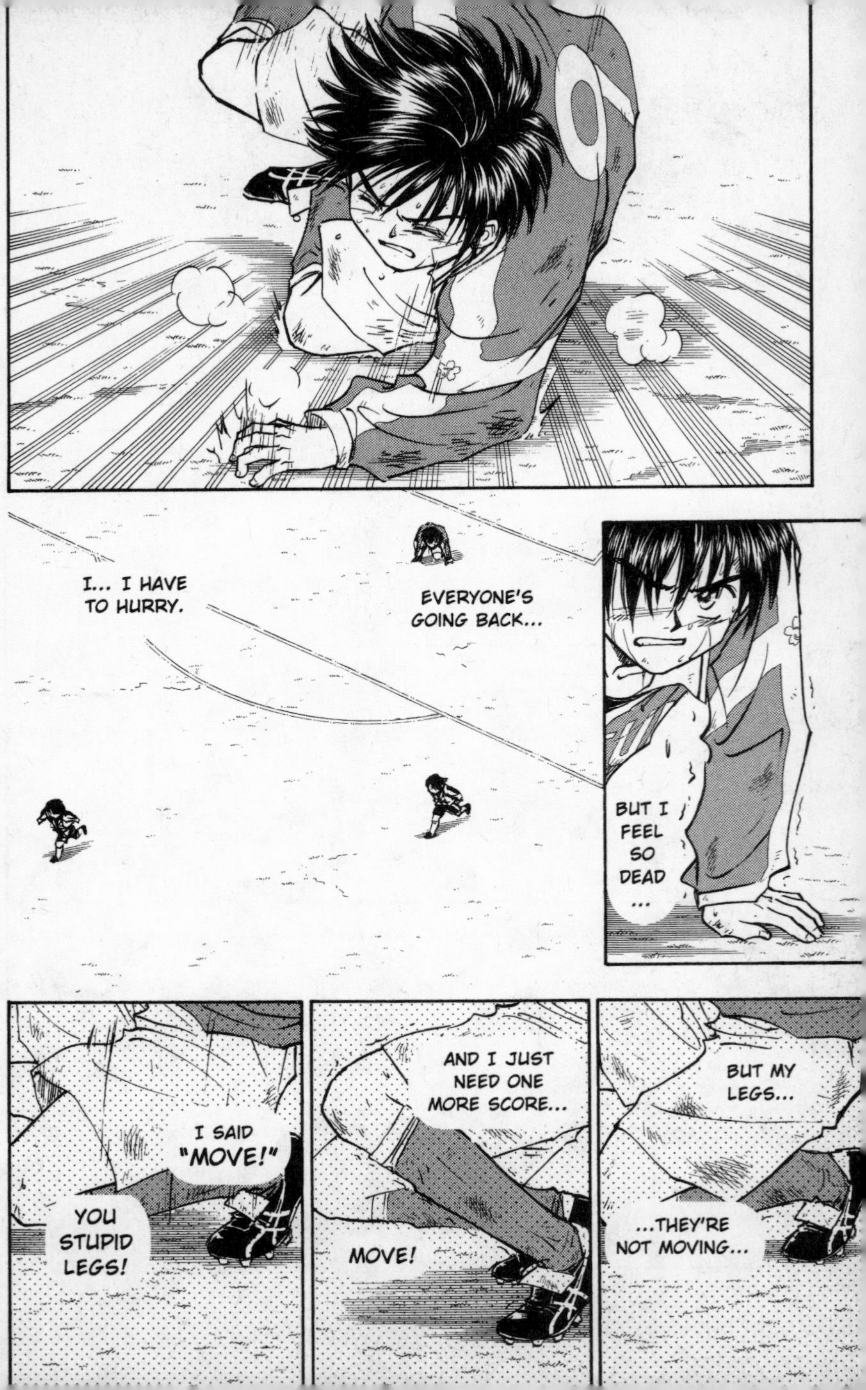
BUT I FEEL SO DEAD...
EVERYONE'S GOING BACK...
I... I HAVE TO HURRY.
BUT MY LEGS...
...THEY'RE NOT MOVING...
AND I JUST NEED ONE MORE SCORE...
MOVE!
I SAID "MOVE!"
YOU STUPID LEGS!

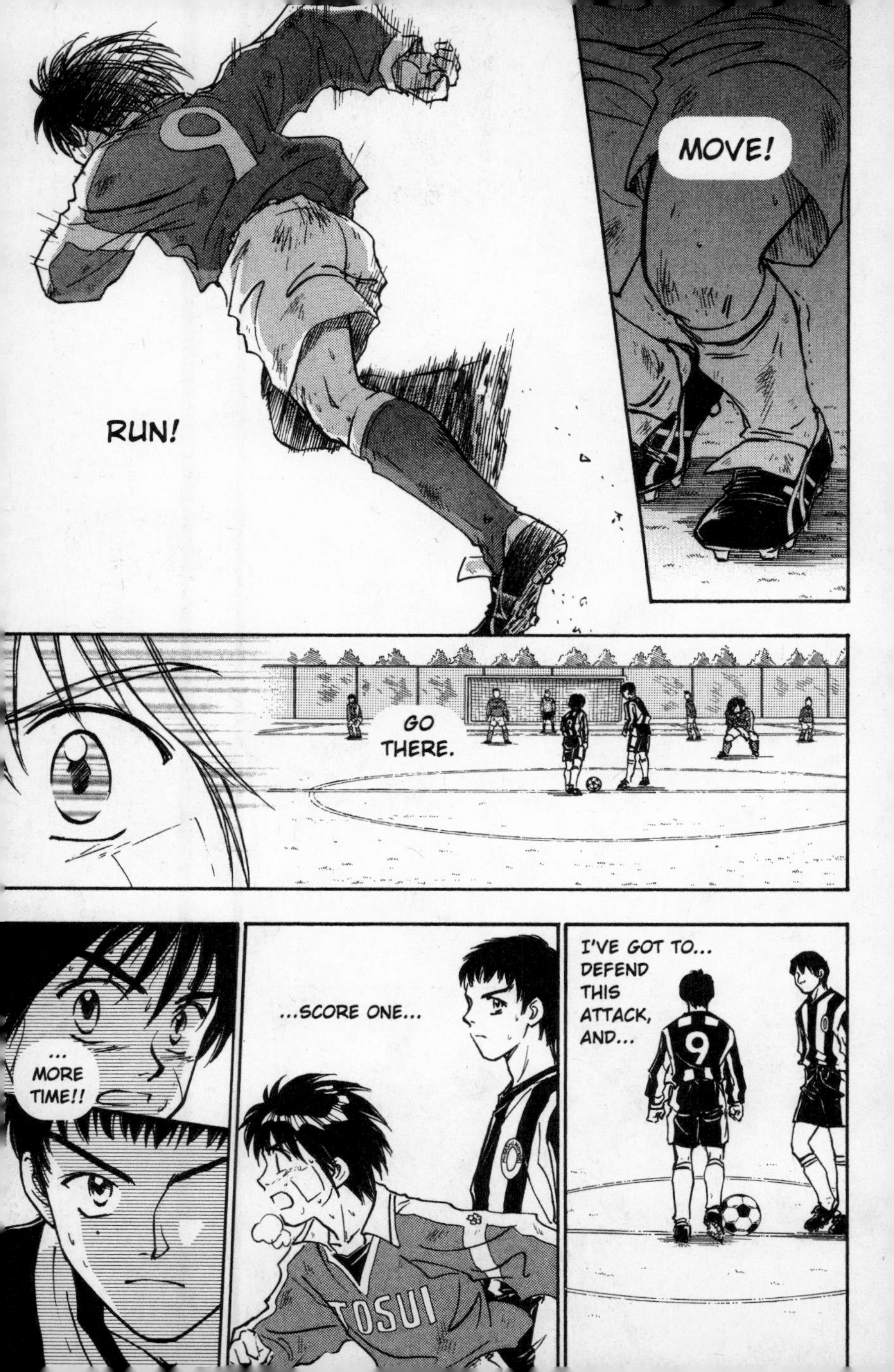
MOVE!
RUN!
GO THERE.
I'VE GOT TO... DEFEND THIS ATTACK, AND...
...SCORE ONE...
... MORE TIME!!
TOSUI

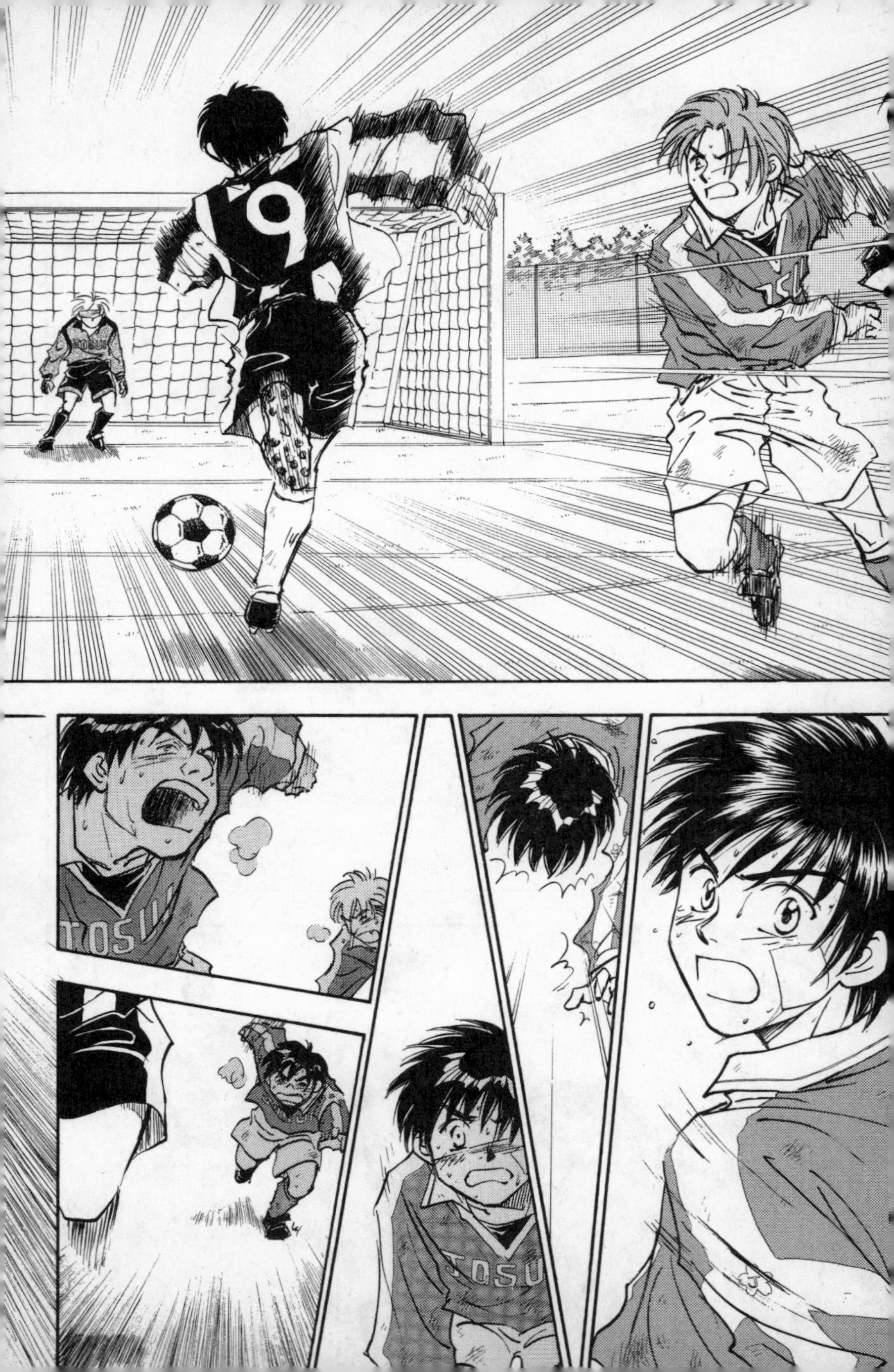

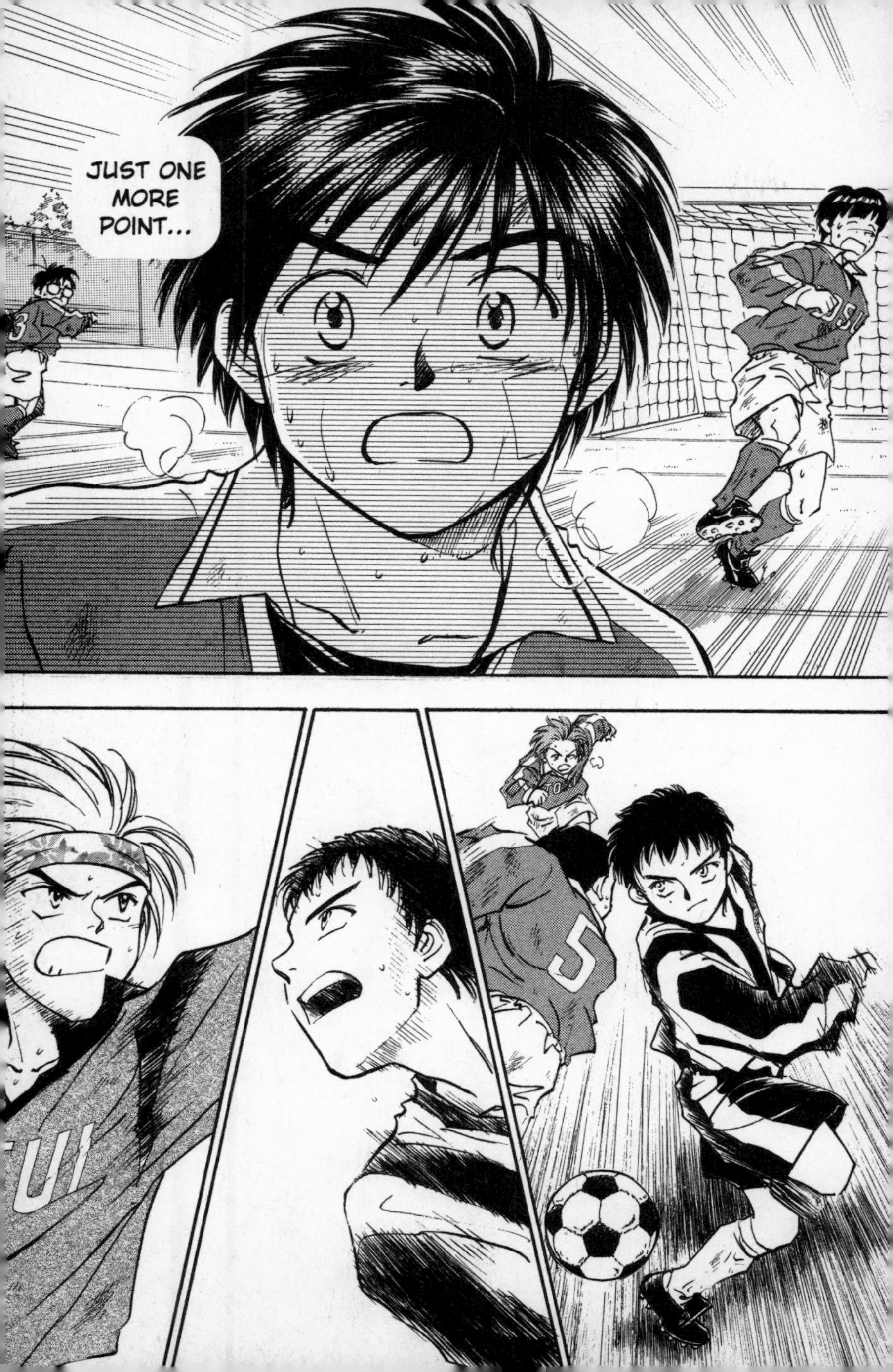
JUST ONE MORE POINT...

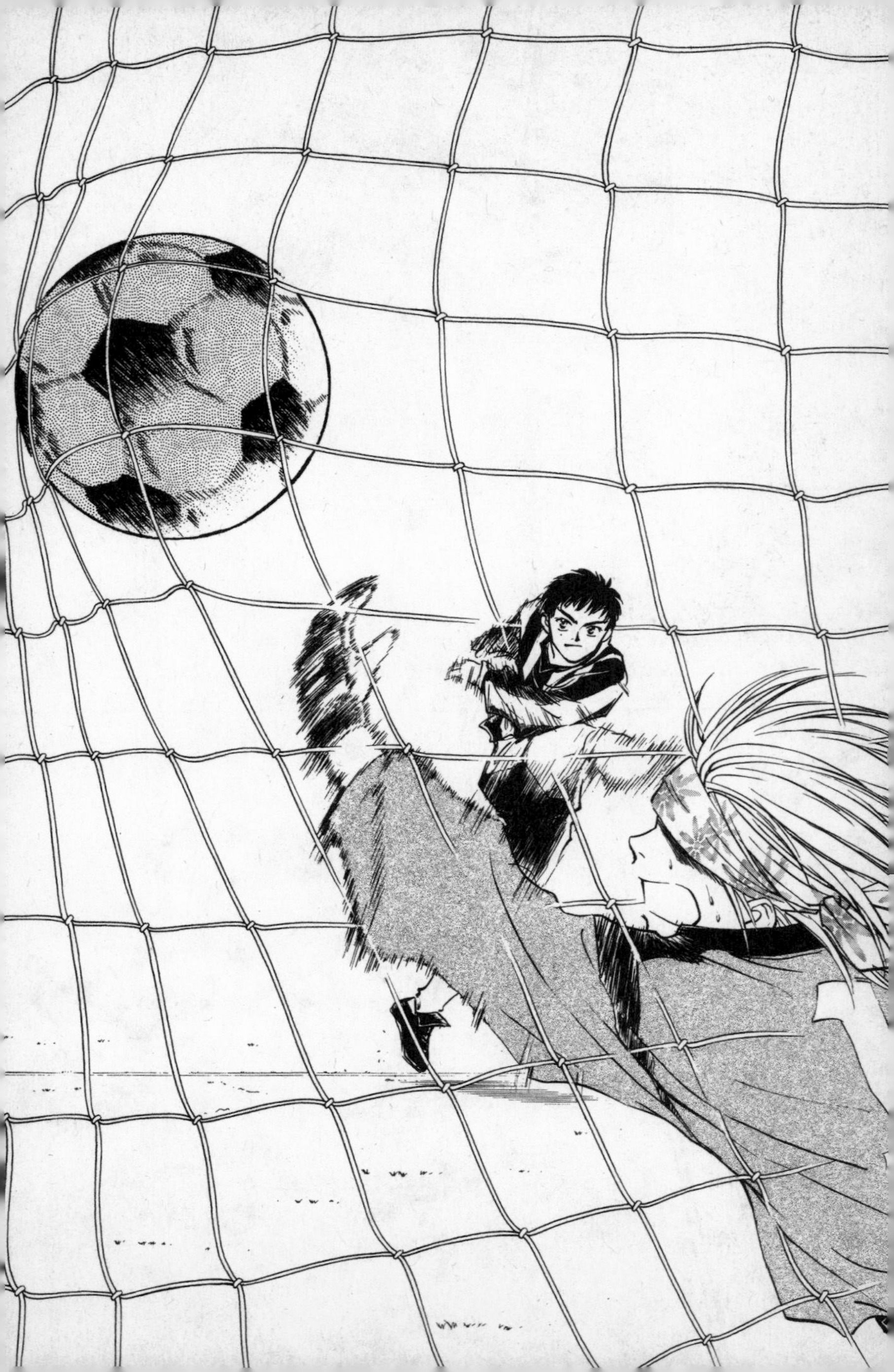

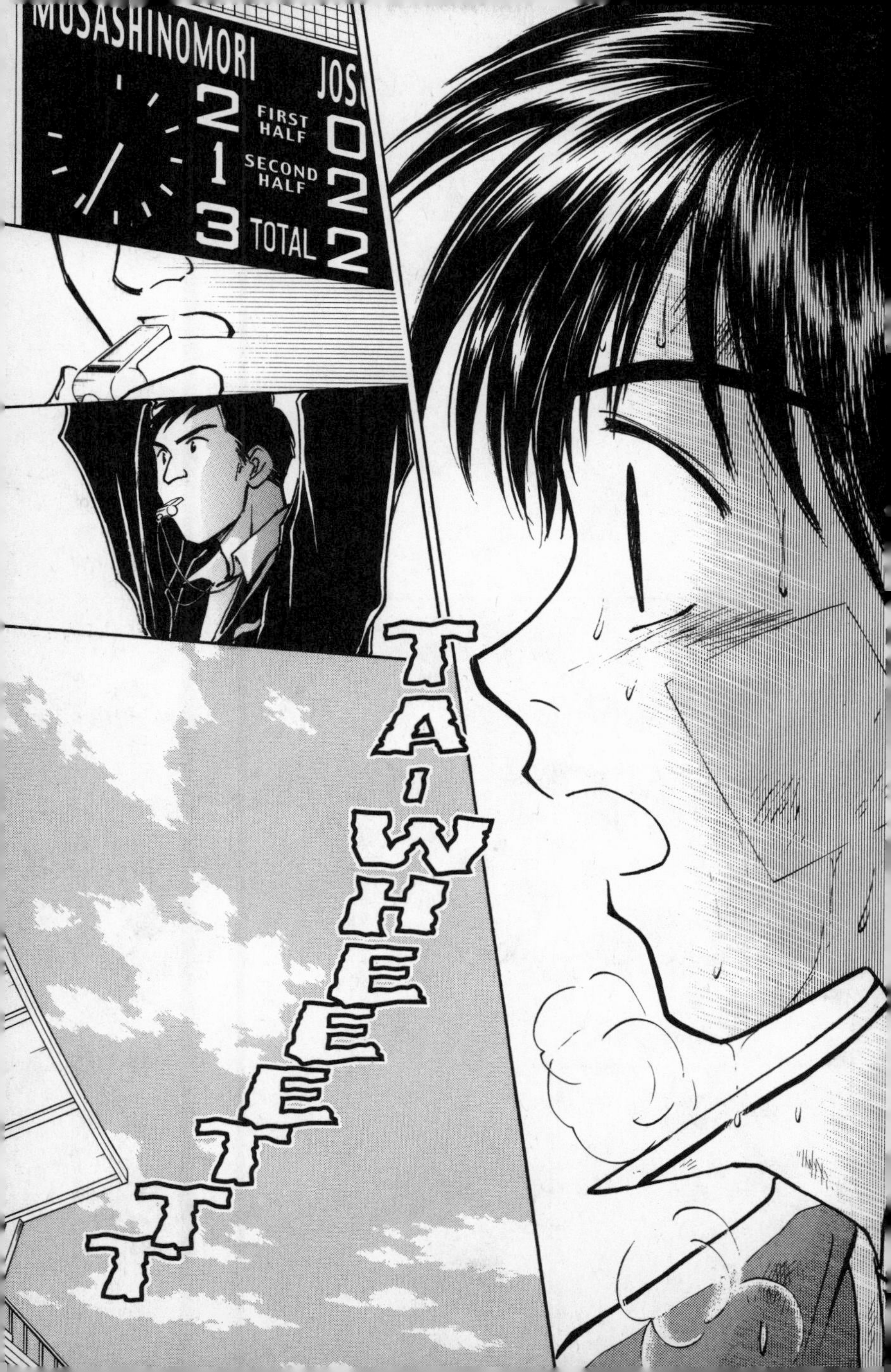

MUSASHINOMORI
JOS
2 FIRST HALF 0
1 SECOND HALF 2
3 TOTAL 2
TA-WHEEETTT

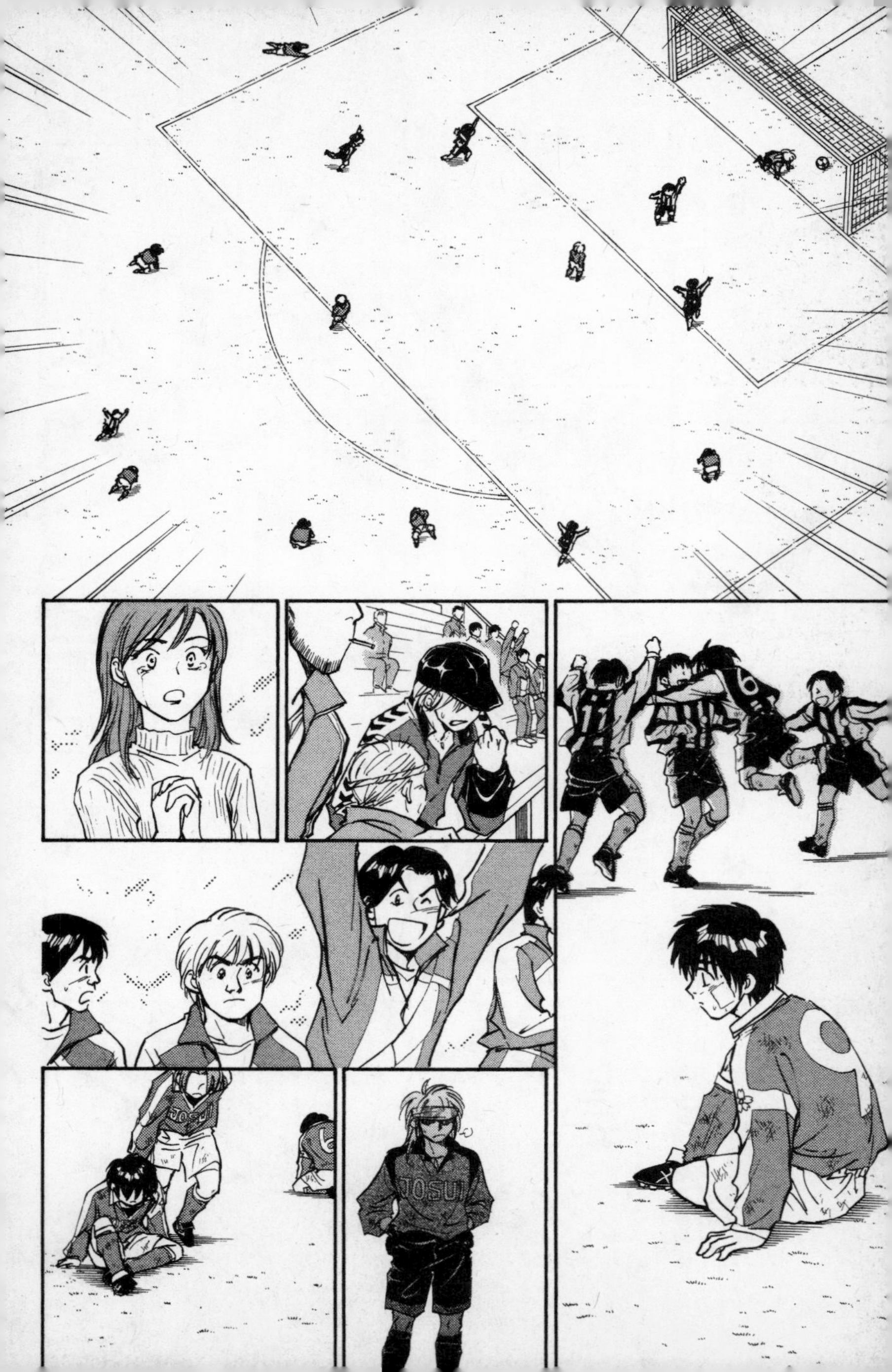
JOSUI

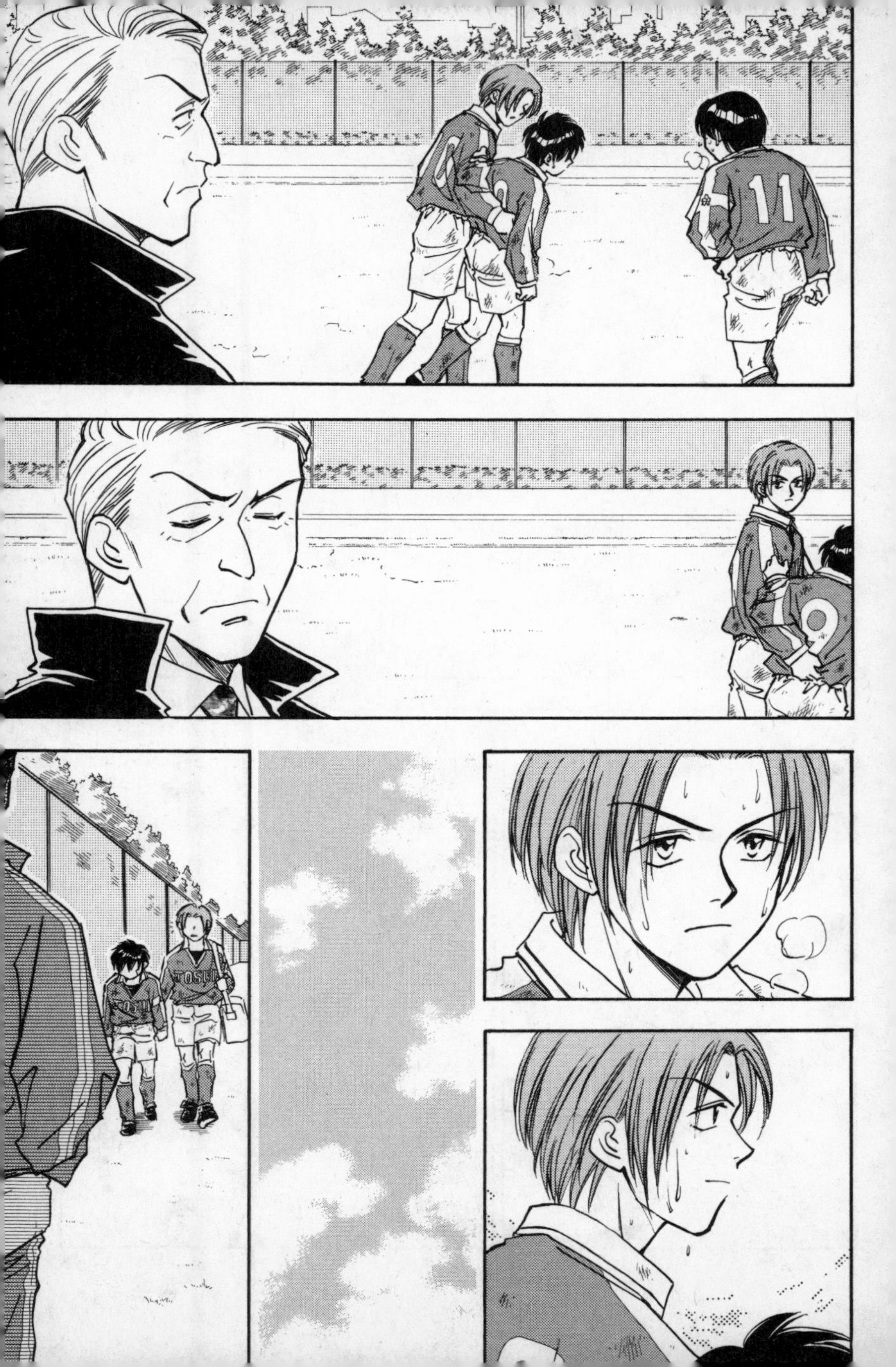

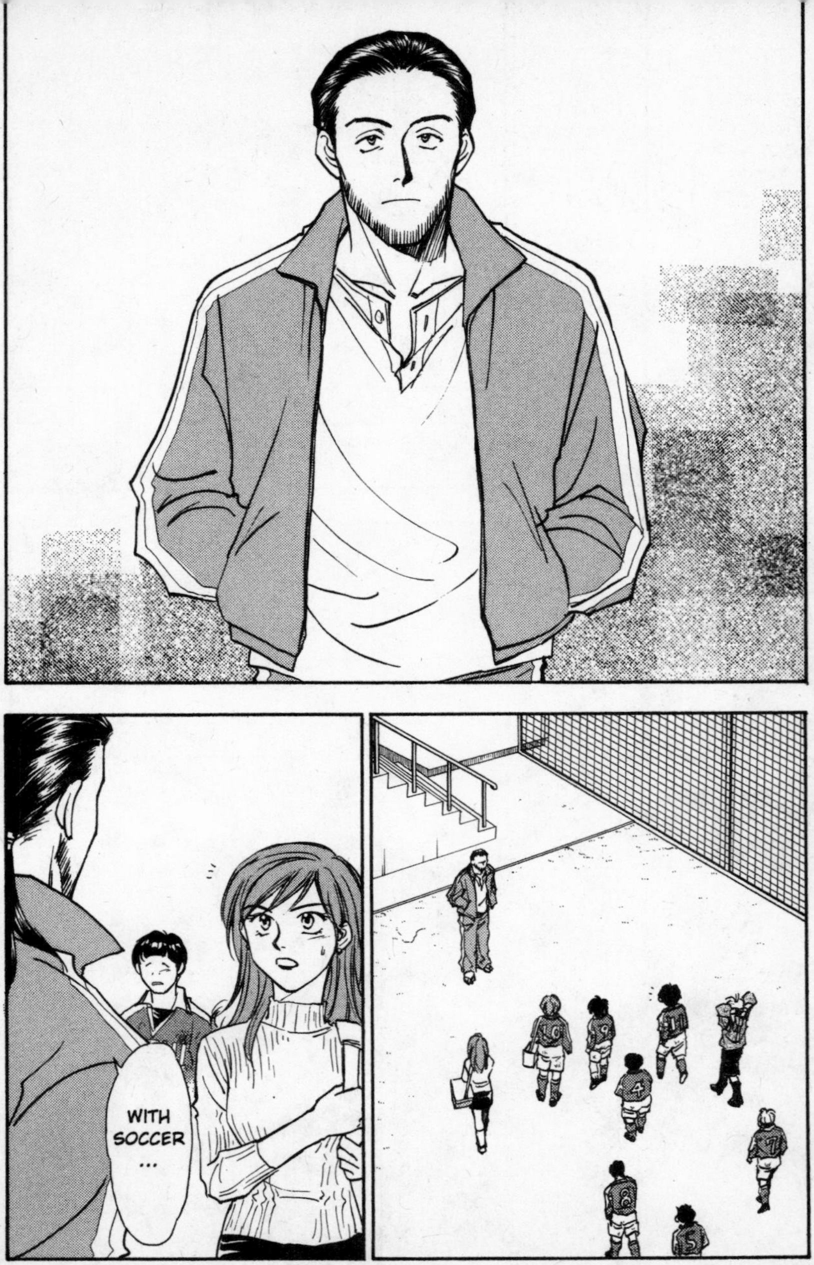
WITH SOCCER ...

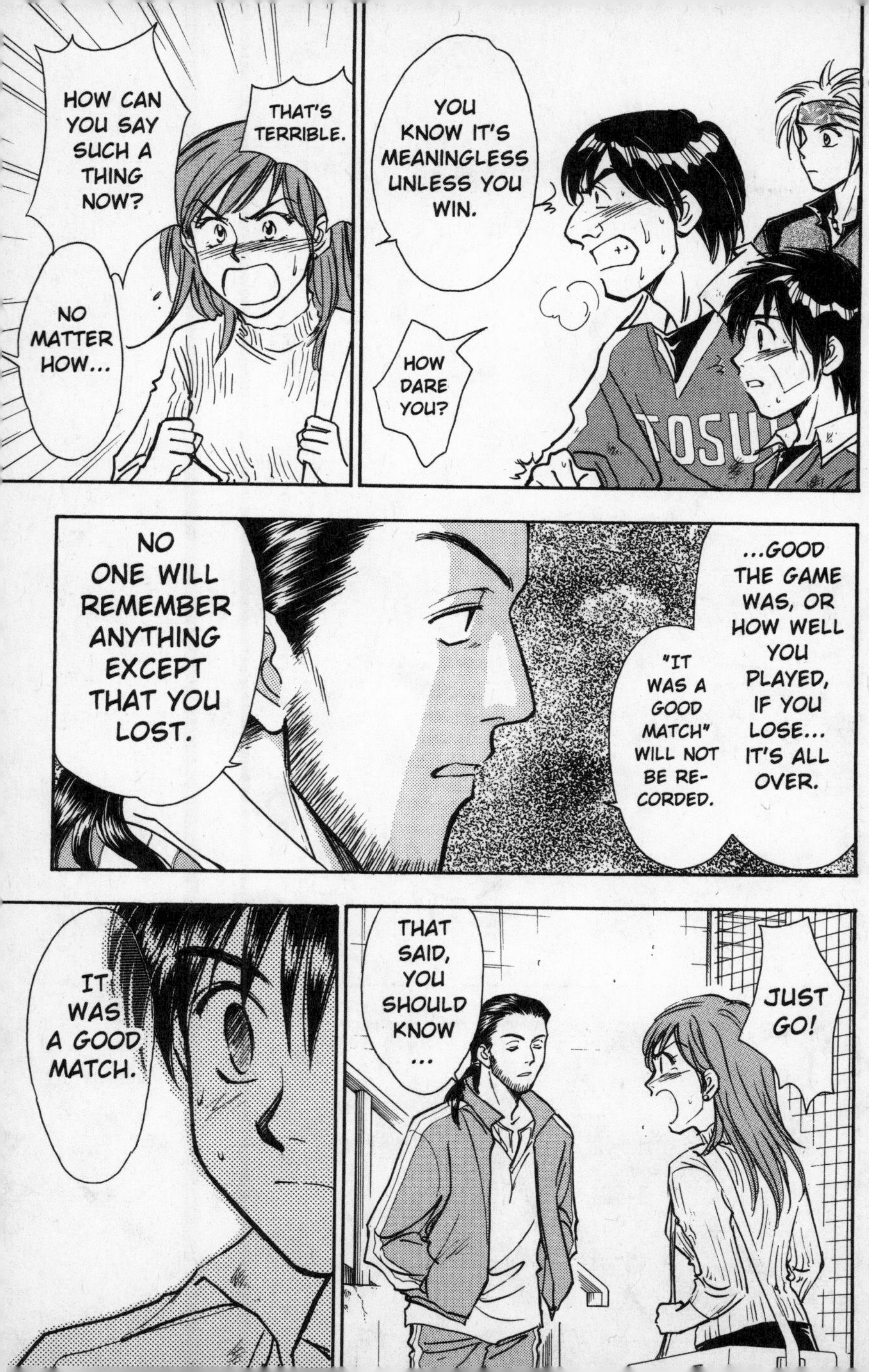
YOU KNOW IT'S MEANINGLESS UNLESS YOU WIN.
HOW DARE YOU?
THAT'S TERRIBLE.
HOW CAN YOU SAY SUCH A THING NOW?
NO MATTER HOW...
TOSU
...GOOD THE GAME WAS, OR HOW WELL YOU PLAYED, IF YOU LOSE... IT'S ALL OVER.
"IT WAS A GOOD MATCH" WILL NOT BE RE-CORDED.
NO ONE WILL REMEMBER ANYTHING EXCEPT THAT YOU LOST.
JUST GO!
THAT SAID, YOU SHOULD KNOW ...
IT WAS A GOOD MATCH.

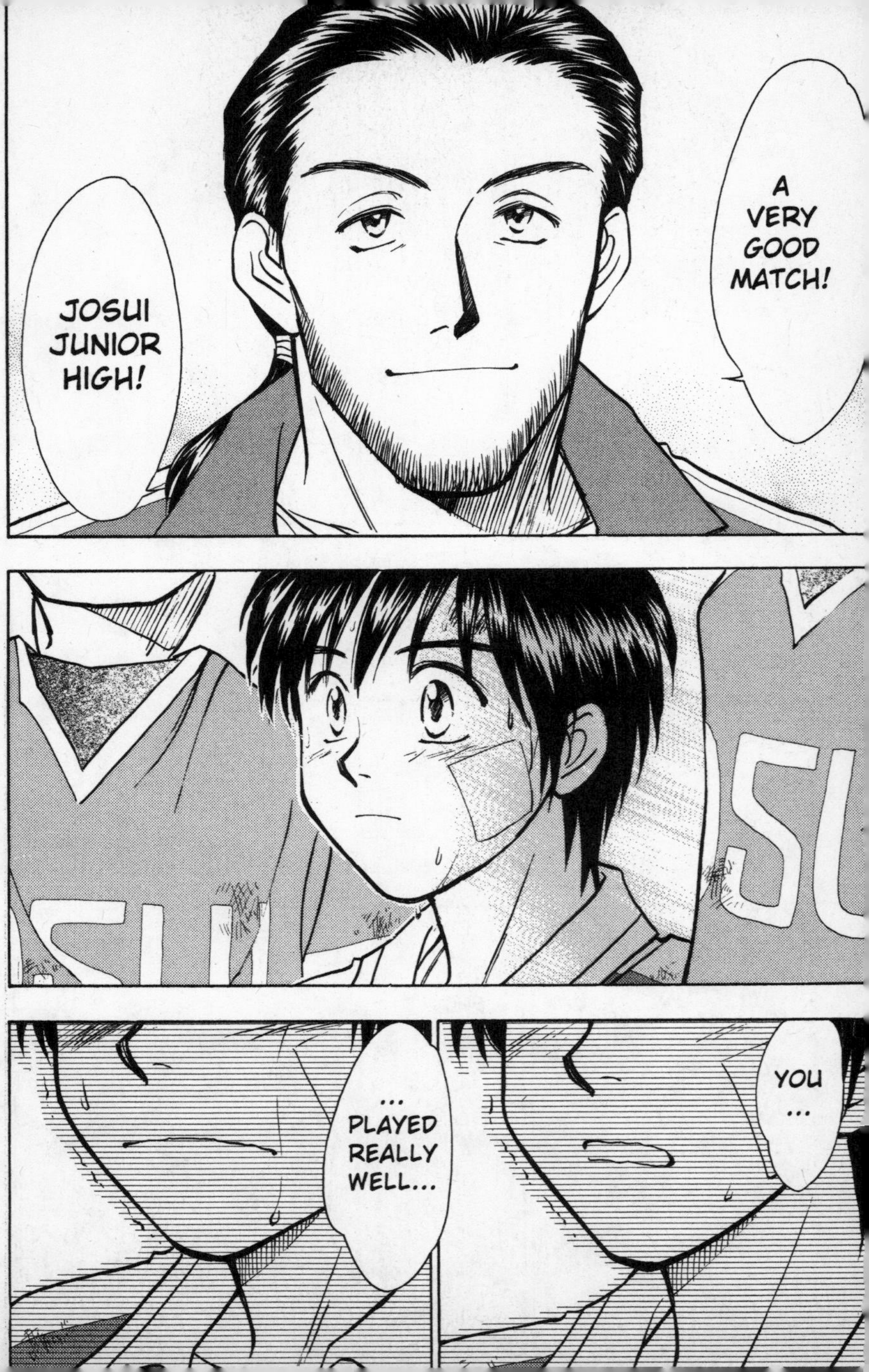
A VERY GOOD MATCH!
JOSUI JUNIOR HIGH!
YOU ...
... PLAYED REALLY WELL...

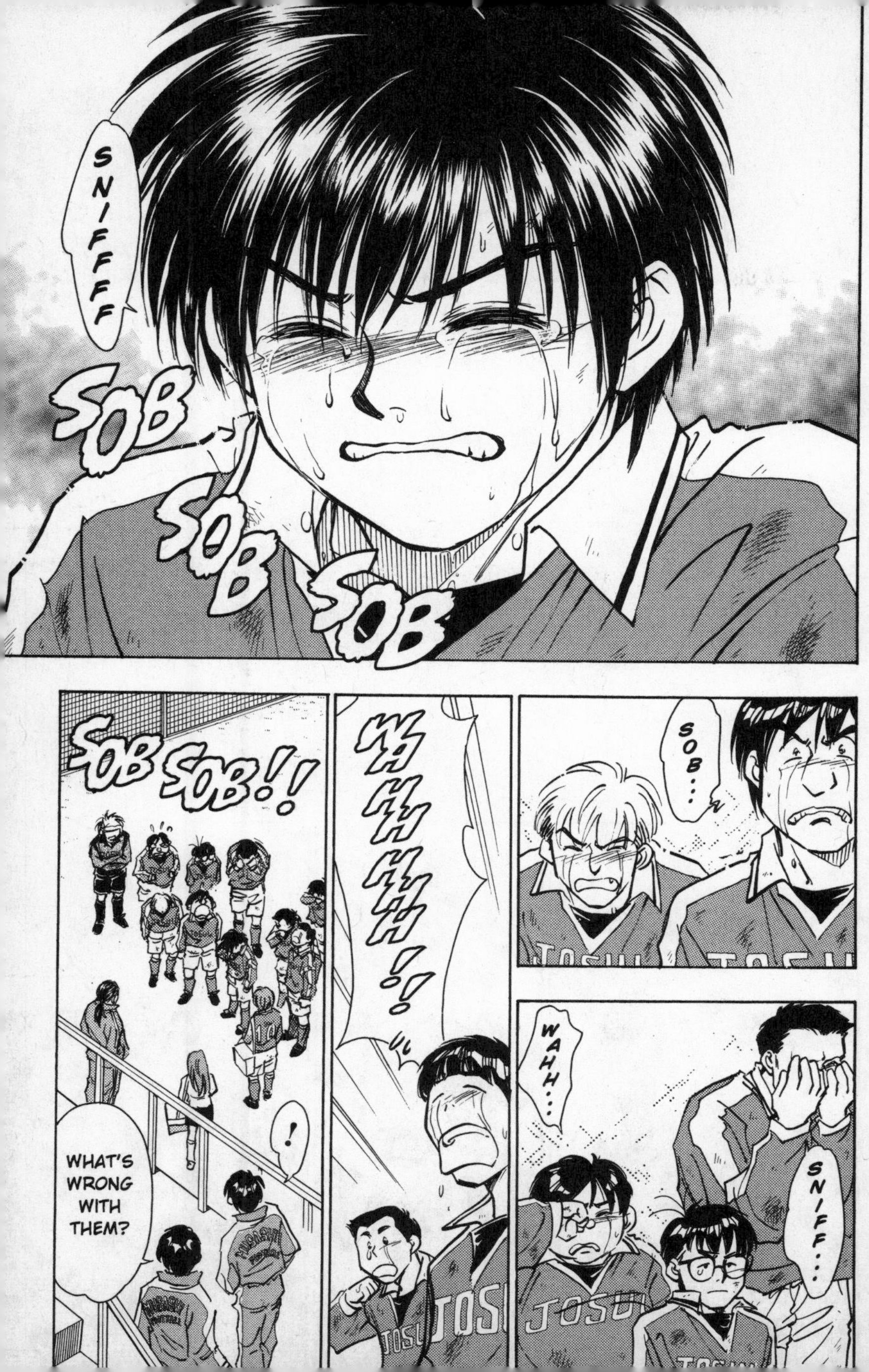
SNIFFFF
SOB
SOB
SOB
SOB...
WAHH...
SNIFF...
WAHHHHHH!!
SOB SOB!!
!
WHAT'S WRONG WITH THEM?

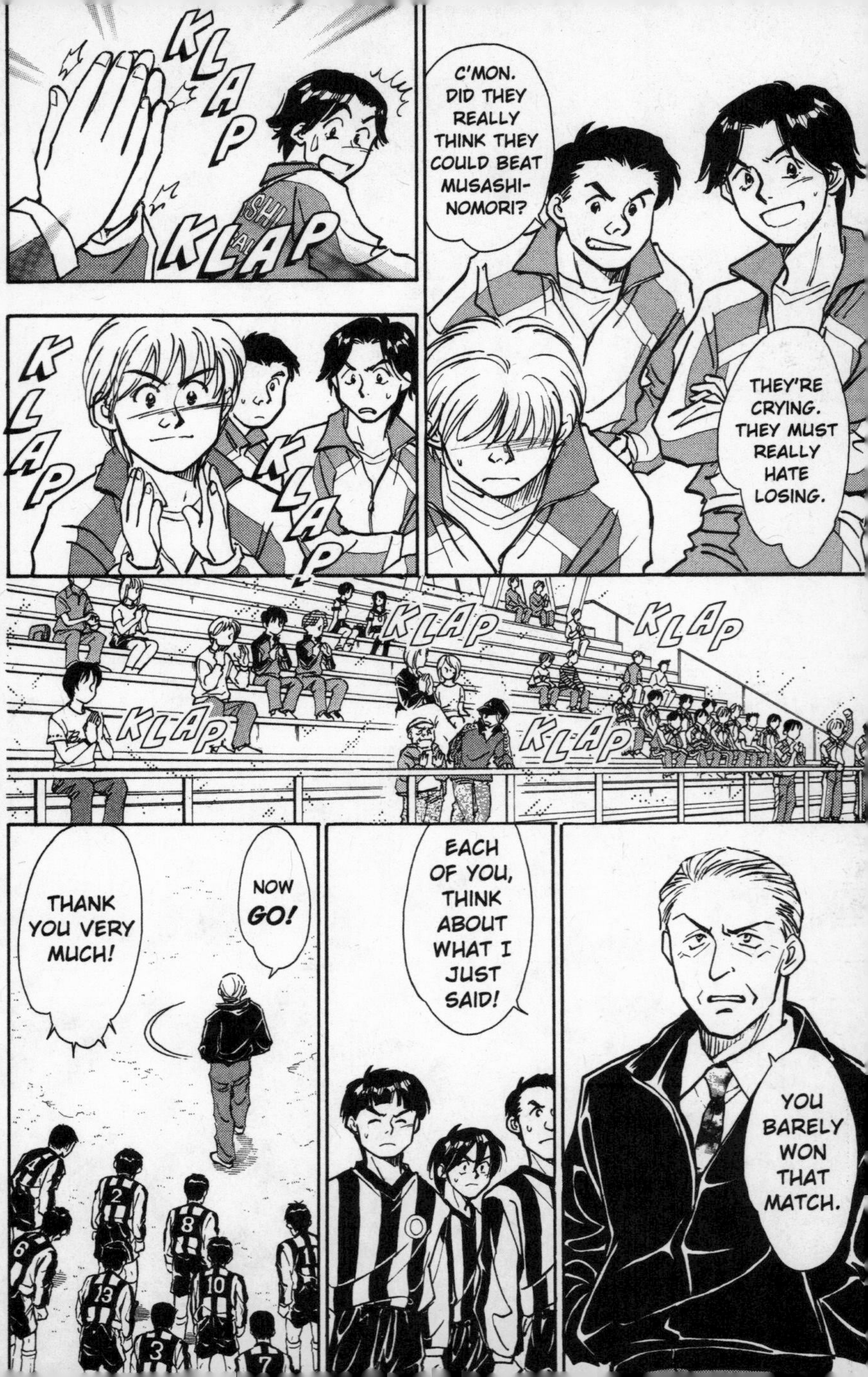
C'MON. DID THEY REALLY THINK THEY COULD BEAT MUSASHI-NOMORI?
THEY'RE CRYING. THEY MUST REALLY HATE LOSING.
KLAP
KLAP
KLAP
KLAP
KLAP
KLAP
KLAP
KLAP
KLAP
YOU BARELY WON THAT MATCH.
EACH OF YOU, THINK ABOUT WHAT I JUST SAID!
NOW GO!
THANK YOU VERY MUCH!

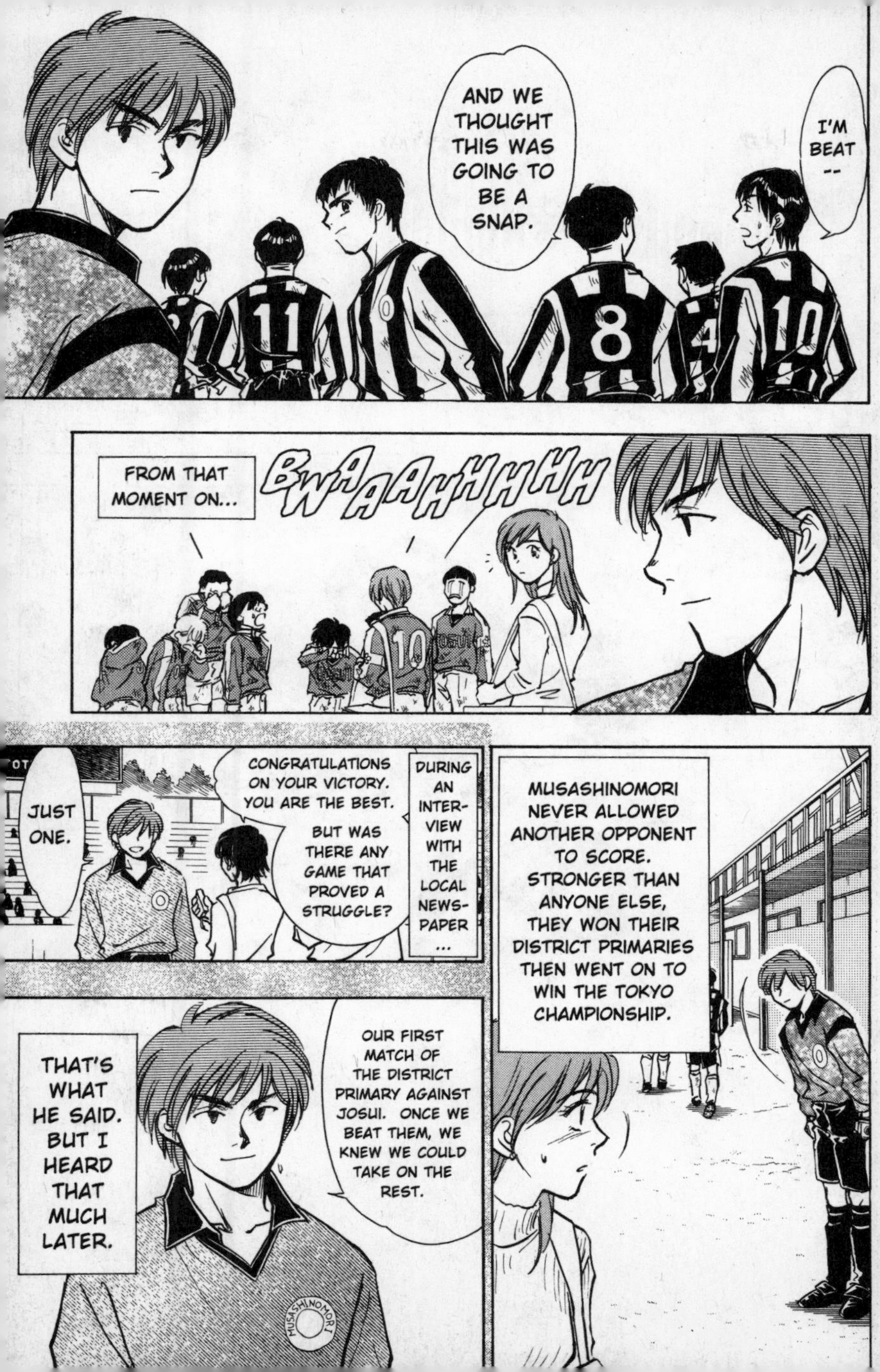
I'M BEAT --
AND WE THOUGHT THIS WAS GOING TO BE A SNAP.
BWAAAHHHHHH
FROM THAT MOMENT ON...
MUSASHINOMORI NEVER ALLOWED ANOTHER OPPONENT TO SCORE. STRONGER THAN ANYONE ELSE, THEY WON THEIR DISTRICT PRIMARIES THEN WENT ON TO WIN THE TOKYO CHAMPIONSHIP.
DURING AN INTERVIEW WITH THE LOCAL NEWSPAPER ...
CONGRATULATIONS ON YOUR VICTORY. YOU ARE THE BEST.
BUT WAS THERE ANY GAME THAT PROVED A STRUGGLE?
JUST ONE.
OUR FIRST MATCH OF THE DISTRICT PRIMARY AGAINST JOSUI. ONCE WE BEAT THEM, WE KNEW WE COULD TAKE ON THE REST.
THAT'S WHAT HE SAID. BUT I HEARD THAT MUCH LATER.

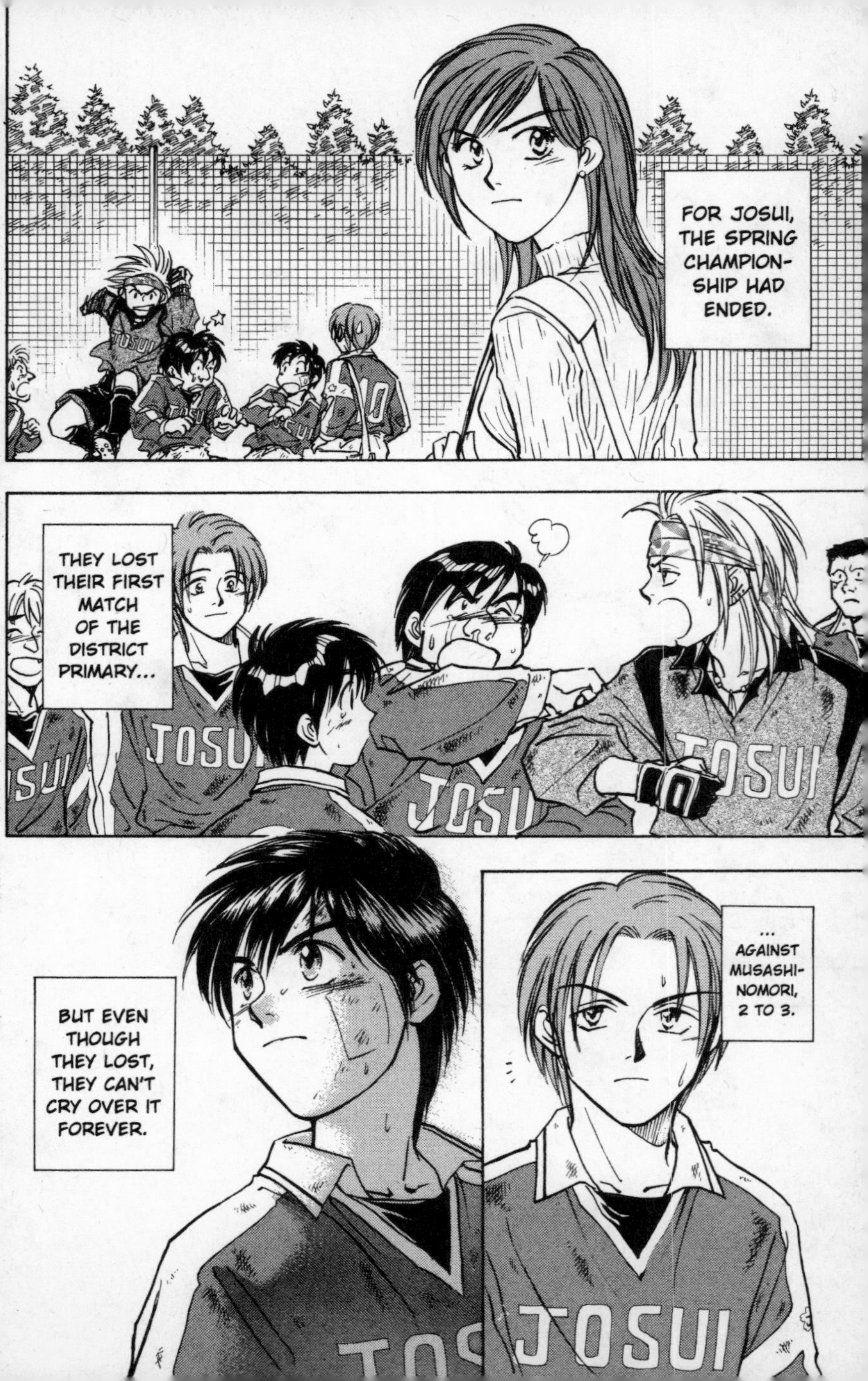
FOR JOSUI, THE SPRING CHAMPIONSHIP HAD ENDED.
THEY LOST THEIR FIRST MATCH OF THE DISTRICT PRIMARY...
...AGAINST MUSASHI-NOMORI, 2 TO 3.
BUT EVEN THOUGH THEY LOST, THEY CAN'T CRY OVER IT FOREVER.

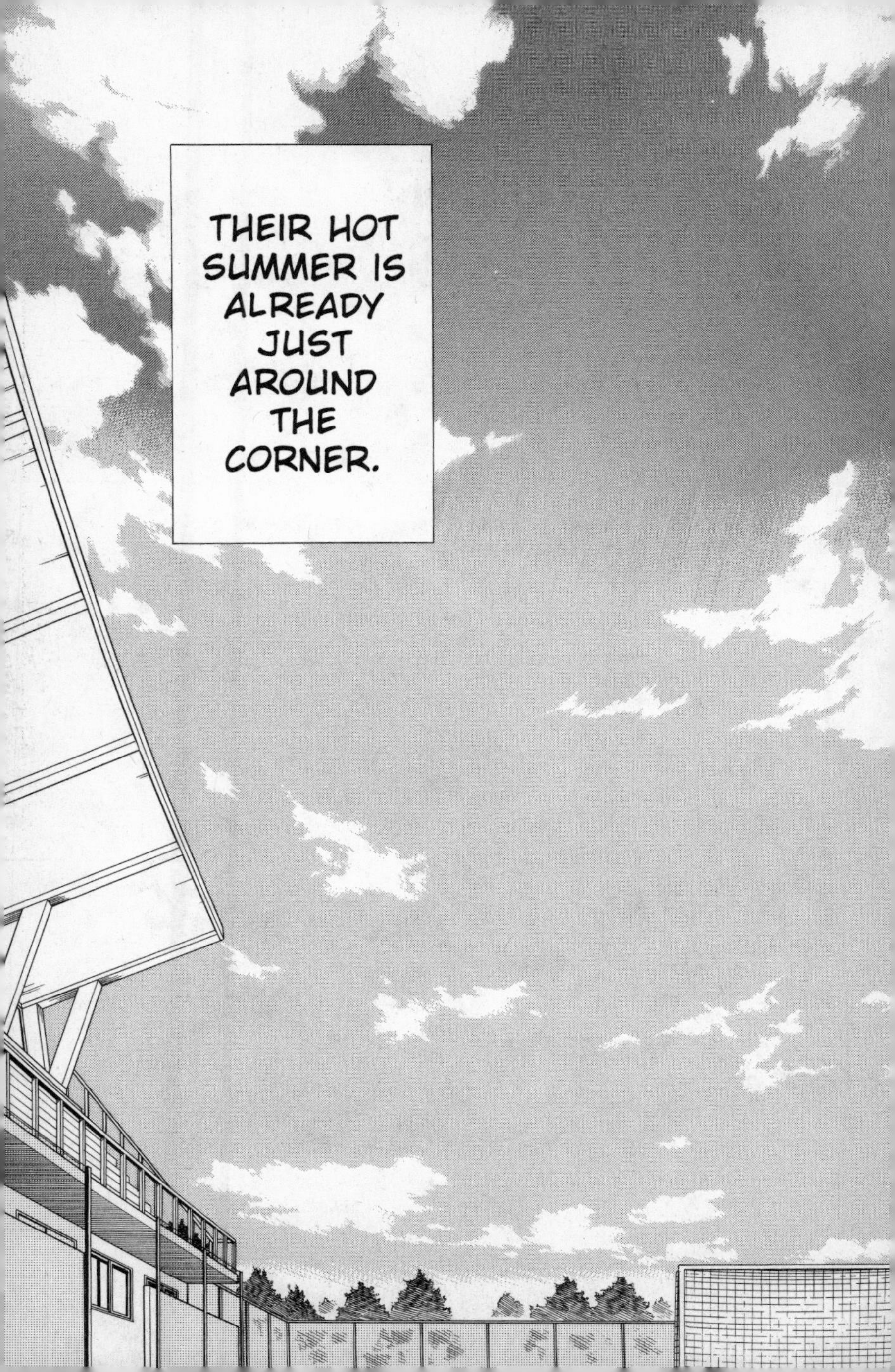
THEIR HOT SUMMER IS ALREADY JUST AROUND THE CORNER.

IMAGINARY DRAWING OF A PARTY HELD FOR FRESHMEN
BY MUSASHINOMORI'S FIRST-TIER SUBSTITUTES.

MUSASHINO'S FOREST IS THE CEMETERY OF THE SOCCER BOYS' DREAM...
CURSED DOLLS' SOCCER HEAVEN, THE THIRD TEAM DREAMS ON SWEETLY.
"A TOMATO CAN NEVER BECOME A MELON."
TALKING ABOUT THE COACH, A DIVORCED MAN WITH THE DROOPING EYES.
WEEDING THE YOUNG MEN'S DREAMS, OH, OLD BACK....

ILLUSTRATED BY
**MESO AIKO**

MUSASHINOMORI, TOO,
IS FEELING INSPIRED.

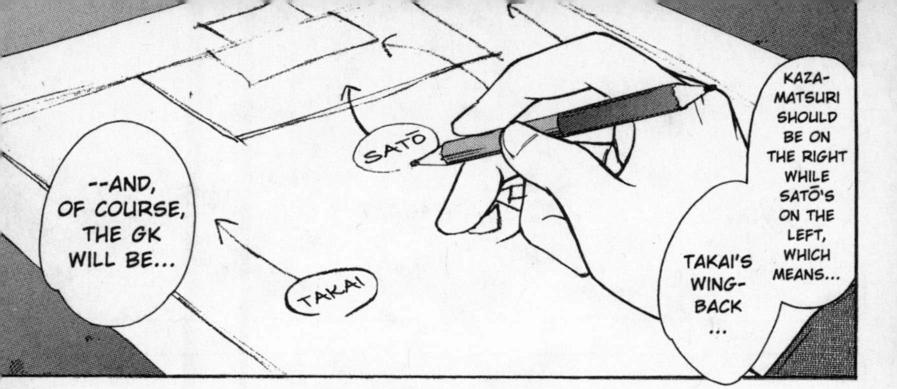
KAZA-MATSURI SHOULD BE ON THE RIGHT WHILE SATŌ'S ON THE LEFT, WHICH MEANS...
TAKAI'S WING-BACK ...
SATŌ
TAKAI
--AND, OF COURSE, THE GK WILL BE...

# STAGE.28
# The Man Who Calls Forth the Storm?!

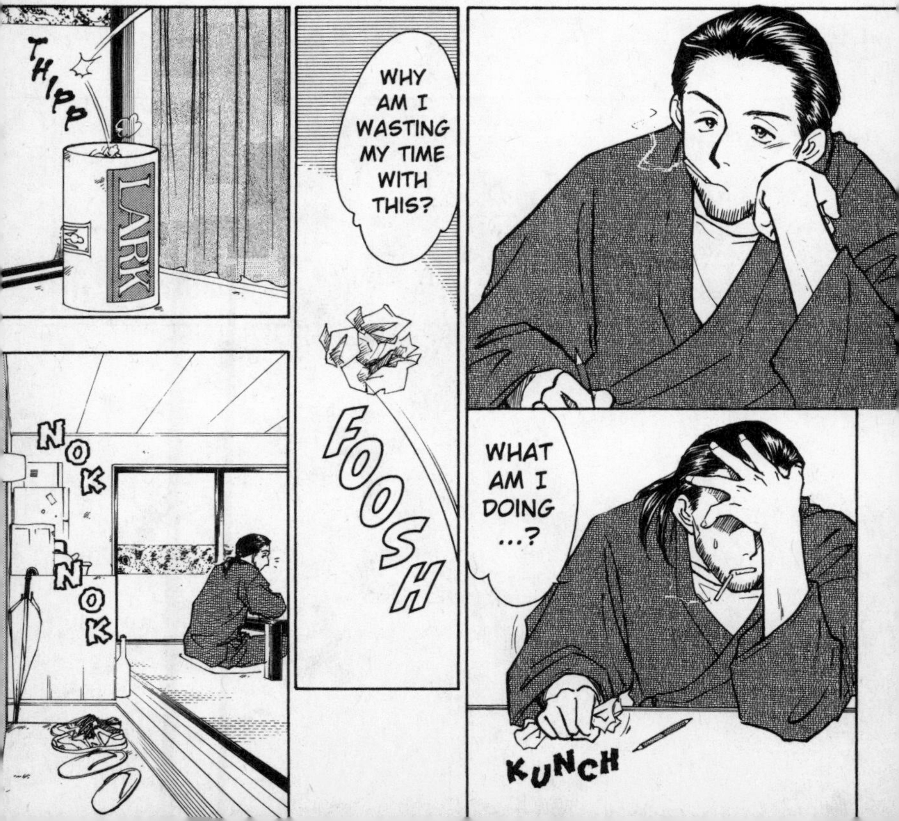
WHAT AM I DOING ...?
KUNCH
WHY AM I WASTING MY TIME WITH THIS?
FOOSH
THIPP
LARK
NOK
NOK
NOK

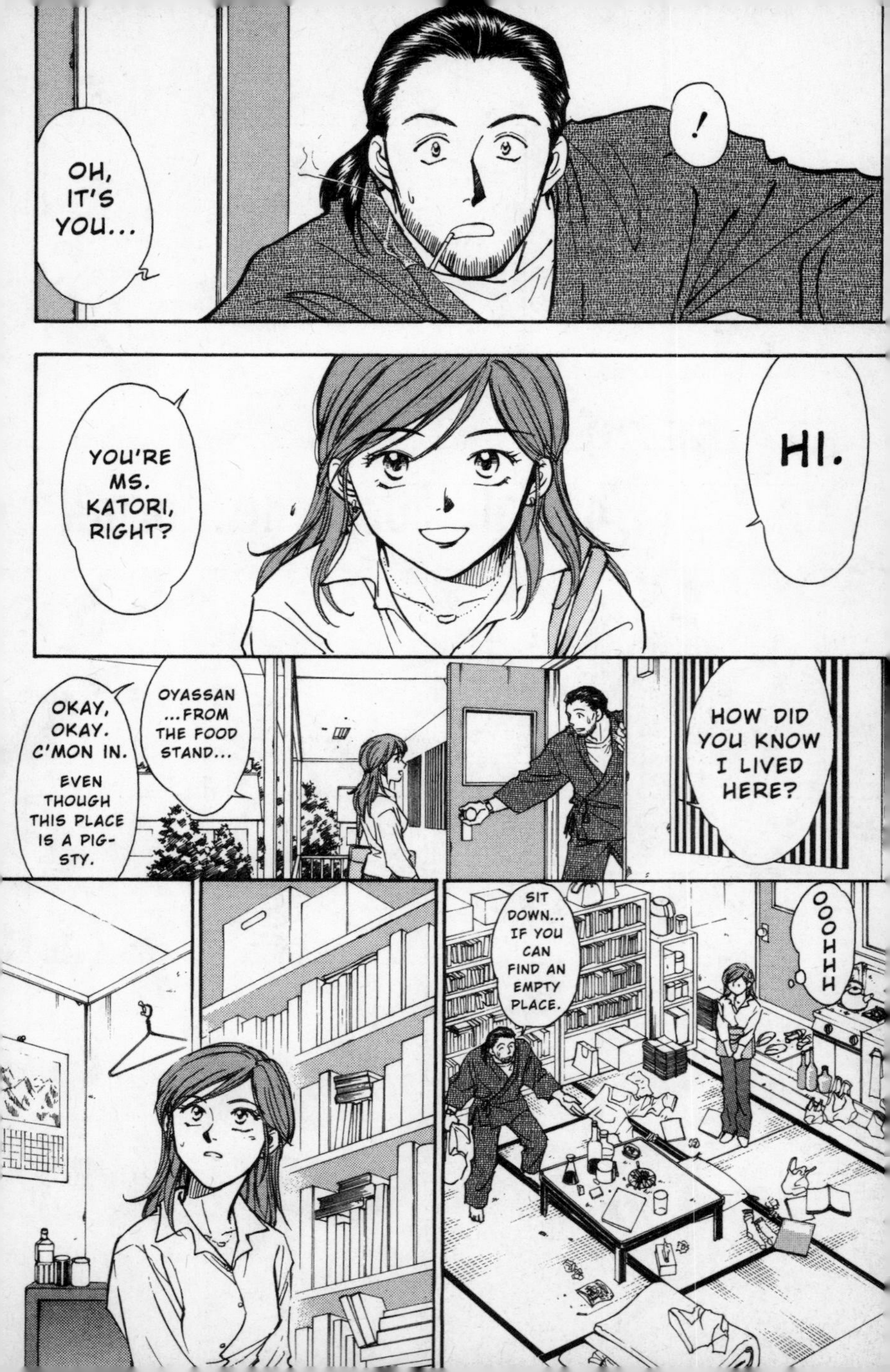
!
OH, IT'S YOU...
HI.
YOU'RE MS. KATORI, RIGHT?
HOW DID YOU KNOW I LIVED HERE?
OYASSAN ...FROM THE FOOD STAND...
OKAY, OKAY. C'MON IN.
EVEN THOUGH THIS PLACE IS A PIG-STY.
OOOHHH
SIT DOWN... IF YOU CAN FIND AN EMPTY PLACE.

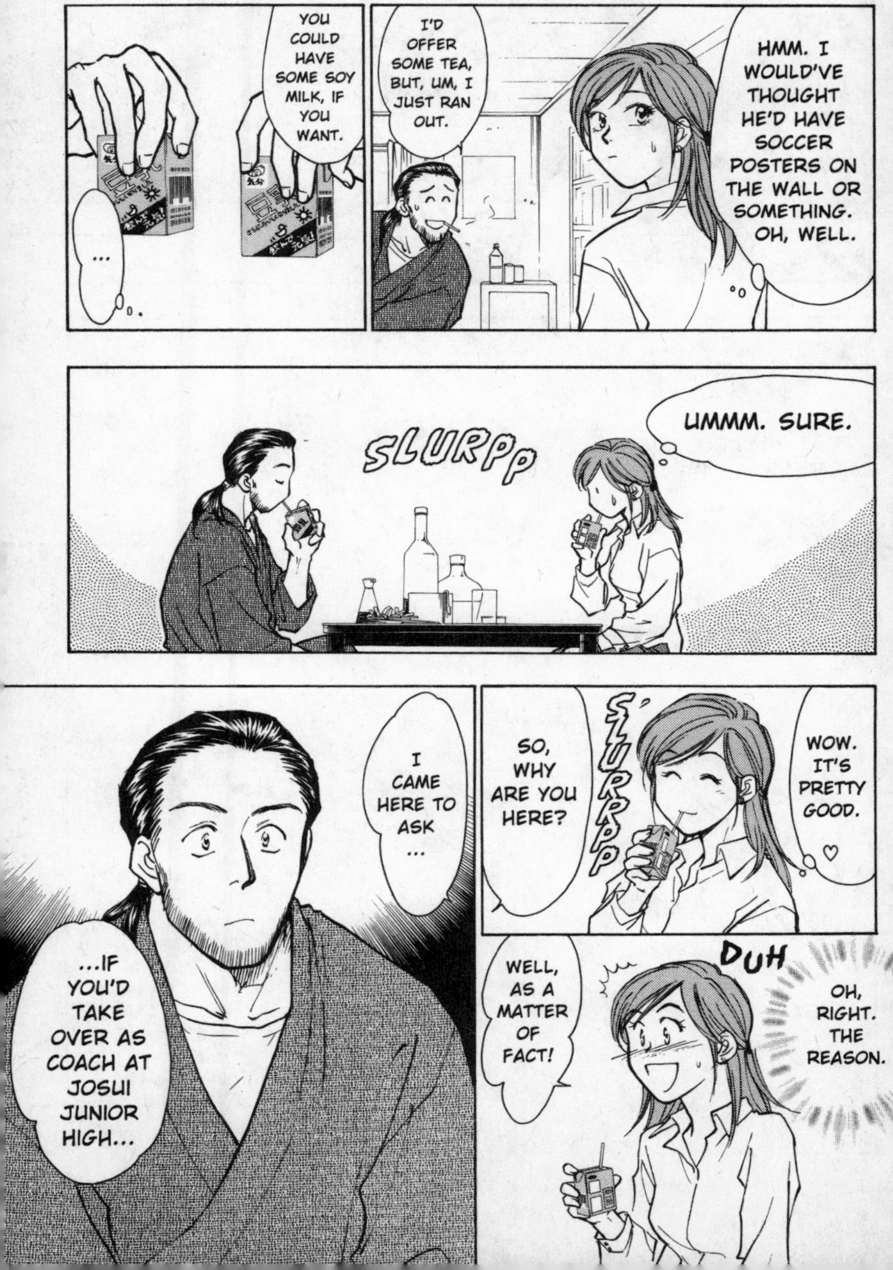
HMM. I WOULD'VE THOUGHT HE'D HAVE SOCCER POSTERS ON THE WALL OR SOMETHING. OH, WELL.
I'D OFFER SOME TEA, BUT, UM, I JUST RAN OUT.
YOU COULD HAVE SOME SOY MILK, IF YOU WANT.
...
UMMM. SURE.
SLURPP
WOW. IT'S PRETTY GOOD. ♡
SLURPP
SO, WHY ARE YOU HERE?
OH, RIGHT. THE REASON.
DUH
WELL, AS A MATTER OF FACT!
I CAME HERE TO ASK ...
...IF YOU'D TAKE OVER AS COACH AT JOSUI JUNIOR HIGH...

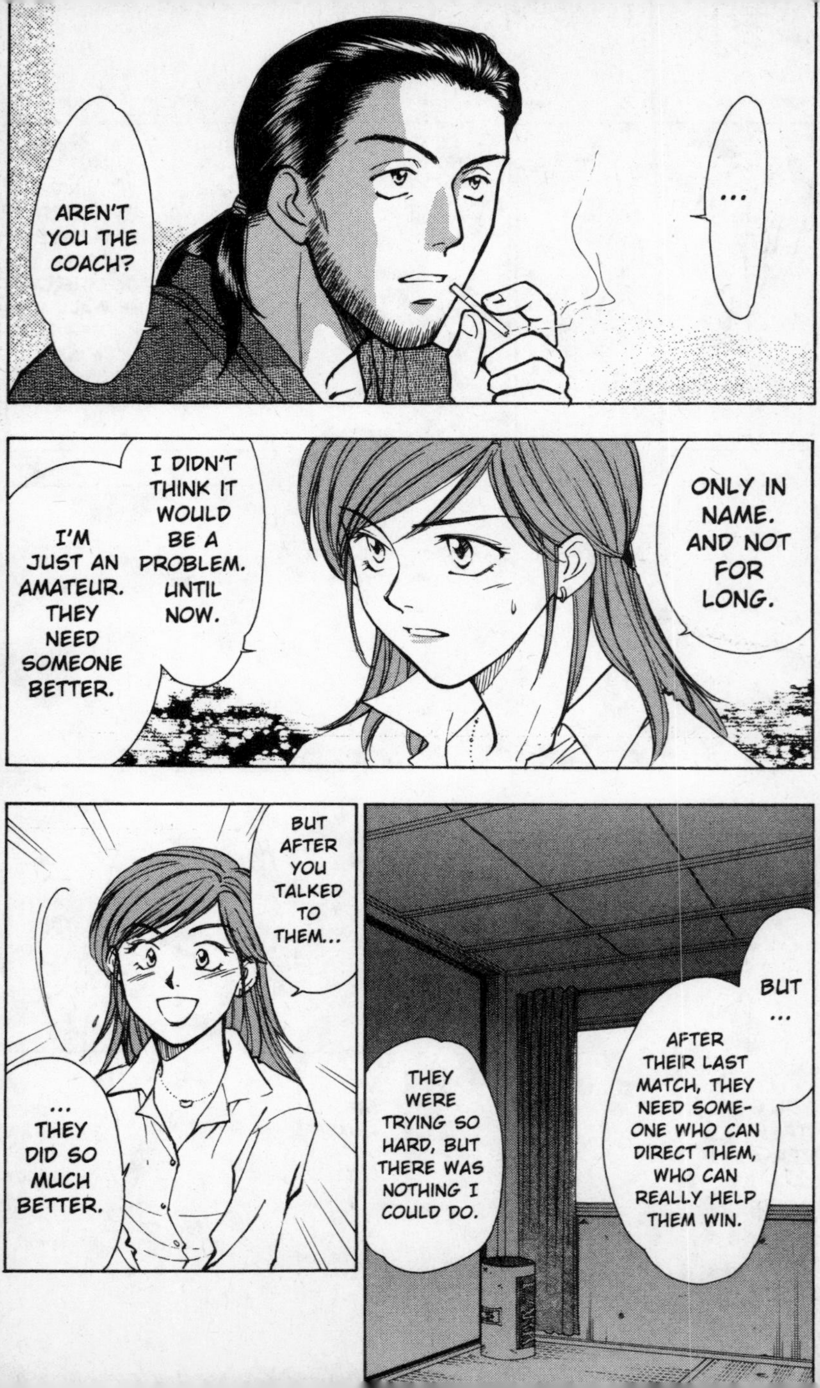
...
AREN'T YOU THE COACH?
ONLY IN NAME. AND NOT FOR LONG.
I DIDN'T THINK IT WOULD BE A PROBLEM. UNTIL NOW.
I'M JUST AN AMATEUR. THEY NEED SOMEONE BETTER.
BUT ...
AFTER THEIR LAST MATCH, THEY NEED SOME-ONE WHO CAN DIRECT THEM, WHO CAN REALLY HELP THEM WIN.
THEY WERE TRYING SO HARD, BUT THERE WAS NOTHING I COULD DO.
BUT AFTER YOU TALKED TO THEM...
... THEY DID SO MUCH BETTER.

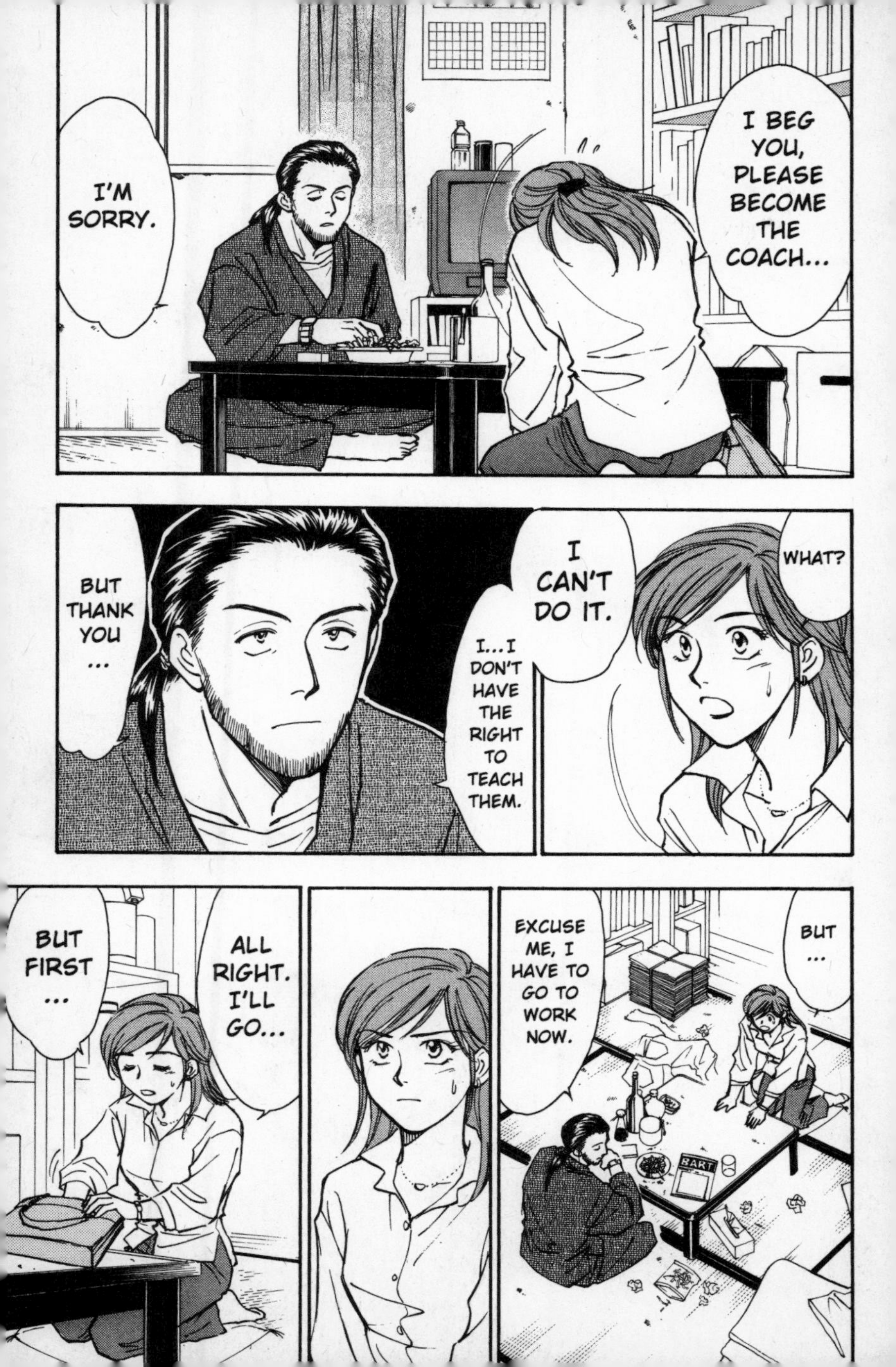
I BEG YOU, PLEASE BECOME THE COACH...
I'M SORRY.
WHAT?
I CAN'T DO IT.
I...I DON'T HAVE THE RIGHT TO TEACH THEM.
BUT THANK YOU...
BUT...
EXCUSE ME, I HAVE TO GO TO WORK NOW.
BART
ALL RIGHT. I'LL GO...
BUT FIRST...

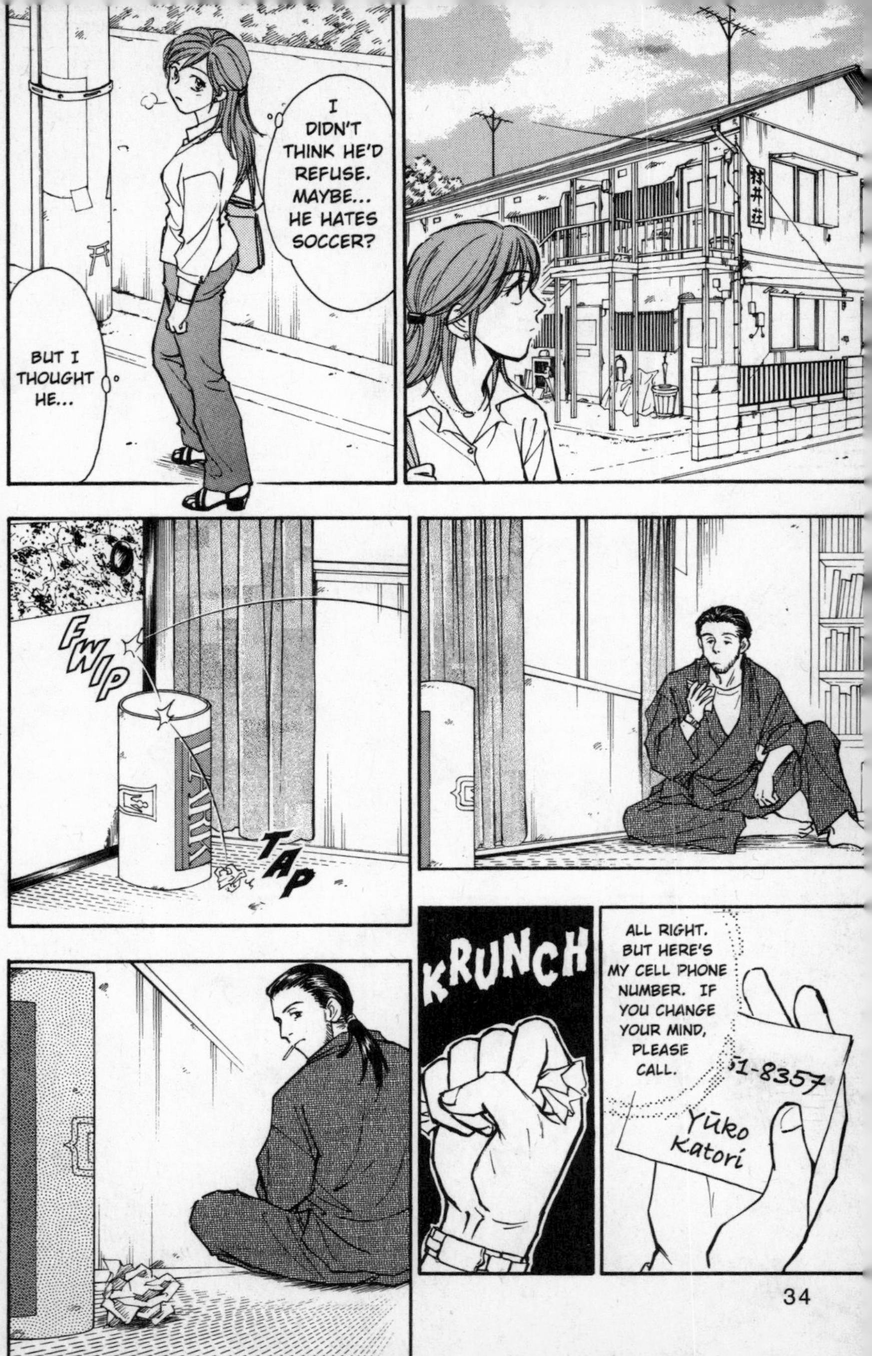
村井荘
I DIDN'T THINK HE'D REFUSE. MAYBE... HE HATES SOCCER?
BUT I THOUGHT HE...
FWIP
TAP
ALL RIGHT. BUT HERE'S MY CELL PHONE NUMBER. IF YOU CHANGE YOUR MIND, PLEASE CALL.
1-8357
Yūko Katori
KRUNCH

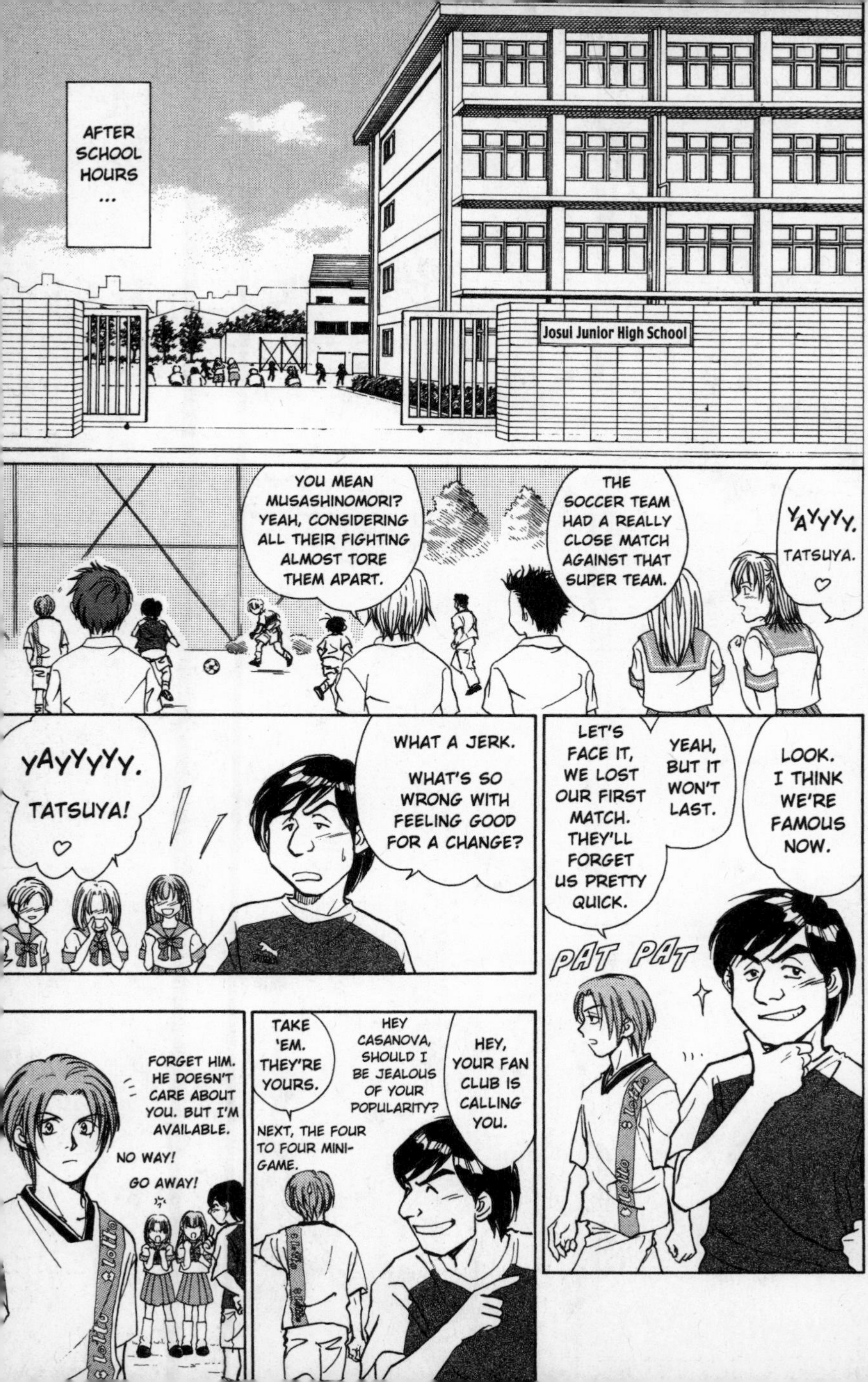
AFTER SCHOOL HOURS ...
Josui Junior High School
YAYYYY. TATSUYA. ♡
THE SOCCER TEAM HAD A REALLY CLOSE MATCH AGAINST THAT SUPER TEAM.
YOU MEAN MUSASHINOMORI? YEAH, CONSIDERING ALL THEIR FIGHTING ALMOST TORE THEM APART.
LOOK. I THINK WE'RE FAMOUS NOW.
YEAH, BUT IT WON'T LAST.
LET'S FACE IT, WE LOST OUR FIRST MATCH. THEY'LL FORGET US PRETTY QUICK.
PAT PAT
WHAT A JERK.
WHAT'S SO WRONG WITH FEELING GOOD FOR A CHANGE?
yAyYyYy. TATSUYA! ♡
HEY, YOUR FAN CLUB IS CALLING YOU.
HEY CASANOVA, SHOULD I BE JEALOUS OF YOUR POPULARITY?
TAKE 'EM. THEY'RE YOURS.
NEXT, THE FOUR TO FOUR MINI-GAME.
FORGET HIM. HE DOESN'T CARE ABOUT YOU. BUT I'M AVAILABLE.
NO WAY!
GO AWAY!

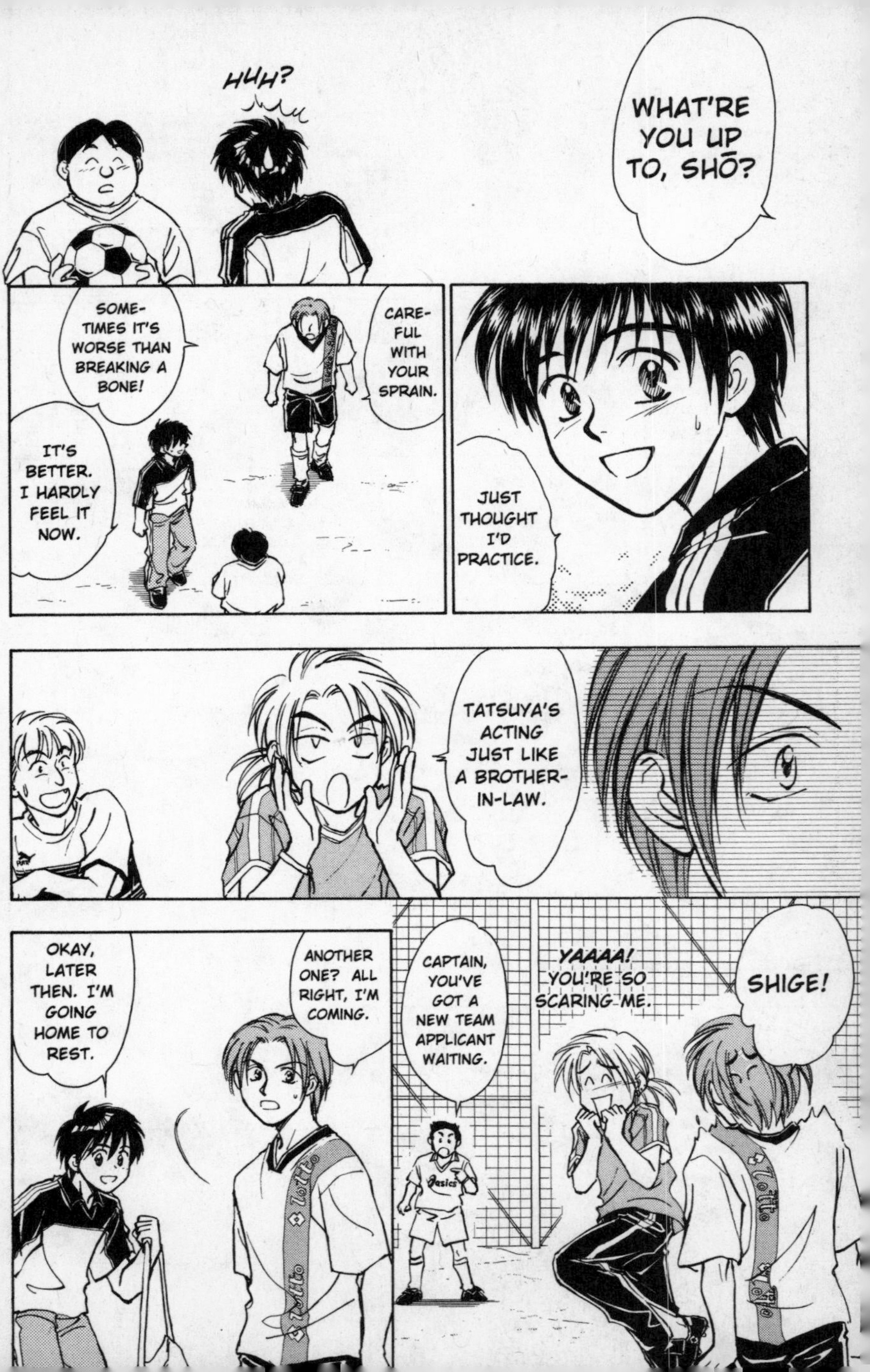
WHAT'RE YOU UP TO, SHŌ?
HUH?
JUST THOUGHT I'D PRACTICE.
CARE-FUL WITH YOUR SPRAIN.
SOME-TIMES IT'S WORSE THAN BREAKING A BONE!
IT'S BETTER. I HARDLY FEEL IT NOW.
TATSUYA'S ACTING JUST LIKE A BROTHER-IN-LAW.
SHIGE!
YAAAA! YOU'RE SO SCARING ME.
CAPTAIN, YOU'VE GOT A NEW TEAM APPLICANT WAITING.
ANOTHER ONE? ALL RIGHT, I'M COMING.
OKAY, LATER THEN. I'M GOING HOME TO REST.

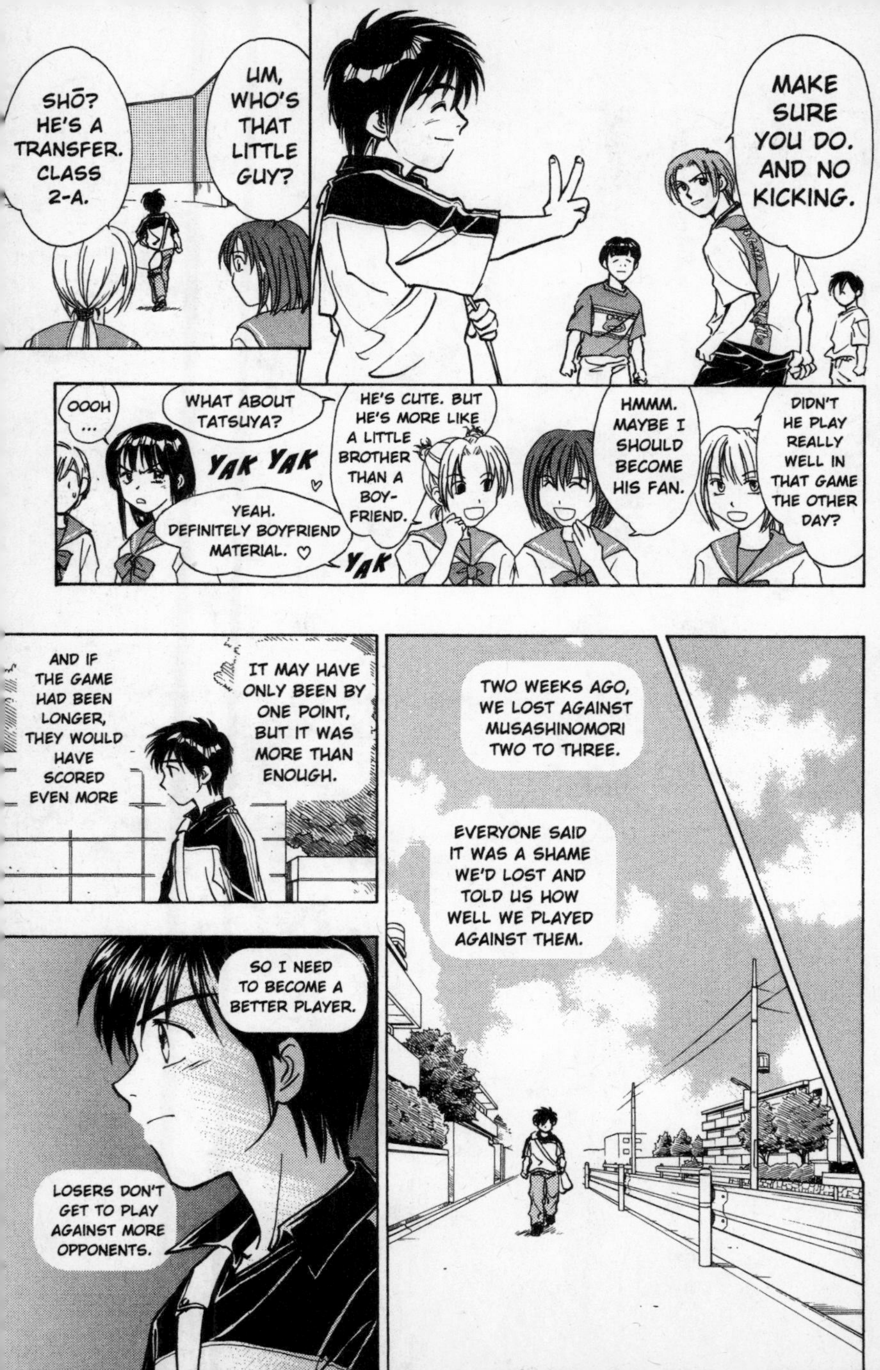
MAKE SURE YOU DO. AND NO KICKING.
UM, WHO'S THAT LITTLE GUY?
SHŌ? HE'S A TRANSFER. CLASS 2-A.
DIDN'T HE PLAY REALLY WELL IN THAT GAME THE OTHER DAY?
HMMM. MAYBE I SHOULD BECOME HIS FAN.
HE'S CUTE. BUT HE'S MORE LIKE A LITTLE BROTHER THAN A BOY-FRIEND.
YAK YAK ♡
WHAT ABOUT TATSUYA?
YEAH. DEFINITELY BOYFRIEND MATERIAL. ♡
YAK
OOOH ...
TWO WEEKS AGO, WE LOST AGAINST MUSASHINOMORI TWO TO THREE.
EVERYONE SAID IT WAS A SHAME WE'D LOST AND TOLD US HOW WELL WE PLAYED AGAINST THEM.
IT MAY HAVE ONLY BEEN BY ONE POINT, BUT IT WAS MORE THAN ENOUGH.
AND IF THE GAME HAD BEEN LONGER, THEY WOULD HAVE SCORED EVEN MORE
SO I NEED TO BECOME A BETTER PLAYER.
LOSERS DON'T GET TO PLAY AGAINST MORE OPPONENTS.

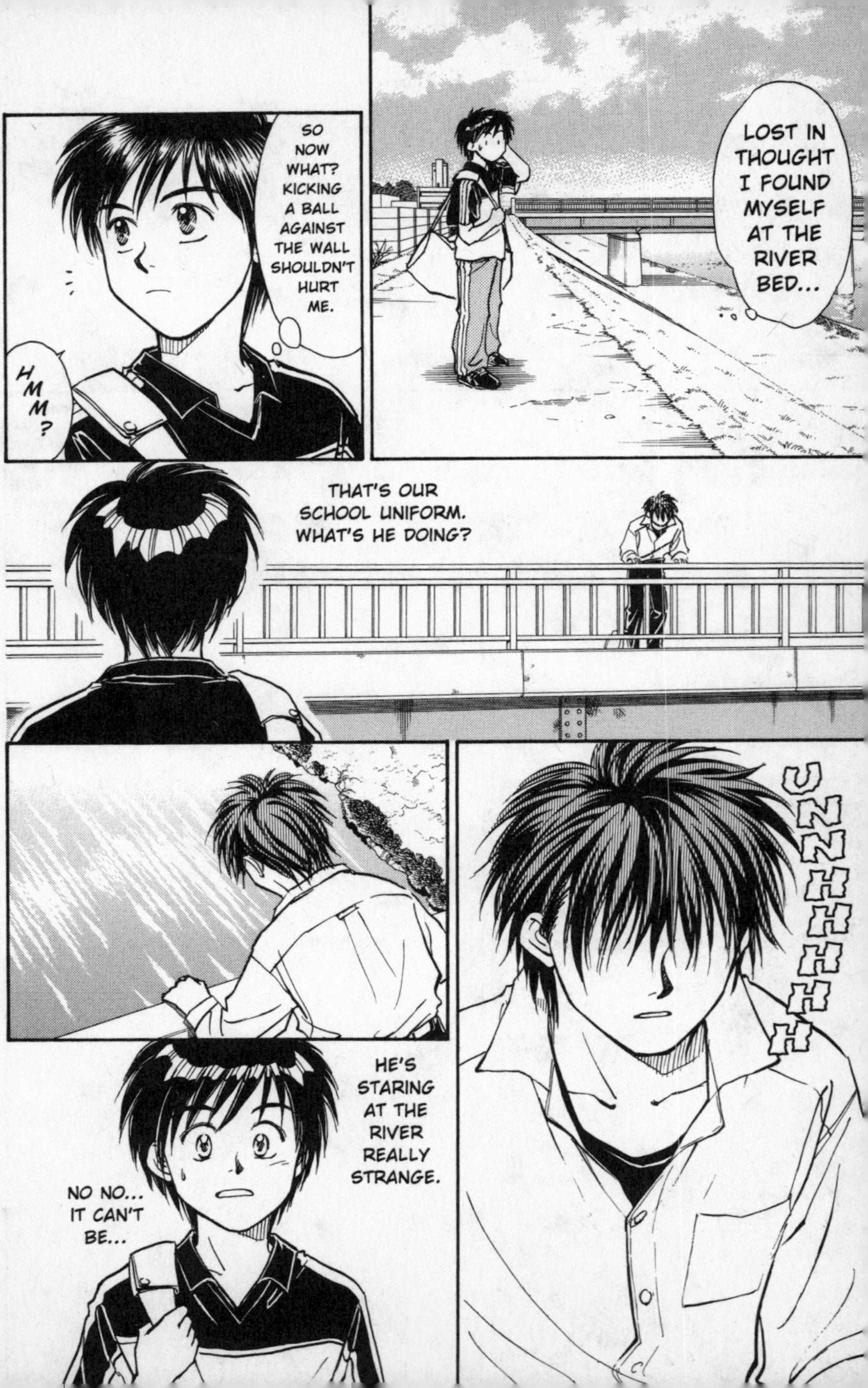
LOST IN THOUGHT I FOUND MYSELF AT THE RIVER BED...
SO NOW WHAT? KICKING A BALL AGAINST THE WALL SHOULDN'T HURT ME.
HMM?
THAT'S OUR SCHOOL UNIFORM. WHAT'S HE DOING?
UNNHHHHH
HE'S STARING AT THE RIVER REALLY STRANGE.
NO NO... IT CAN'T BE...

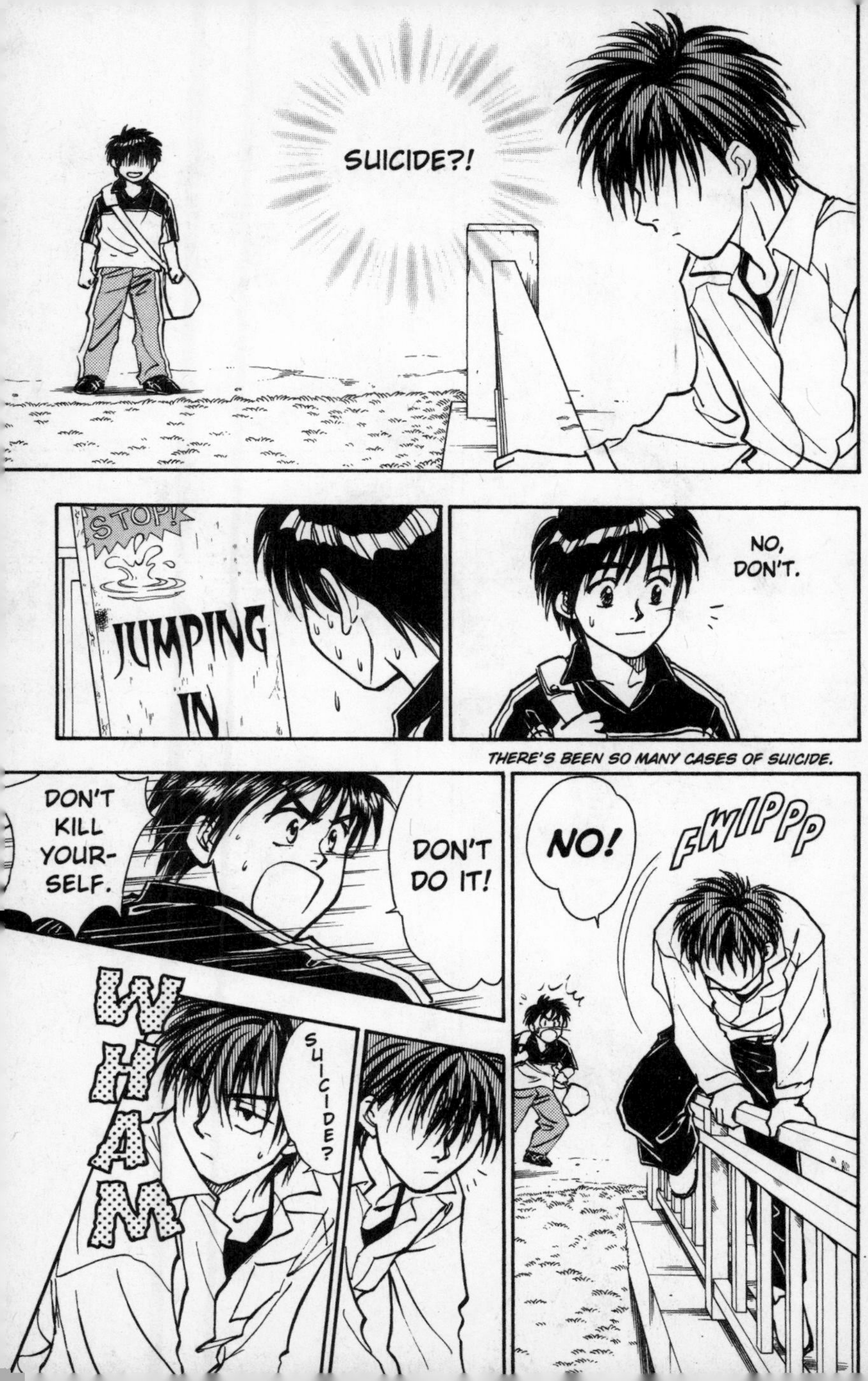
SUICIDE?!
NO, DON'T.
STOP!
JUMPING IN
THERE'S BEEN SO MANY CASES OF SUICIDE.
NO!
FWIPPP
DON'T DO IT!
DON'T KILL YOUR-SELF.
SUICIDE?
WHAM

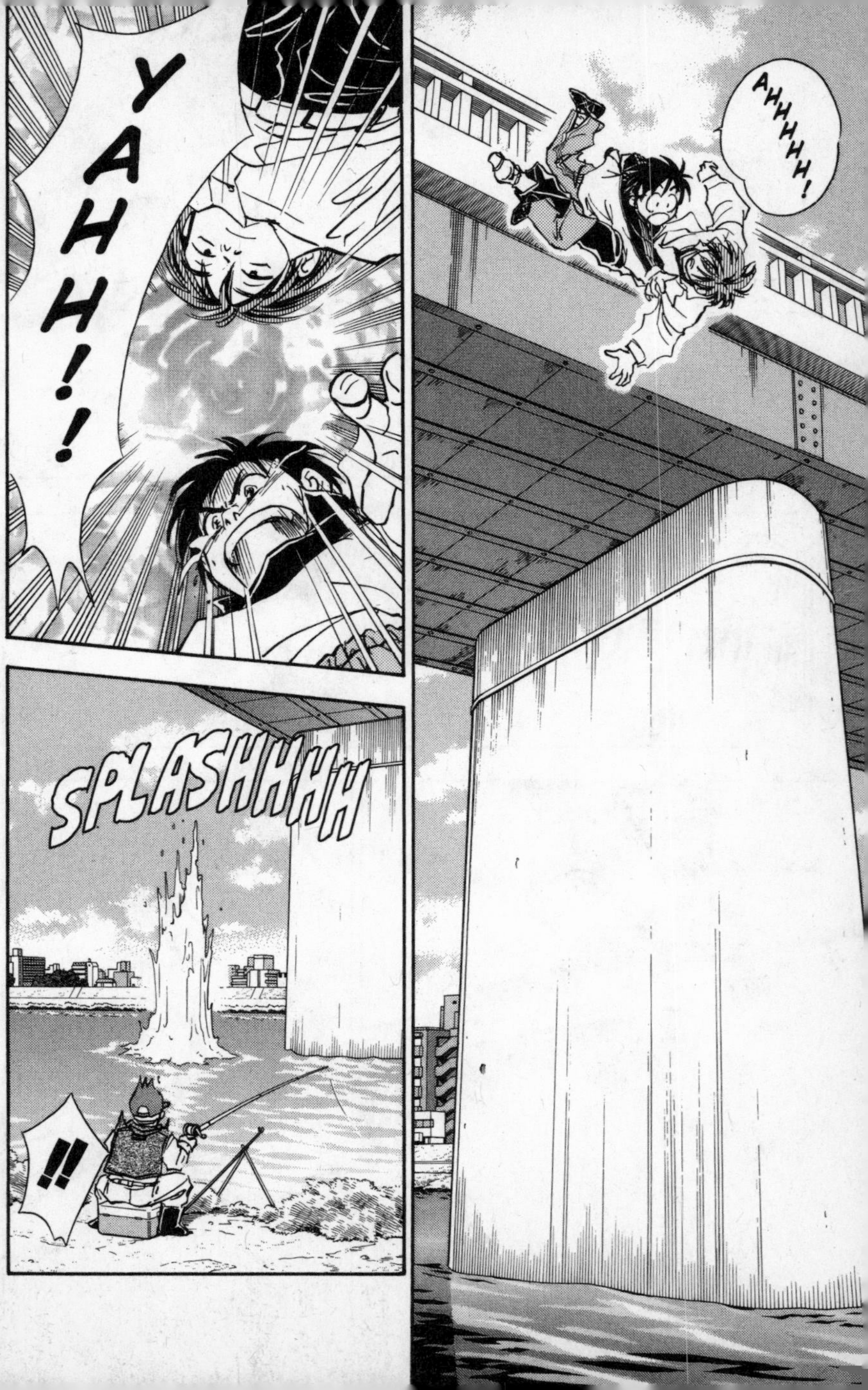
AHHHHH!
YAHHH!!!
SPLASHHHH
!!

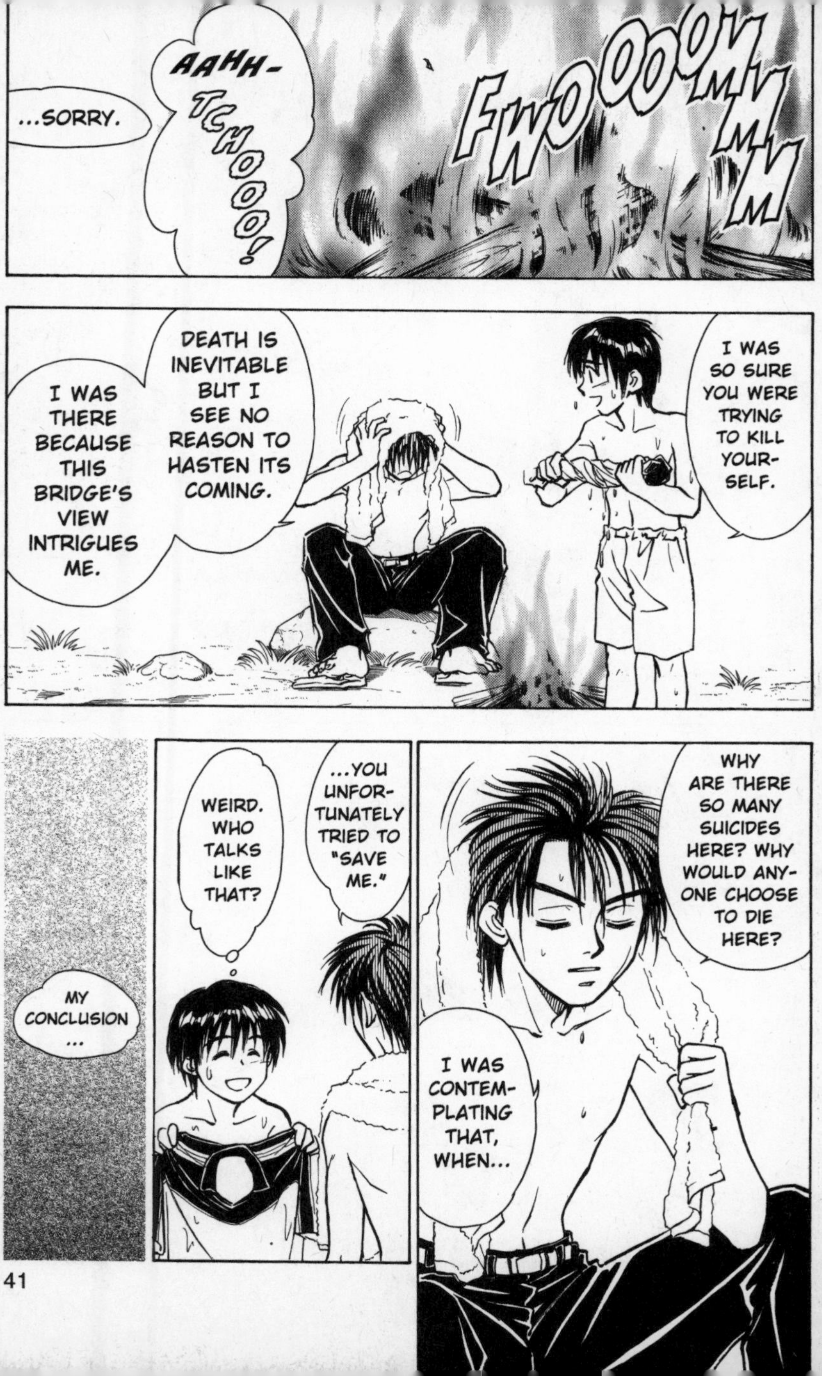
FWOOOOMMM
AAHH-TCHOOOO!
...SORRY.
I WAS SO SURE YOU WERE TRYING TO KILL YOURSELF.
DEATH IS INEVITABLE BUT I SEE NO REASON TO HASTEN ITS COMING.
I WAS THERE BECAUSE THIS BRIDGE'S VIEW INTRIGUES ME.
WHY ARE THERE SO MANY SUICIDES HERE? WHY WOULD ANYONE CHOOSE TO DIE HERE?
I WAS CONTEMPLATING THAT, WHEN...
...YOU UNFORTUNATELY TRIED TO "SAVE ME."
WEIRD. WHO TALKS LIKE THAT?
MY CONCLUSION ...

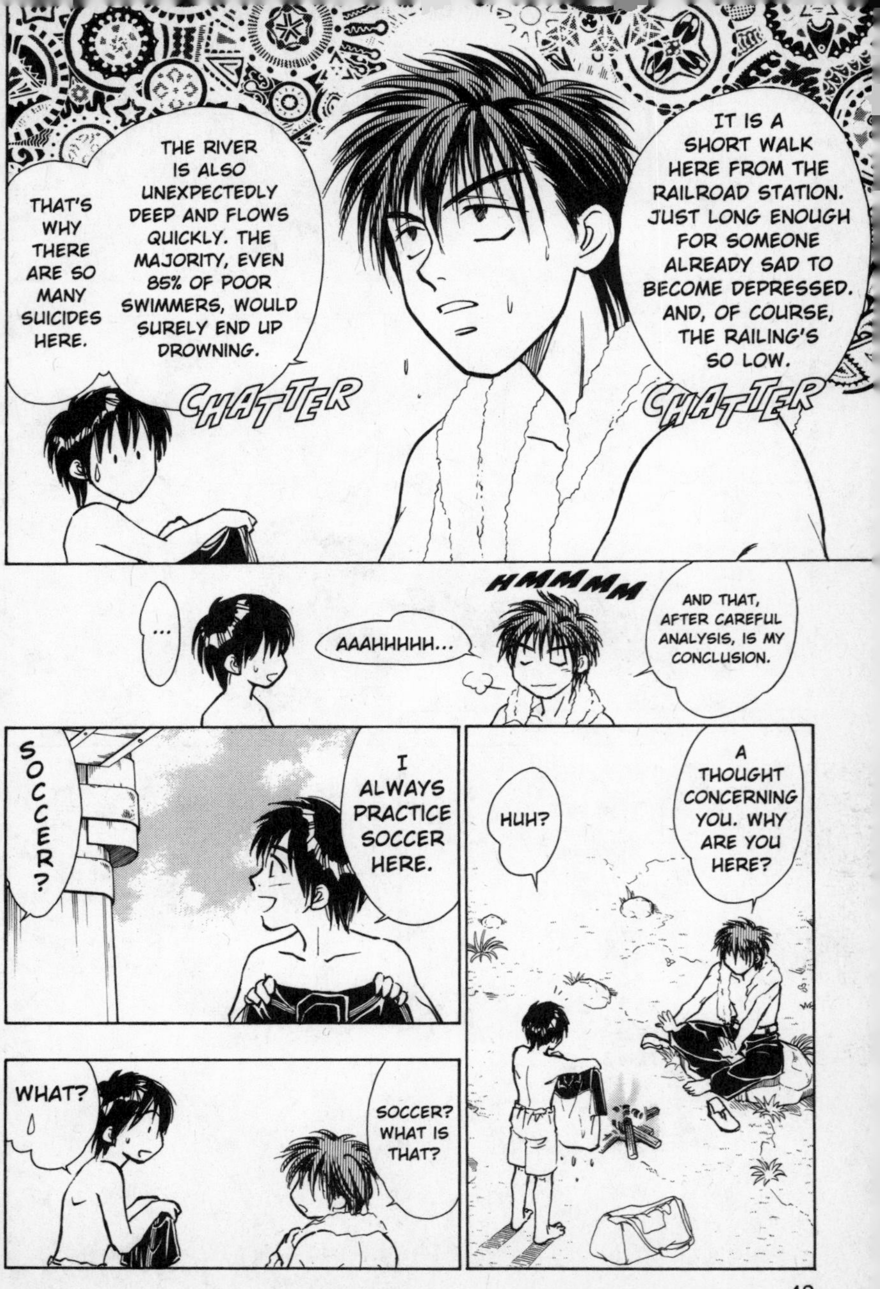
IT IS A SHORT WALK HERE FROM THE RAILROAD STATION. JUST LONG ENOUGH FOR SOMEONE ALREADY SAD TO BECOME DEPRESSED. AND, OF COURSE, THE RAILING'S SO LOW.
CHATTER
THE RIVER IS ALSO UNEXPECTEDLY DEEP AND FLOWS QUICKLY. THE MAJORITY, EVEN 85% OF POOR SWIMMERS, WOULD SURELY END UP DROWNING.
THAT'S WHY THERE ARE SO MANY SUICIDES HERE.
CHATTER
AND THAT, AFTER CAREFUL ANALYSIS, IS MY CONCLUSION.
HMMMMM
AAAHHHHH...
...
A THOUGHT CONCERNING YOU. WHY ARE YOU HERE?
HUH?
I ALWAYS PRACTICE SOCCER HERE.
SOCCER?
SOCCER? WHAT IS THAT?
WHAT?

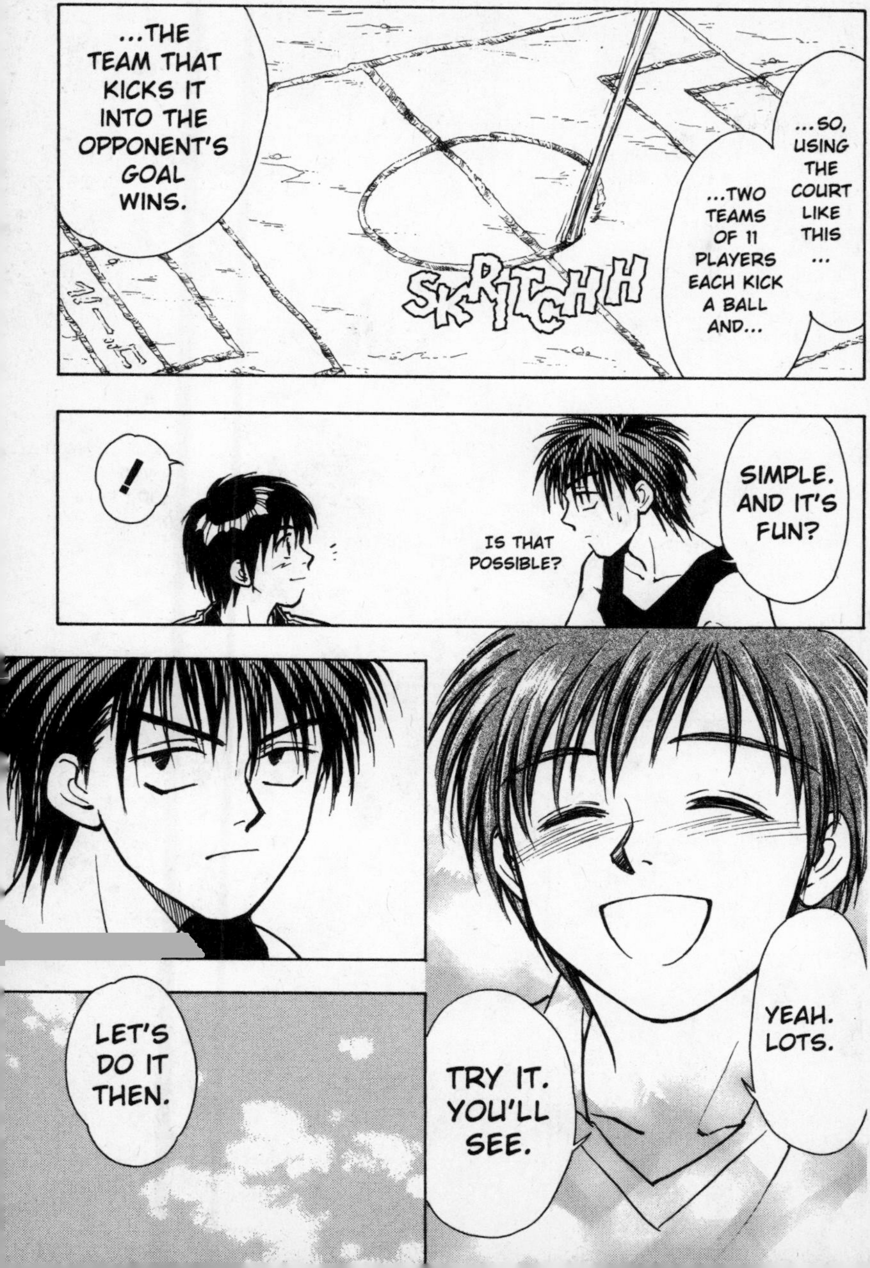
...SO, USING THE COURT LIKE THIS ...
...TWO TEAMS OF 11 PLAYERS EACH KICK A BALL AND...
SKRITCHH
...THE TEAM THAT KICKS IT INTO THE OPPONENT'S GOAL WINS.
SIMPLE. AND IT'S FUN?
IS THAT POSSIBLE?
!
YEAH. LOTS.
TRY IT. YOU'LL SEE.
LET'S DO IT THEN.

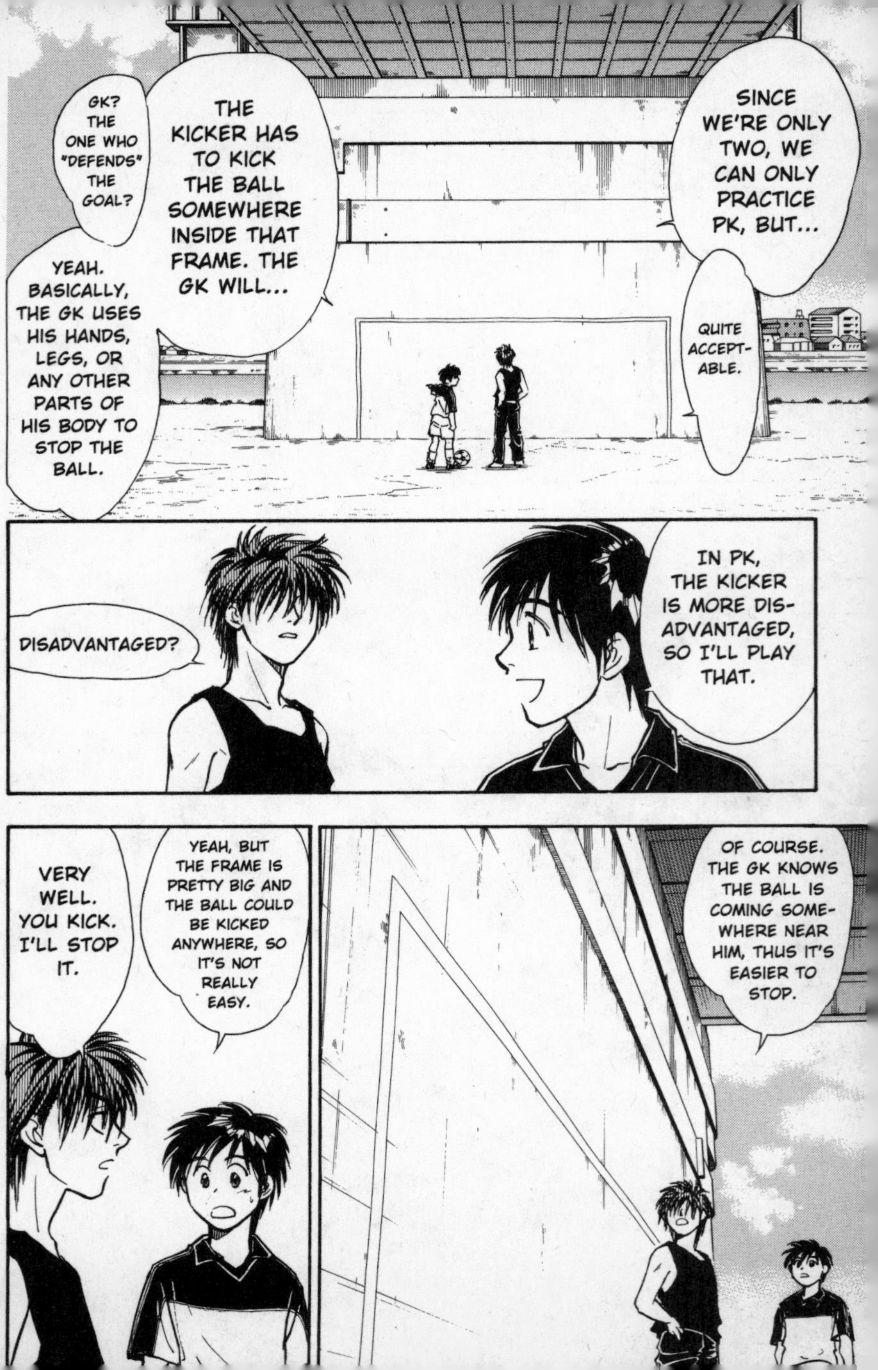
SINCE WE'RE ONLY TWO, WE CAN ONLY PRACTICE PK, BUT...
QUITE ACCEPT-ABLE.
THE KICKER HAS TO KICK THE BALL SOMEWHERE INSIDE THAT FRAME. THE GK WILL...
GK? THE ONE WHO "DEFENDS" THE GOAL?
YEAH. BASICALLY, THE GK USES HIS HANDS, LEGS, OR ANY OTHER PARTS OF HIS BODY TO STOP THE BALL.
IN PK, THE KICKER IS MORE DIS-ADVANTAGED, SO I'LL PLAY THAT.
DISADVANTAGED?
OF COURSE. THE GK KNOWS THE BALL IS COMING SOME-WHERE NEAR HIM, THUS IT'S EASIER TO STOP.
YEAH, BUT THE FRAME IS PRETTY BIG AND THE BALL COULD BE KICKED ANYWHERE, SO IT'S NOT REALLY EASY.
VERY WELL. YOU KICK. I'LL STOP IT.

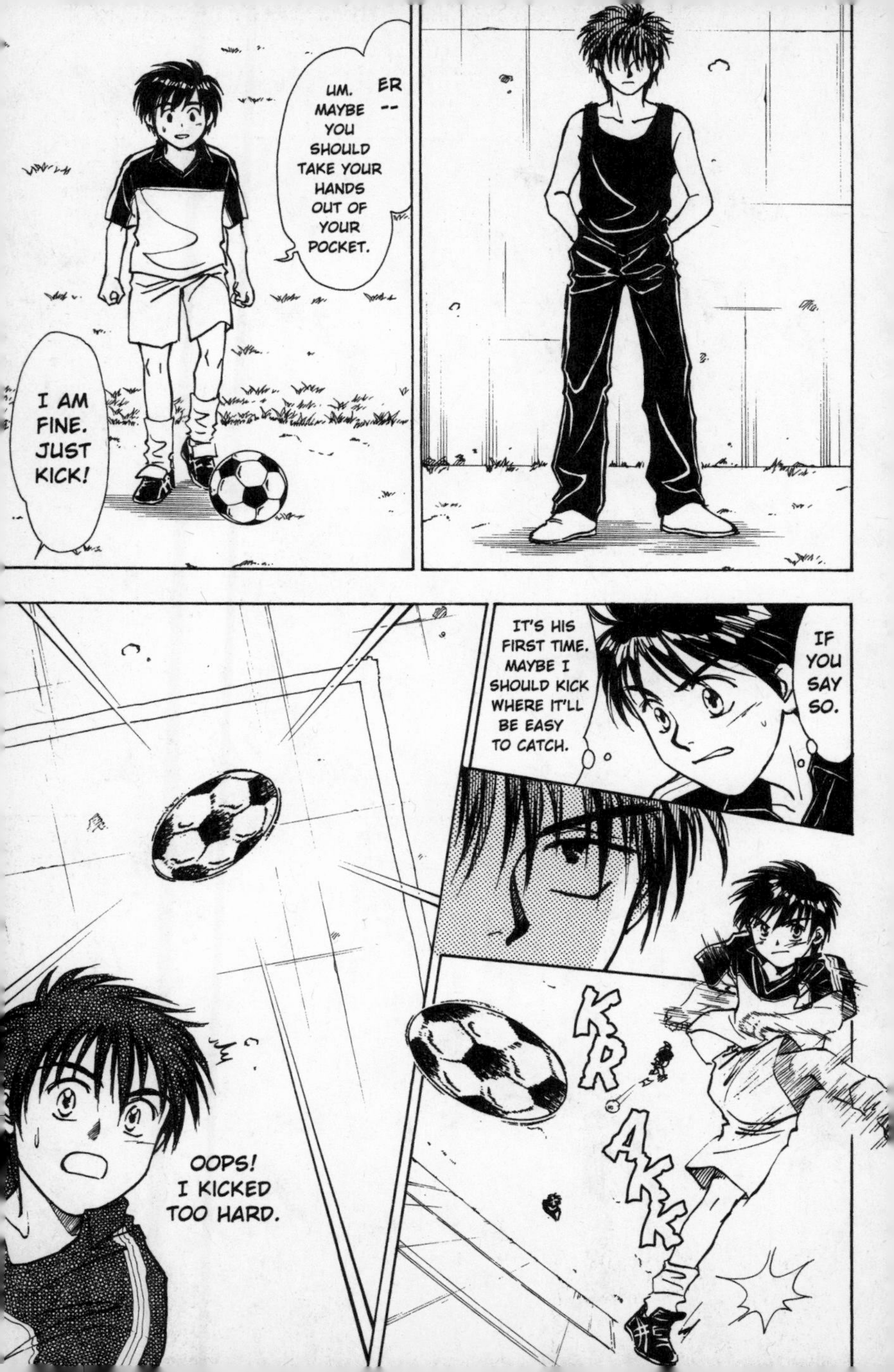
UM. ER -- MAYBE YOU SHOULD TAKE YOUR HANDS OUT OF YOUR POCKET.
I AM FINE. JUST KICK!
IF YOU SAY SO.
IT'S HIS FIRST TIME. MAYBE I SHOULD KICK WHERE IT'LL BE EASY TO CATCH.
KRAKK
OOPS! I KICKED TOO HARD.

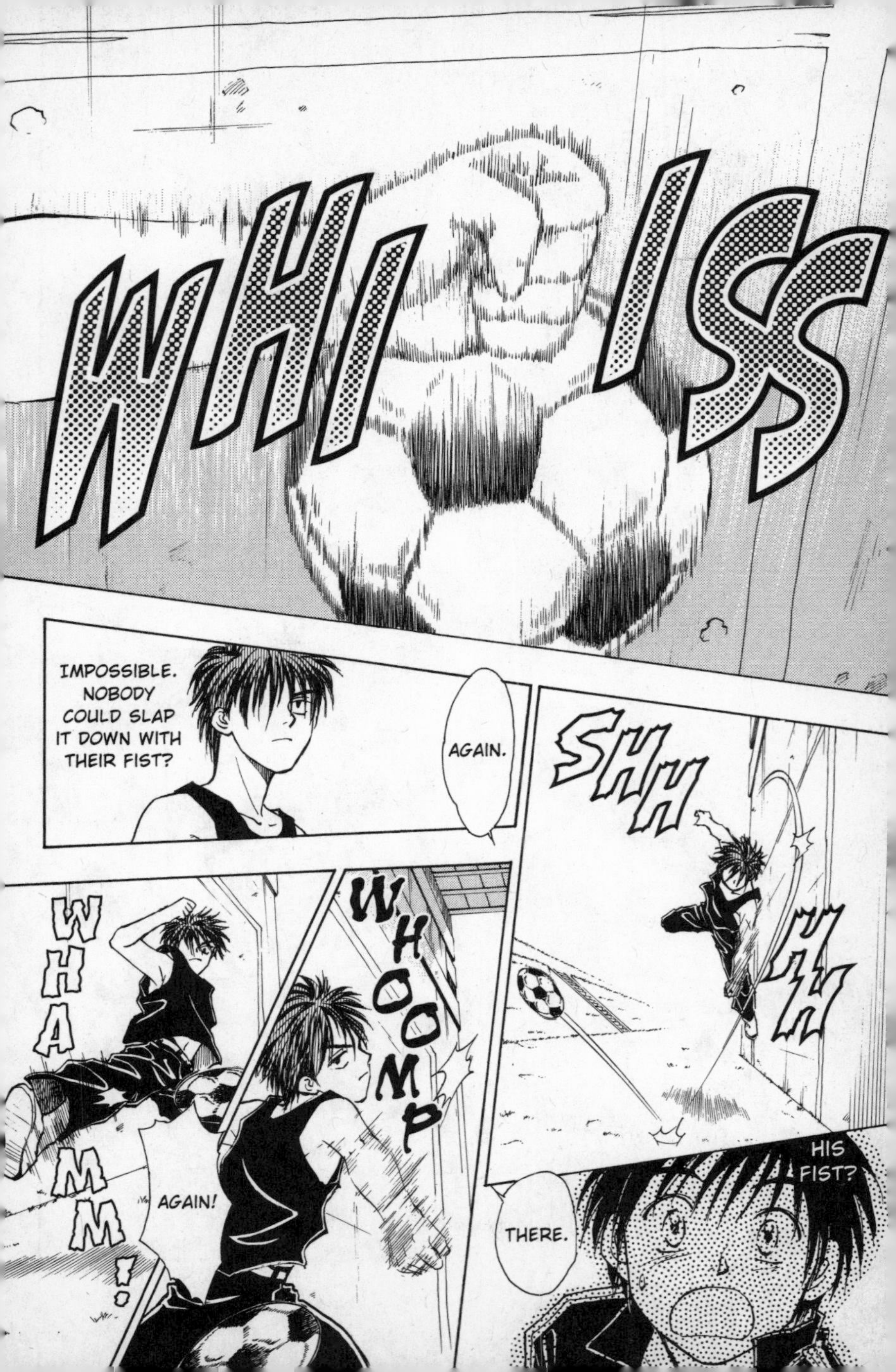
WHIISS
SHH
H
IMPOSSIBLE. NOBODY COULD SLAP IT DOWN WITH THEIR FIST?
AGAIN.
WHOOMP
AGAIN!
WHAMM!
HIS FIST?
THERE.

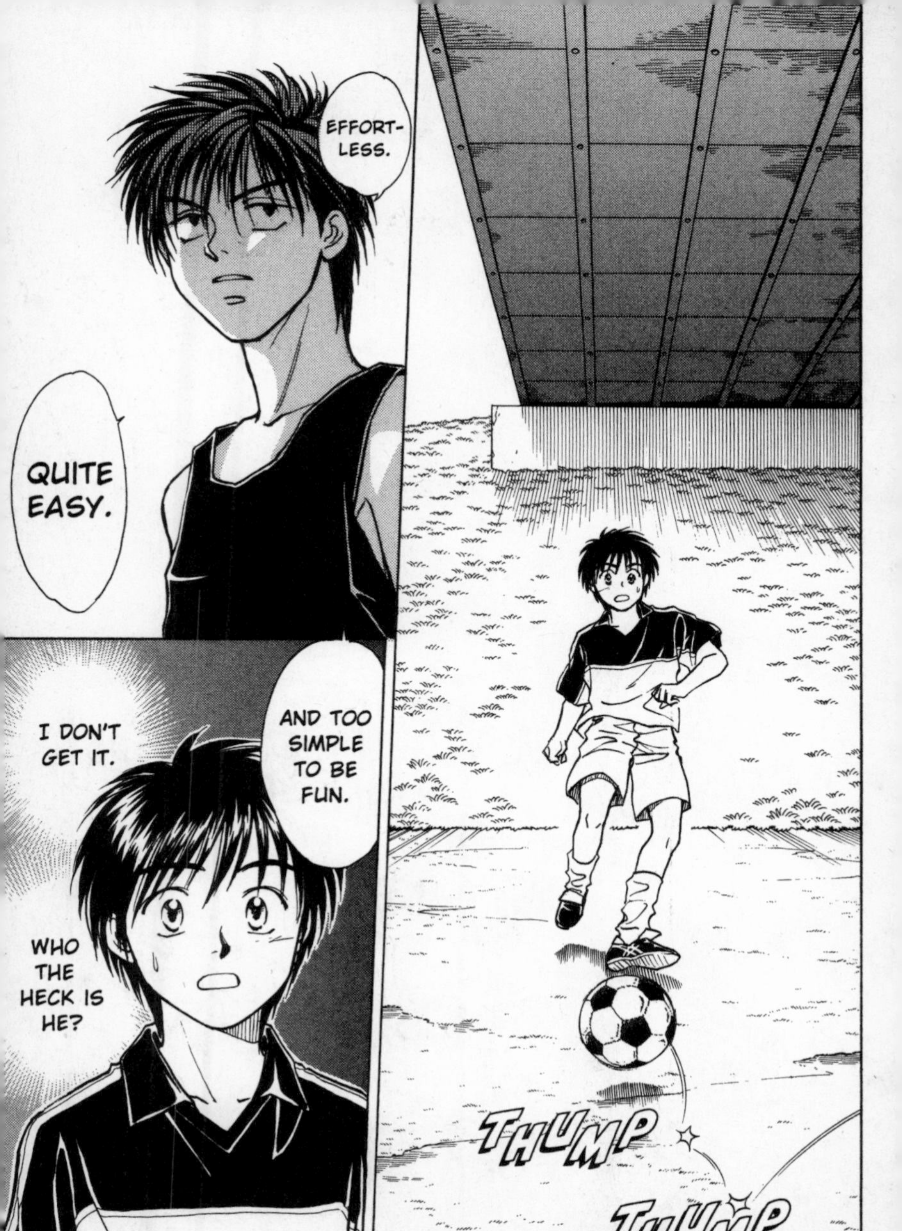
THUMP
THUMP
EFFORT-LESS.
QUITE EASY.
AND TOO SIMPLE TO BE FUN.
I DON'T GET IT.
WHO THE HECK IS HE?

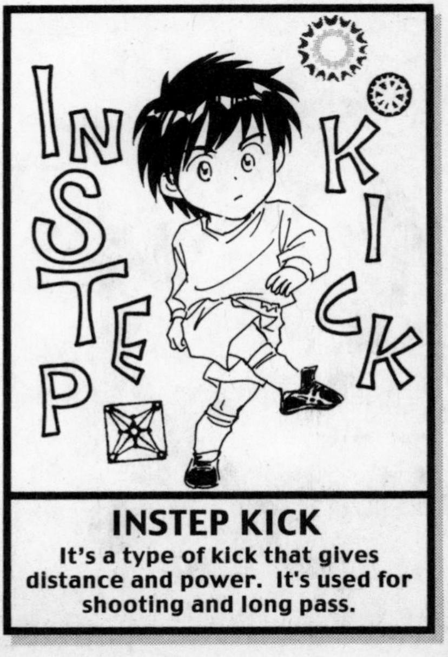
INSTEP
KICK

**INSTEP KICK**

**It's a type of kick that gives distance and power. It's used for shooting and long pass.**

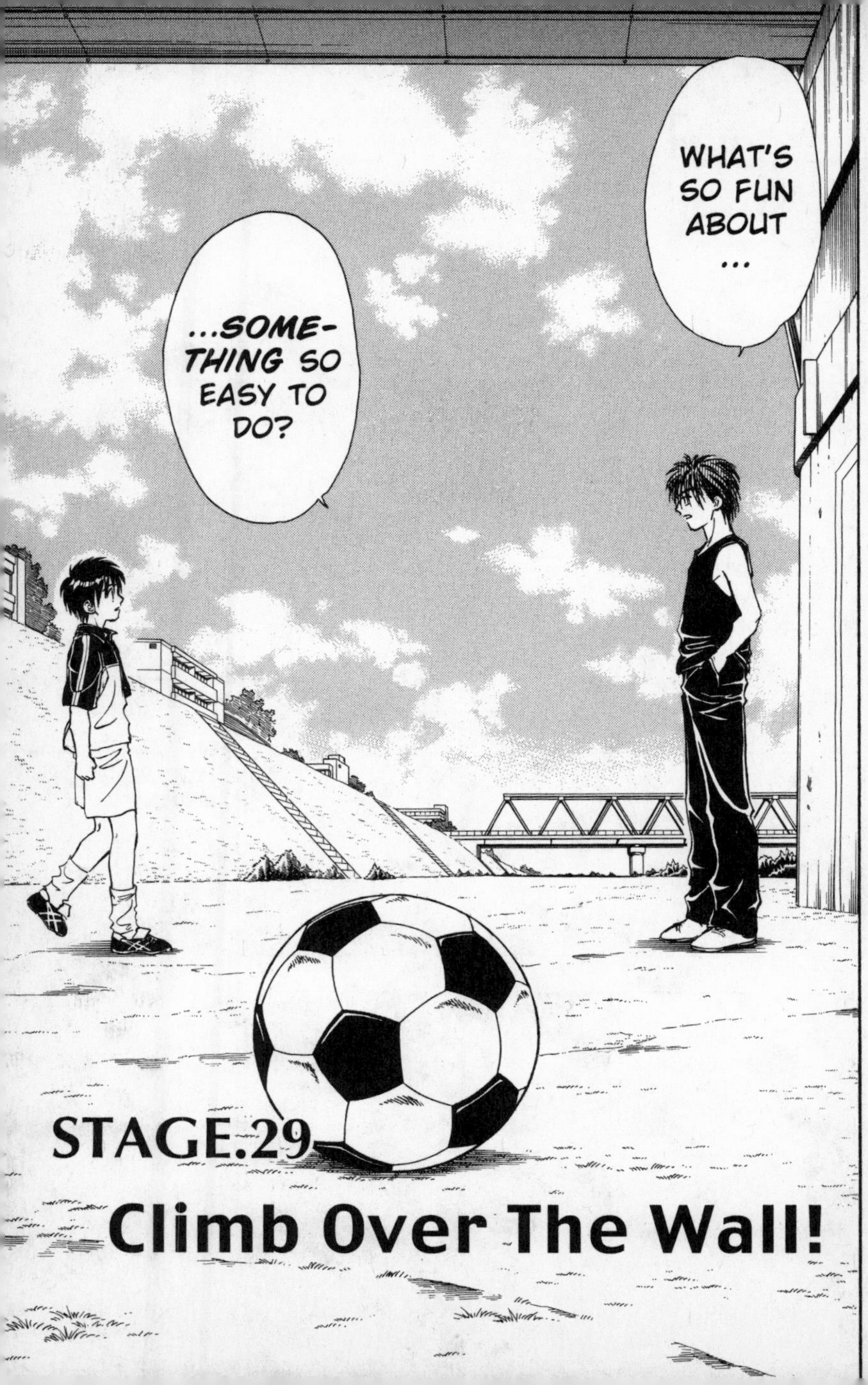
WHAT'S SO FUN ABOUT ...
...SOMETHING SO EASY TO DO?

# STAGE.29 Climb Over The Wall!

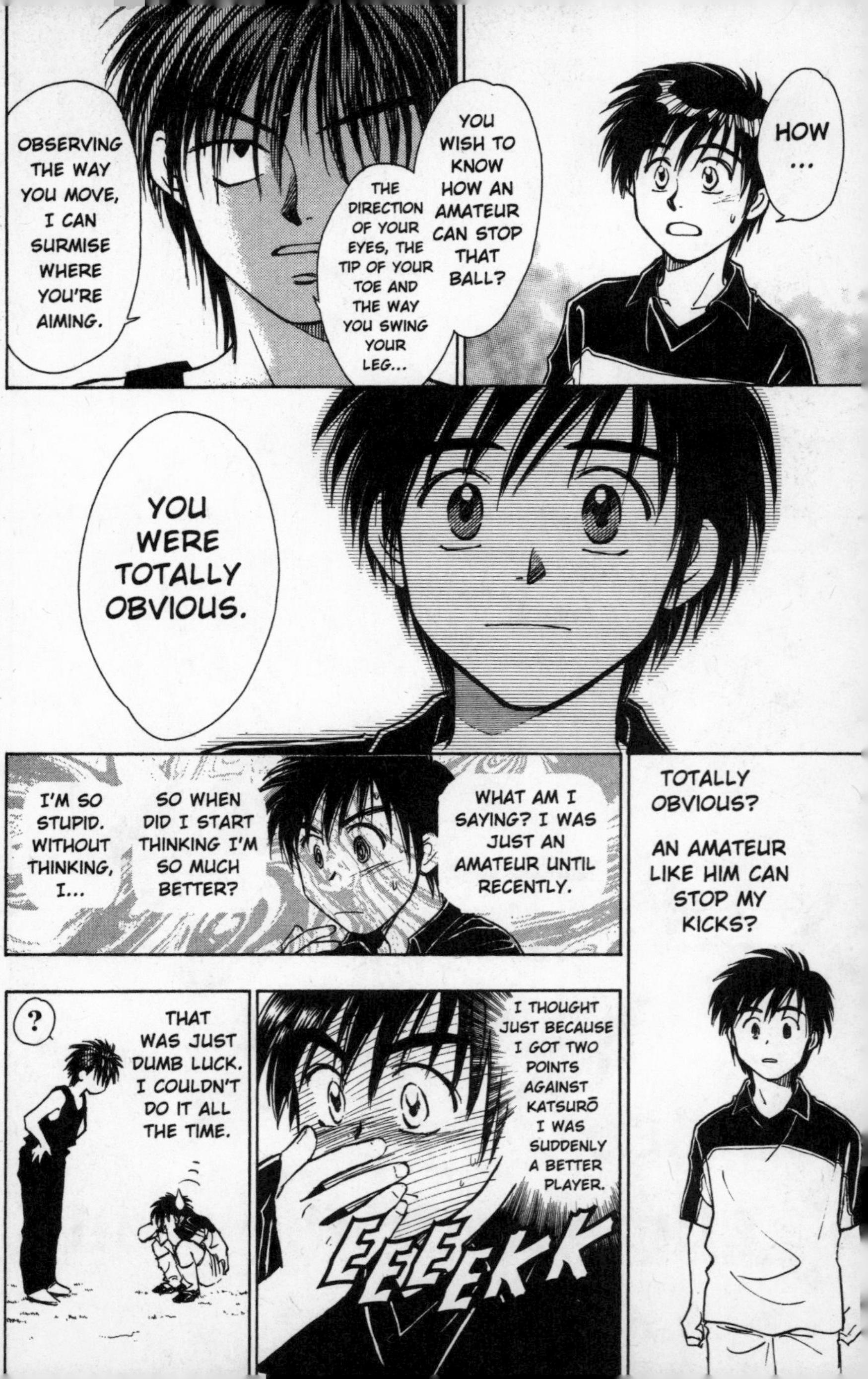

HOW ...
YOU WISH TO KNOW HOW AN AMATEUR CAN STOP THAT BALL?
THE DIRECTION OF YOUR EYES, THE TIP OF YOUR TOE AND THE WAY YOU SWING YOUR LEG...
OBSERVING THE WAY YOU MOVE, I CAN SURMISE WHERE YOU'RE AIMING.
YOU WERE TOTALLY OBVIOUS.
TOTALLY OBVIOUS?
AN AMATEUR LIKE HIM CAN STOP MY KICKS?
WHAT AM I SAYING? I WAS JUST AN AMATEUR UNTIL RECENTLY.
SO WHEN DID I START THINKING I'M SO MUCH BETTER?
I'M SO STUPID. WITHOUT THINKING, I...
I THOUGHT JUST BECAUSE I GOT TWO POINTS AGAINST KATSURŌ I WAS SUDDENLY A BETTER PLAYER.
EEEEKK
?
THAT WAS JUST DUMB LUCK. I COULDN'T DO IT ALL THE TIME.

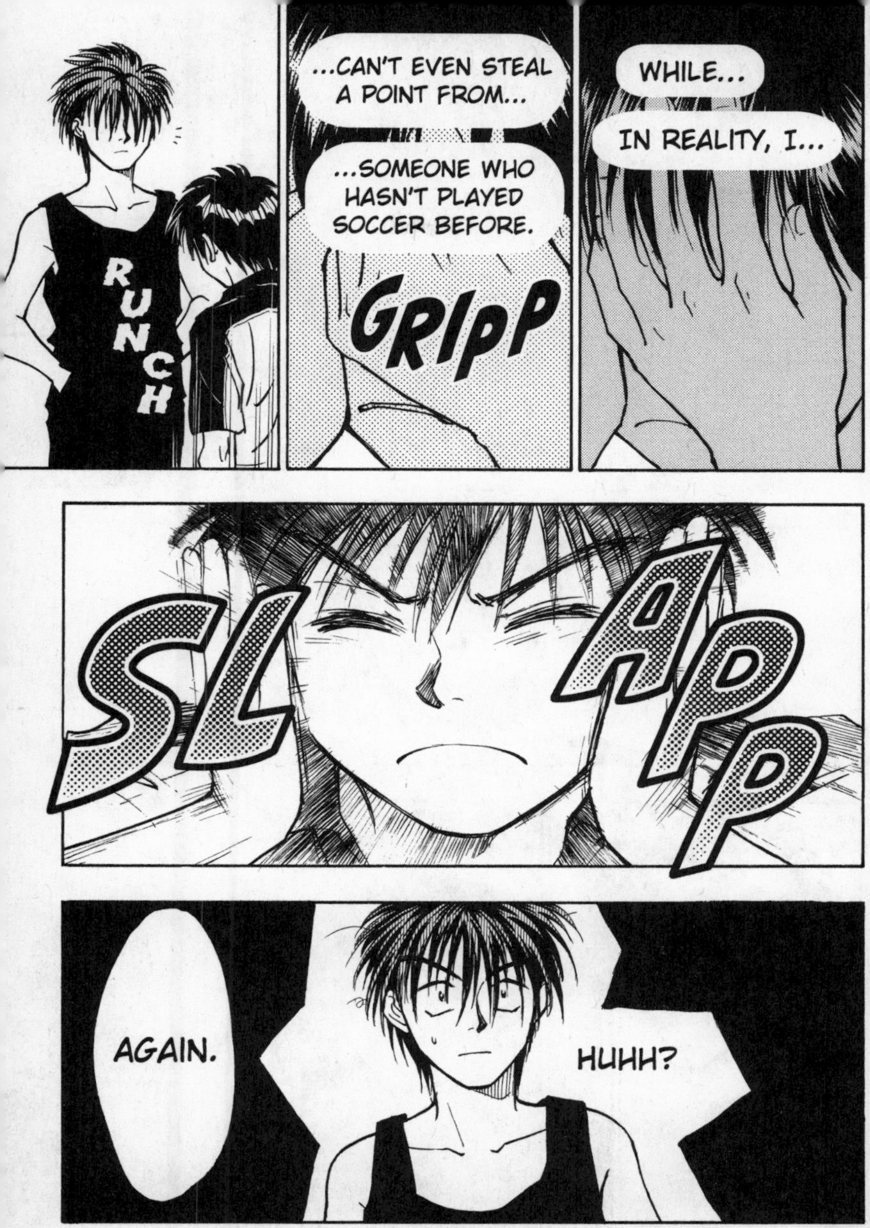
WHILE...
IN REALITY, I...
...CAN'T EVEN STEAL A POINT FROM...
...SOMEONE WHO HASN'T PLAYED SOCCER BEFORE.
GRIPP
RUNCH
SLAPP
HUHH?
AGAIN.

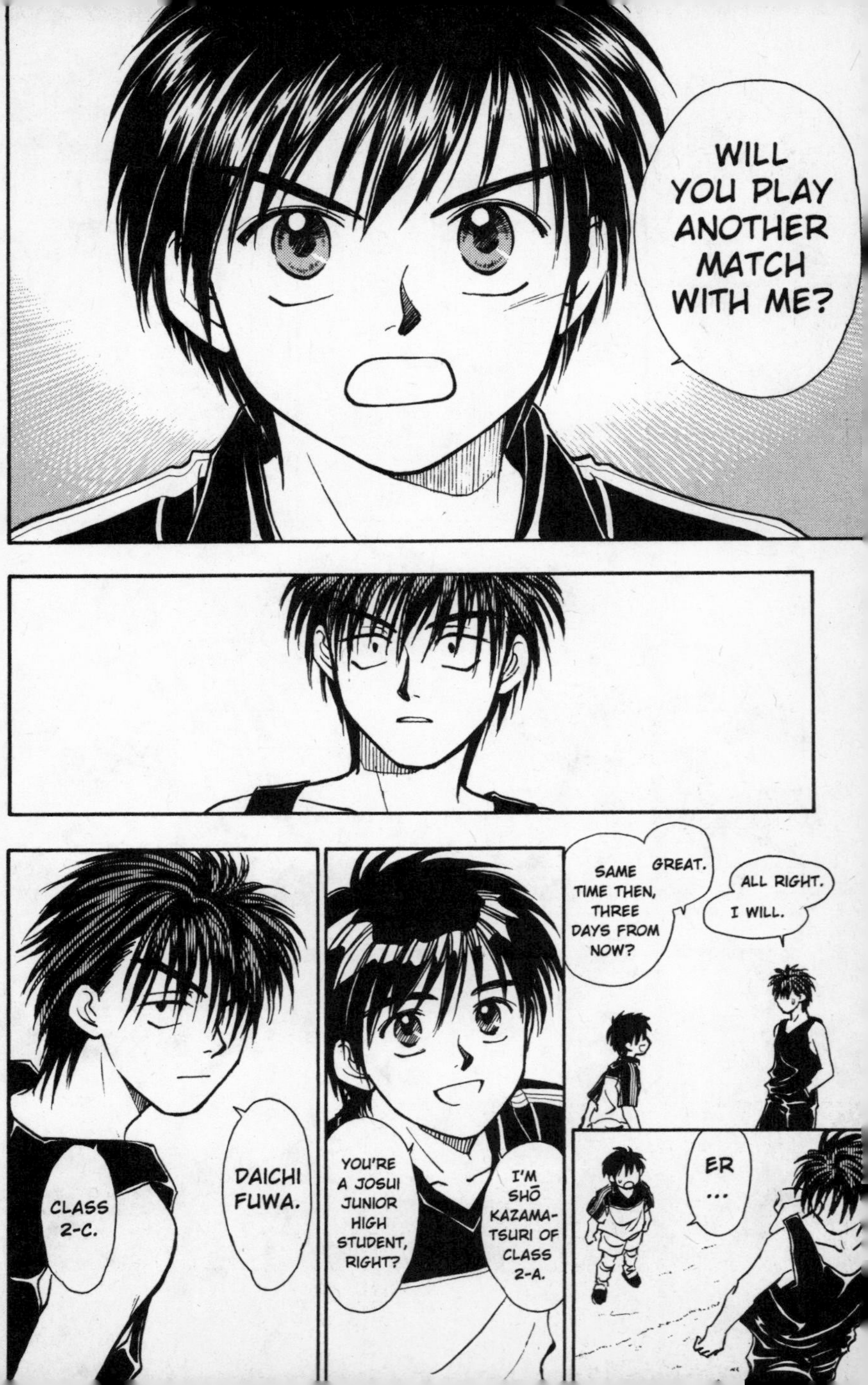
WILL YOU PLAY ANOTHER MATCH WITH ME?
ALL RIGHT. I WILL.
GREAT. SAME TIME THEN, THREE DAYS FROM NOW?
ER ...
I'M SHŌ KAZAMATSURI OF CLASS 2-A.
YOU'RE A JOSUI JUNIOR HIGH STUDENT, RIGHT?
DAICHI FUWA.
CLASS 2-C.

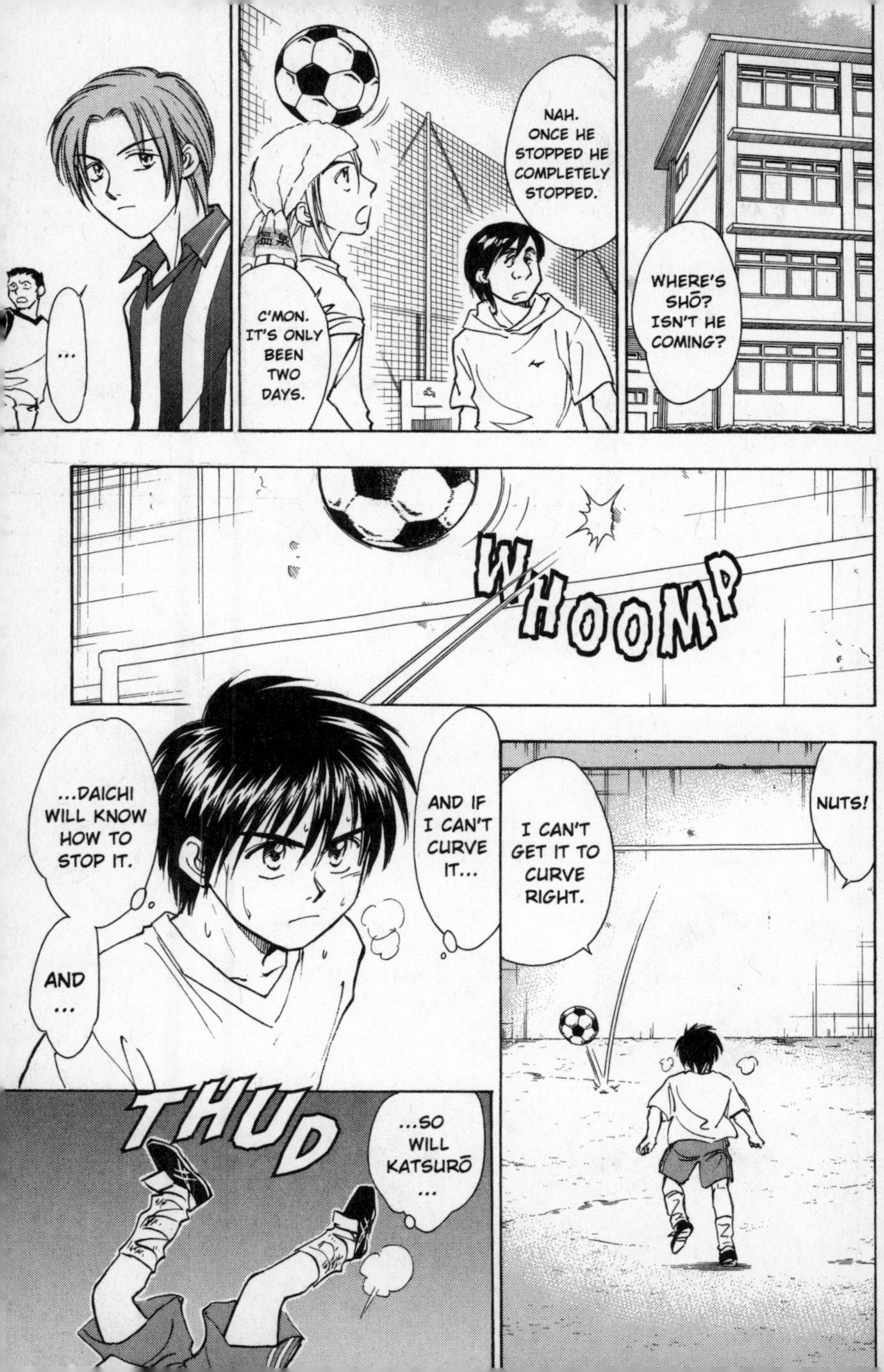
WHERE'S SHŌ? ISN'T HE COMING?
NAH. ONCE HE STOPPED HE COMPLETELY STOPPED.
C'MON. IT'S ONLY BEEN TWO DAYS.
...
WHOOMP
NUTS!
I CAN'T GET IT TO CURVE RIGHT.
AND IF I CAN'T CURVE IT...
...DAICHI WILL KNOW HOW TO STOP IT.
AND ...
THUD
...SO WILL KATSURŌ ...

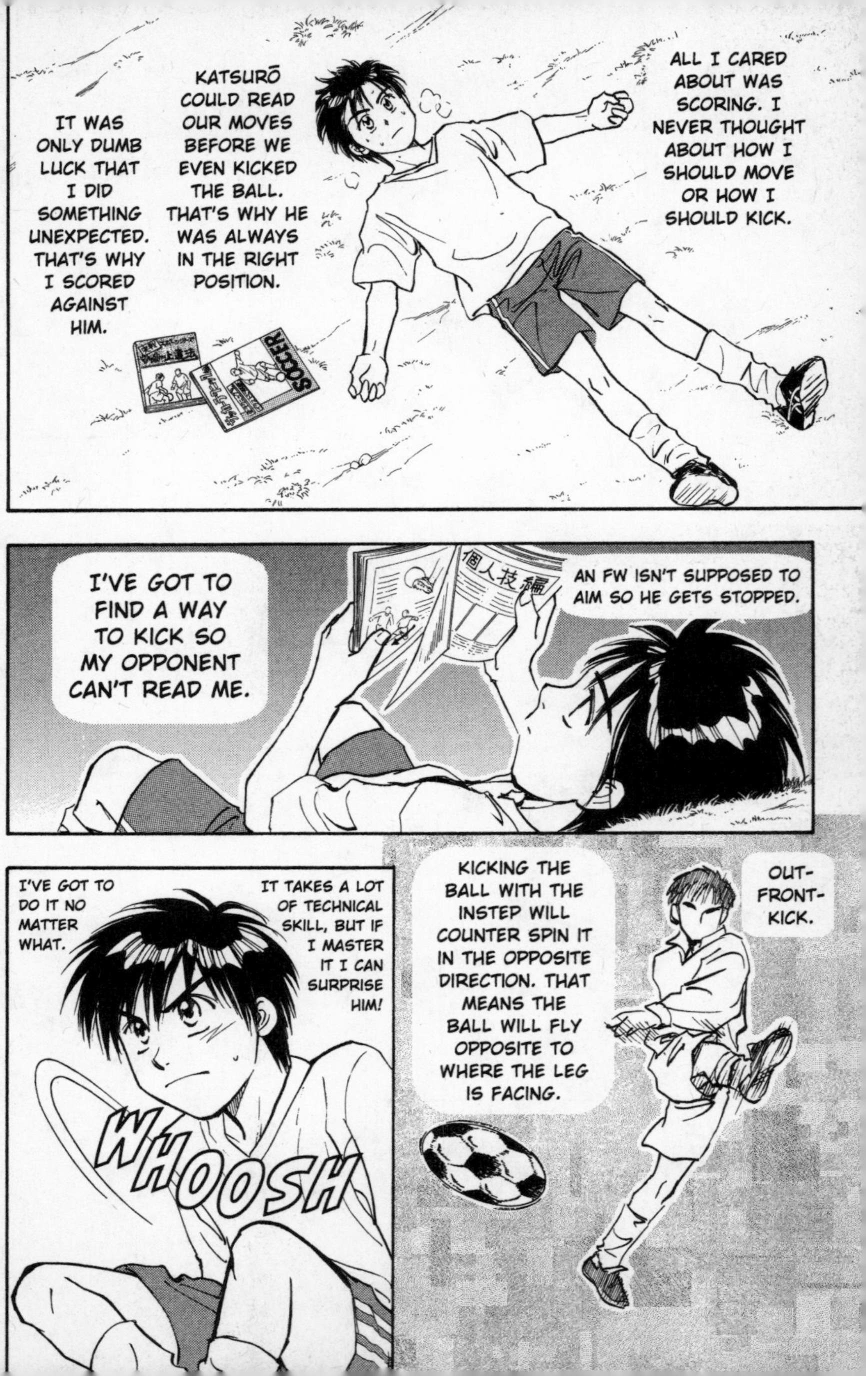
ALL I CARED ABOUT WAS SCORING. I NEVER THOUGHT ABOUT HOW I SHOULD MOVE OR HOW I SHOULD KICK.
KATSURŌ COULD READ OUR MOVES BEFORE WE EVEN KICKED THE BALL. THAT'S WHY HE WAS ALWAYS IN THE RIGHT POSITION.
IT WAS ONLY DUMB LUCK THAT I DID SOMETHING UNEXPECTED. THAT'S WHY I SCORED AGAINST HIM.
SOCCER
個人技編
AN FW ISN'T SUPPOSED TO AIM SO HE GETS STOPPED.
I'VE GOT TO FIND A WAY TO KICK SO MY OPPONENT CAN'T READ ME.
OUT-FRONT-KICK.
KICKING THE BALL WITH THE INSTEP WILL COUNTER SPIN IT IN THE OPPOSITE DIRECTION. THAT MEANS THE BALL WILL FLY OPPOSITE TO WHERE THE LEG IS FACING.
IT TAKES A LOT OF TECHNICAL SKILL, BUT IF I MASTER IT I CAN SURPRISE HIM!
I'VE GOT TO DO IT NO MATTER WHAT.
WHOOSH

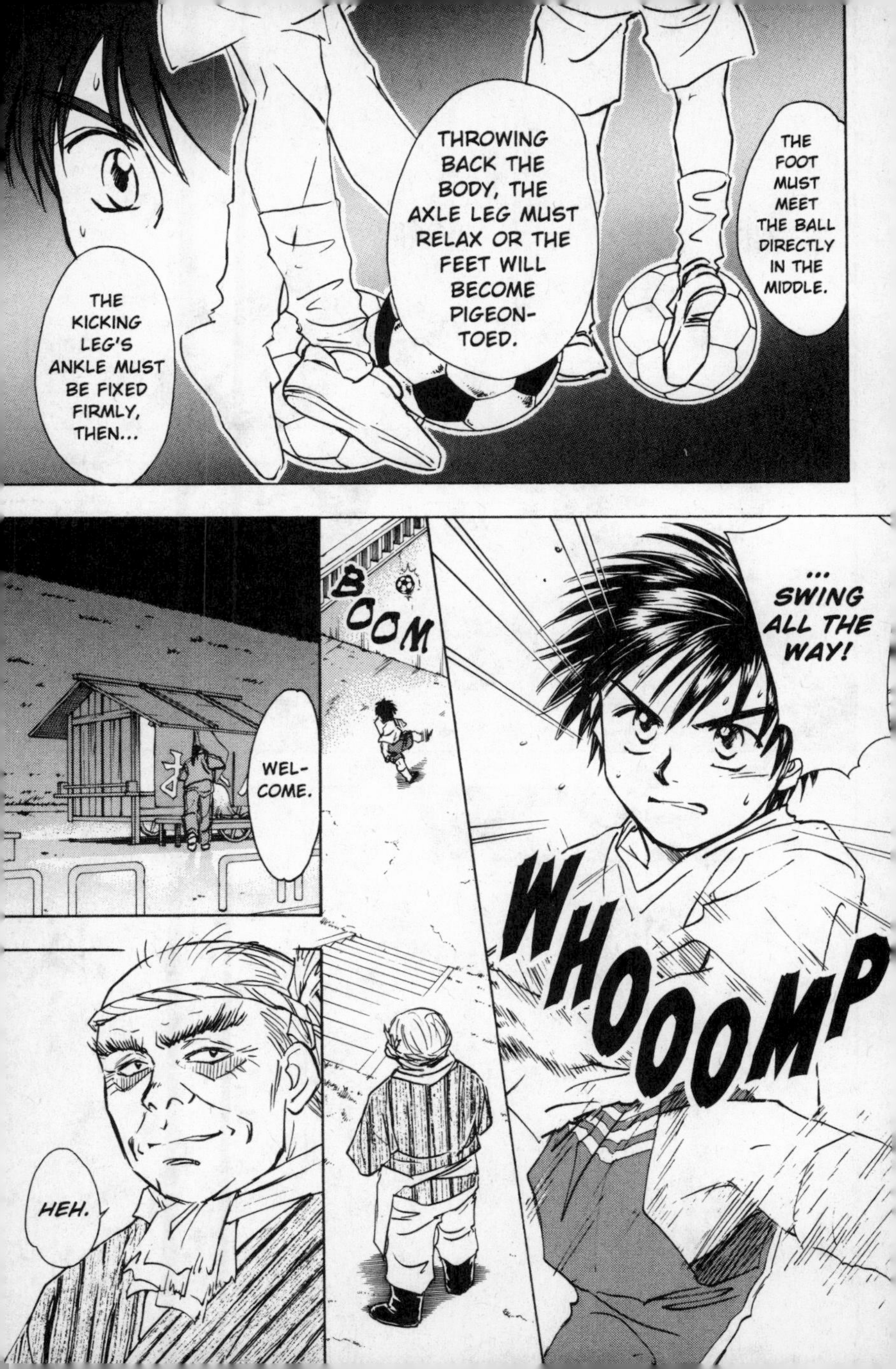
THE FOOT MUST MEET THE BALL DIRECTLY IN THE MIDDLE.
THROWING BACK THE BODY, THE AXLE LEG MUST RELAX OR THE FEET WILL BECOME PIGEON-TOED.
THE KICKING LEG'S ANKLE MUST BE FIXED FIRMLY, THEN...
... SWING ALL THE WAY!
WHOOOMP
BOOM
WEL-COME.
HEH.

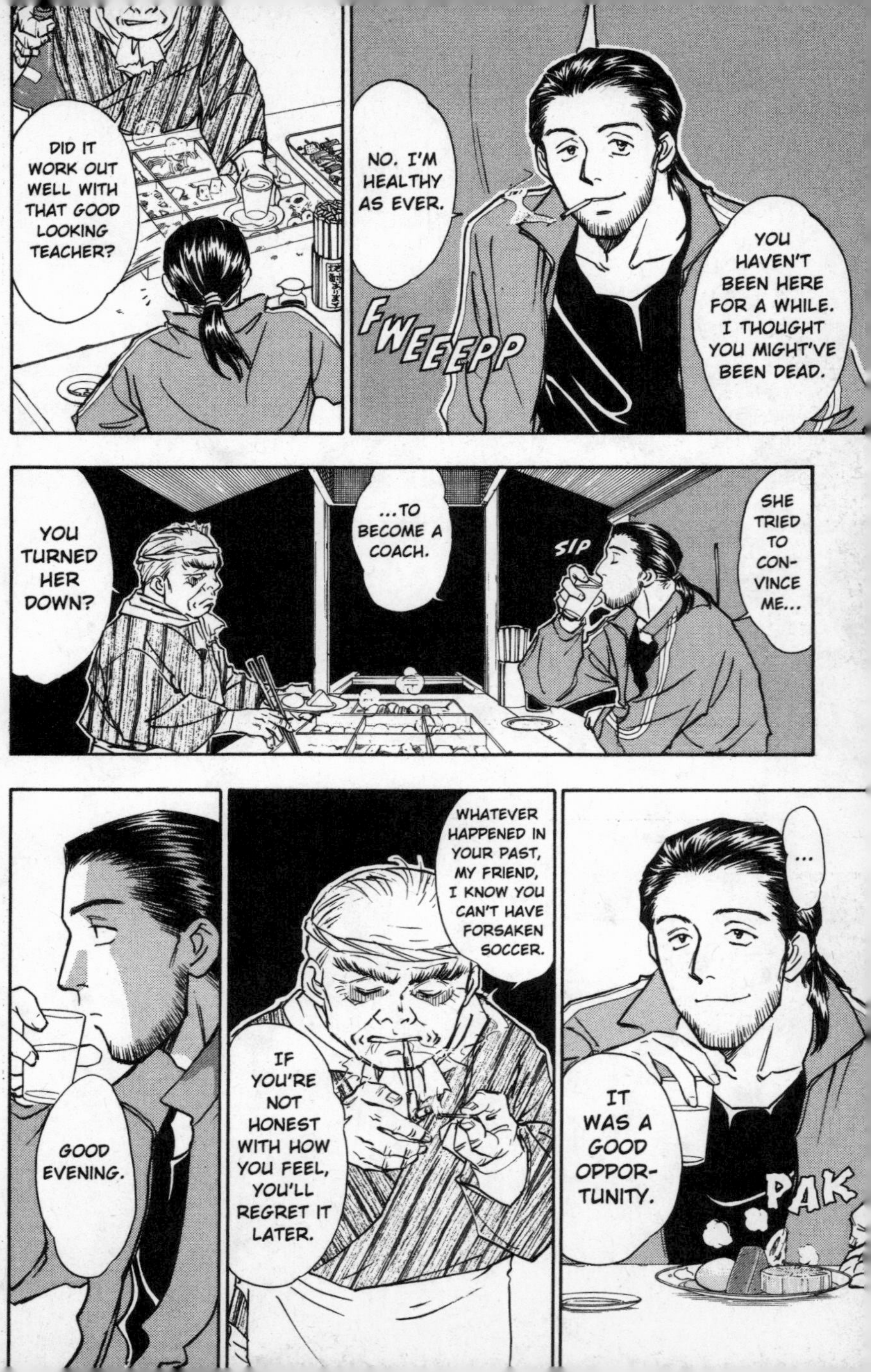
YOU HAVEN'T BEEN HERE FOR A WHILE. I THOUGHT YOU MIGHT'VE BEEN DEAD.
NO. I'M HEALTHY AS EVER.
FWEEEPP
DID IT WORK OUT WELL WITH THAT GOOD LOOKING TEACHER?
SHE TRIED TO CON-VINCE ME...
SIP
...TO BECOME A COACH.
YOU TURNED HER DOWN?
...
IT WAS A GOOD OPPOR-TUNITY.
PAK
WHATEVER HAPPENED IN YOUR PAST, MY FRIEND, I KNOW YOU CAN'T HAVE FORSAKEN SOCCER.
IF YOU'RE NOT HONEST WITH HOW YOU FEEL, YOU'LL REGRET IT LATER.
GOOD EVENING.

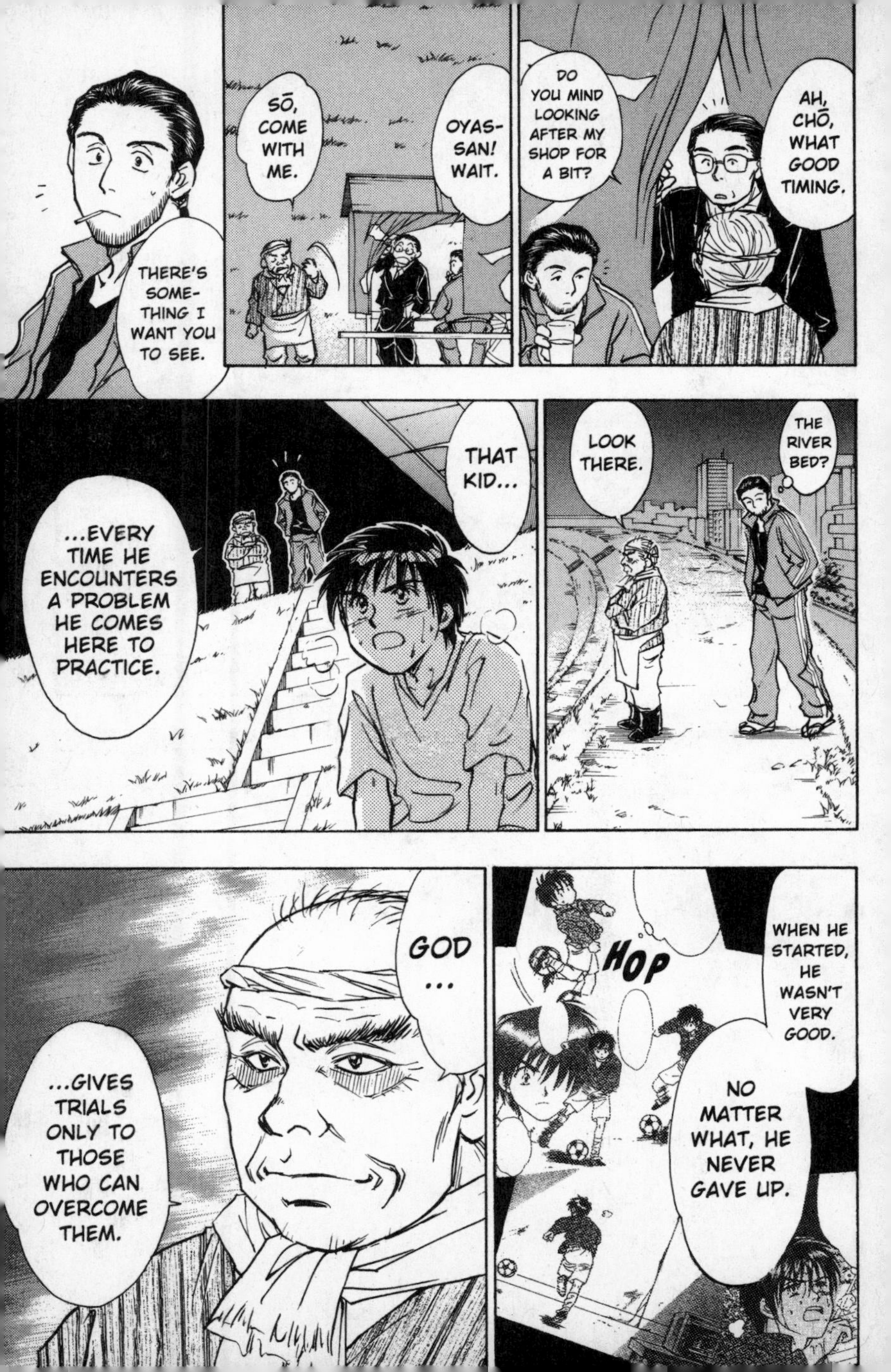
AH, CHŌ, WHAT GOOD TIMING.
DO YOU MIND LOOKING AFTER MY SHOP FOR A BIT?
OYAS-SAN! WAIT.
SŌ, COME WITH ME.
THERE'S SOME-THING I WANT YOU TO SEE.
THE RIVER BED?
LOOK THERE.
THAT KID...
...EVERY TIME HE ENCOUNTERS A PROBLEM HE COMES HERE TO PRACTICE.
WHEN HE STARTED, HE WASN'T VERY GOOD.
HOP
NO MATTER WHAT, HE NEVER GAVE UP.
GOD ...
...GIVES TRIALS ONLY TO THOSE WHO CAN OVERCOME THEM.

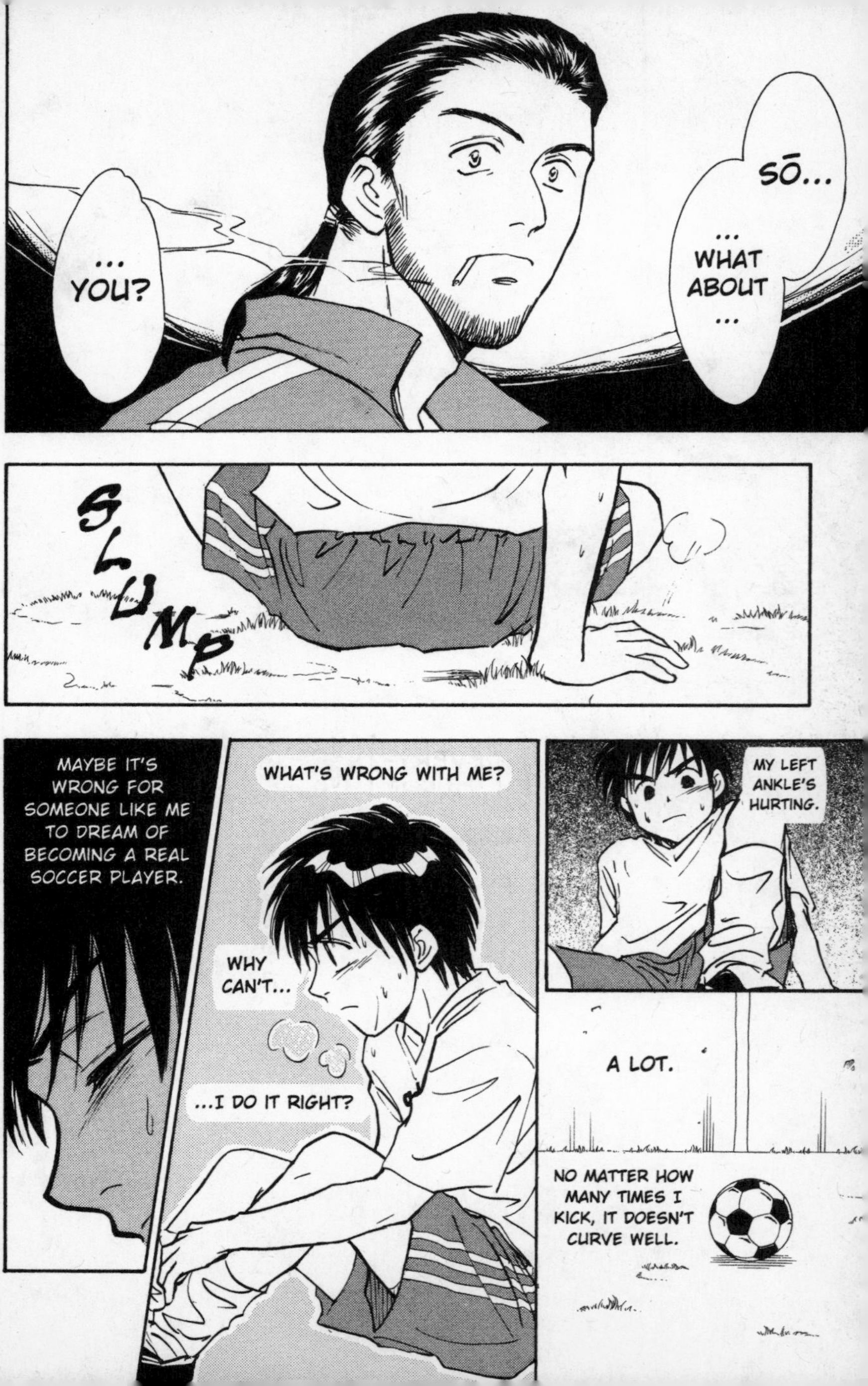
SŌ...
... WHAT ABOUT ...
... YOU?
SLUMP
MY LEFT ANKLE'S HURTING.
A LOT.
NO MATTER HOW MANY TIMES I KICK, IT DOESN'T CURVE WELL.
WHAT'S WRONG WITH ME?
WHY CAN'T...
...I DO IT RIGHT?
MAYBE IT'S WRONG FOR SOMEONE LIKE ME TO DREAM OF BECOMING A REAL SOCCER PLAYER.

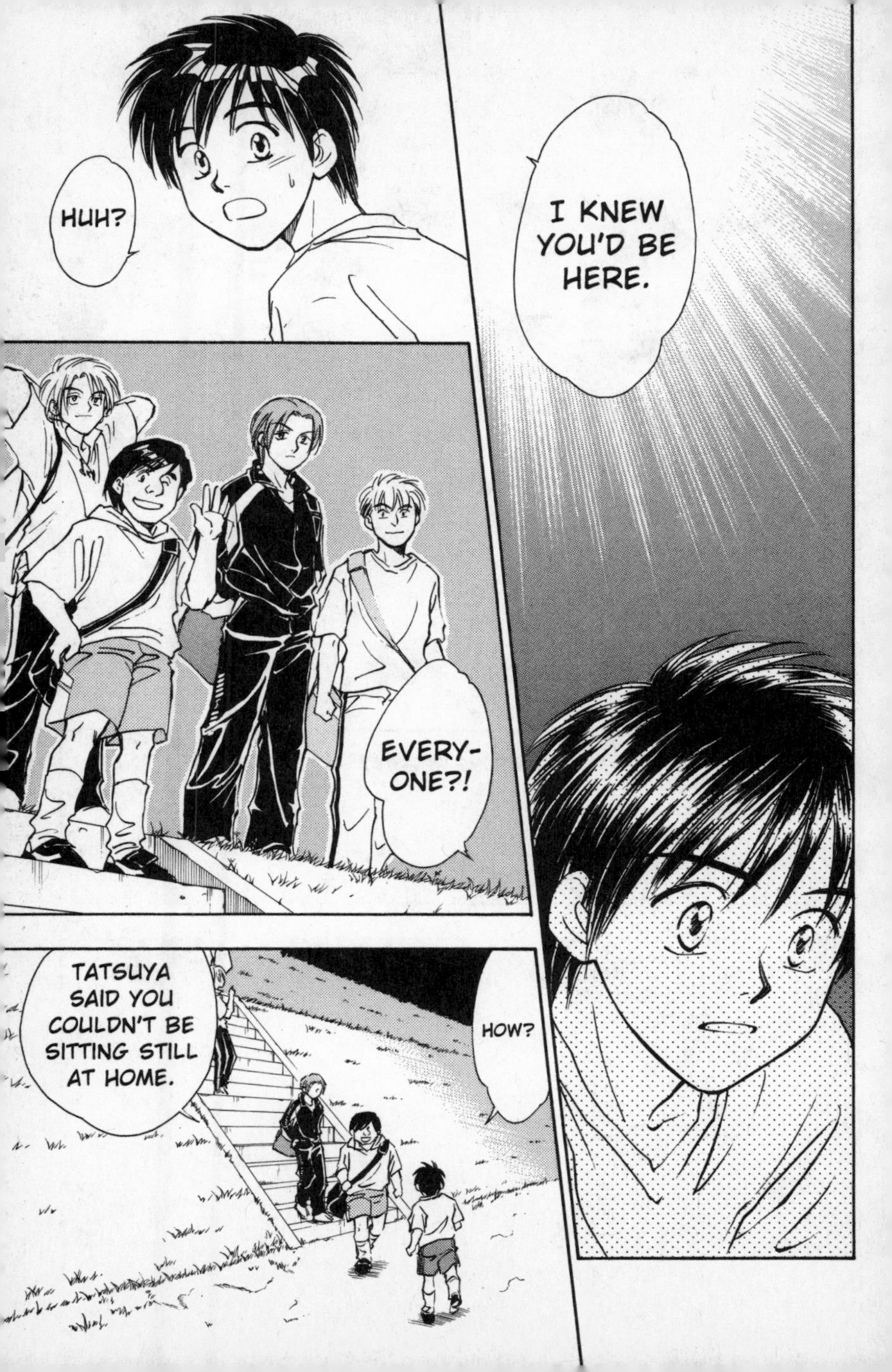
I KNEW YOU'D BE HERE.
HUH?
EVERY-ONE?!
HOW?
TATSUYA SAID YOU COULDN'T BE SITTING STILL AT HOME.

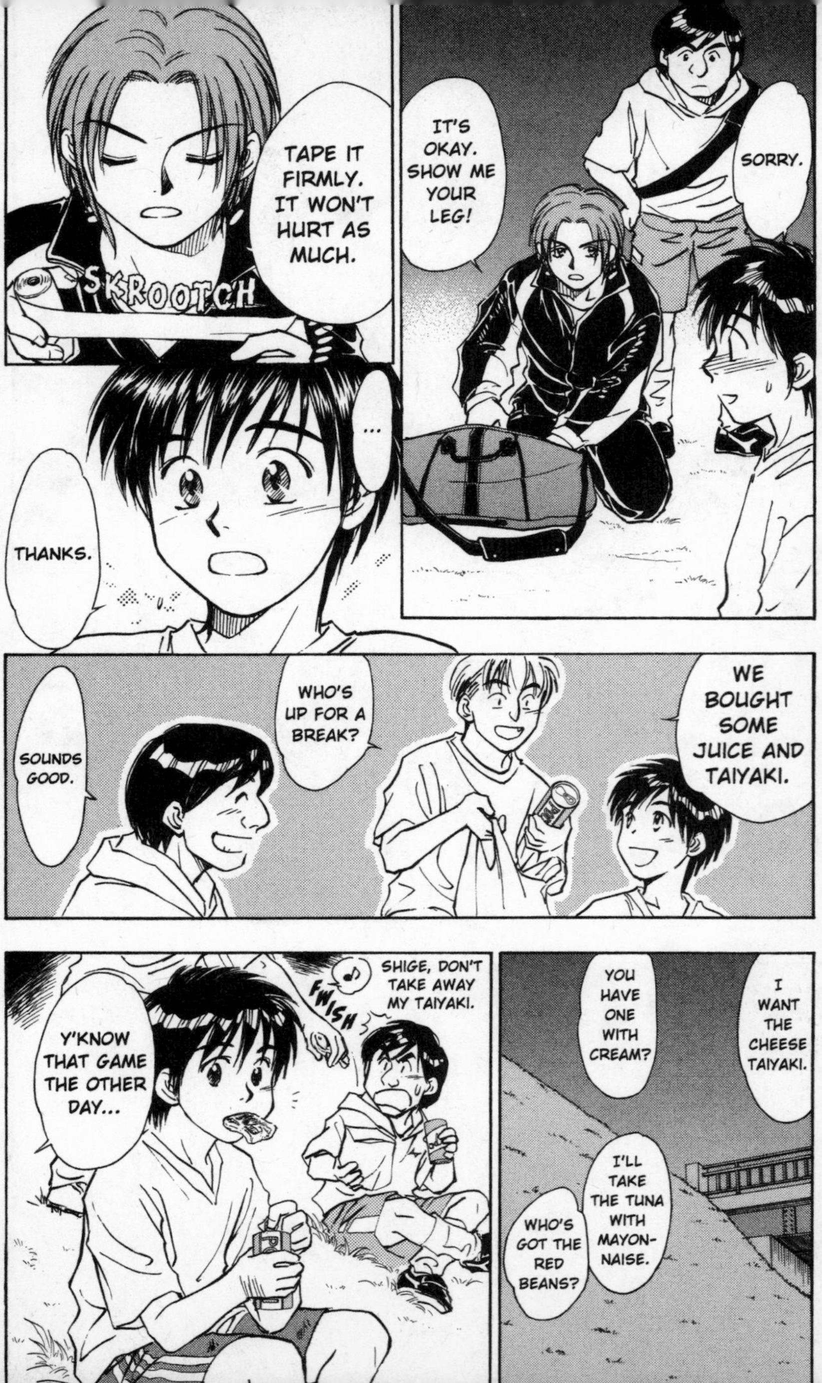
SORRY.
IT'S OKAY. SHOW ME YOUR LEG!
TAPE IT FIRMLY. IT WON'T HURT AS MUCH.
SKROOTCH
...
THANKS.
WE BOUGHT SOME JUICE AND TAIYAKI.
WHO'S UP FOR A BREAK?
SOUNDS GOOD.
I WANT THE CHEESE TAIYAKI.
YOU HAVE ONE WITH CREAM?
I'LL TAKE THE TUNA WITH MAYON-NAISE.
WHO'S GOT THE RED BEANS?
SHIGE, DON'T TAKE AWAY MY TAIYAKI.
FWISH
Y'KNOW THAT GAME THE OTHER DAY...

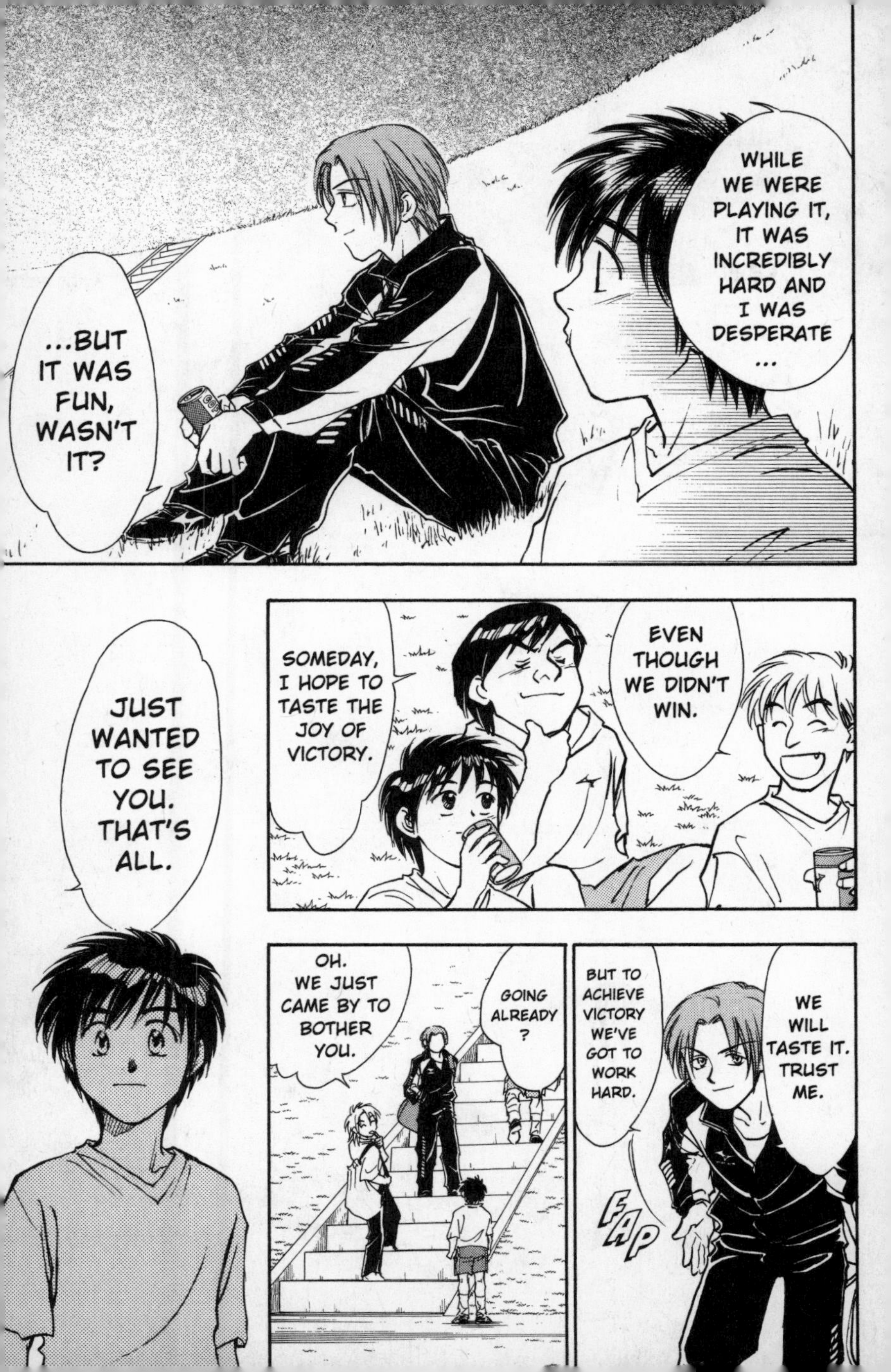
WHILE WE WERE PLAYING IT, IT WAS INCREDIBLY HARD AND I WAS DESPERATE ...
...BUT IT WAS FUN, WASN'T IT?
EVEN THOUGH WE DIDN'T WIN.
SOMEDAY, I HOPE TO TASTE THE JOY OF VICTORY.
WE WILL TASTE IT. TRUST ME.
BUT TO ACHIEVE VICTORY WE'VE GOT TO WORK HARD.
FAP
GOING ALREADY ?
OH. WE JUST CAME BY TO BOTHER YOU.
JUST WANTED TO SEE YOU. THAT'S ALL.

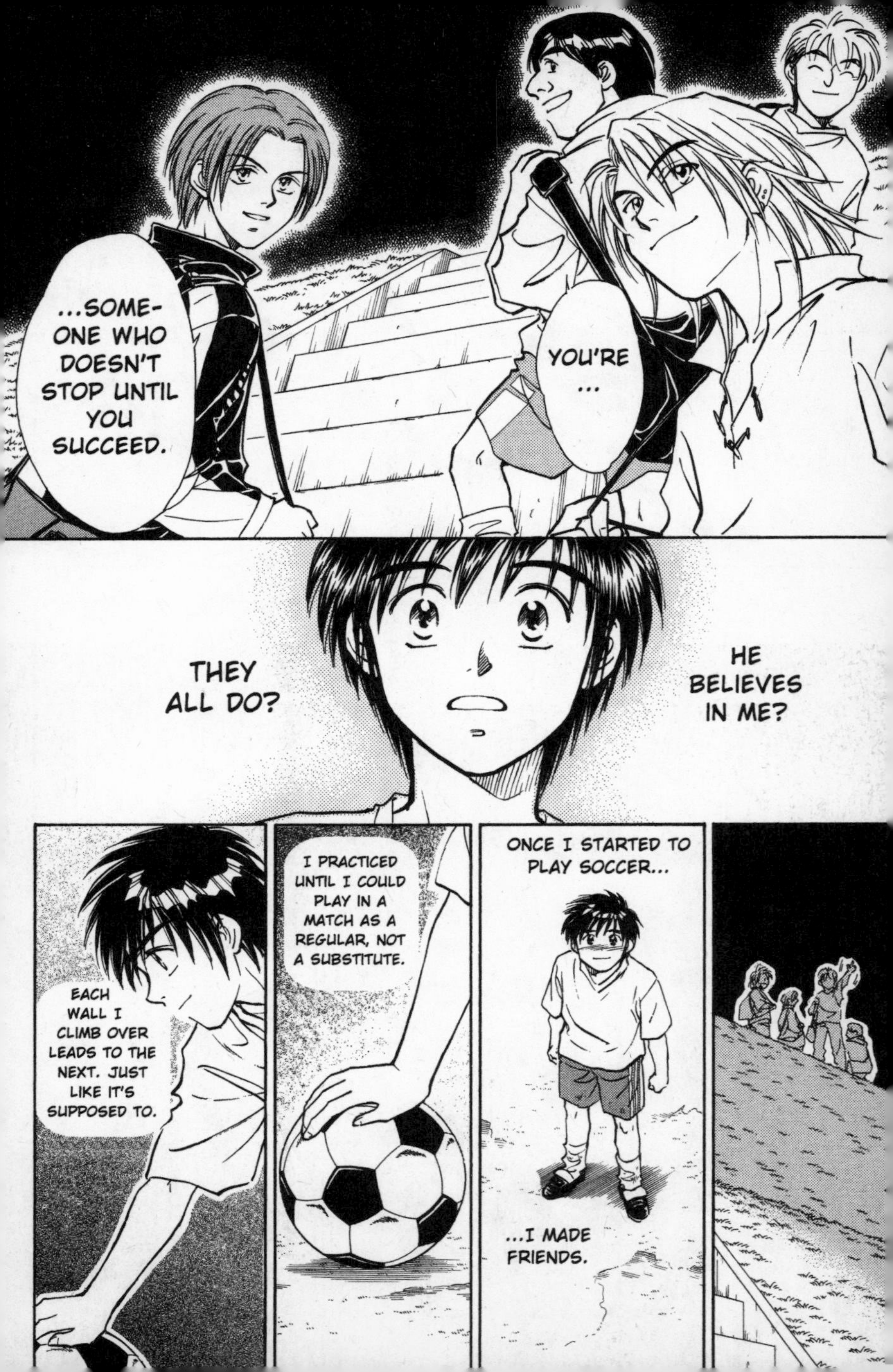
YOU'RE ...
...SOME-ONE WHO DOESN'T STOP UNTIL YOU SUCCEED.
HE BELIEVES IN ME?
THEY ALL DO?
ONCE I STARTED TO PLAY SOCCER...
...I MADE FRIENDS.
I PRACTICED UNTIL I COULD PLAY IN A MATCH AS A REGULAR, NOT A SUBSTITUTE.
EACH WALL I CLIMB OVER LEADS TO THE NEXT. JUST LIKE IT'S SUPPOSED TO.

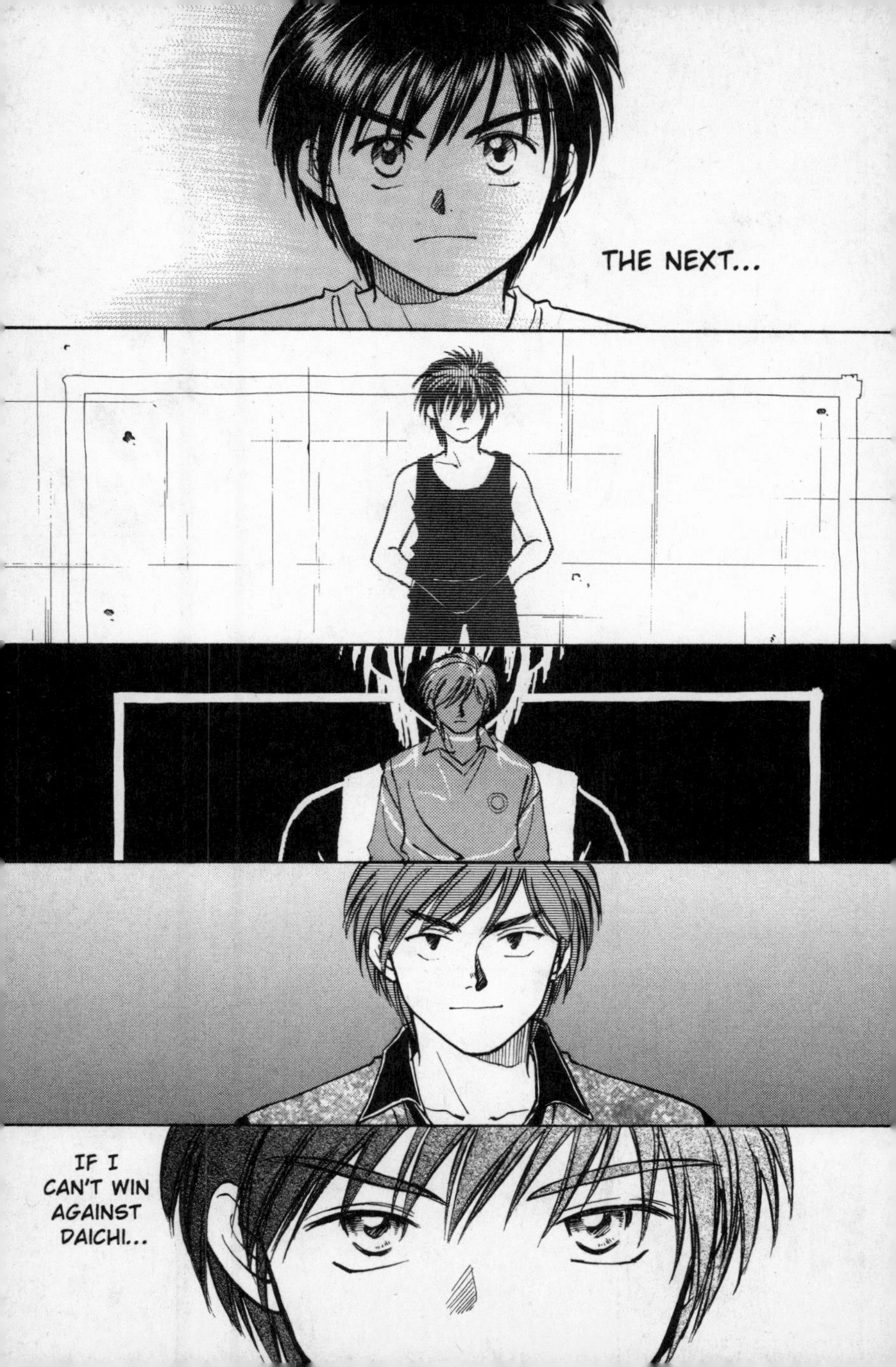
THE NEXT...
IF I CAN'T WIN AGAINST DAICHI...

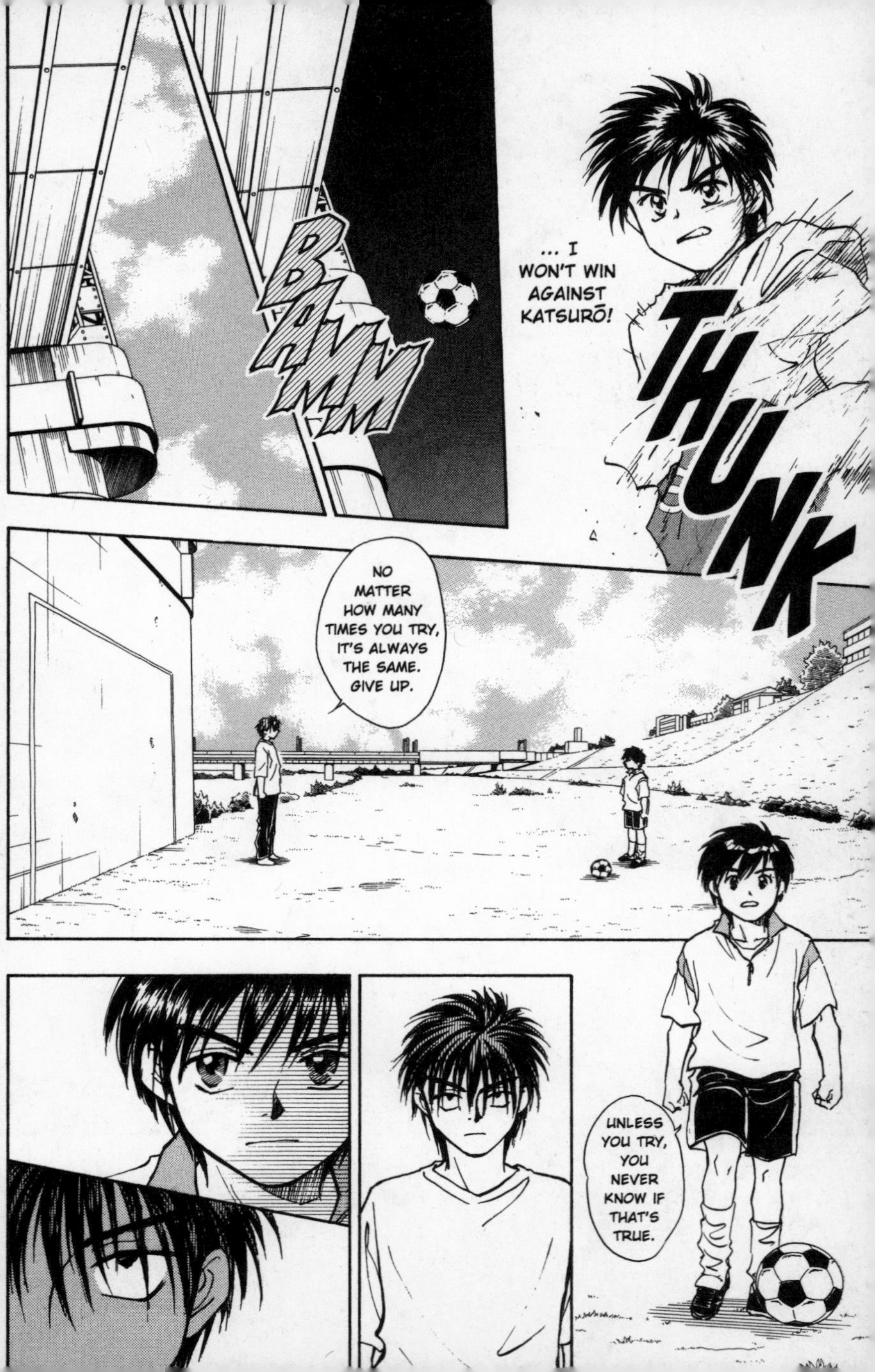
... I WON'T WIN AGAINST KATSURŌ!
THUNK
BAMM
NO MATTER HOW MANY TIMES YOU TRY, IT'S ALWAYS THE SAME. GIVE UP.
UNLESS YOU TRY, YOU NEVER KNOW IF THAT'S TRUE.

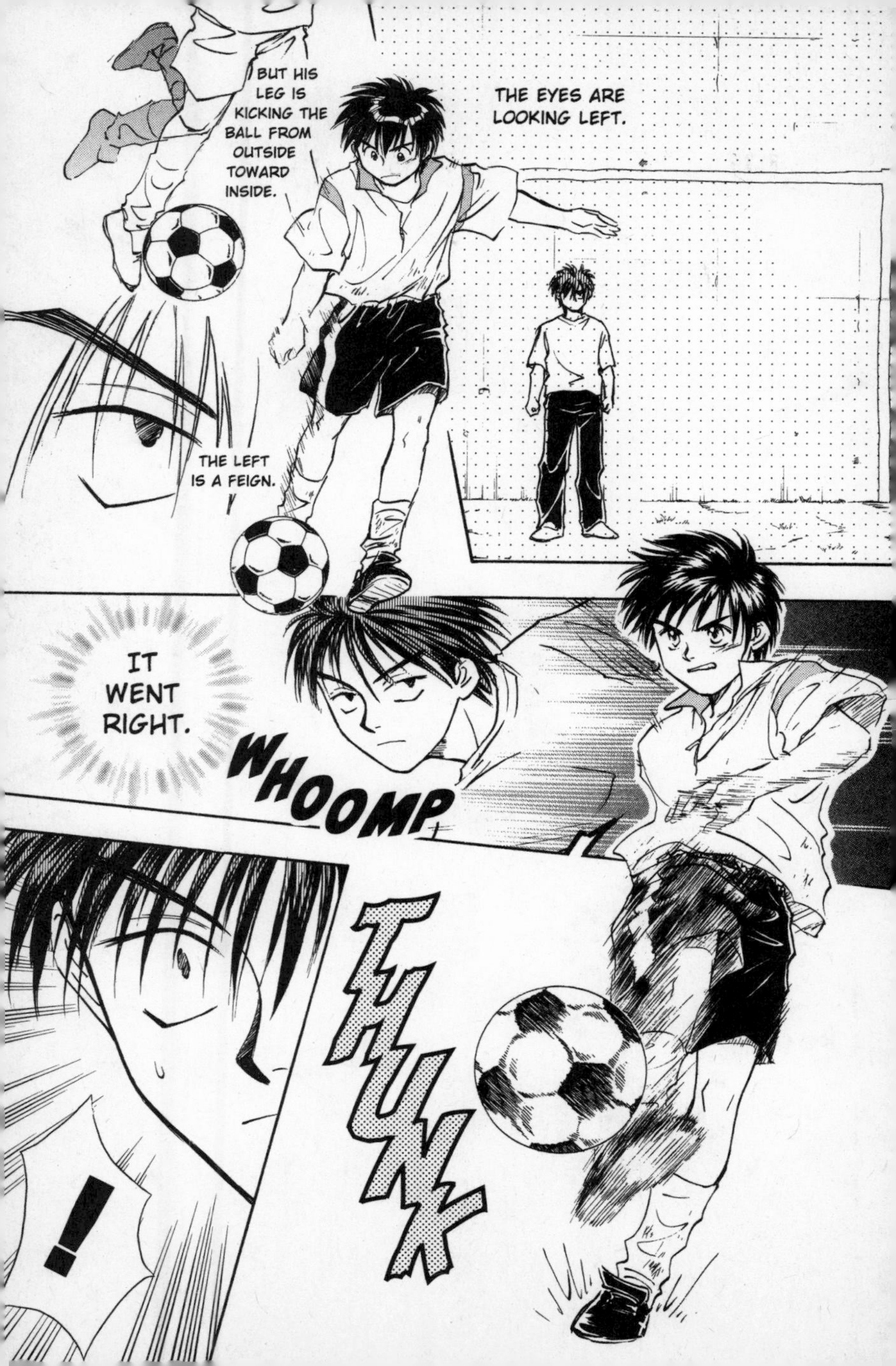
THE EYES ARE LOOKING LEFT.
BUT HIS LEG IS KICKING THE BALL FROM OUTSIDE TOWARD INSIDE.
THE LEFT IS A FEIGN.
WHOOMP
IT WENT RIGHT.
THUNK
!

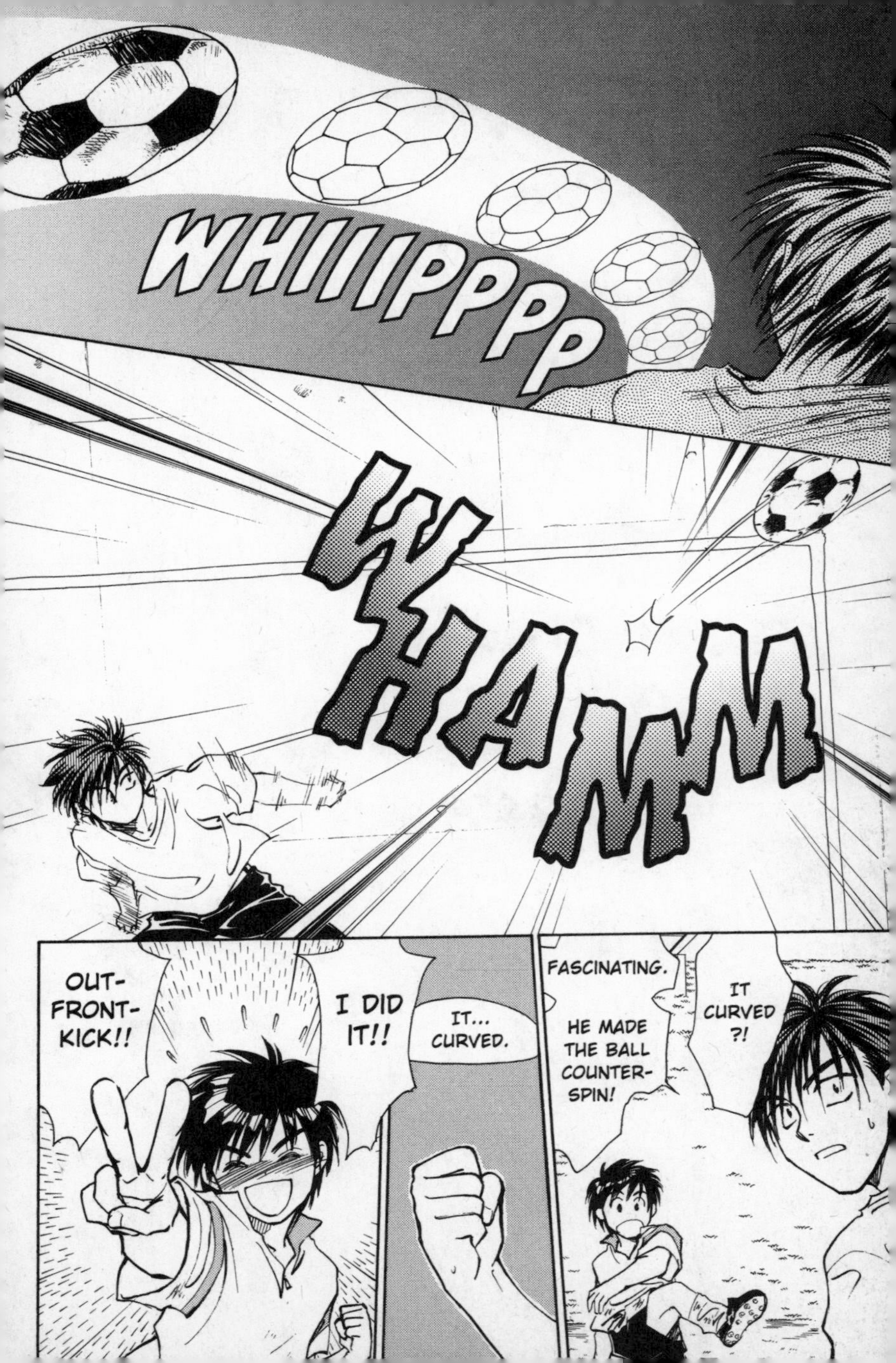
WHIIIPPPP
WHAMM
IT CURVED ?!
FASCINATING.
HE MADE THE BALL COUNTER-SPIN!
IT... CURVED.
I DID IT!!
OUT-FRONT-KICK!!

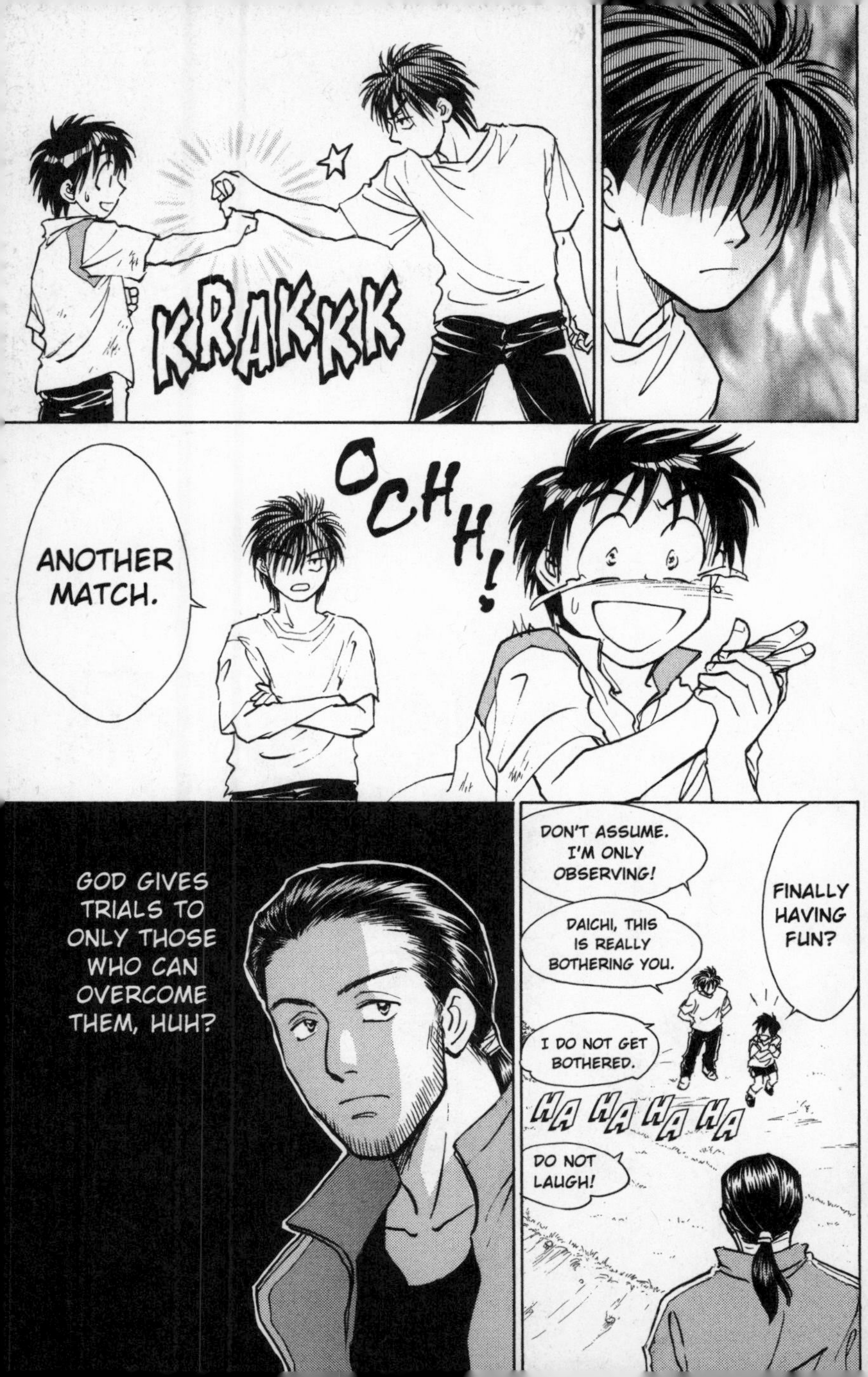
KRAKKK
OCHH!
ANOTHER MATCH.
FINALLY HAVING FUN?
DON'T ASSUME. I'M ONLY OBSERVING!
DAICHI, THIS IS REALLY BOTHERING YOU.
I DO NOT GET BOTHERED.
HA HA HA HA HA
DO NOT LAUGH!
GOD GIVES TRIALS TO ONLY THOSE WHO CAN OVERCOME THEM, HUH?

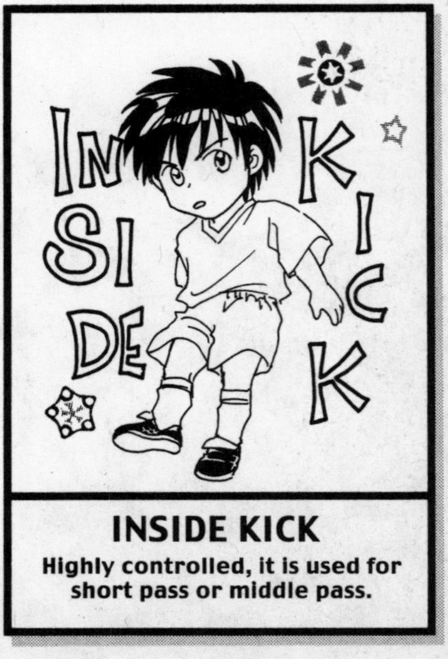
INSIDE KICK

**INSIDE KICK**

**Highly controlled, it is used for short pass or middle pass.**

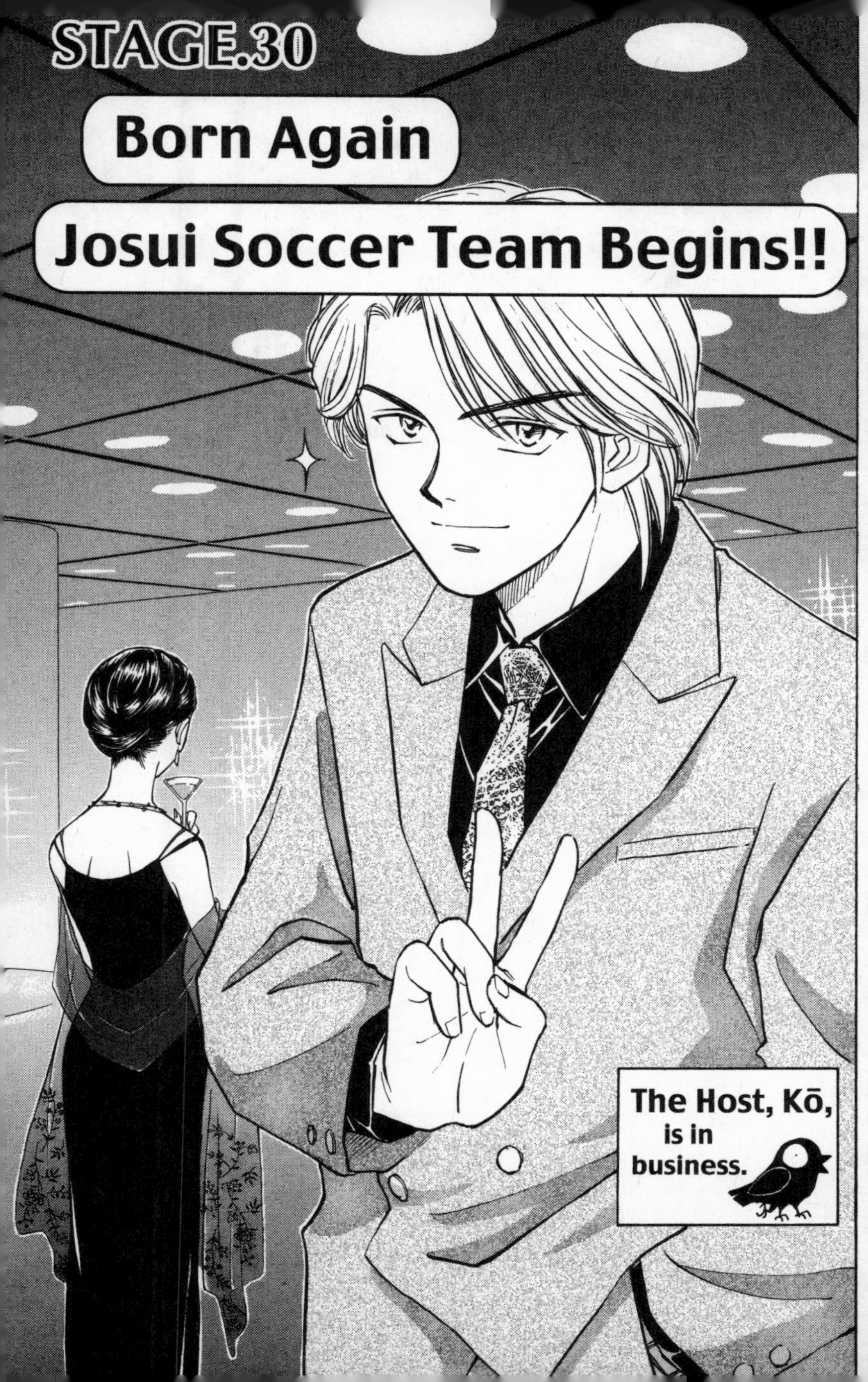
STAGE.30
Born Again
Josui Soccer Team Begins!!
The Host, Kō, is in business.

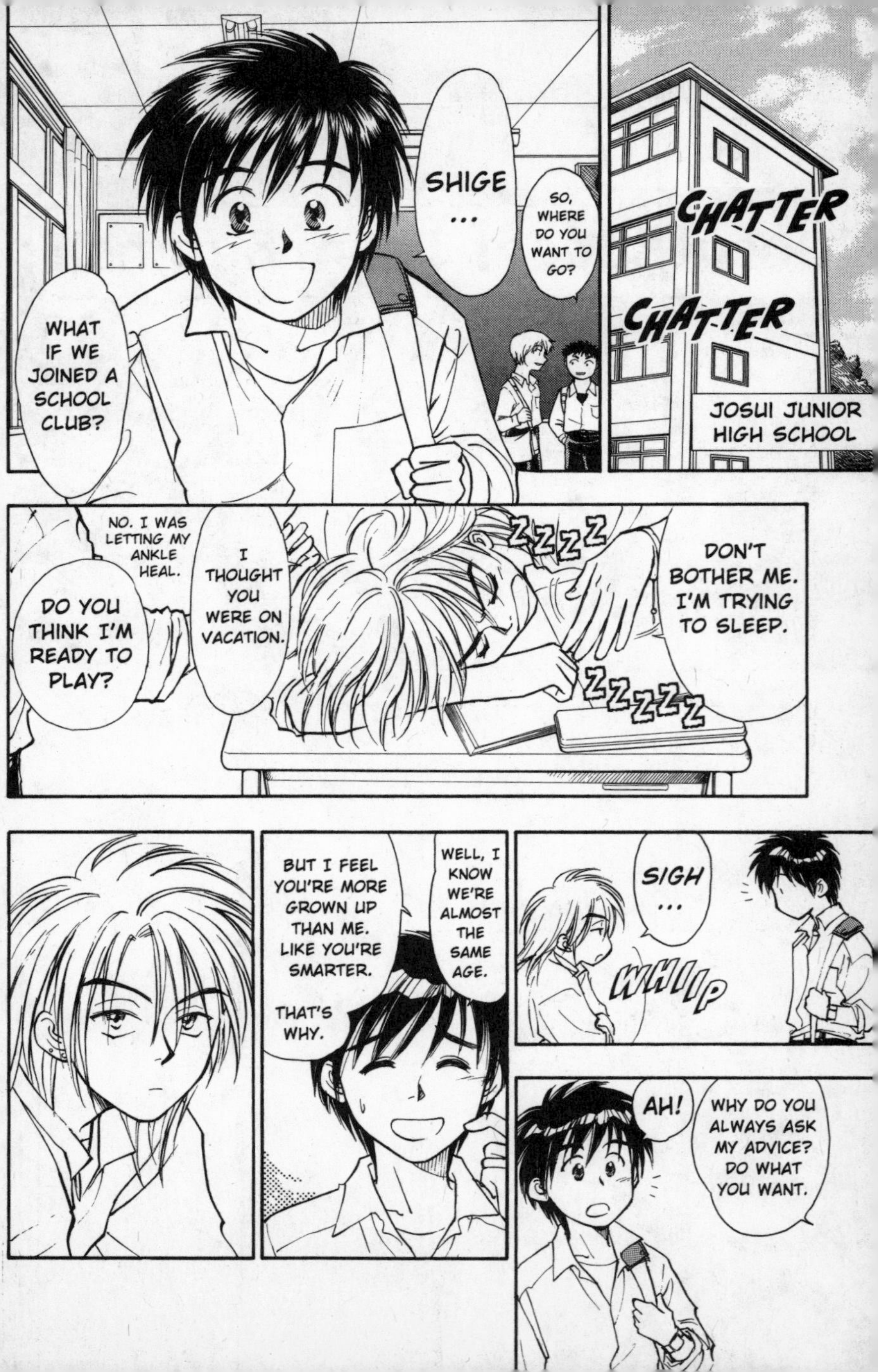
CHATTER
CHATTER
JOSUI JUNIOR HIGH SCHOOL
SO, WHERE DO YOU WANT TO GO?
SHIGE ...
WHAT IF WE JOINED A SCHOOL CLUB?
ZZZZ
DON'T BOTHER ME. I'M TRYING TO SLEEP.
ZZZZZ
I THOUGHT YOU WERE ON VACATION.
NO. I WAS LETTING MY ANKLE HEAL.
DO YOU THINK I'M READY TO PLAY?
SIGH ...
WHIIP
AH!
WHY DO YOU ALWAYS ASK MY ADVICE? DO WHAT YOU WANT.
WELL, I KNOW WE'RE ALMOST THE SAME AGE.
BUT I FEEL YOU'RE MORE GROWN UP THAN ME. LIKE YOU'RE SMARTER.
THAT'S WHY.

READ THIS WAY

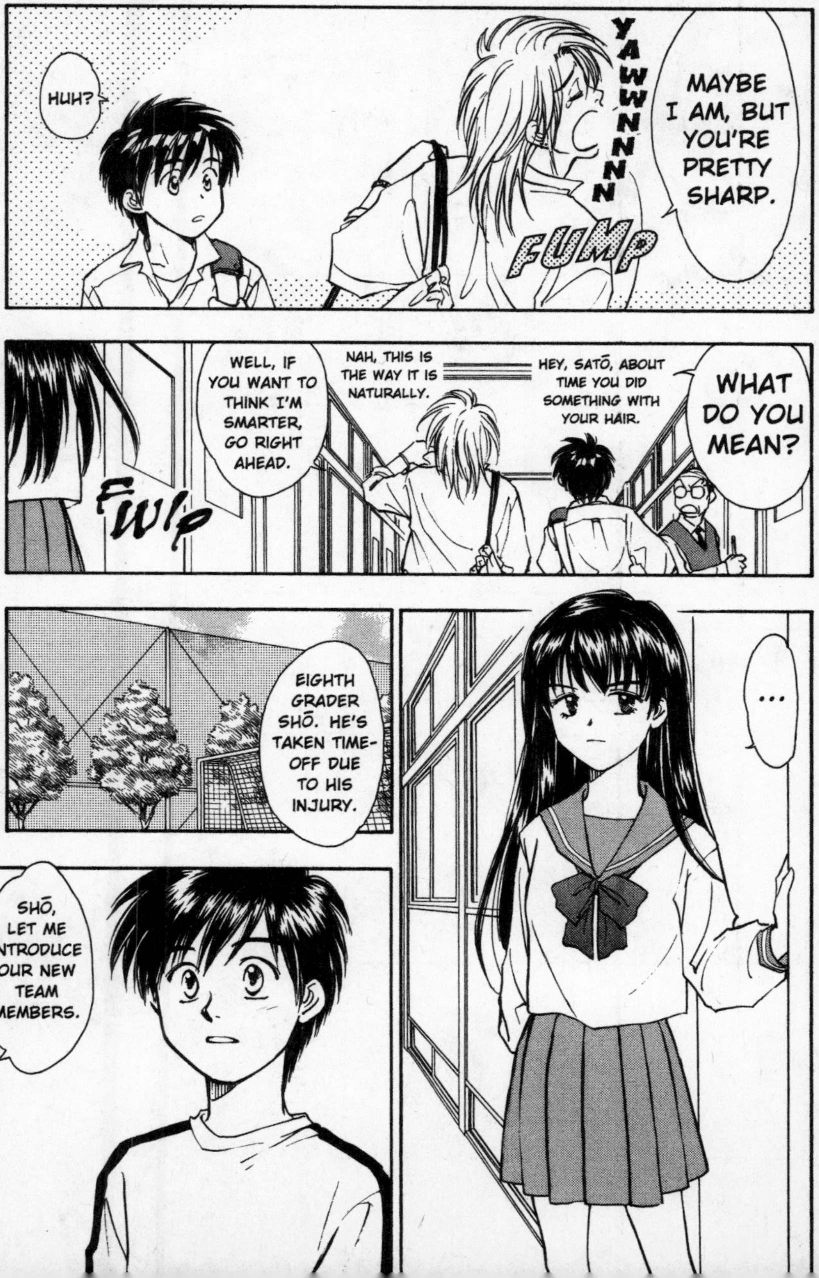

MAYBE I AM, BUT YOU'RE PRETTY SHARP.
YAWWNNNN
FUMP
HUH?
WHAT DO YOU MEAN?
HEY, SATŌ, ABOUT TIME YOU DID SOMETHING WITH YOUR HAIR.
NAH, THIS IS THE WAY IT IS NATURALLY.
WELL, IF YOU WANT TO THINK I'M SMARTER, GO RIGHT AHEAD.
FWIP
...
EIGHTH GRADER SHŌ. HE'S TAKEN TIME-OFF DUE TO HIS INJURY.
SHŌ, LET ME INTRODUCE OUR NEW TEAM MEMBERS.

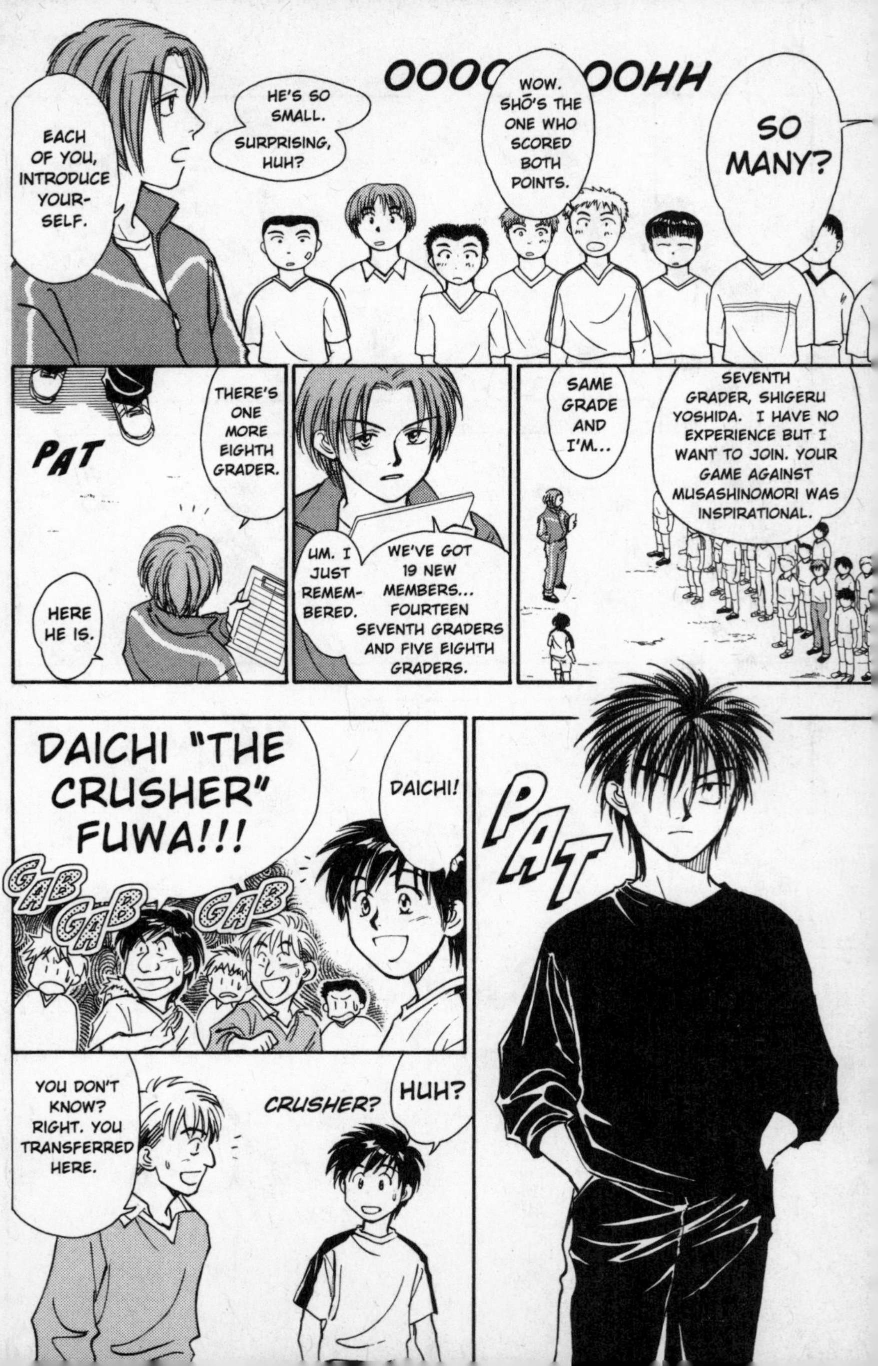
SO MANY?
OOOO OOHH
WOW. SHŌ'S THE ONE WHO SCORED BOTH POINTS.
HE'S SO SMALL. SURPRISING, HUH?
EACH OF YOU, INTRODUCE YOUR-SELF.
SEVENTH GRADER, SHIGERU YOSHIDA. I HAVE NO EXPERIENCE BUT I WANT TO JOIN. YOUR GAME AGAINST MUSASHINOMORI WAS INSPIRATIONAL.
SAME GRADE AND I'M...
WE'VE GOT 19 NEW MEMBERS... FOURTEEN SEVENTH GRADERS AND FIVE EIGHTH GRADERS.
UM. I JUST REMEM-BERED.
THERE'S ONE MORE EIGHTH GRADER.
PAT
HERE HE IS.
PAT
DAICHI!
DAICHI "THE CRUSHER" FUWA!!!
GAB GAB GAB
HUH?
CRUSHER?
YOU DON'T KNOW? RIGHT. YOU TRANSFERRED HERE.

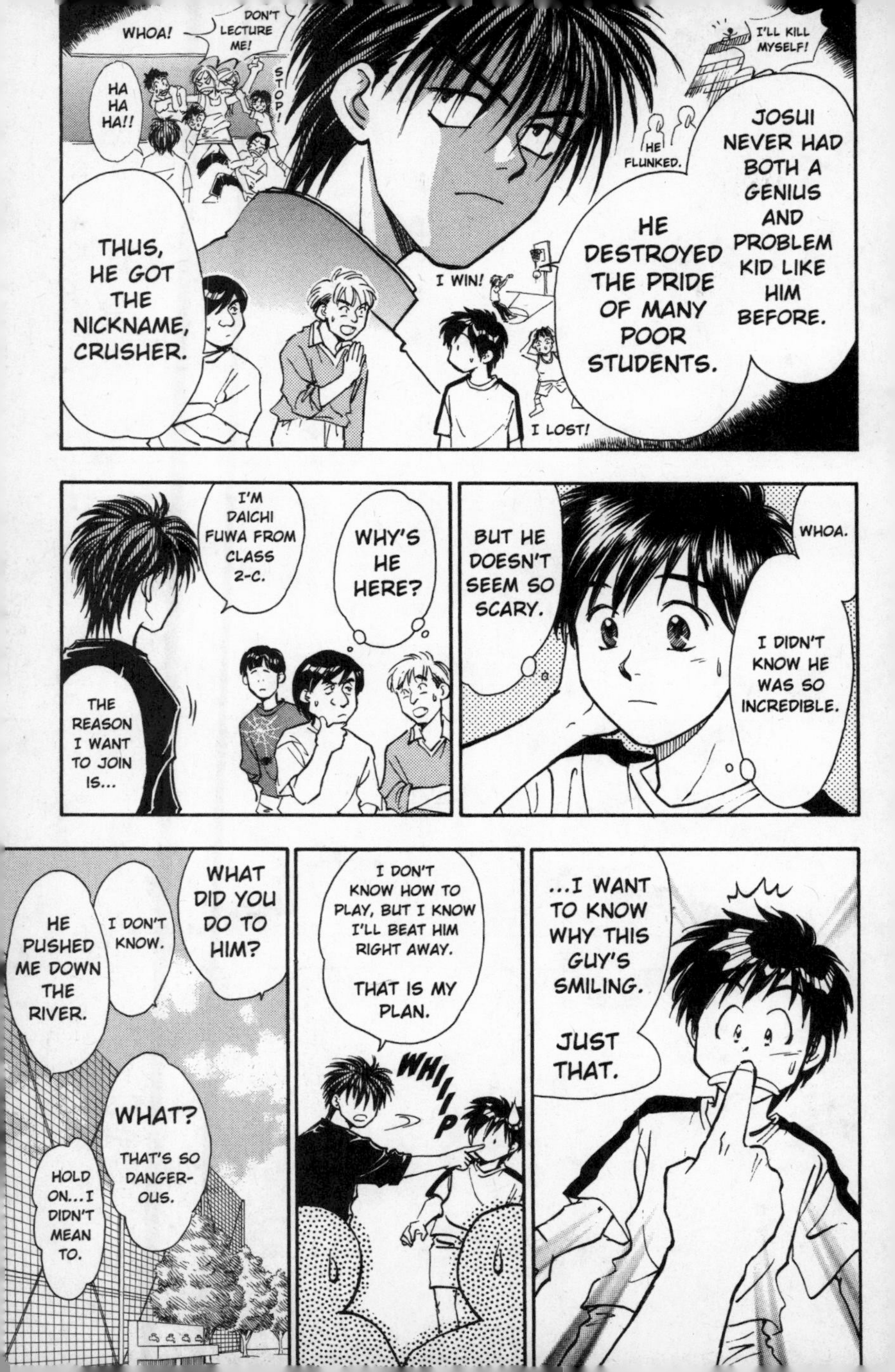
I'LL KILL MYSELF!
JOSUI NEVER HAD BOTH A GENIUS AND PROBLEM KID LIKE HIM BEFORE.
HE FLUNKED.
HE DESTROYED THE PRIDE OF MANY POOR STUDENTS.
I WIN!
I LOST!
DON'T LECTURE ME!
WHOA!
STOP!
HA HA HA!!
THUS, HE GOT THE NICKNAME, CRUSHER.
WHOA.
I DIDN'T KNOW HE WAS SO INCREDIBLE.
BUT HE DOESN'T SEEM SO SCARY.
WHY'S HE HERE?
I'M DAICHI FUWA FROM CLASS 2-C.
THE REASON I WANT TO JOIN IS...
...I WANT TO KNOW WHY THIS GUY'S SMILING.
JUST THAT.
I DON'T KNOW HOW TO PLAY, BUT I KNOW I'LL BEAT HIM RIGHT AWAY.
THAT IS MY PLAN.
WHIIIP
WHAT DID YOU DO TO HIM?
I DON'T KNOW.
HE PUSHED ME DOWN THE RIVER.
WHAT?
THAT'S SO DANGER-OUS.
HOLD ON...I DIDN'T MEAN TO.

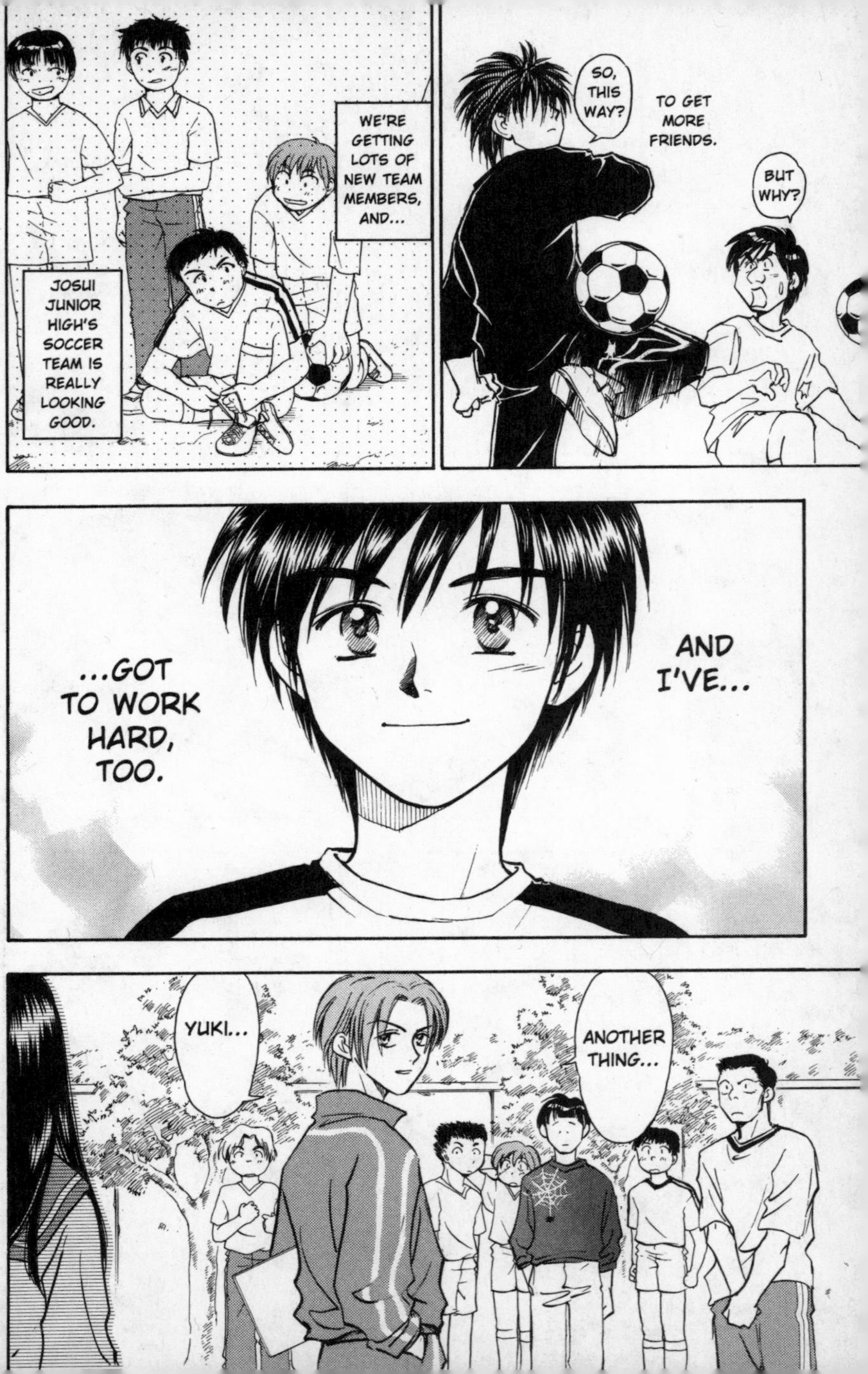
BUT WHY?
TO GET MORE FRIENDS.
SO, THIS WAY?
WE'RE GETTING LOTS OF NEW TEAM MEMBERS, AND...
JOSUI JUNIOR HIGH'S SOCCER TEAM IS REALLY LOOKING GOOD.
AND I'VE...
...GOT TO WORK HARD, TOO.
ANOTHER THING...
YUKI...

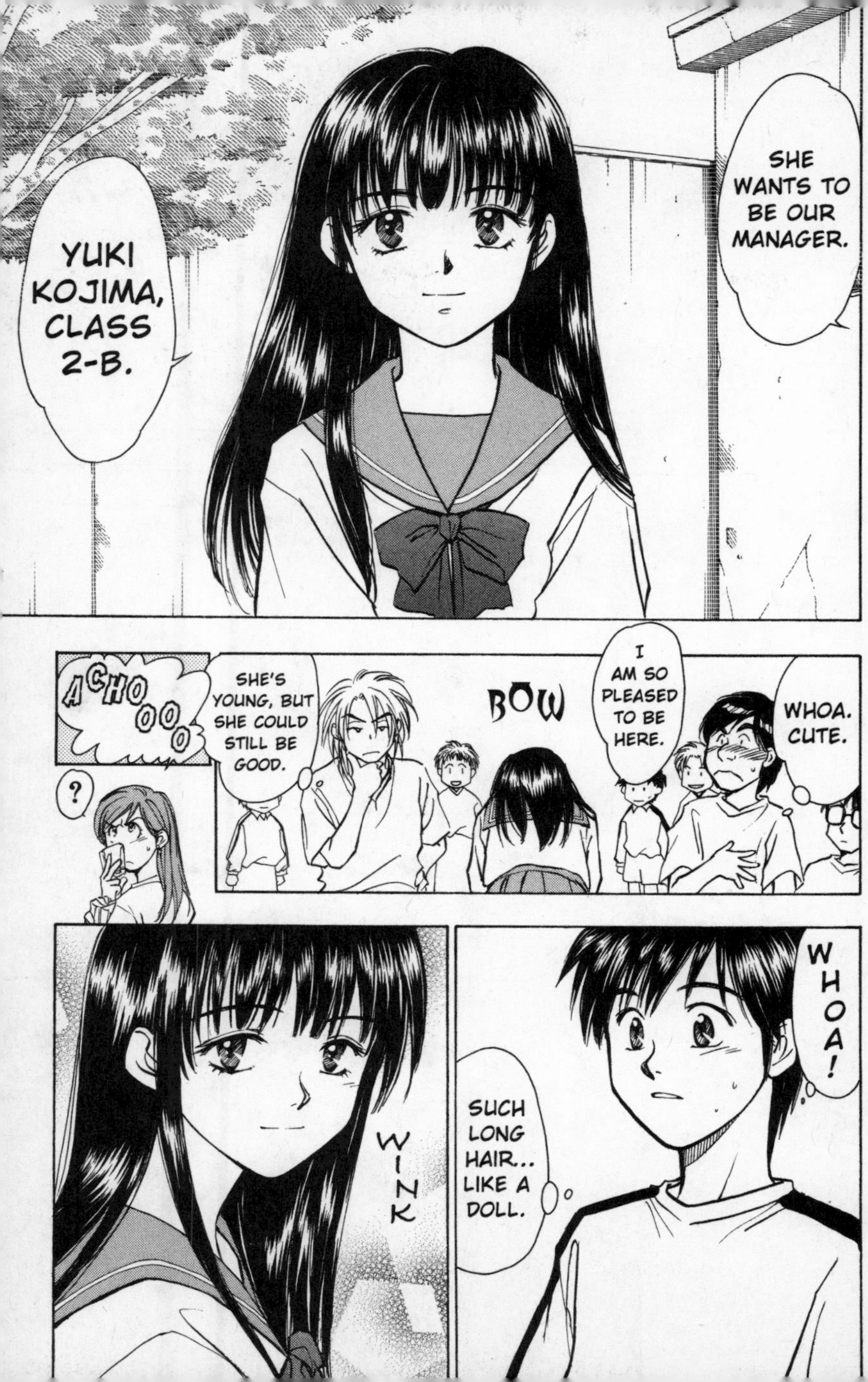
SHE WANTS TO BE OUR MANAGER.
YUKI KOJIMA, CLASS 2-B.
WHOA. CUTE.
I AM SO PLEASED TO BE HERE.
BOW
SHE'S YOUNG, BUT SHE COULD STILL BE GOOD.
ACHOOOOO
?
WHOA!
SUCH LONG HAIR... LIKE A DOLL.
WINK

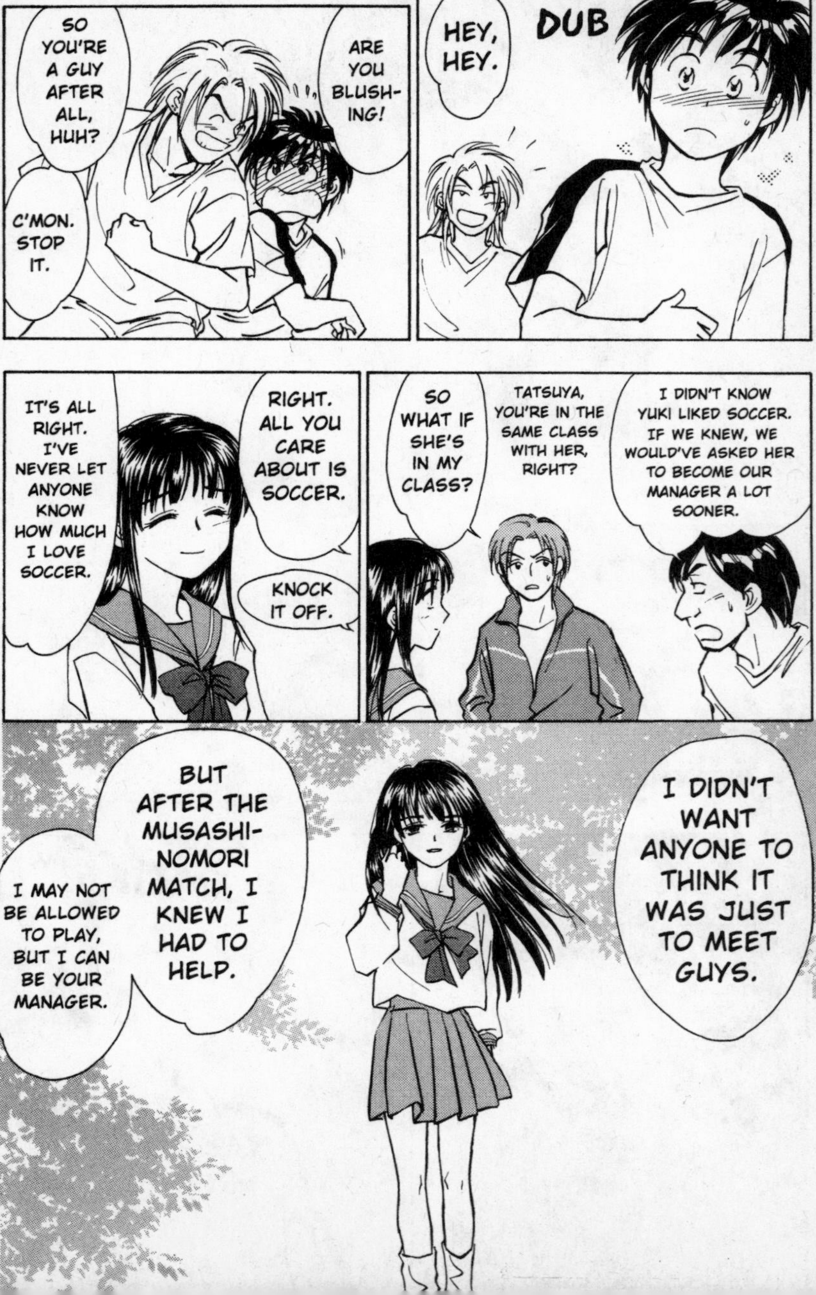
LUB DUB
HEY, HEY.
ARE YOU BLUSH-ING!
SO YOU'RE A GUY AFTER ALL, HUH?
C'MON. STOP IT.
I DIDN'T KNOW YUKI LIKED SOCCER. IF WE KNEW, WE WOULD'VE ASKED HER TO BECOME OUR MANAGER A LOT SOONER.
TATSUYA, YOU'RE IN THE SAME CLASS WITH HER, RIGHT?
SO WHAT IF SHE'S IN MY CLASS?
RIGHT. ALL YOU CARE ABOUT IS SOCCER.
KNOCK IT OFF.
IT'S ALL RIGHT. I'VE NEVER LET ANYONE KNOW HOW MUCH I LOVE SOCCER.
I DIDN'T WANT ANYONE TO THINK IT WAS JUST TO MEET GUYS.
BUT AFTER THE MUSASHI-NOMORI MATCH, I KNEW I HAD TO HELP.
I MAY NOT BE ALLOWED TO PLAY, BUT I CAN BE YOUR MANAGER.

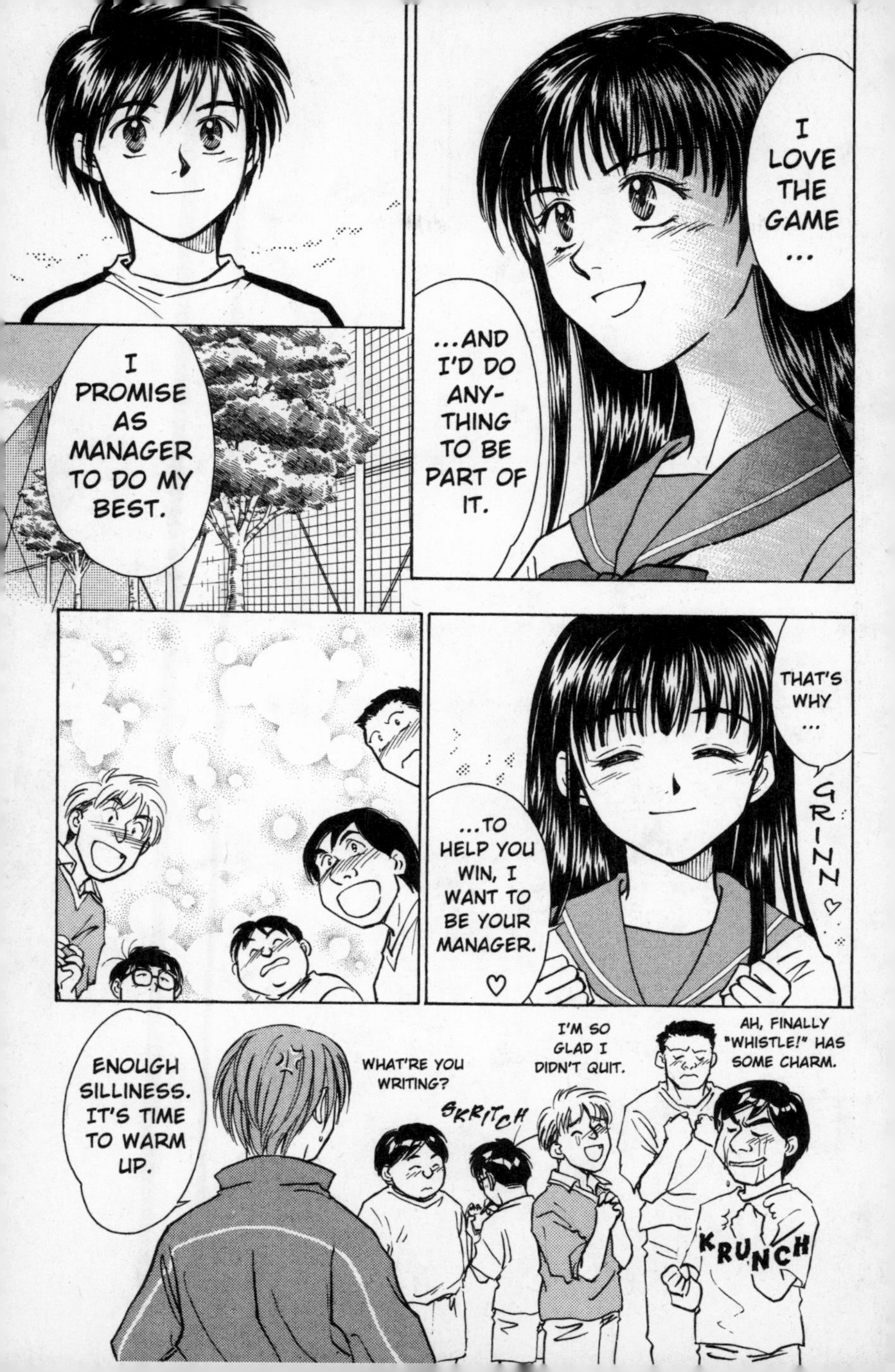
I LOVE THE GAME...
...AND I'D DO ANY-THING TO BE PART OF IT.
I PROMISE AS MANAGER TO DO MY BEST.
THAT'S WHY...
GRINN
...TO HELP YOU WIN, I WANT TO BE YOUR MANAGER.
AH, FINALLY "WHISTLE!" HAS SOME CHARM.
KRUNCH
I'M SO GLAD I DIDN'T QUIT.
WHAT'RE YOU WRITING?
SKRITCH
ENOUGH SILLINESS. IT'S TIME TO WARM UP.

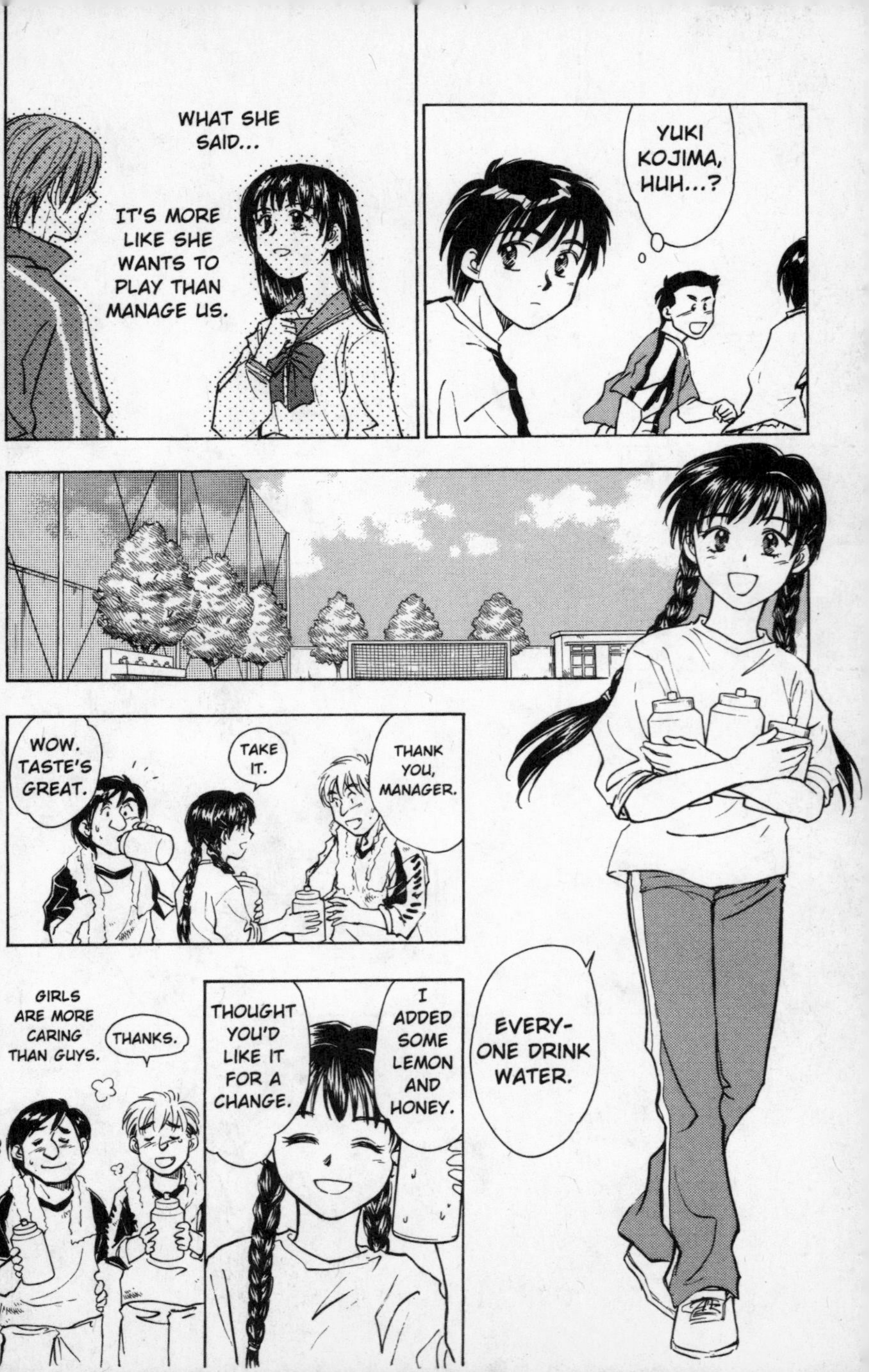
YUKI KOJIMA, HUH...?
WHAT SHE SAID...
IT'S MORE LIKE SHE WANTS TO PLAY THAN MANAGE US.
EVERY-ONE DRINK WATER.
THANK YOU, MANAGER.
TAKE IT.
WOW. TASTE'S GREAT.
I ADDED SOME LEMON AND HONEY.
THOUGHT YOU'D LIKE IT FOR A CHANGE.
THANKS.
GIRLS ARE MORE CARING THAN GUYS.

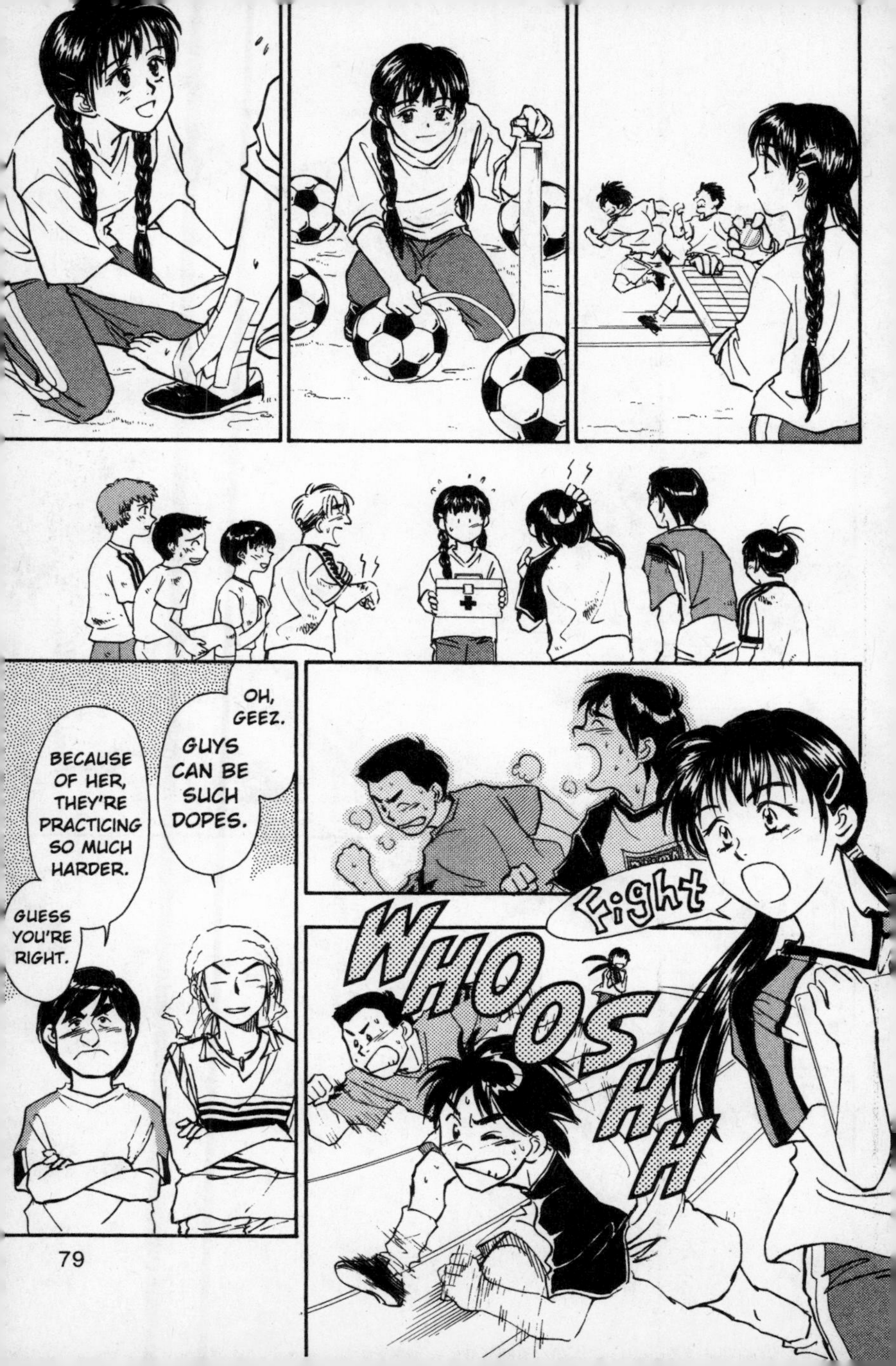
Fight
WHOOSHH
OH, GEEZ. GUYS CAN BE SUCH DOPES.
BECAUSE OF HER, THEY'RE PRACTICING SO MUCH HARDER.
GUESS YOU'RE RIGHT.

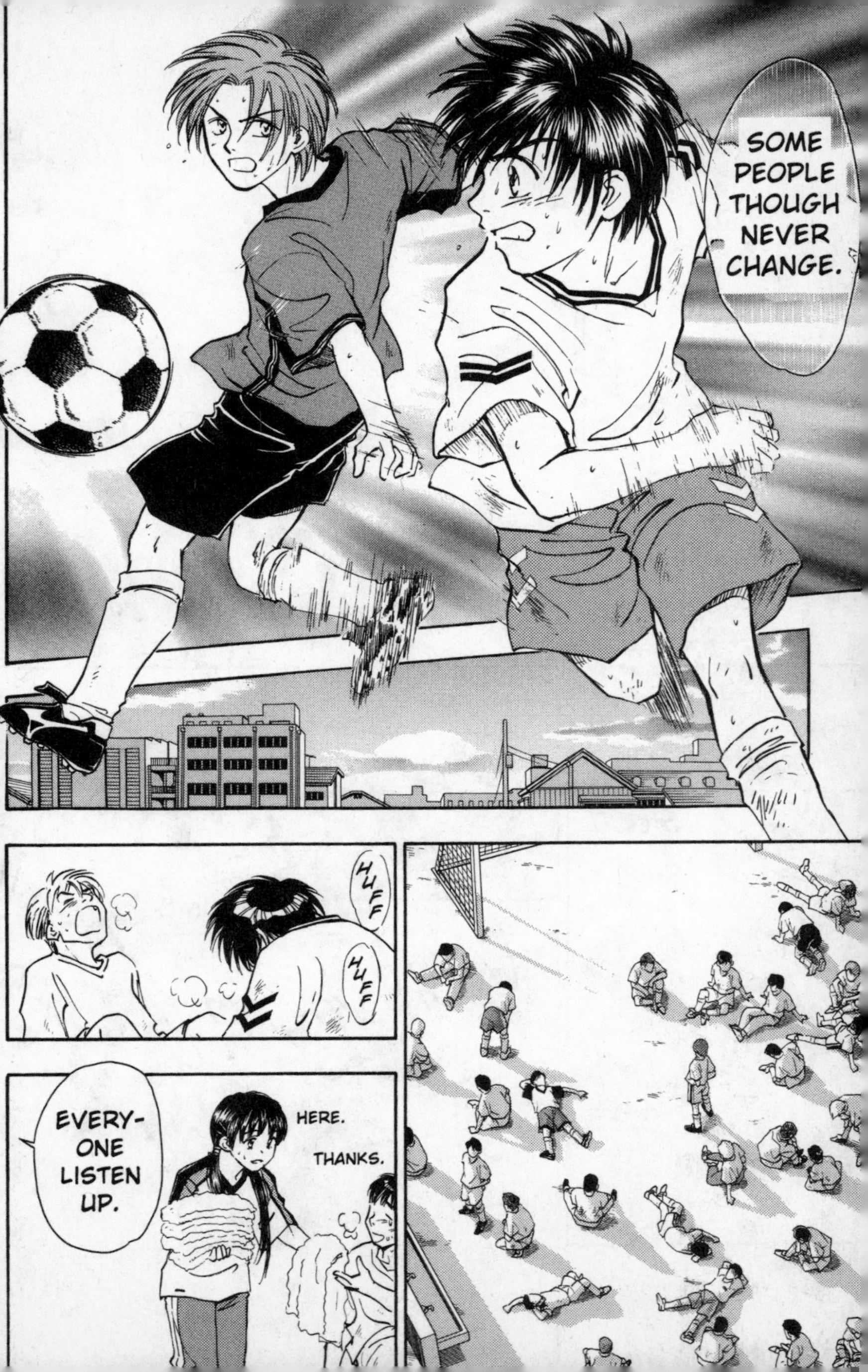
SOME PEOPLE THOUGH NEVER CHANGE.
HUFF
HUFF
HERE.
THANKS.
EVERY-ONE LISTEN UP.

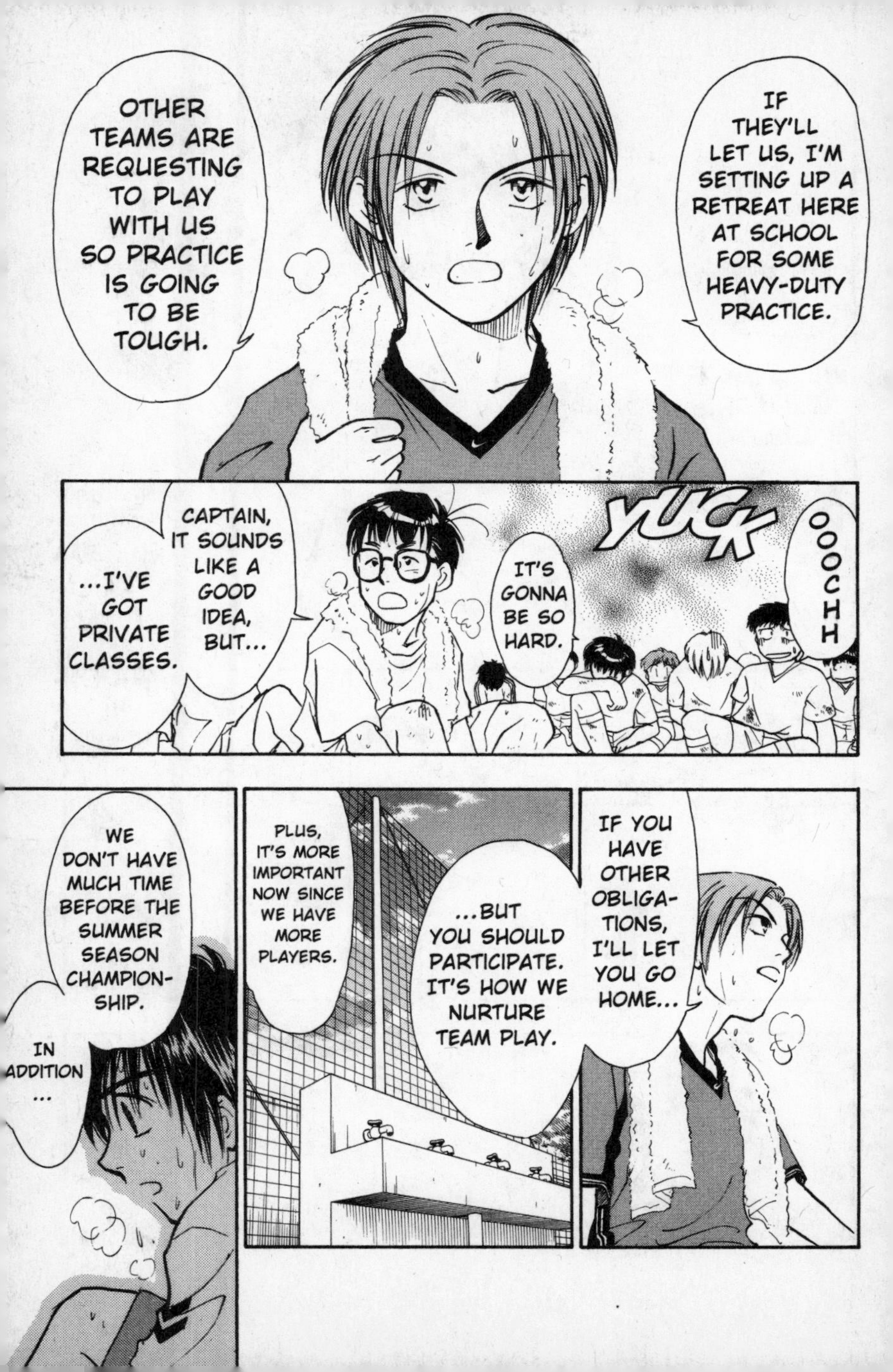
IF THEY'LL LET US, I'M SETTING UP A RETREAT HERE AT SCHOOL FOR SOME HEAVY-DUTY PRACTICE.
OTHER TEAMS ARE REQUESTING TO PLAY WITH US SO PRACTICE IS GOING TO BE TOUGH.
OOOCHH
YUCK
IT'S GONNA BE SO HARD.
CAPTAIN, IT SOUNDS LIKE A GOOD IDEA, BUT...
...I'VE GOT PRIVATE CLASSES.
IF YOU HAVE OTHER OBLIGA-TIONS, I'LL LET YOU GO HOME...
...BUT YOU SHOULD PARTICIPATE. IT'S HOW WE NURTURE TEAM PLAY.
PLUS, IT'S MORE IMPORTANT NOW SINCE WE HAVE MORE PLAYERS.
WE DON'T HAVE MUCH TIME BEFORE THE SUMMER SEASON CHAMPION-SHIP.
IN ADDITION...

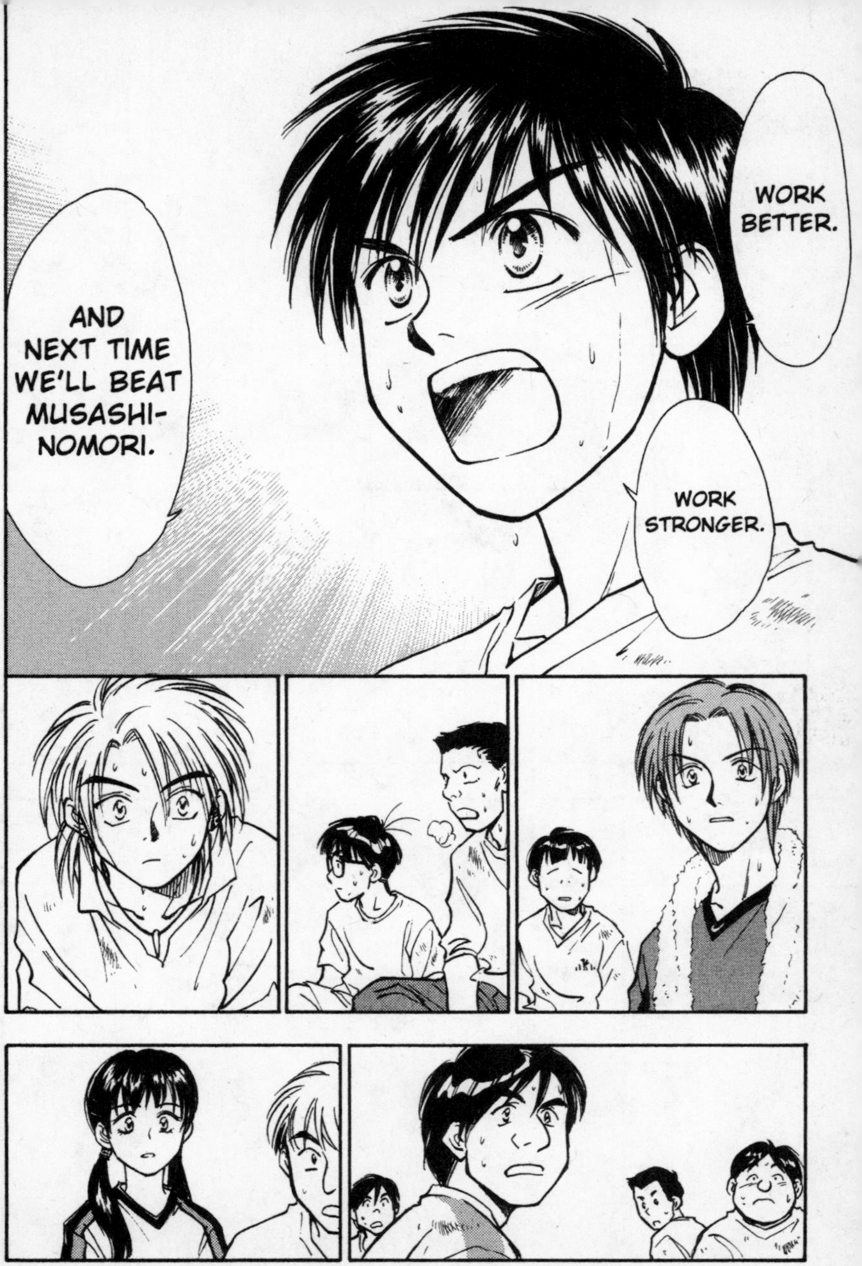
WORK BETTER.
WORK STRONGER.
AND NEXT TIME WE'LL BEAT MUSASHI-NOMORI.

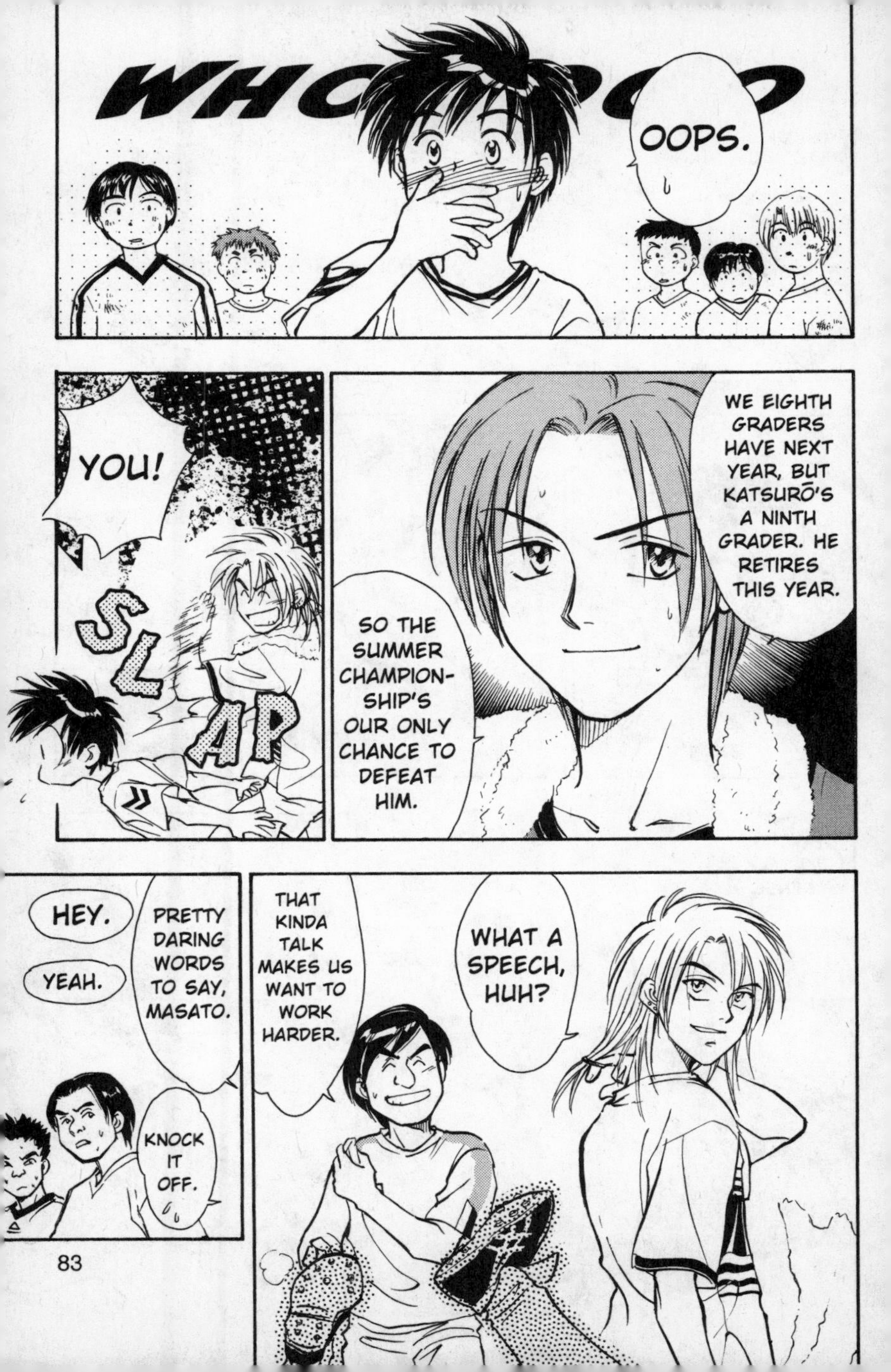
OOPS.
WE EIGHTH GRADERS HAVE NEXT YEAR, BUT KATSURŌ'S A NINTH GRADER. HE RETIRES THIS YEAR.
SO THE SUMMER CHAMPIONSHIP'S OUR ONLY CHANCE TO DEFEAT HIM.
YOU!
SLAP
WHAT A SPEECH, HUH?
THAT KINDA TALK MAKES US WANT TO WORK HARDER.
PRETTY DARING WORDS TO SAY, MASATO.
HEY.
YEAH.
KNOCK IT OFF.

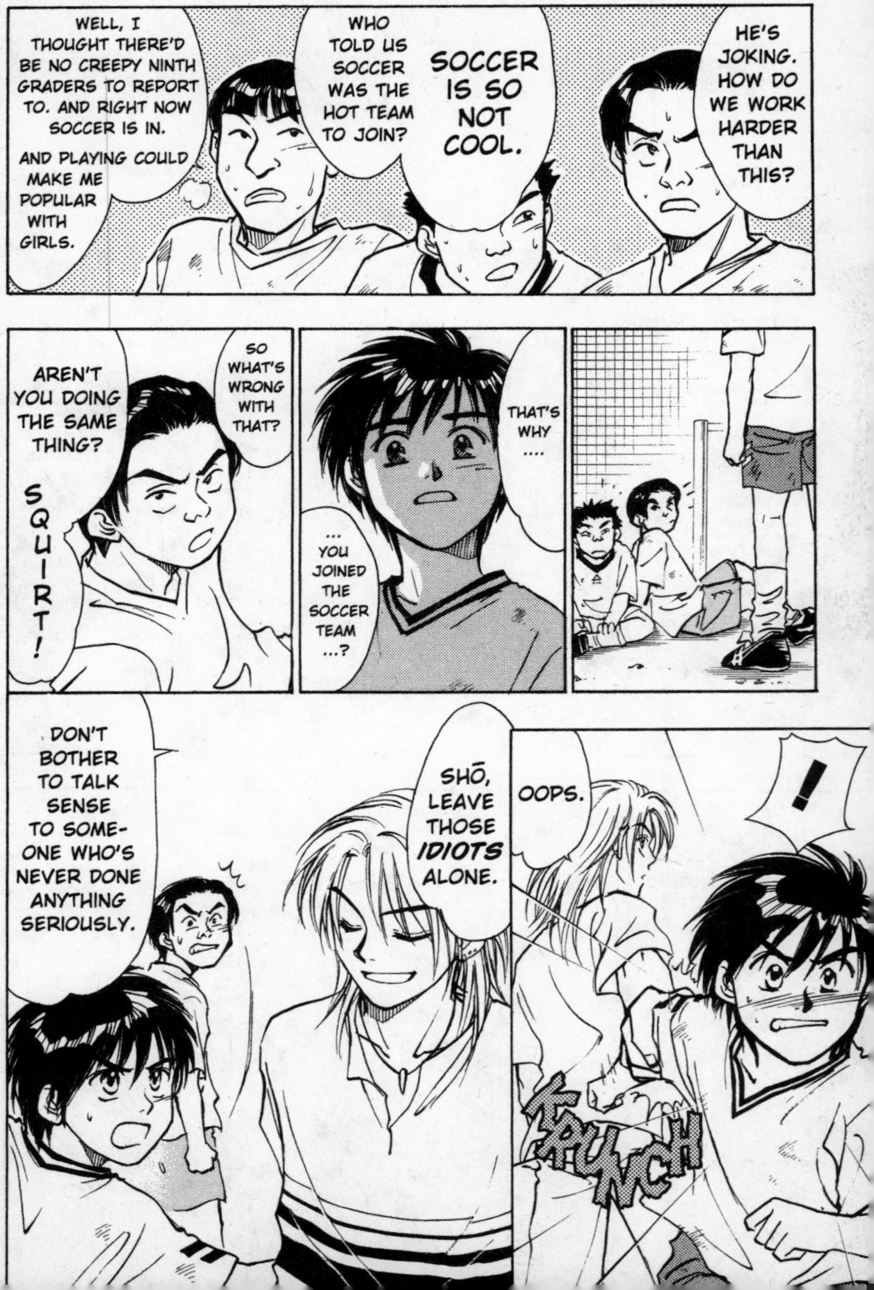
HE'S JOKING. HOW DO WE WORK HARDER THAN THIS?
SOCCER IS SO NOT COOL.
WHO TOLD US SOCCER WAS THE HOT TEAM TO JOIN?
WELL, I THOUGHT THERE'D BE NO CREEPY NINTH GRADERS TO REPORT TO. AND RIGHT NOW SOCCER IS IN.
AND PLAYING COULD MAKE ME POPULAR WITH GIRLS.
THAT'S WHY ....
... YOU JOINED THE SOCCER TEAM ...?
SO WHAT'S WRONG WITH THAT?
AREN'T YOU DOING THE SAME THING?
SQUIRT!
!
OOPS.
TPUNCH
SHŌ, LEAVE THOSE *IDIOTS* ALONE.
DON'T BOTHER TO TALK SENSE TO SOME-ONE WHO'S NEVER DONE ANYTHING SERIOUSLY.

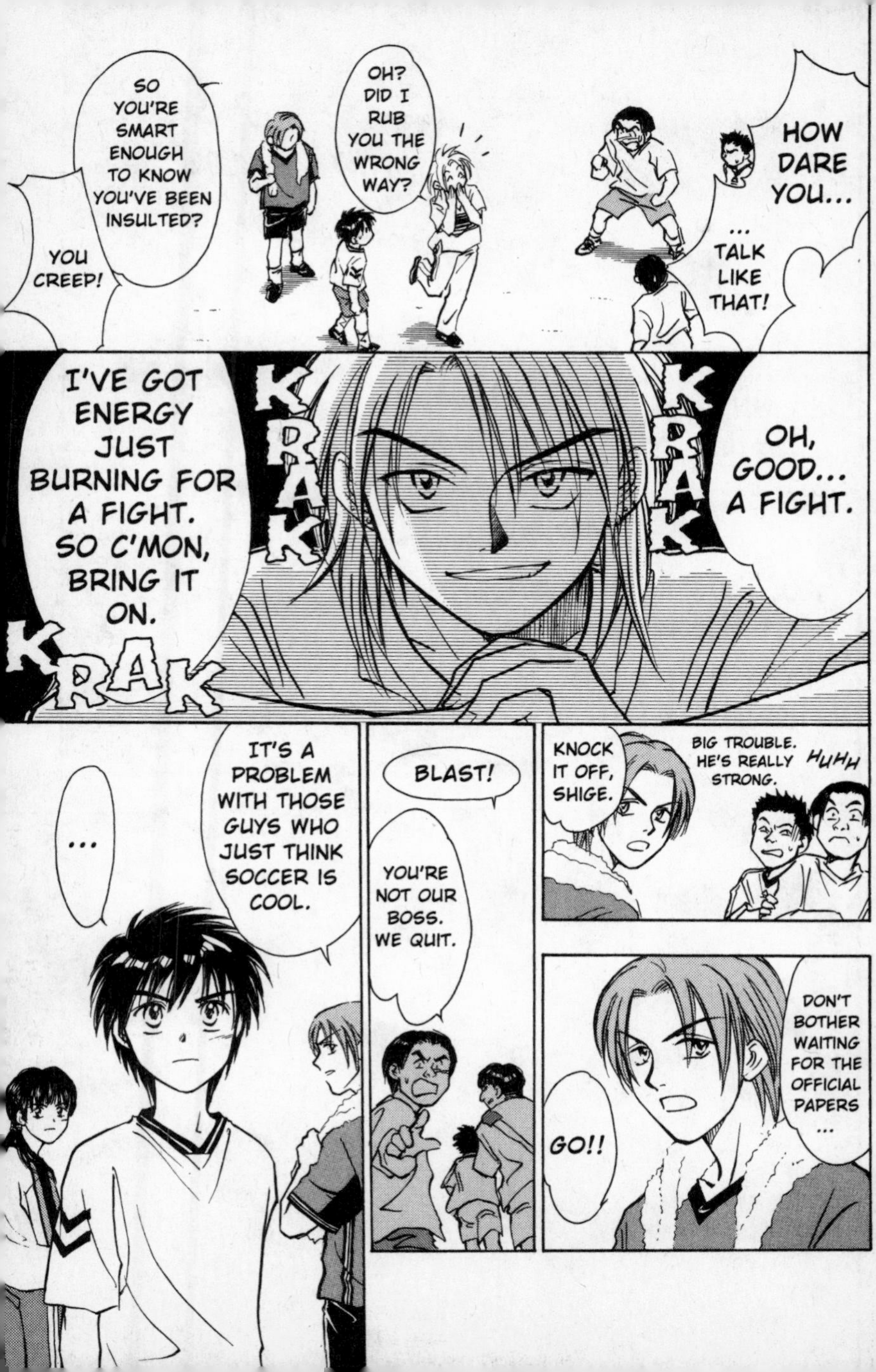
HOW DARE YOU...
...TALK LIKE THAT!
OH? DID I RUB YOU THE WRONG WAY?
SO YOU'RE SMART ENOUGH TO KNOW YOU'VE BEEN INSULTED?
YOU CREEP!
KRAK
OH, GOOD... A FIGHT.
KRAK
I'VE GOT ENERGY JUST BURNING FOR A FIGHT. SO C'MON, BRING IT ON.
KRAK
HUHH
BIG TROUBLE. HE'S REALLY STRONG.
KNOCK IT OFF, SHIGE.
DON'T BOTHER WAITING FOR THE OFFICIAL PAPERS...
GO!!
BLAST!
YOU'RE NOT OUR BOSS. WE QUIT.
IT'S A PROBLEM WITH THOSE GUYS WHO JUST THINK SOCCER IS COOL.
...

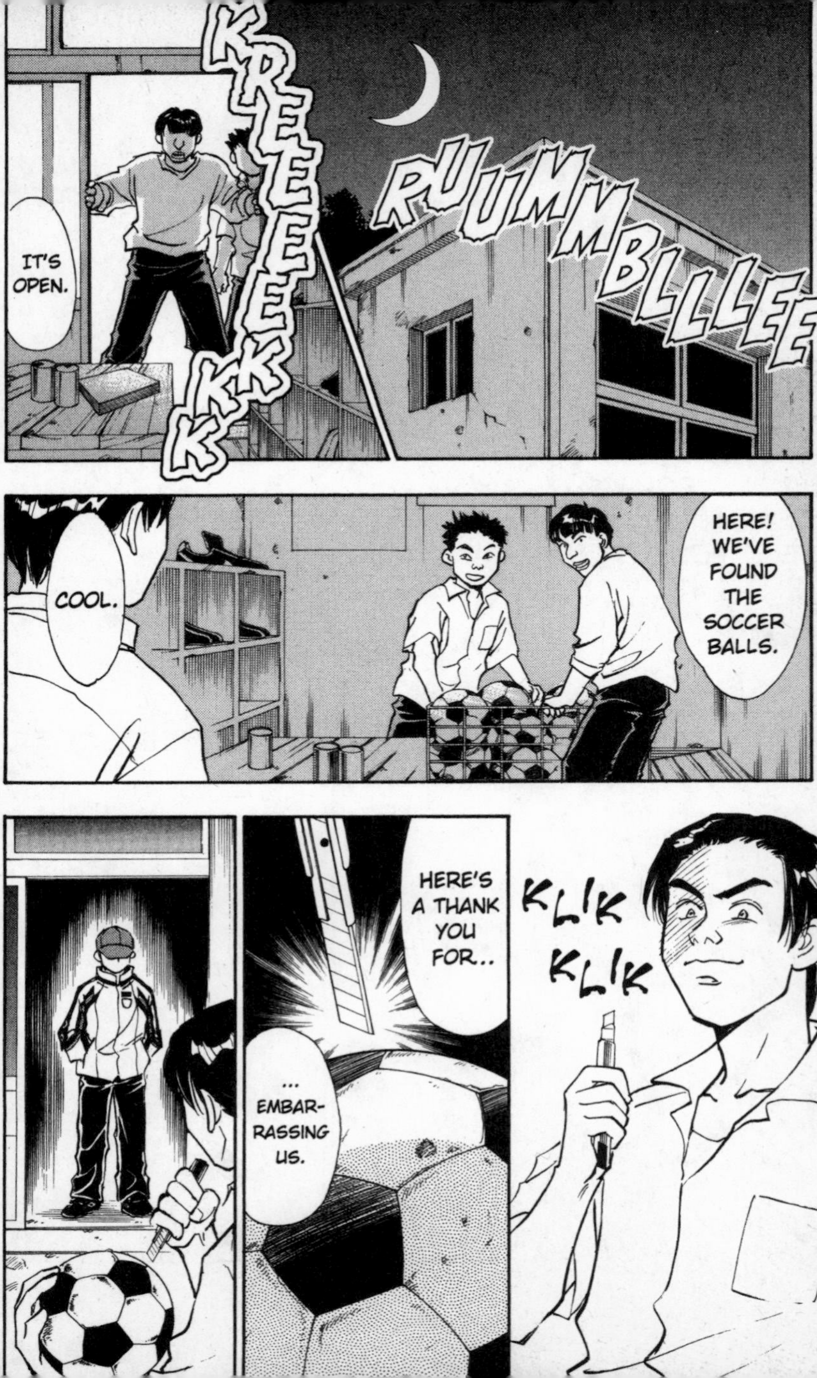
RUUMMBLLLEE
KREEEEKKK
IT'S OPEN.
HERE! WE'VE FOUND THE SOCCER BALLS.
COOL.
KLIK KLIK
HERE'S A THANK YOU FOR...
... EMBARRASSING US.

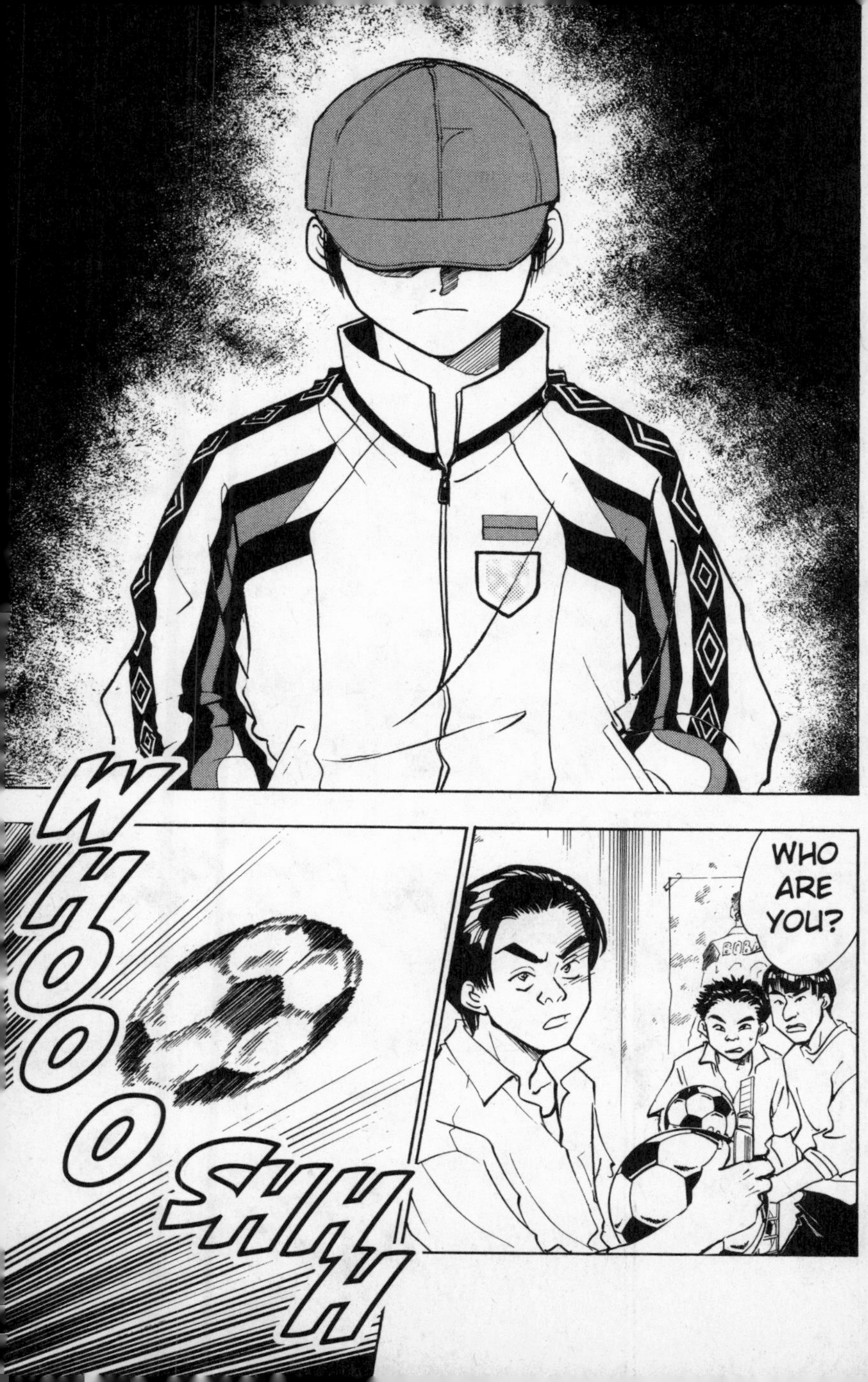
WHO ARE YOU?
WHOOOSHH

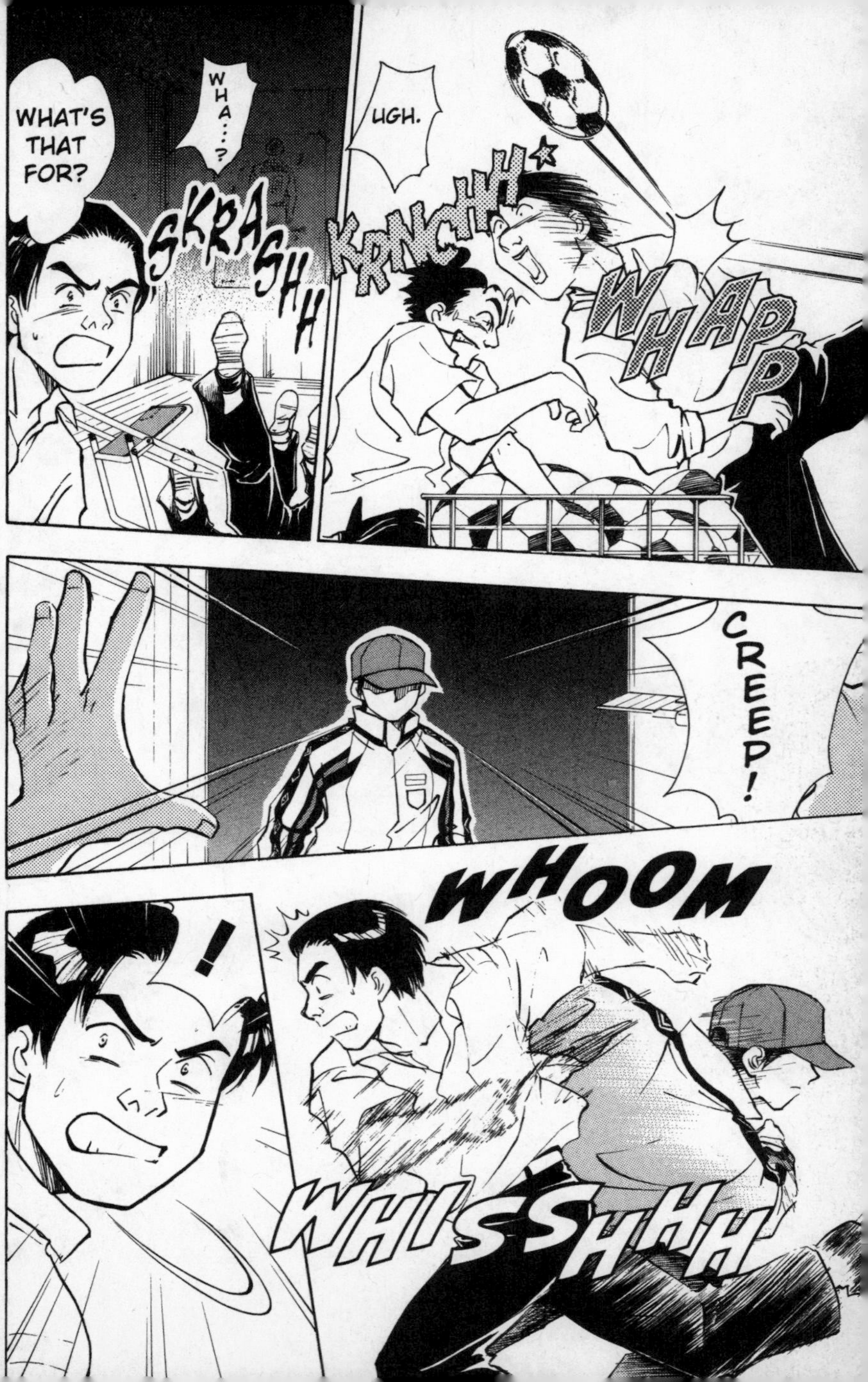
UGH.
KRNCHH
WHAPP
WHA...?
WHAT'S THAT FOR?
SKRASHH
CREEP!
WHOOM
WHISSHHH
!

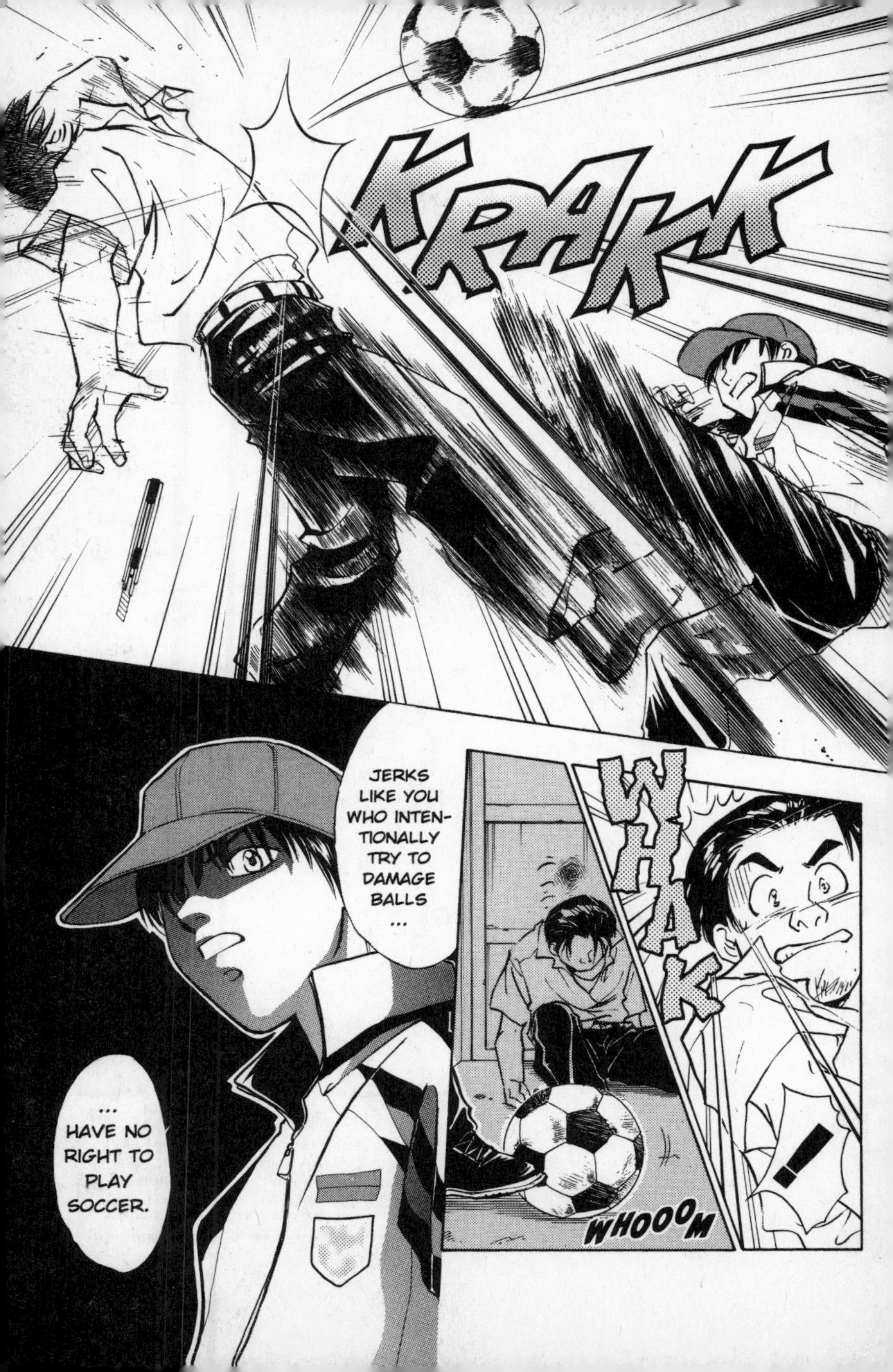
KRAKK
WHAK
!
WHOOOM
JERKS LIKE YOU WHO INTEN-TIONALLY TRY TO DAMAGE BALLS ...
... HAVE NO RIGHT TO PLAY SOCCER.

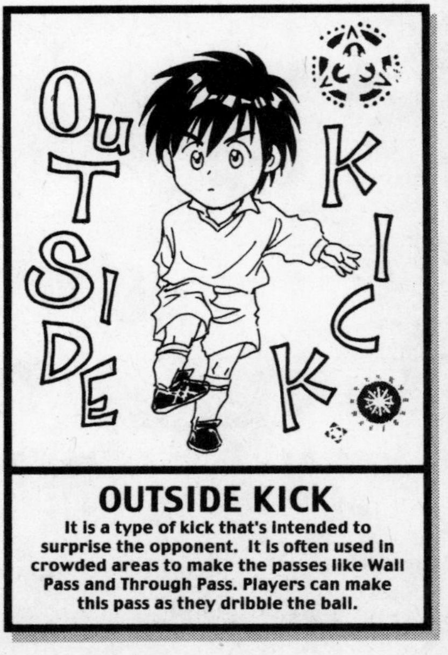
OuTSIDE
KICK

**OUTSIDE KICK**

**It is a type of kick that's intended to surprise the opponent. It is often used in crowded areas to make the passes like Wall Pass and Through Pass. Players can make this pass as they dribble the ball.**

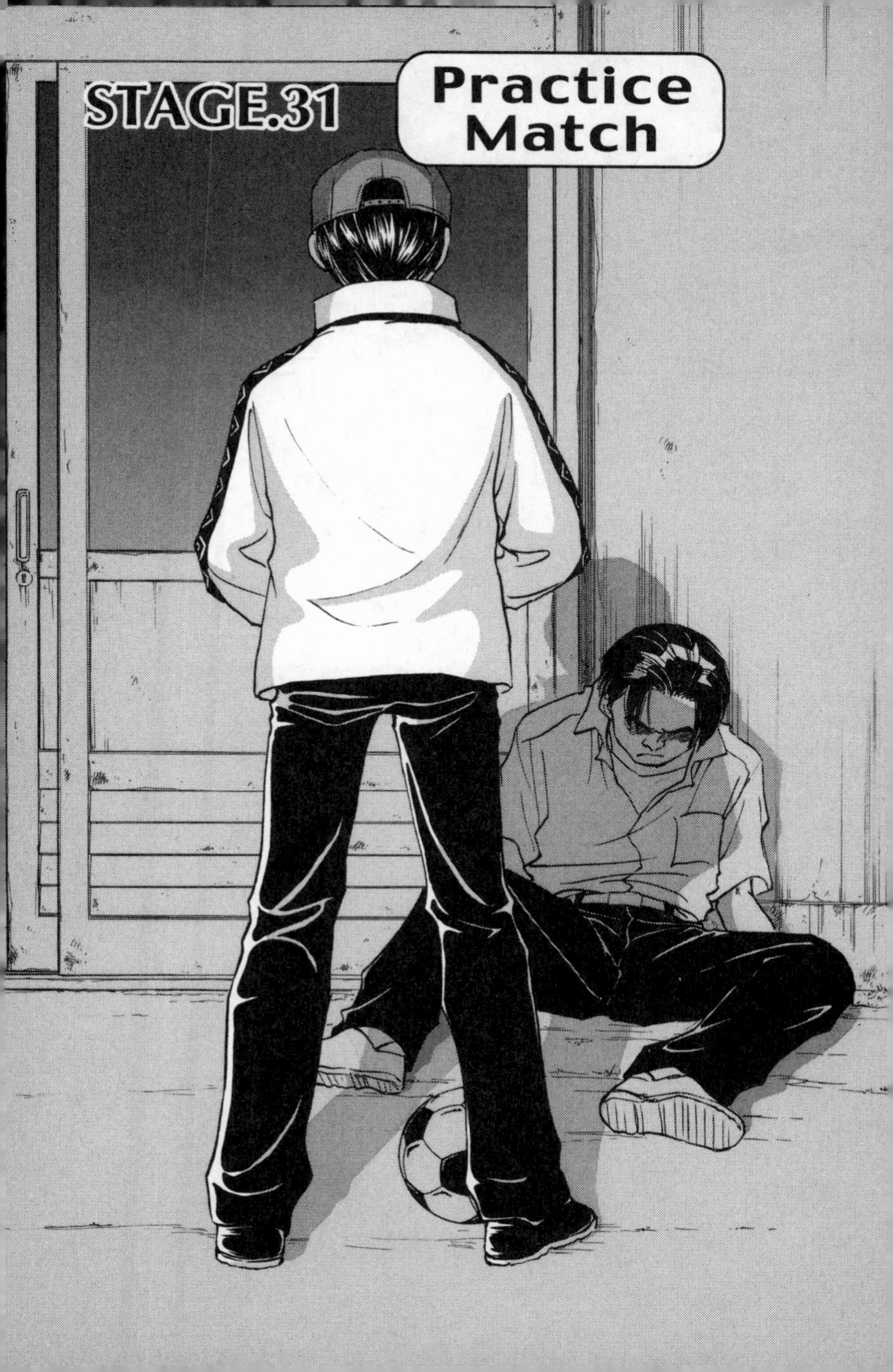
STAGE.31
Practice Match

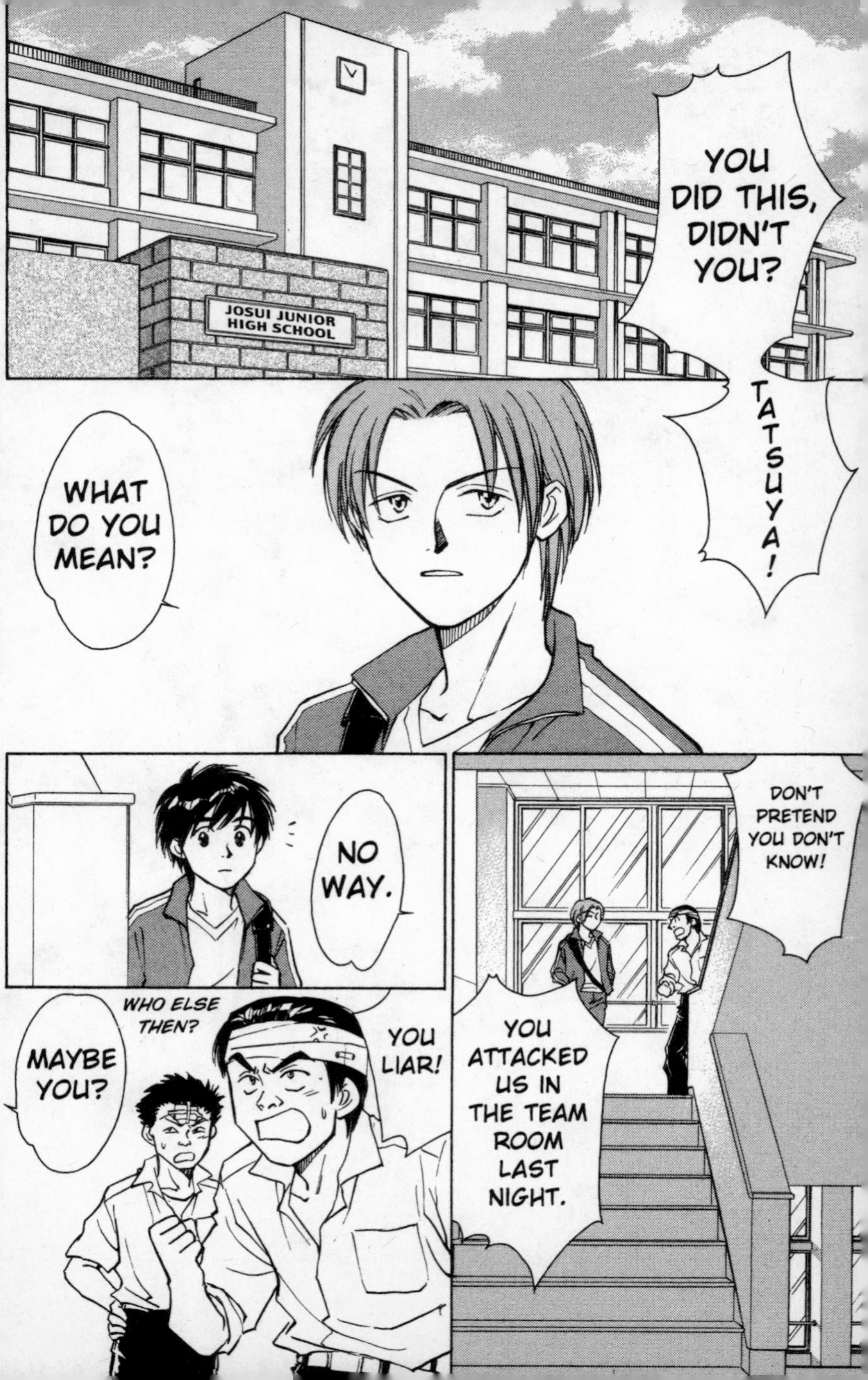
JOSUI JUNIOR HIGH SCHOOL
YOU DID THIS, DIDN'T YOU?
TATSUYA!
WHAT DO YOU MEAN?
DON'T PRETEND YOU DON'T KNOW!
YOU ATTACKED US IN THE TEAM ROOM LAST NIGHT.
NO WAY.
YOU LIAR!
WHO ELSE THEN?
MAYBE YOU?

READ THIS WAY

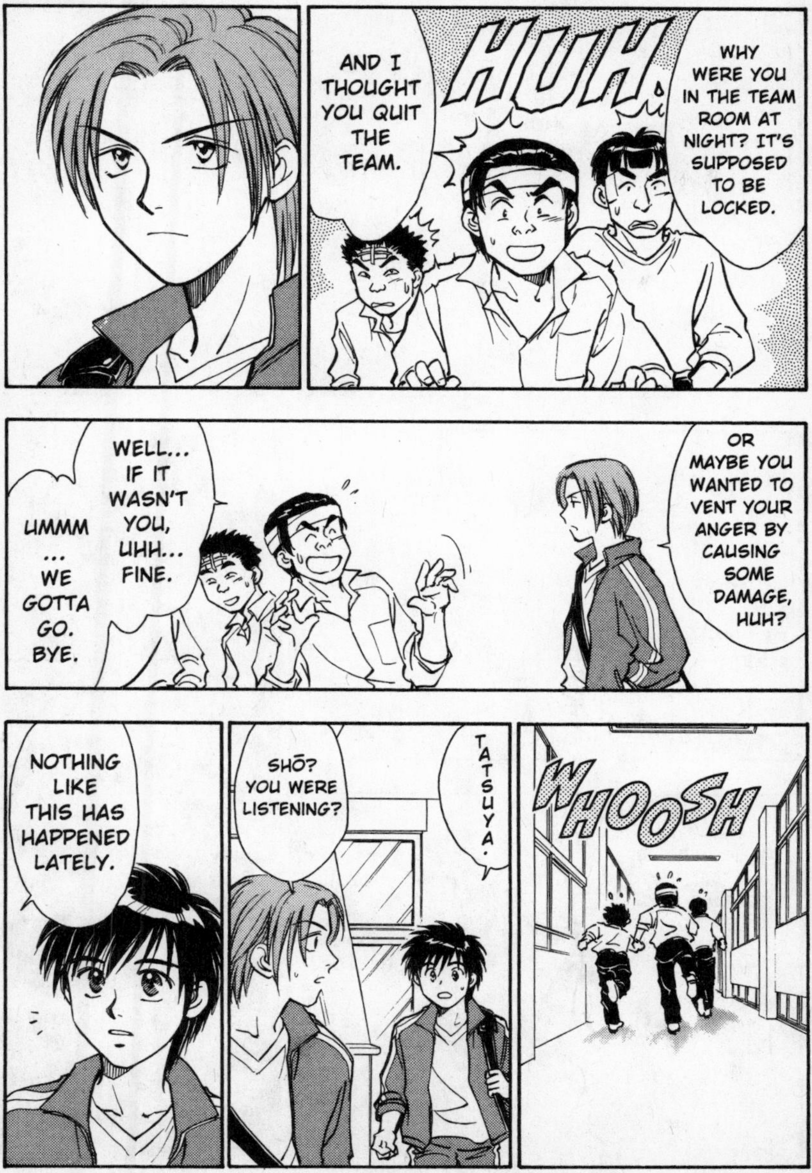
WHY WERE YOU IN THE TEAM ROOM AT NIGHT? IT'S SUPPOSED TO BE LOCKED.
HUH.
AND I THOUGHT YOU QUIT THE TEAM.
OR MAYBE YOU WANTED TO VENT YOUR ANGER BY CAUSING SOME DAMAGE, HUH?
WELL... IF IT WASN'T YOU, UHH... FINE.
UMMM ... WE GOTTA GO. BYE.
WHOOSH
TATSUYA.
SHŌ? YOU WERE LISTENING?
NOTHING LIKE THIS HAS HAPPENED LATELY.

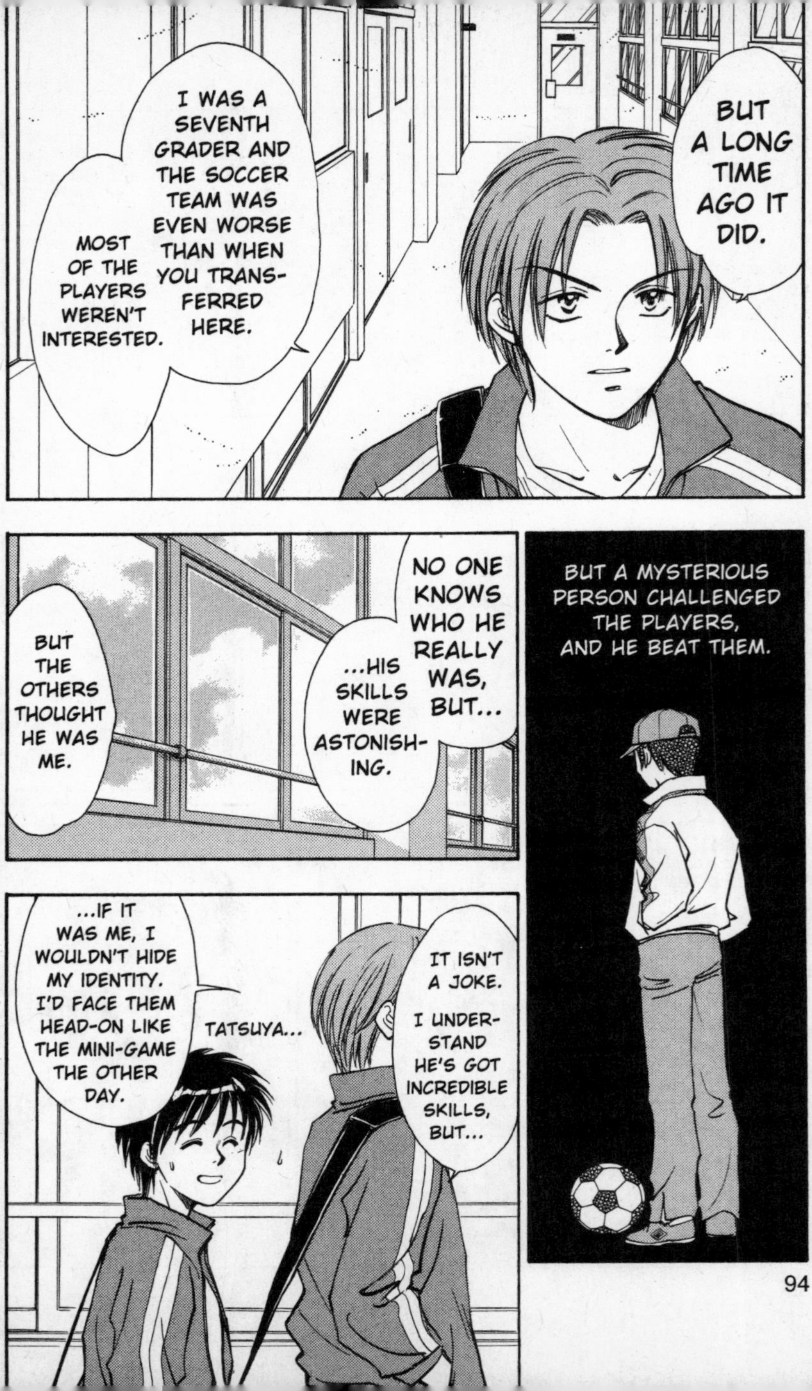
BUT A LONG TIME AGO IT DID.
I WAS A SEVENTH GRADER AND THE SOCCER TEAM WAS EVEN WORSE THAN WHEN YOU TRANSFERRED HERE.
MOST OF THE PLAYERS WEREN'T INTERESTED.
BUT A MYSTERIOUS PERSON CHALLENGED THE PLAYERS, AND HE BEAT THEM.
NO ONE KNOWS WHO HE REALLY WAS, BUT...
...HIS SKILLS WERE ASTONISHING.
BUT THE OTHERS THOUGHT HE WAS ME.
IT ISN'T A JOKE.
I UNDERSTAND HE'S GOT INCREDIBLE SKILLS, BUT...
TATSUYA...
...IF IT WAS ME, I WOULDN'T HIDE MY IDENTITY. I'D FACE THEM HEAD-ON LIKE THE MINI-GAME THE OTHER DAY.

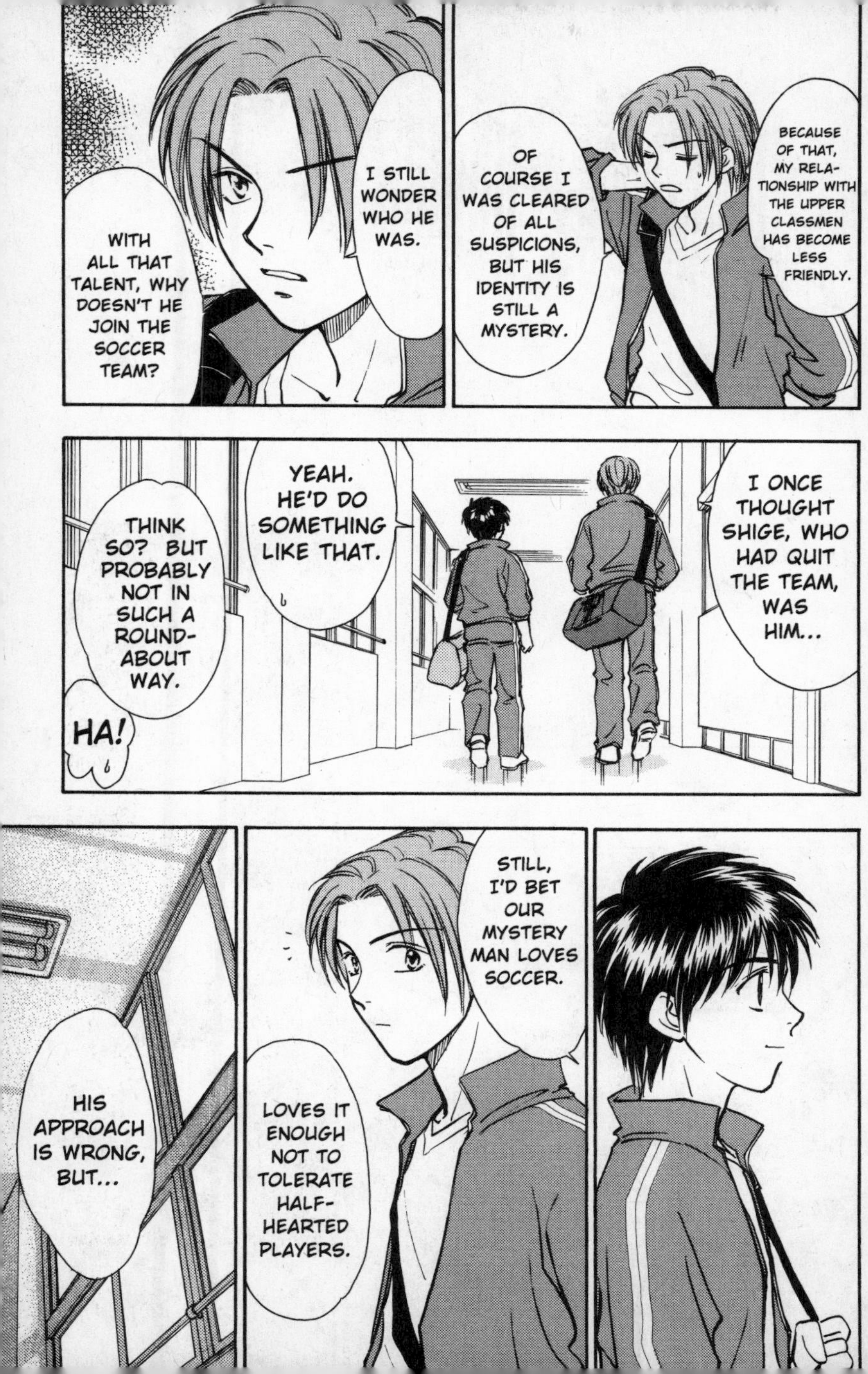
BECAUSE OF THAT, MY RELATIONSHIP WITH THE UPPER CLASSMEN HAS BECOME LESS FRIENDLY.
OF COURSE I WAS CLEARED OF ALL SUSPICIONS, BUT HIS IDENTITY IS STILL A MYSTERY.
I STILL WONDER WHO HE WAS.
WITH ALL THAT TALENT, WHY DOESN'T HE JOIN THE SOCCER TEAM?
I ONCE THOUGHT SHIGE, WHO HAD QUIT THE TEAM, WAS HIM...
YEAH. HE'D DO SOMETHING LIKE THAT.
THINK SO? BUT PROBABLY NOT IN SUCH A ROUND-ABOUT WAY.
HA!
STILL, I'D BET OUR MYSTERY MAN LOVES SOCCER.
LOVES IT ENOUGH NOT TO TOLERATE HALF-HEARTED PLAYERS.
HIS APPROACH IS WRONG, BUT...

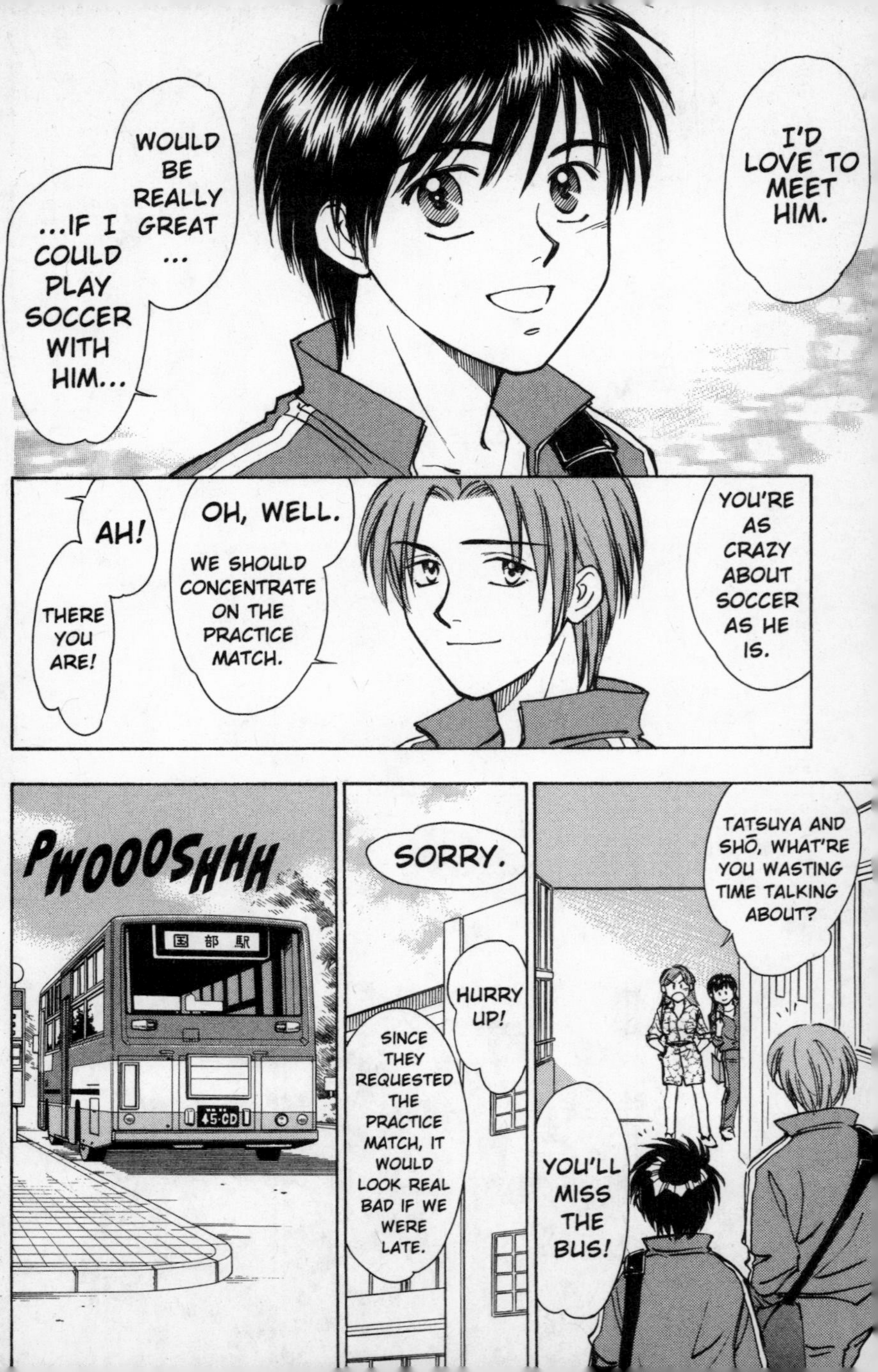
I'D LOVE TO MEET HIM.
WOULD BE REALLY GREAT ...
...IF I COULD PLAY SOCCER WITH HIM...
YOU'RE AS CRAZY ABOUT SOCCER AS HE IS.
OH, WELL.
WE SHOULD CONCENTRATE ON THE PRACTICE MATCH.
AH!
THERE YOU ARE!
TATSUYA AND SHŌ, WHAT'RE YOU WASTING TIME TALKING ABOUT?
YOU'LL MISS THE BUS!
SORRY.
HURRY UP!
SINCE THEY REQUESTED THE PRACTICE MATCH, IT WOULD LOOK REAL BAD IF WE WERE LATE.
PWOOOSHHH
国部駅
45-CD

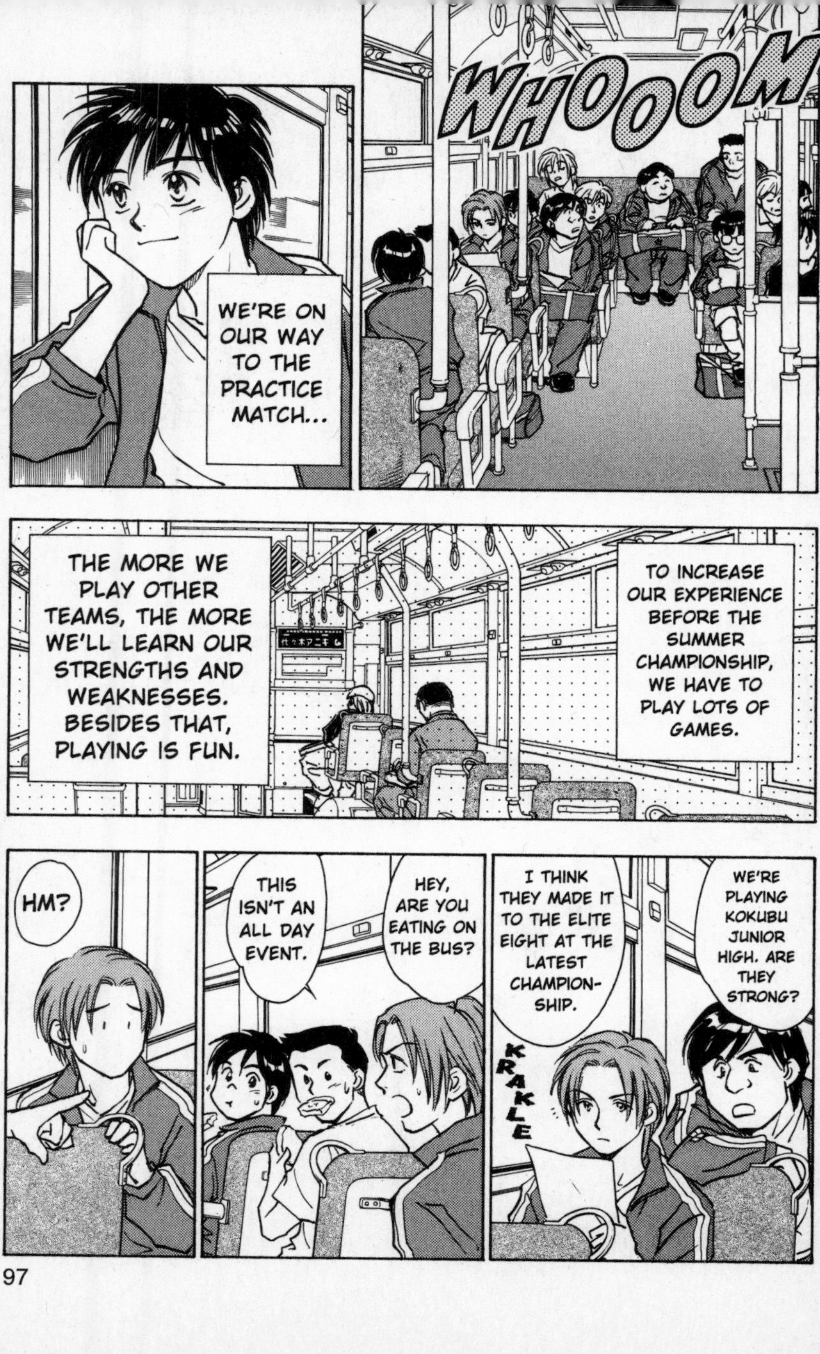
WHOOOM
WE'RE ON OUR WAY TO THE PRACTICE MATCH...
TO INCREASE OUR EXPERIENCE BEFORE THE SUMMER CHAMPIONSHIP, WE HAVE TO PLAY LOTS OF GAMES.
THE MORE WE PLAY OTHER TEAMS, THE MORE WE'LL LEARN OUR STRENGTHS AND WEAKNESSES. BESIDES THAT, PLAYING IS FUN.
WE'RE PLAYING KOKUBU JUNIOR HIGH. ARE THEY STRONG?
I THINK THEY MADE IT TO THE ELITE EIGHT AT THE LATEST CHAMPIONSHIP.
KRAKLE
HEY, ARE YOU EATING ON THE BUS?
THIS ISN'T AN ALL DAY EVENT.
HM?

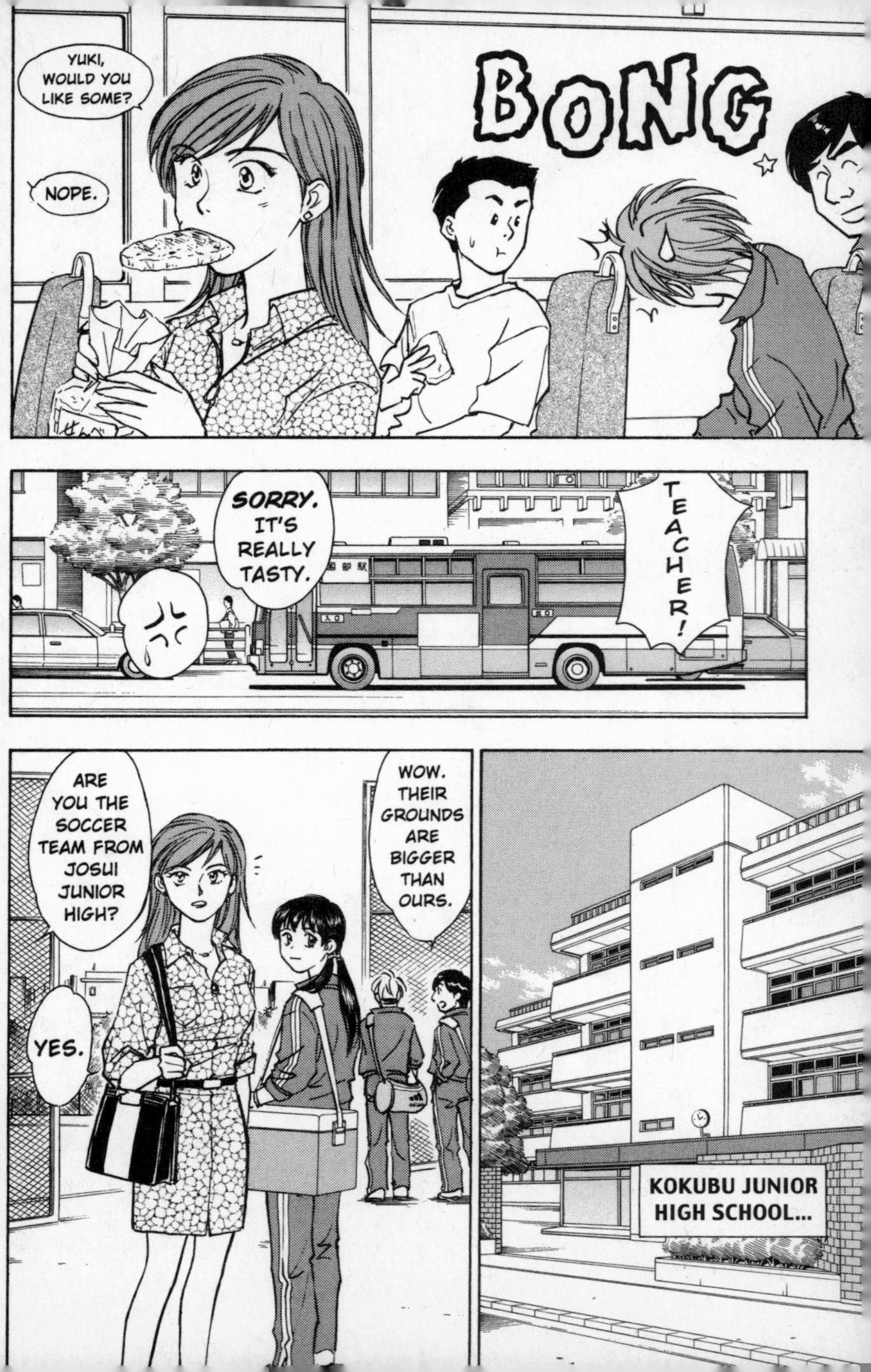
YUKI, WOULD YOU LIKE SOME?
NOPE.
BONG
TEACHER!
SORRY. IT'S REALLY TASTY.
KOKUBU JUNIOR HIGH SCHOOL...
WOW. THEIR GROUNDS ARE BIGGER THAN OURS.
ARE YOU THE SOCCER TEAM FROM JOSUI JUNIOR HIGH?
YES.

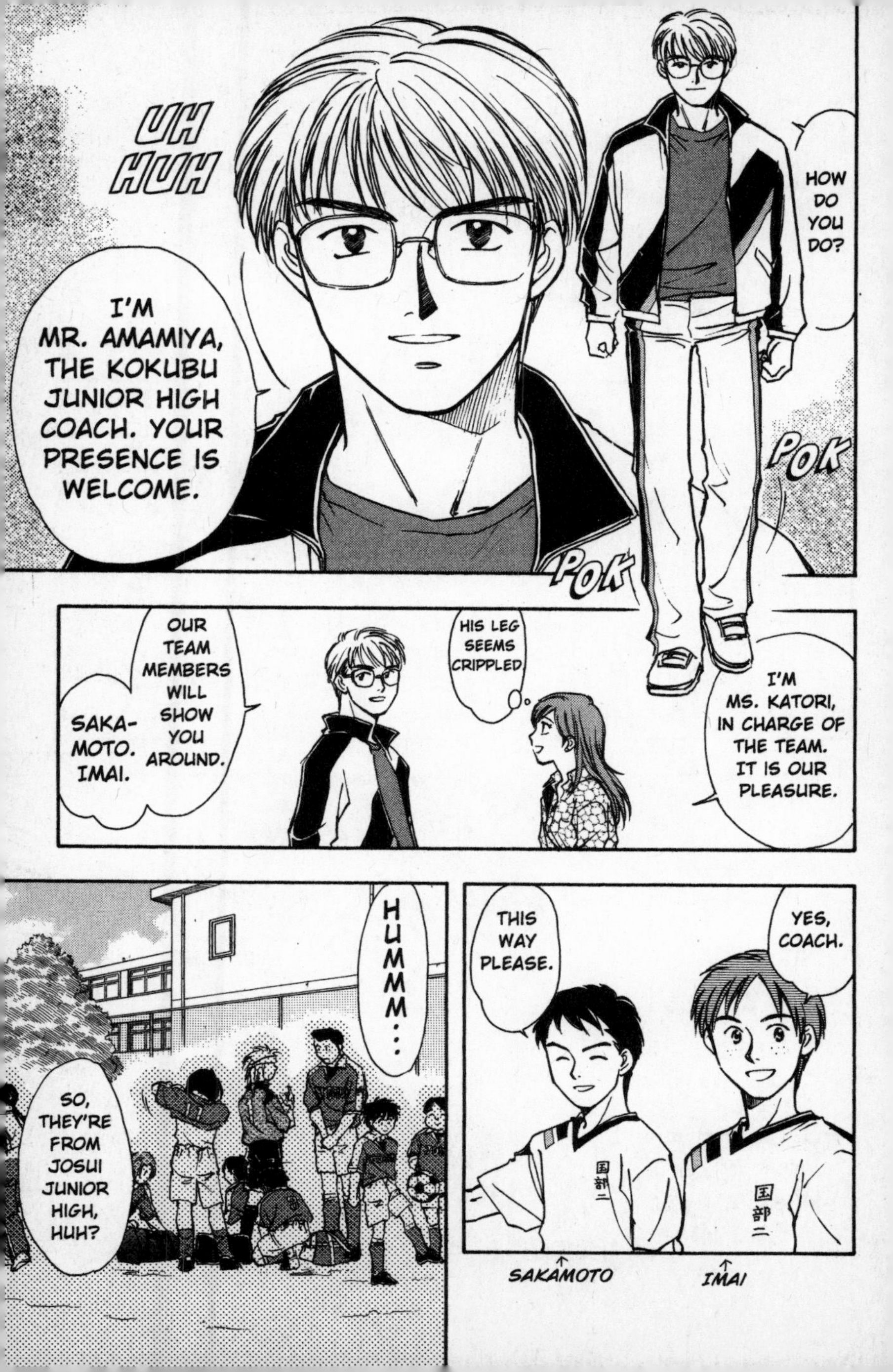
HOW DO YOU DO?
POK
POK
I'M MS. KATORI, IN CHARGE OF THE TEAM. IT IS OUR PLEASURE.
UH HUH
I'M MR. AMAMIYA, THE KOKUBU JUNIOR HIGH COACH. YOUR PRESENCE IS WELCOME.
HIS LEG SEEMS CRIPPLED
OUR TEAM MEMBERS WILL SHOW YOU AROUND.
SAKAMOTO. IMAI.
YES, COACH.
THIS WAY PLEASE.
SAKAMOTO
IMAI
HUMMM...
SO, THEY'RE FROM JOSUI JUNIOR HIGH, HUH?

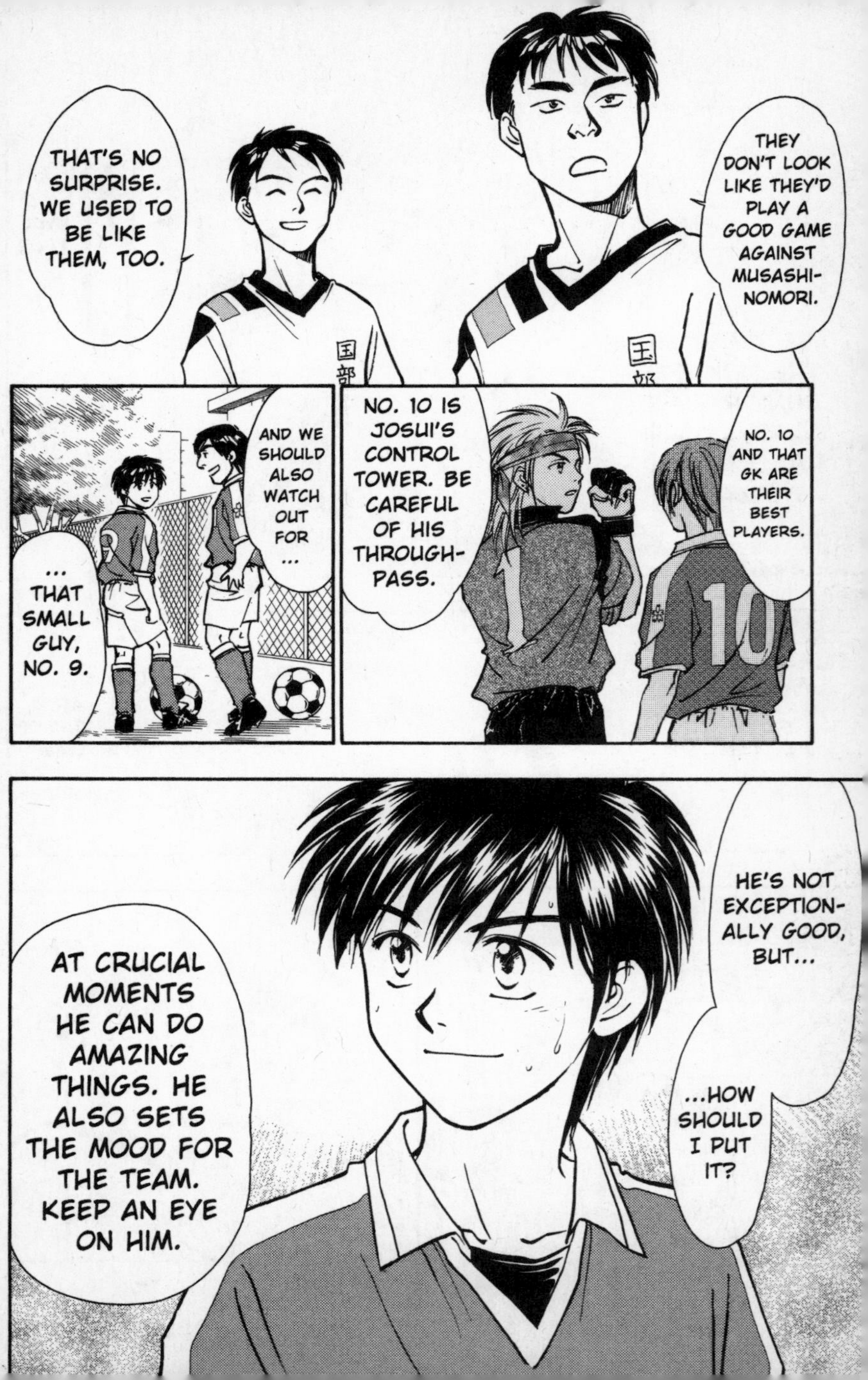
THEY DON'T LOOK LIKE THEY'D PLAY A GOOD GAME AGAINST MUSASHI-NOMORI.
THAT'S NO SURPRISE. WE USED TO BE LIKE THEM, TOO.
NO. 10 AND THAT GK ARE THEIR BEST PLAYERS.
NO. 10 IS JOSUI'S CONTROL TOWER. BE CAREFUL OF HIS THROUGH-PASS.
AND WE SHOULD ALSO WATCH OUT FOR ...
... THAT SMALL GUY, NO. 9.
HE'S NOT EXCEPTION-ALLY GOOD, BUT...
...HOW SHOULD I PUT IT?
AT CRUCIAL MOMENTS HE CAN DO AMAZING THINGS. HE ALSO SETS THE MOOD FOR THE TEAM. KEEP AN EYE ON HIM.

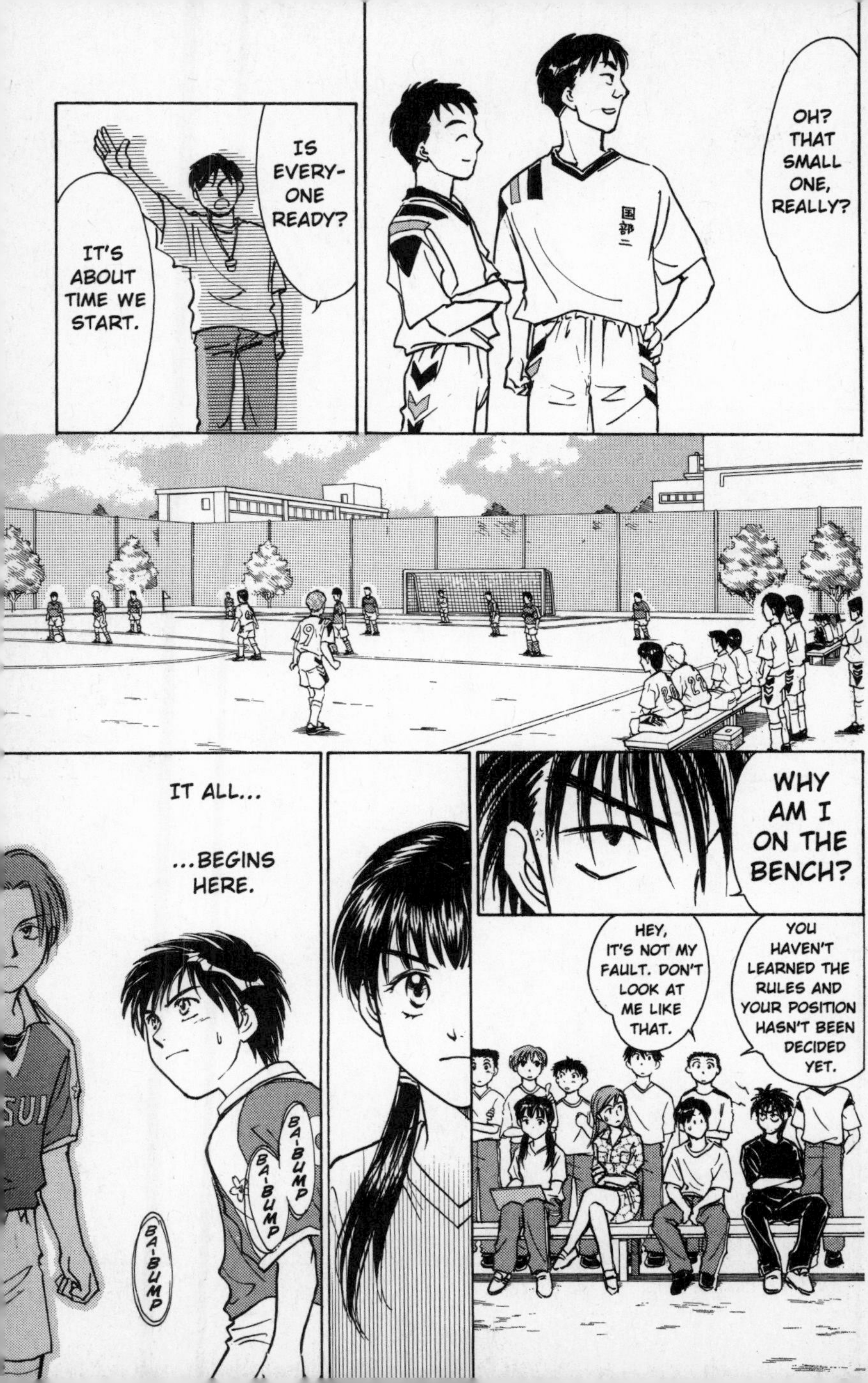
OH? THAT SMALL ONE, REALLY?
IS EVERY-ONE READY?
IT'S ABOUT TIME WE START.
WHY AM I ON THE BENCH?
YOU HAVEN'T LEARNED THE RULES AND YOUR POSITION HASN'T BEEN DECIDED YET.
HEY, IT'S NOT MY FAULT. DON'T LOOK AT ME LIKE THAT.
IT ALL...
...BEGINS HERE.
BA-BUMP
BA-BUMP
BA-BUMP

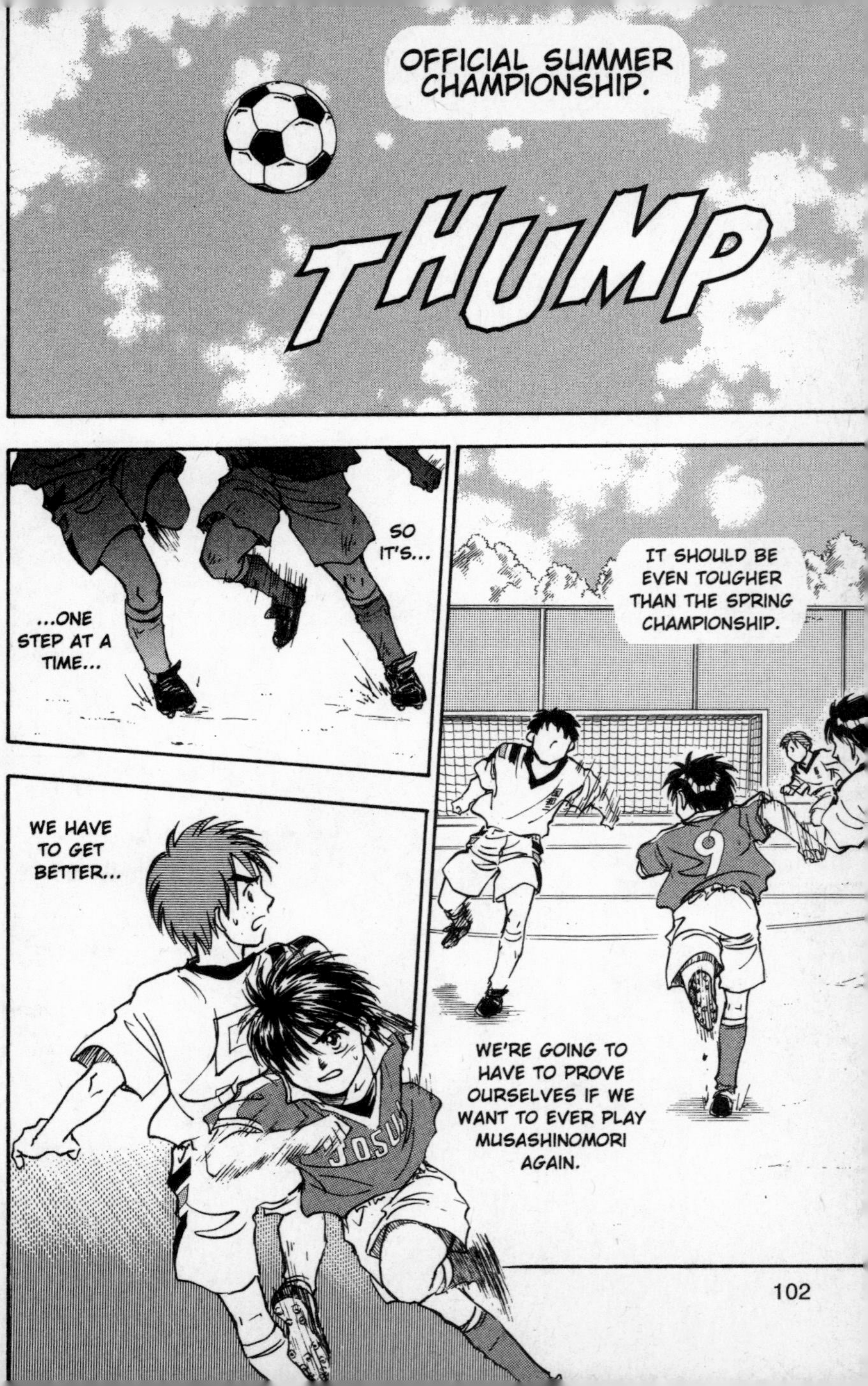
OFFICIAL SUMMER CHAMPIONSHIP.
THUMP
IT SHOULD BE EVEN TOUGHER THAN THE SPRING CHAMPIONSHIP.
WE'RE GOING TO HAVE TO PROVE OURSELVES IF WE WANT TO EVER PLAY MUSASHINOMORI AGAIN.
SO IT'S...
...ONE STEP AT A TIME...
WE HAVE TO GET BETTER...

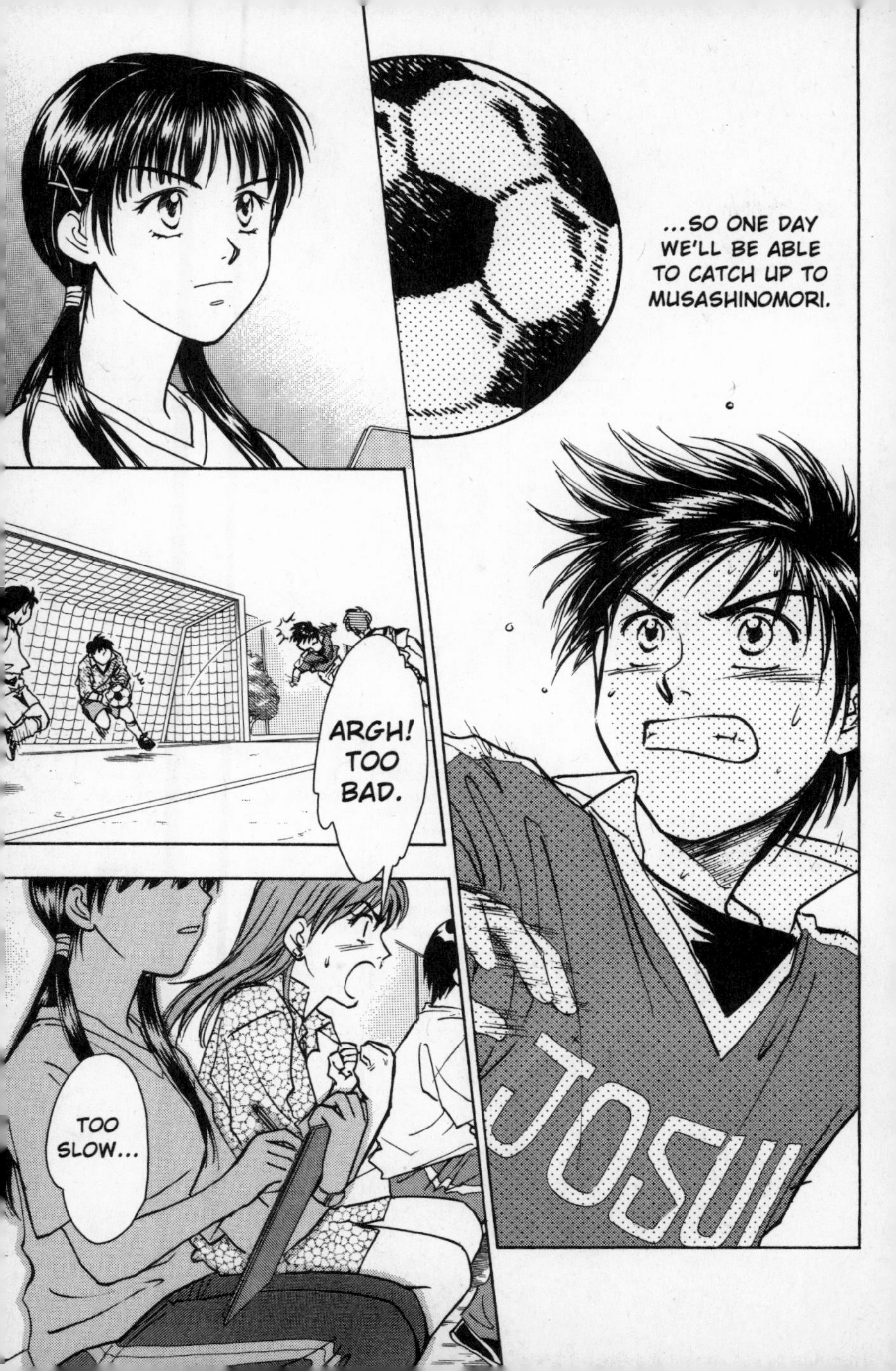
...SO ONE DAY WE'LL BE ABLE TO CATCH UP TO MUSASHINOMORI.
JOSUI
ARGH! TOO BAD.
TOO SLOW...

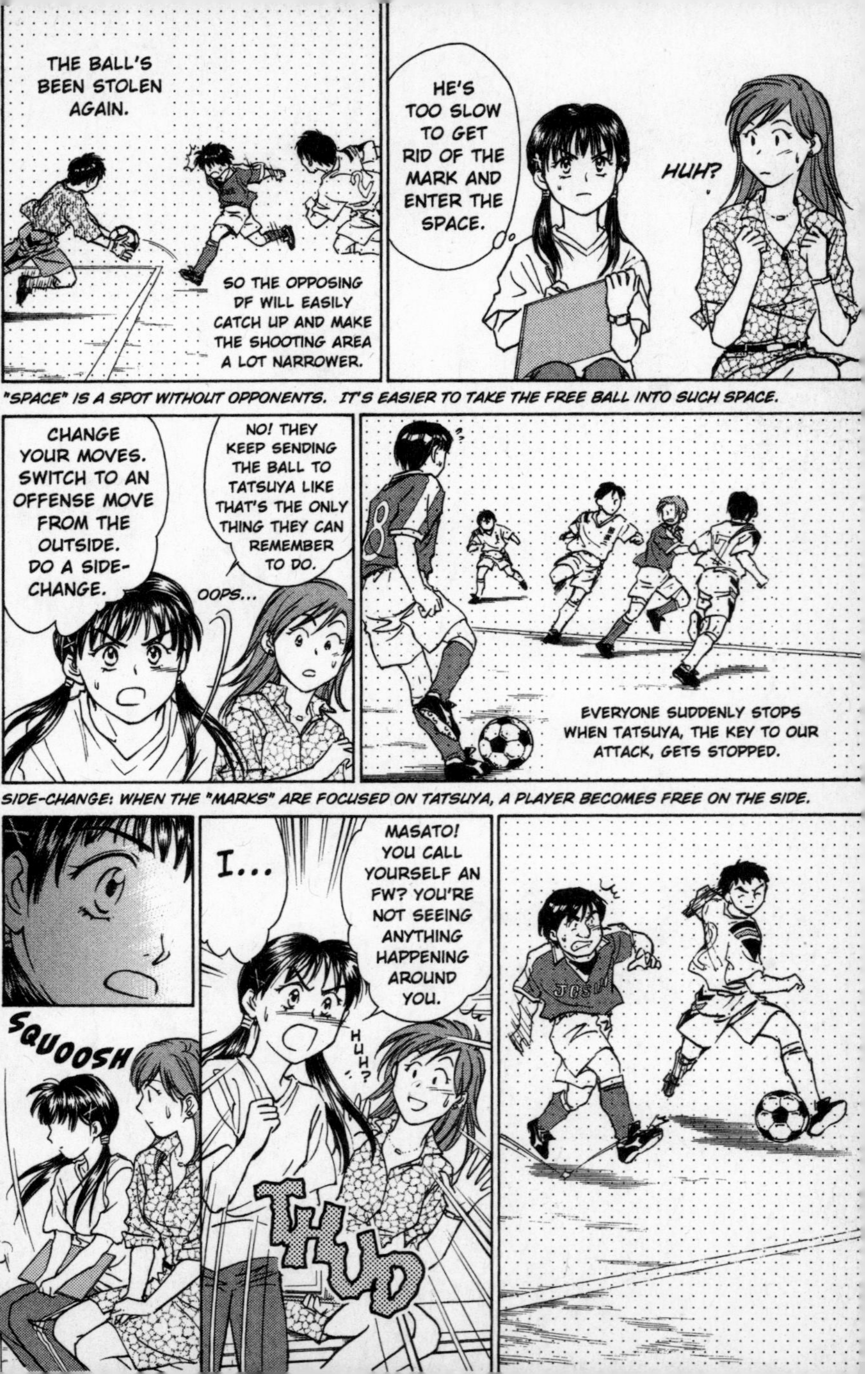
HE'S TOO SLOW TO GET RID OF THE MARK AND ENTER THE SPACE.
HUH?
THE BALL'S BEEN STOLEN AGAIN.
SO THE OPPOSING DF WILL EASILY CATCH UP AND MAKE THE SHOOTING AREA A LOT NARROWER.
"SPACE" IS A SPOT WITHOUT OPPONENTS. IT'S EASIER TO TAKE THE FREE BALL INTO SUCH SPACE.
EVERYONE SUDDENLY STOPS WHEN TATSUYA, THE KEY TO OUR ATTACK, GETS STOPPED.
NO! THEY KEEP SENDING THE BALL TO TATSUYA LIKE THAT'S THE ONLY THING THEY CAN REMEMBER TO DO.
CHANGE YOUR MOVES. SWITCH TO AN OFFENSE MOVE FROM THE OUTSIDE. DO A SIDE-CHANGE.
OOPS...
SIDE-CHANGE: WHEN THE "MARKS" ARE FOCUSED ON TATSUYA, A PLAYER BECOMES FREE ON THE SIDE.
MASATO! YOU CALL YOURSELF AN FW? YOU'RE NOT SEEING ANYTHING HAPPENING AROUND YOU.
I...
HUH?
THUD
SQUOOSH

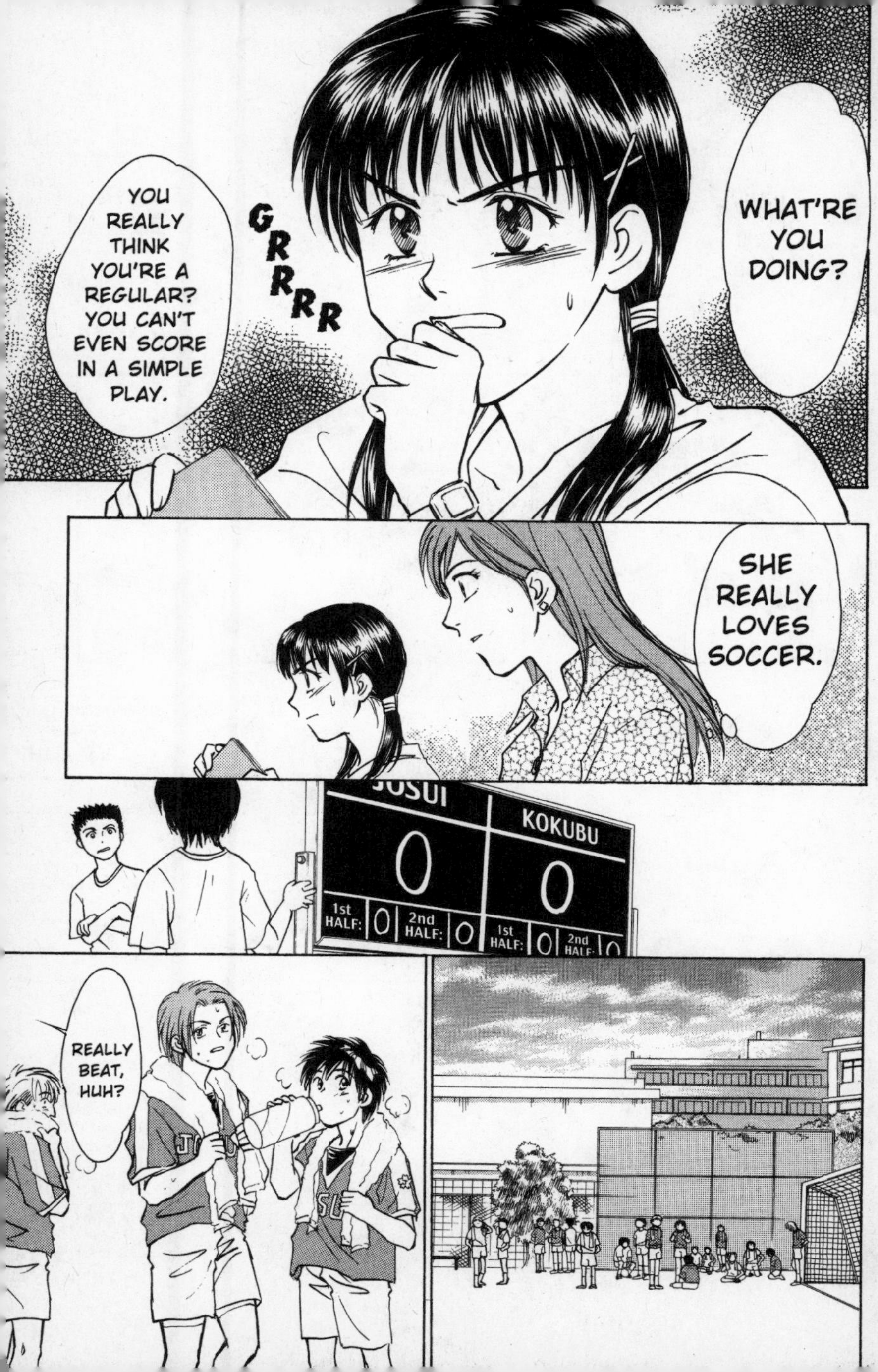
WHAT'RE YOU DOING?
GRRRR
YOU REALLY THINK YOU'RE A REGULAR? YOU CAN'T EVEN SCORE IN A SIMPLE PLAY.
SHE REALLY LOVES SOCCER.
JOSUI
KOKUBU
0
0
1st HALF: 0
2nd HALF: 0
1st HALF: 0
REALLY BEAT, HUH?

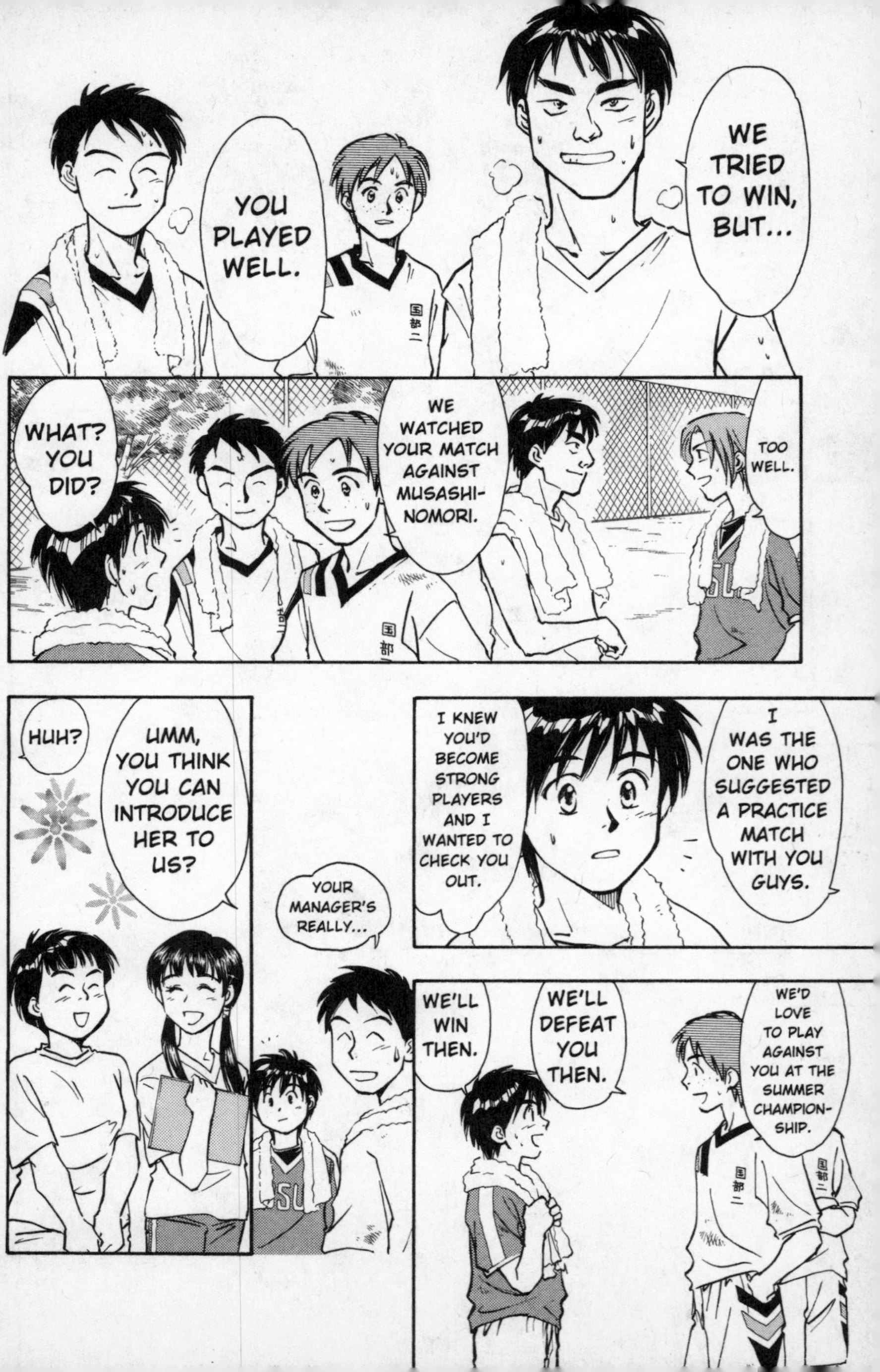
WE TRIED TO WIN, BUT...
YOU PLAYED WELL.
TOO WELL.
WE WATCHED YOUR MATCH AGAINST MUSASHI-NOMORI.
WHAT? YOU DID?
I WAS THE ONE WHO SUGGESTED A PRACTICE MATCH WITH YOU GUYS.
I KNEW YOU'D BECOME STRONG PLAYERS AND I WANTED TO CHECK YOU OUT.
WE'D LOVE TO PLAY AGAINST YOU AT THE SUMMER CHAMPIONSHIP.
WE'LL DEFEAT YOU THEN.
WE'LL WIN THEN.
UMM, YOU THINK YOU CAN INTRODUCE HER TO US?
HUH?
YOUR MANAGER'S REALLY...

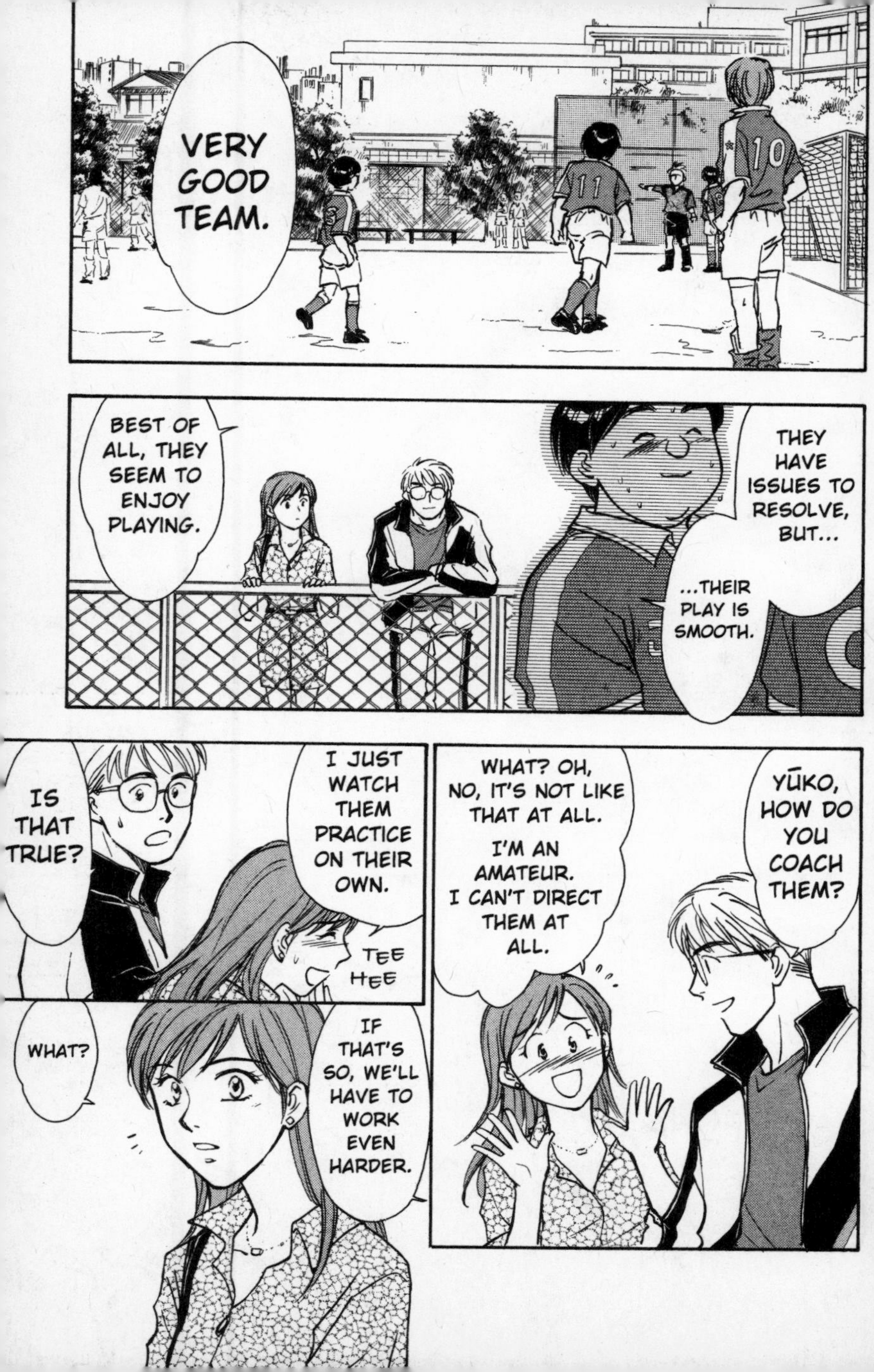
VERY GOOD TEAM.
THEY HAVE ISSUES TO RESOLVE, BUT...
...THEIR PLAY IS SMOOTH.
BEST OF ALL, THEY SEEM TO ENJOY PLAYING.
YŪKO, HOW DO YOU COACH THEM?
WHAT? OH, NO, IT'S NOT LIKE THAT AT ALL.
I'M AN AMATEUR. I CAN'T DIRECT THEM AT ALL.
I JUST WATCH THEM PRACTICE ON THEIR OWN.
TEE HEE
IS THAT TRUE?
IF THAT'S SO, WE'LL HAVE TO WORK EVEN HARDER.
WHAT?

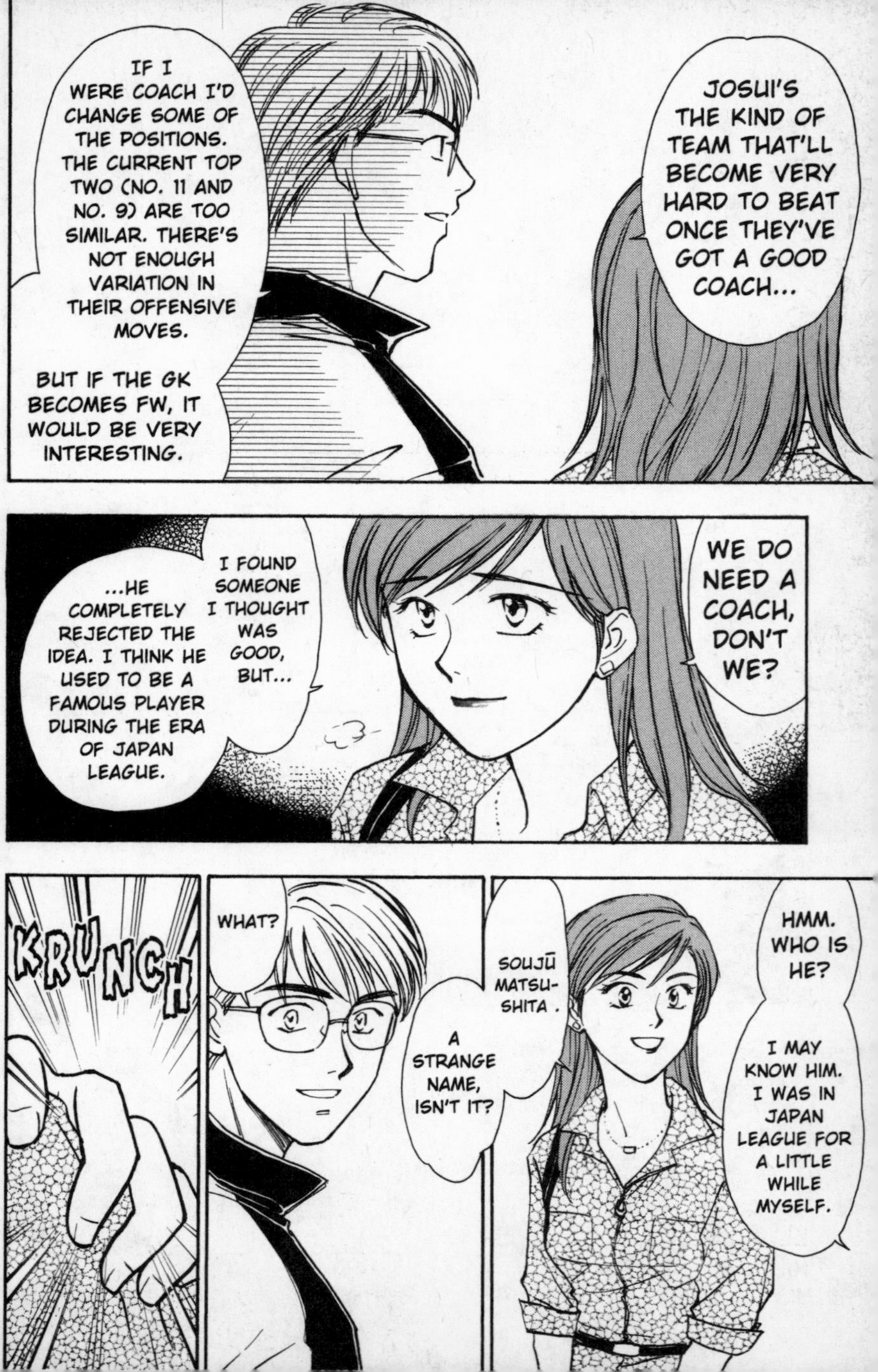
JOSUI'S THE KIND OF TEAM THAT'LL BECOME VERY HARD TO BEAT ONCE THEY'VE GOT A GOOD COACH...
IF I WERE COACH I'D CHANGE SOME OF THE POSITIONS. THE CURRENT TOP TWO (NO. 11 AND NO. 9) ARE TOO SIMILAR. THERE'S NOT ENOUGH VARIATION IN THEIR OFFENSIVE MOVES.
BUT IF THE GK BECOMES FW, IT WOULD BE VERY INTERESTING.
WE DO NEED A COACH, DON'T WE?
I FOUND SOMEONE I THOUGHT WAS GOOD, BUT...
...HE COMPLETELY REJECTED THE IDEA. I THINK HE USED TO BE A FAMOUS PLAYER DURING THE ERA OF JAPAN LEAGUE.
HMM. WHO IS HE?
SOUJŪ MATSU-SHITA.
I MAY KNOW HIM. I WAS IN JAPAN LEAGUE FOR A LITTLE WHILE MYSELF.
A STRANGE NAME, ISN'T IT?
WHAT?
KRUNCH

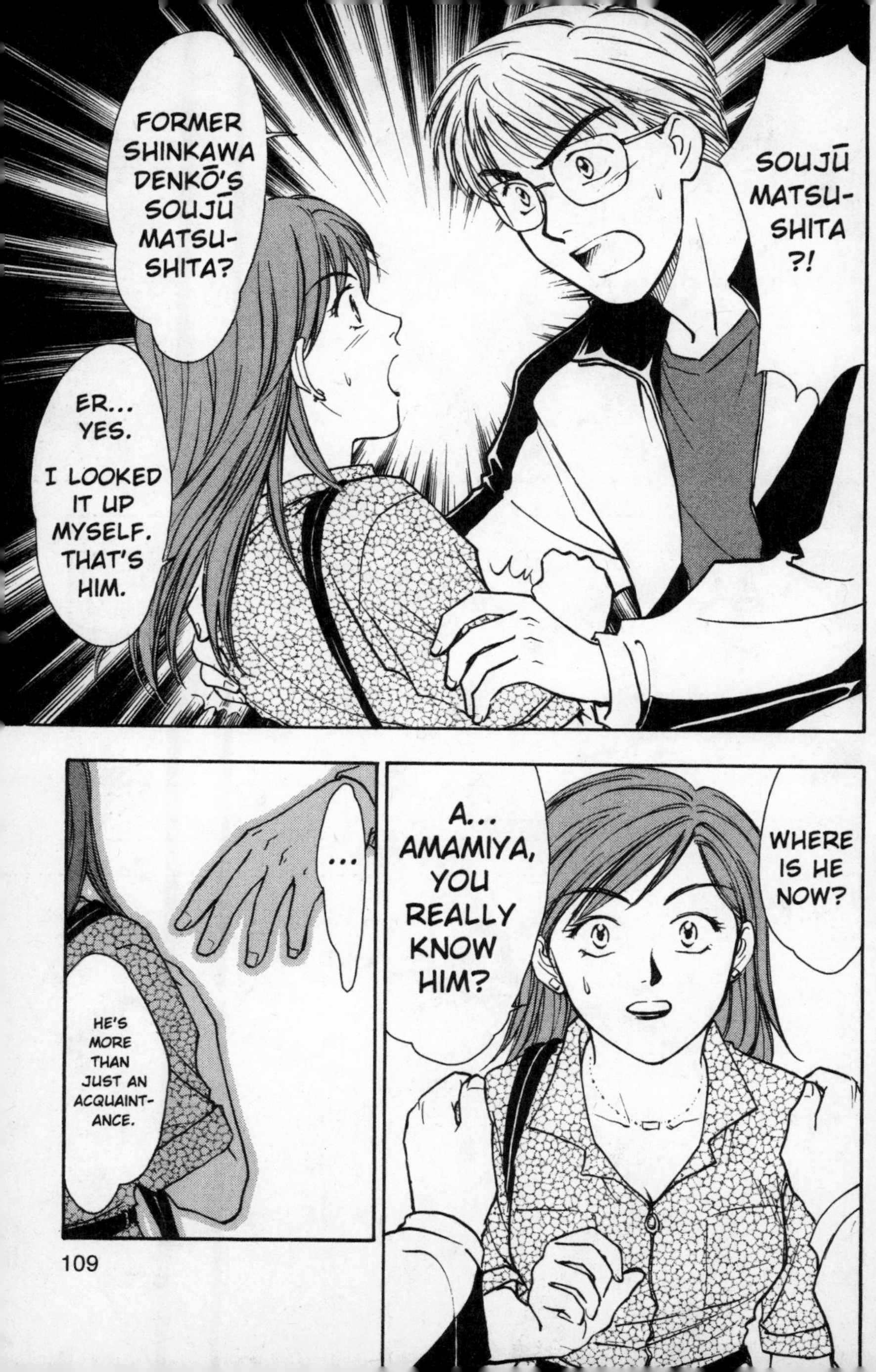
SOUJŪ MATSU-SHITA ?!
FORMER SHINKAWA DENKŌ'S SOUJŪ MATSU-SHITA?
ER... YES.
I LOOKED IT UP MYSELF. THAT'S HIM.
WHERE IS HE NOW?
A... AMAMIYA, YOU REALLY KNOW HIM?
...
HE'S MORE THAN JUST AN ACQUAINT-ANCE.

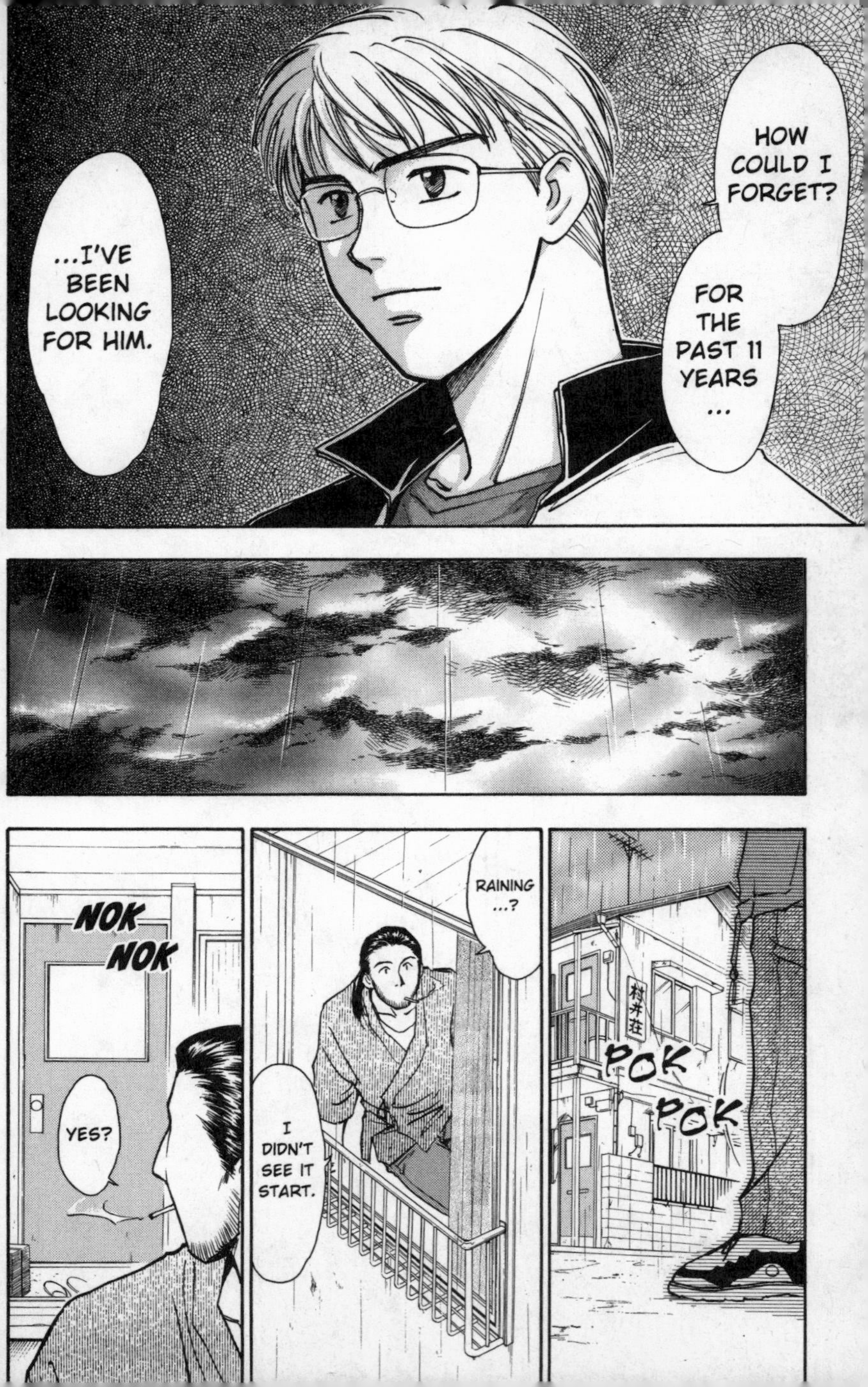
HOW COULD I FORGET?
FOR THE PAST 11 YEARS ...
...I'VE BEEN LOOKING FOR HIM.
村井荘
POK POK
RAINING ...?
I DIDN'T SEE IT START.
NOK NOK
YES?

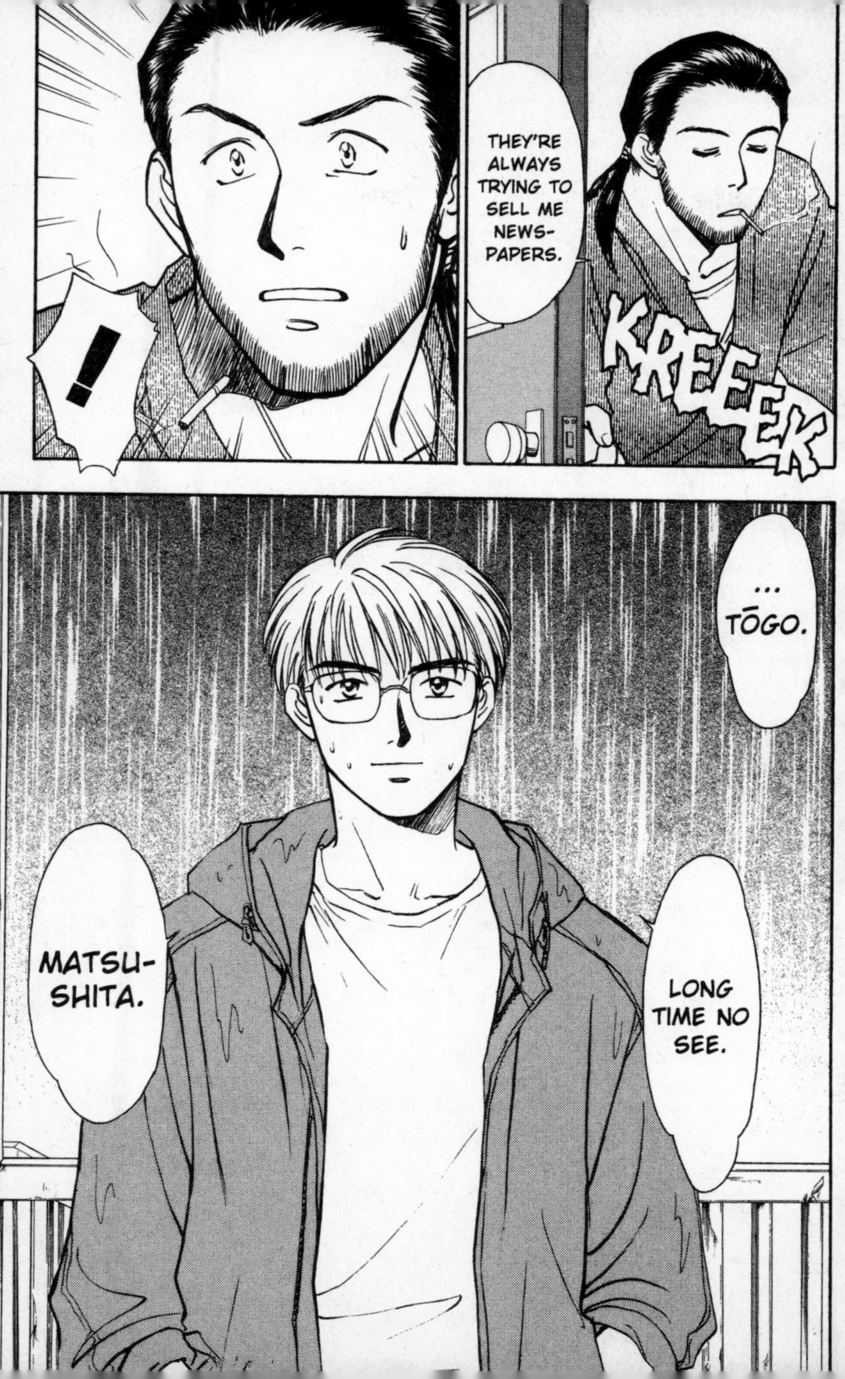
THEY'RE ALWAYS TRYING TO SELL ME NEWS-PAPERS.
KREEEK
!
... TŌGO.
LONG TIME NO SEE.
MATSU-SHITA.

# ● '86 MEXICO WORLD CUP PRIMARY

DURING THE '64 TOKYO OLYMPICS, JAPAN'S SOCCER TEAM MADE IT TO THE BEST EIGHT. THIS PROMPTED JAPAN TO ESTABLISH THE NATIONWIDE "JAPAN SOCCER LEAGUE" IN 1965 TO "STRENGTHEN" JAPAN'S SOCCER TEAMS. ITS EFFECT WAS IMMEDIATELY SHOWN BY THE JAPAN TEAM SEIZING THE BRONZE MEDAL AT THE MEXICO OLYMPICS IN 1968.

AFTER THAT, JAPAN'S SOCCER TEAMS DIDN'T DO WELL UNTIL LATER IN THE 1970S WHEN TWO TEAMS APPEARED SHARING THE SAME GOAL OF BECOMING PROFESSIONAL. THE TWO TEAMS WERE THE YOMIURI CLUB (CURRENT VELDY KAWASAKI) AND NISSAN AUTOMOBILE (CURRENT YOKOHAMA MARINERS).

YOMIURI WAS A HEAVY DUTY EUROPEAN TYPE CLUB, WHICH TRAINED PLAYERS FROM GRADE-SCHOOL AGE. THE TEAM RULED WITH THE MEMBERS LIKE SATOSHI TSUNAMI (FORMER BELMARLE), YASUTARŌ MATSUKI (FORMER COACH AT SELESSO ŌSAKA), RAMOS FROM BRAZIL, AND THE JAPANESE REPRESENTATIVE, HISASHI KATŌ (FORMER COACH AT VELDY), WHO WERE RECRUITED FROM WASEDA UNIVERSITY.

MEANWHILE, NISSAN PUT SHŪ KAMO IN CHARGE AS THEIR COACH AND RECRUITED THE JAPANESE REPRESENTATIVE, KAZUSHI KIMURA (FORMER MARINERS), ALTHOUGH HE WAS STILL A COLLEGE STUDENT, ALONG WITH NOBUTOSHI KANNA (CURRENT COMMENTATOR). FURTHERMORE, THEY HIRED KŌICHI HASHIRATANI (FORMER LEISOL) AND TAKASHI MIZUNUMA (FORMER MARINERS). THEIR GOAL WAS TO DEFEAT YOMIURI.

AT THE TIME, JAPAN'S REPRESENTATIVE TEAM WAS MAINLY MADE UP OF THE TWO TEAMS MENTIONED ABOVE, AND IN 1985, UNDER THE DIRECTION OF THE COACH TAKAJI MORI (FORMER COACH AT ABISPA), THEY WORKED HARD FOR THE MEXICO WORLD CUP. THEY CONTINUED TO WIN AND MADE IT TO THE FINAL GAME AGAINST THEIR ARCH-ENEMY, KOREA. THE FINAL GAME OF HOME & AWAY AGAINST KOREA WAS TO DETERMINE WHICH TEAM WOULD BE SELECTED TO PLAY AT THE MEXICO WORLD CUP. THE FIRST GAME WAS HELD AT NATIONAL SPORTS ARENA. IT WAS UNUSUALLY FILLED TO THE BRIM WITH SPECTATORS. UNFORTUNATELY, HOWEVER, THE JAPAN TEAM LOST -- ONE TO TWO. THE JAPAN TEAM LOST AGAIN AT THE SECOND GAME THAT FOLLOWED IN SOUL -- ZERO TO ONE. THUS, THEIR EARNEST WISH (TO GO TO THE MEXICO WORLD CUP) DID NOT MATERIALIZE.

THEREAFTER, YOMIURI RECRUITED YASUTOSHI AND KAZU, THE MIURA BROTHERS. THEY ALSO TOOK KITAZAWA FROM HONDA GIKEN. NISSAN, ON THE OTHER HAND, RECRUITED TETSUJI HASHIRATANI AND KENTA HASEGAWA (CURRENT ESPAL). THUS, THESE TWO STRONG TEAMS LED JAPAN UNTIL THE J-LEAGUE OPENED.

## --TATSUYA WATANABE (WINNING RUN)

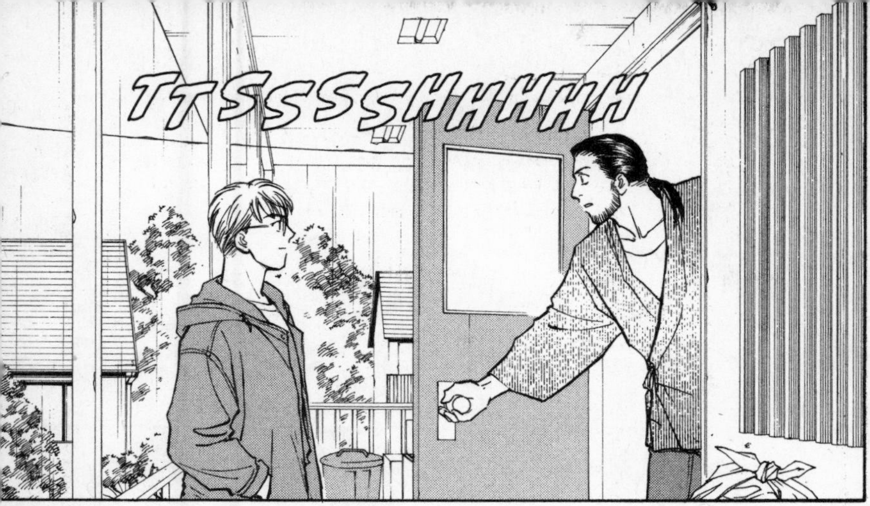
TTSSSSHHHHHH

# STAGE.32 Moon After the Rain

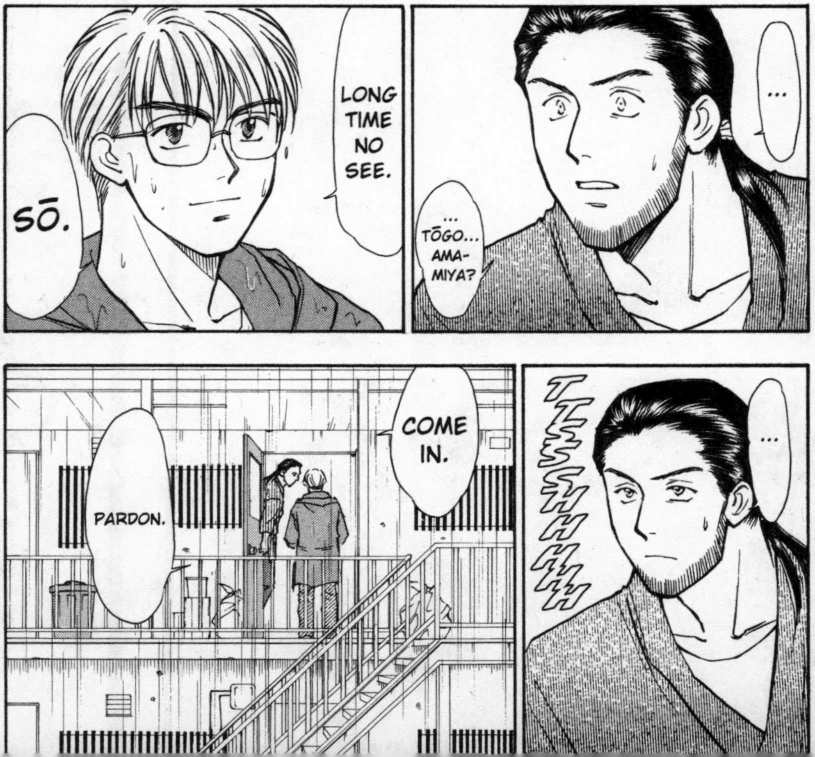
...
... TŌGO... AMAMIYA?
LONG TIME NO SEE.
SŌ.
TTSSHHHHH
...
COME IN.
PARDON.

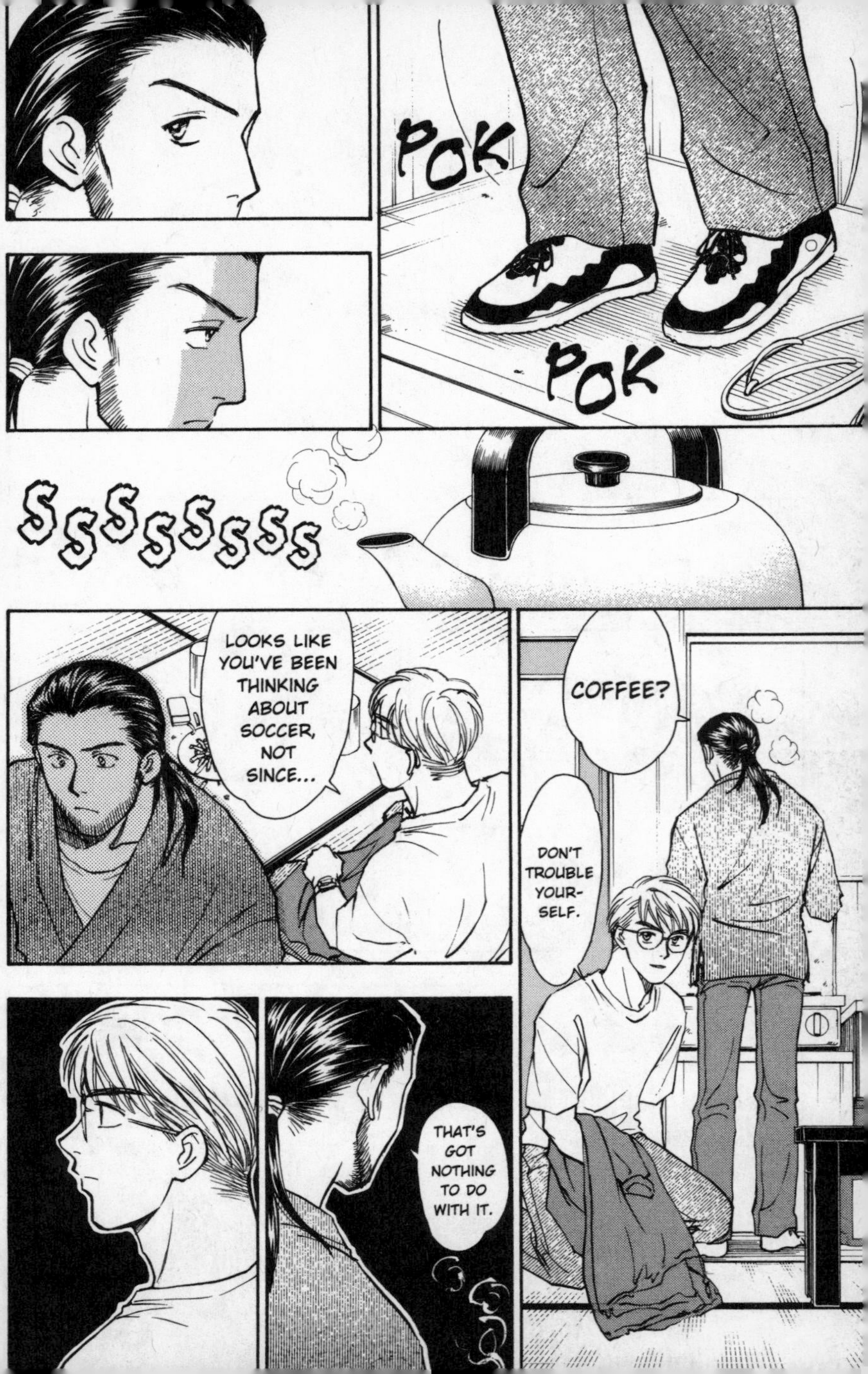

POK
POK
SsSsSsSs
COFFEE?
DON'T TROUBLE YOUR-SELF.
LOOKS LIKE YOU'VE BEEN THINKING ABOUT SOCCER, NOT SINCE...
THAT'S GOT NOTHING TO DO WITH IT.

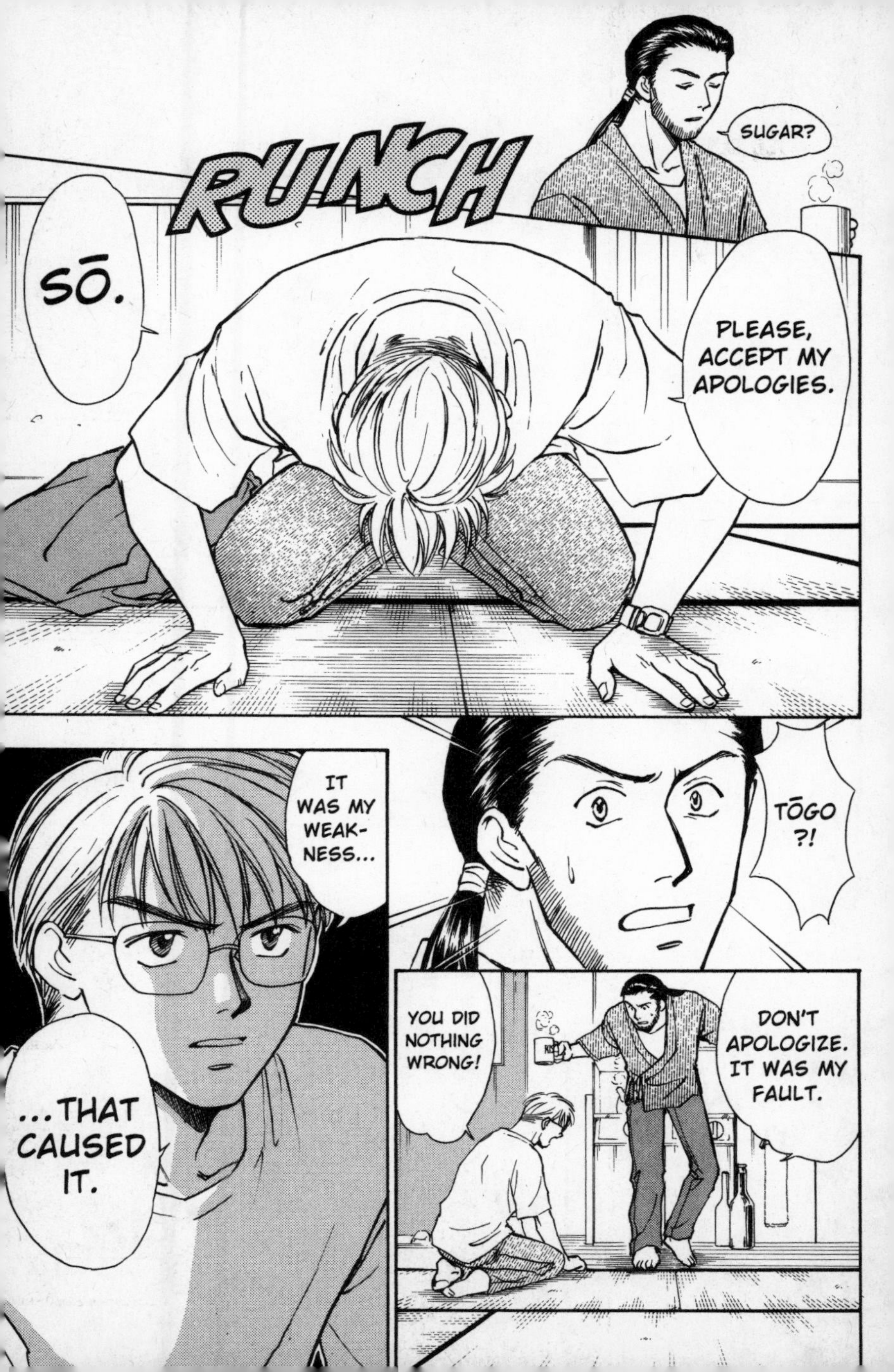
SUGAR?
RUNCH
PLEASE, ACCEPT MY APOLOGIES.
SŌ.
TŌGO?!
DON'T APOLOGIZE. IT WAS MY FAULT.
YOU DID NOTHING WRONG!
IT WAS MY WEAKNESS...
...THAT CAUSED IT.

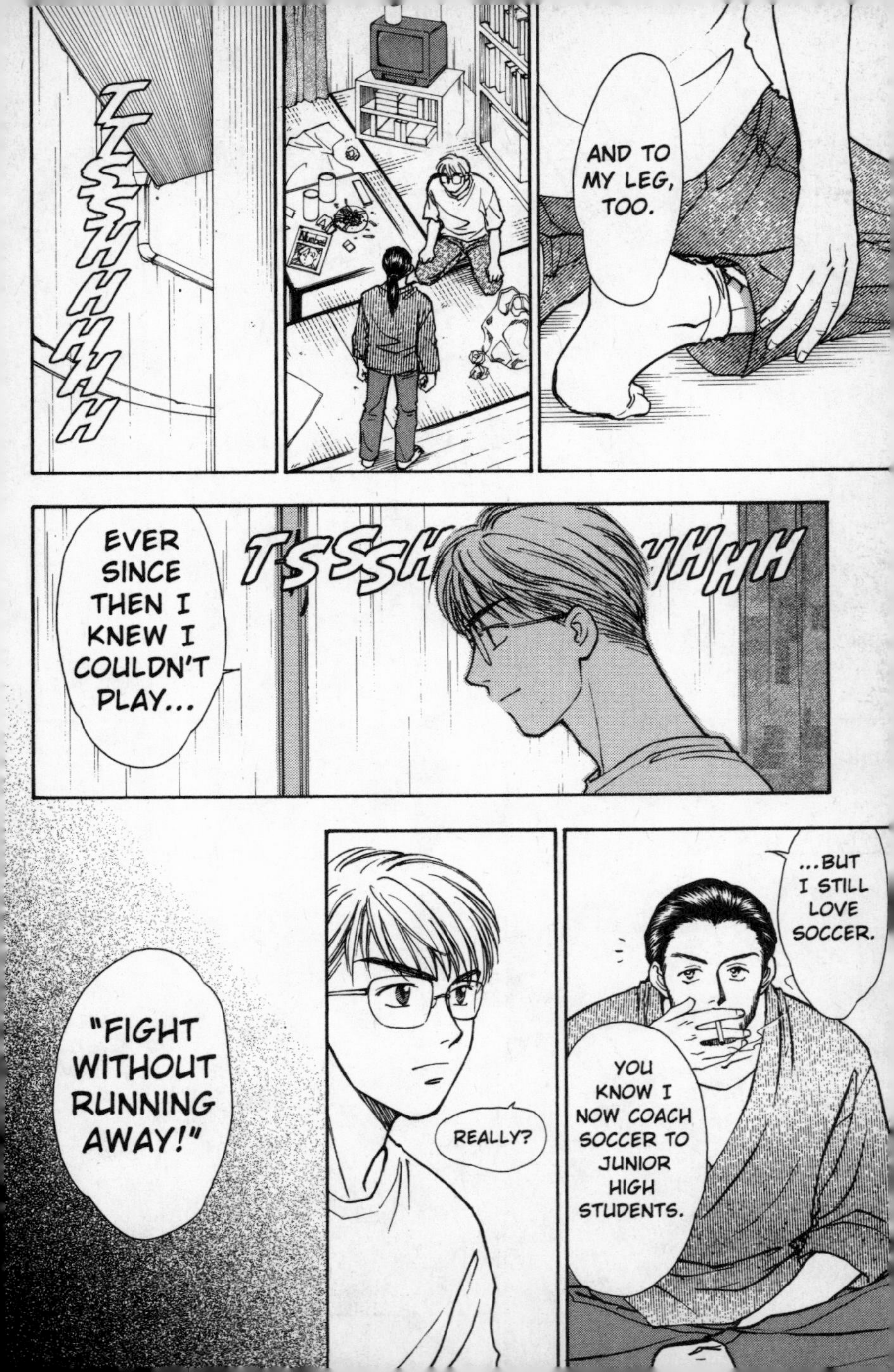
AND TO MY LEG, TOO.
TSSHHHHHHH
TSSSH HHHH
EVER SINCE THEN I KNEW I COULDN'T PLAY...
...BUT I STILL LOVE SOCCER.
YOU KNOW I NOW COACH SOCCER TO JUNIOR HIGH STUDENTS.
REALLY?
"FIGHT WITHOUT RUNNING AWAY!"

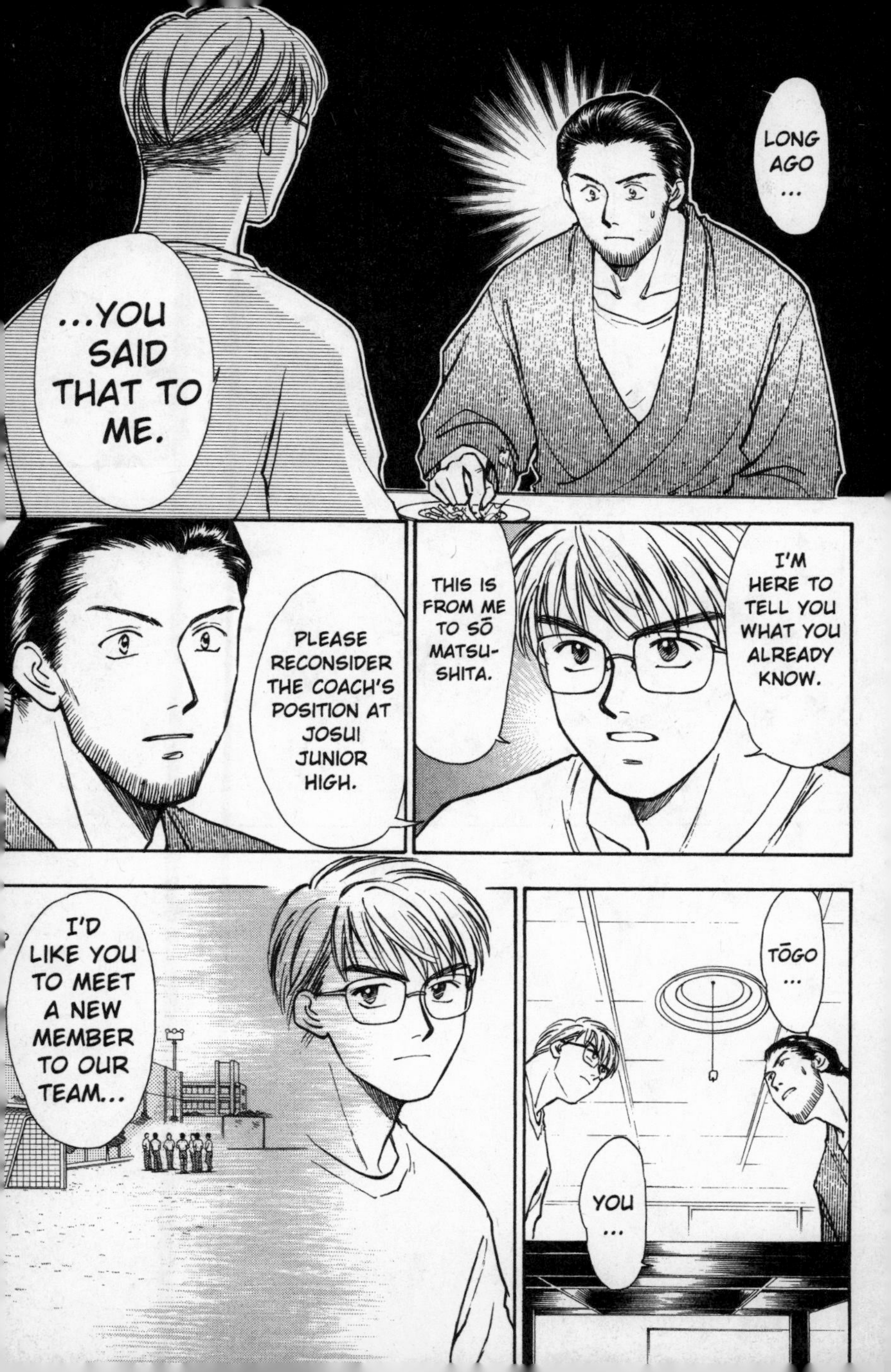
LONG AGO ...
...YOU SAID THAT TO ME.
I'M HERE TO TELL YOU WHAT YOU ALREADY KNOW.
THIS IS FROM ME TO SŌ MATSU-SHITA.
PLEASE RECONSIDER THE COACH'S POSITION AT JOSUI JUNIOR HIGH.
TŌGO ...
YOU ...
I'D LIKE YOU TO MEET A NEW MEMBER TO OUR TEAM...

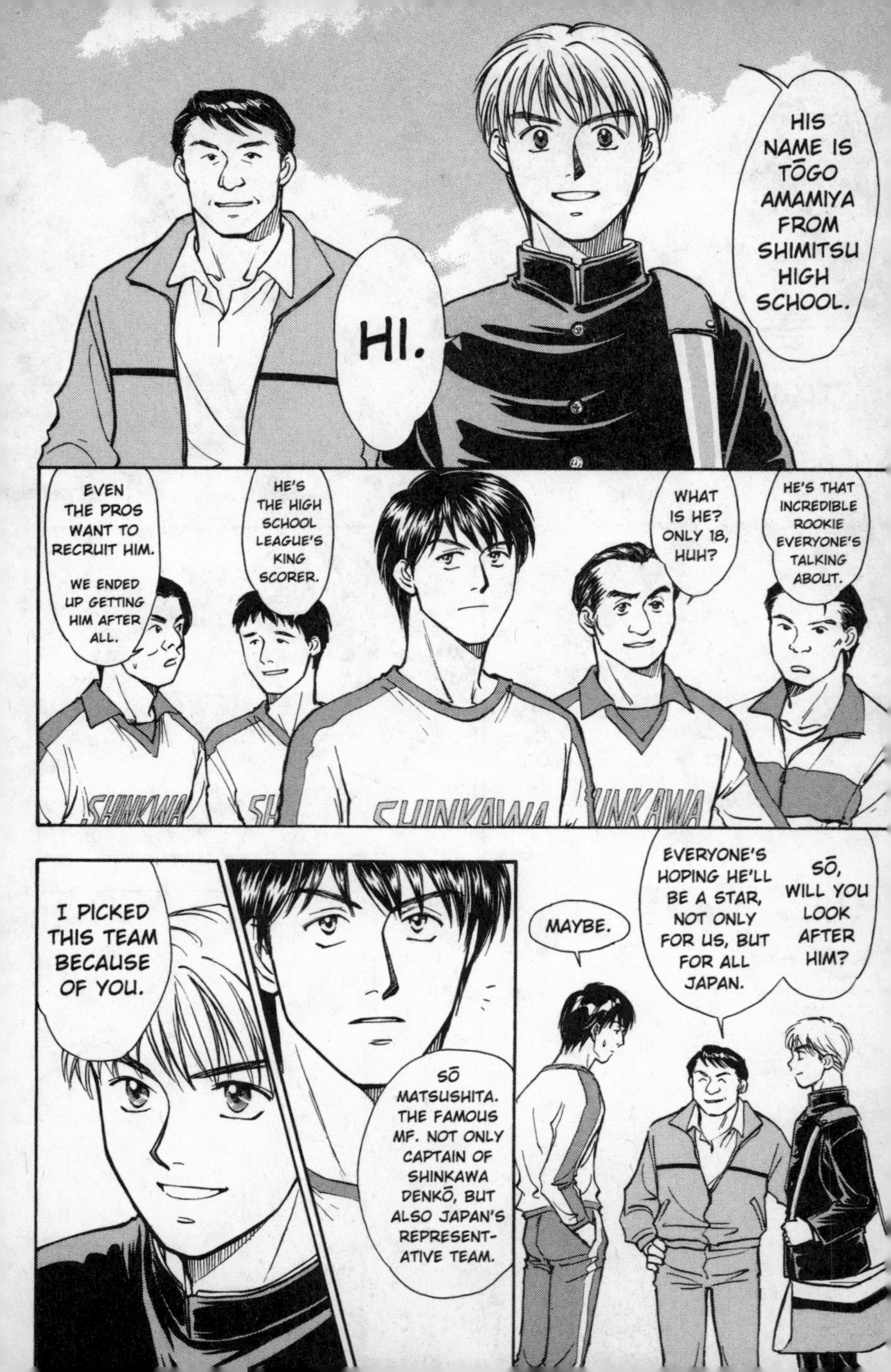
HIS NAME IS TŌGO AMAMIYA FROM SHIMITSU HIGH SCHOOL.
HI.
HE'S THAT INCREDIBLE ROOKIE EVERYONE'S TALKING ABOUT.
WHAT IS HE? ONLY 18, HUH?
HE'S THE HIGH SCHOOL LEAGUE'S KING SCORER.
EVEN THE PROS WANT TO RECRUIT HIM.
WE ENDED UP GETTING HIM AFTER ALL.
SŌ, WILL YOU LOOK AFTER HIM?
EVERYONE'S HOPING HE'LL BE A STAR, NOT ONLY FOR US, BUT FOR ALL JAPAN.
MAYBE.
SŌ MATSUSHITA. THE FAMOUS MF. NOT ONLY CAPTAIN OF SHINKAWA DENKŌ, BUT ALSO JAPAN'S REPRESENTATIVE TEAM.
I PICKED THIS TEAM BECAUSE OF YOU.

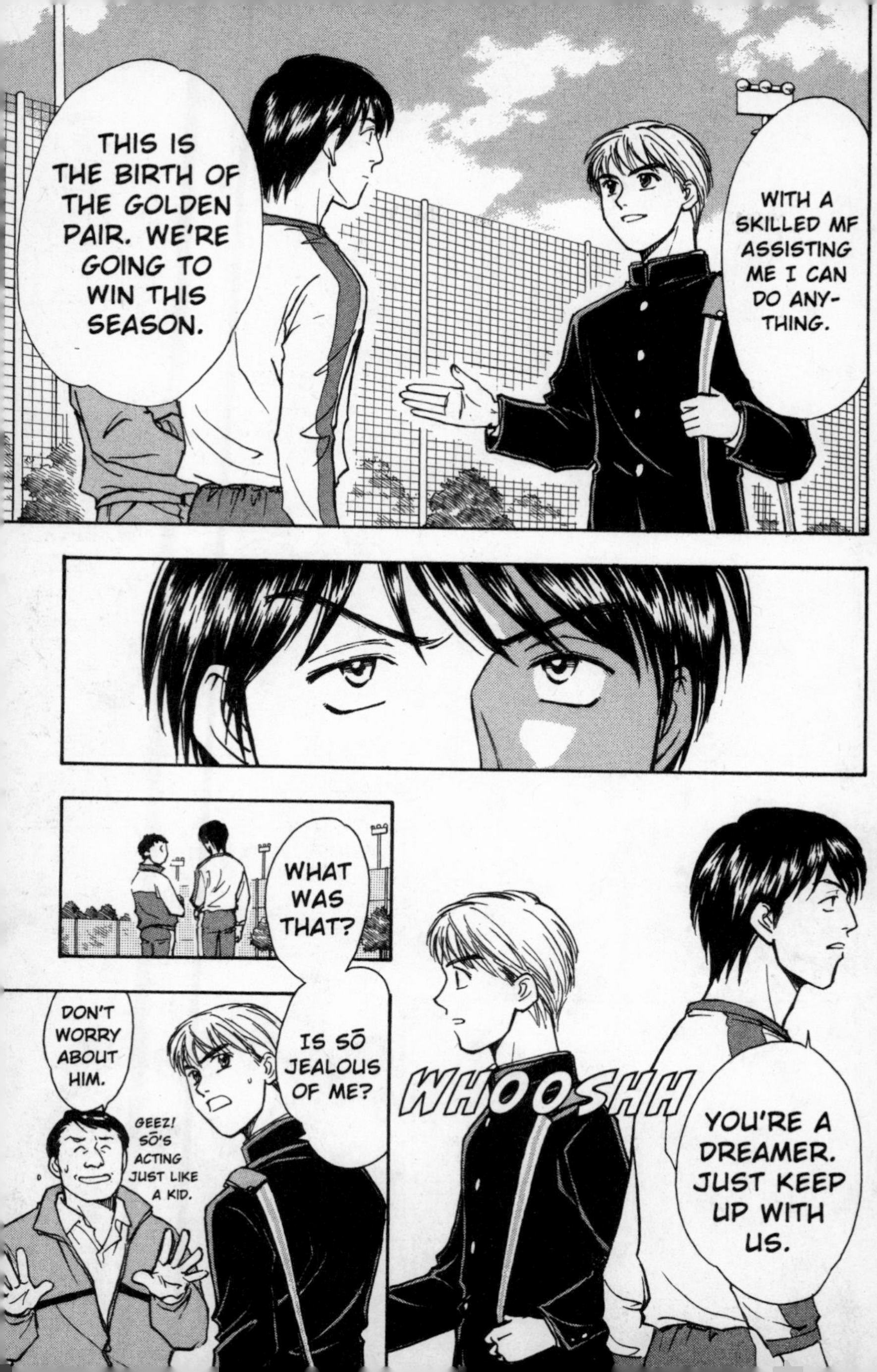
WITH A SKILLED MF ASSISTING ME I CAN DO ANY-THING.
THIS IS THE BIRTH OF THE GOLDEN PAIR. WE'RE GOING TO WIN THIS SEASON.
YOU'RE A DREAMER. JUST KEEP UP WITH US.
WHOOSHH
WHAT WAS THAT?
IS SŌ JEALOUS OF ME?
DON'T WORRY ABOUT HIM.
GEEZ! SŌ'S ACTING JUST LIKE A KID.

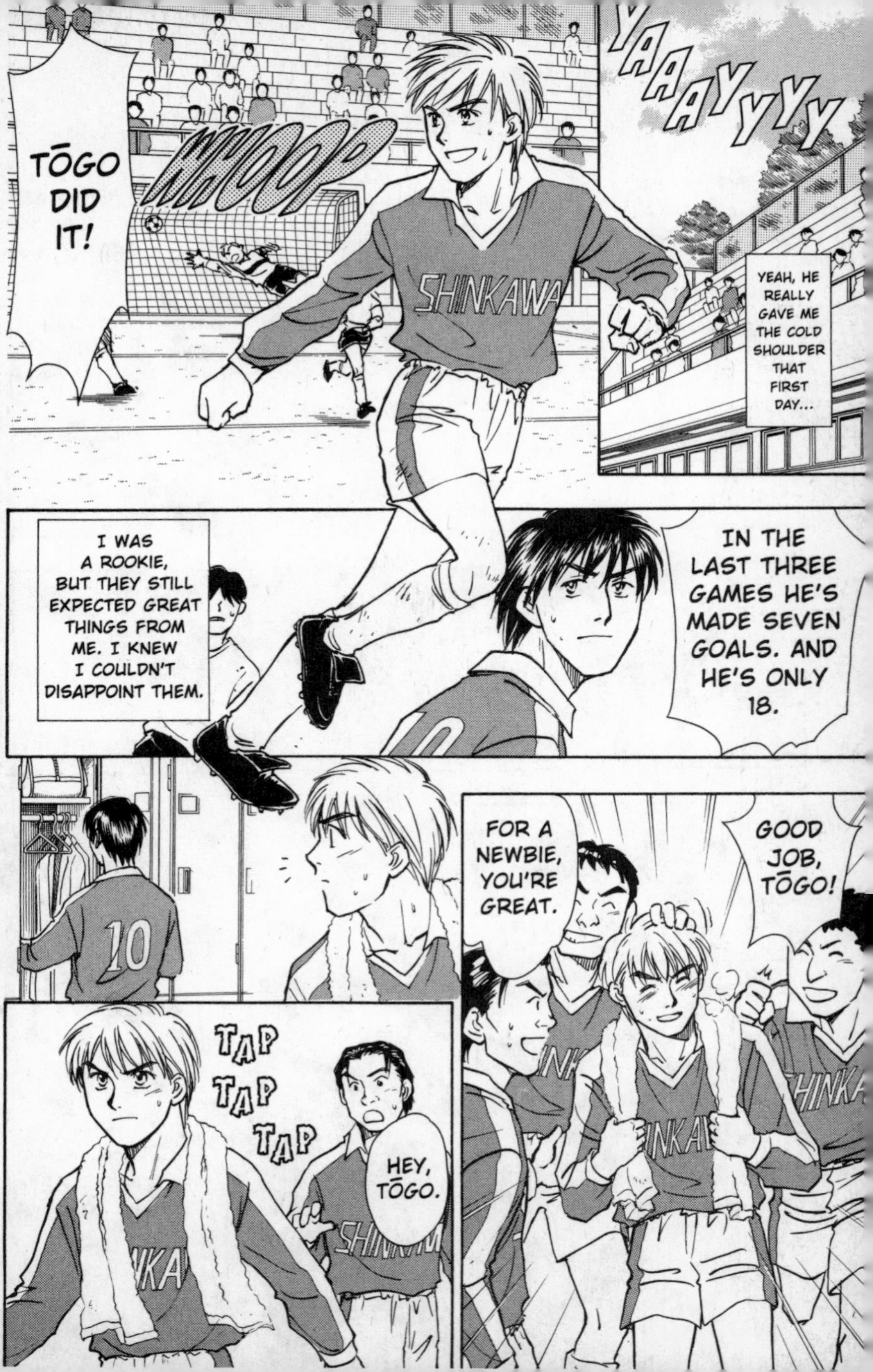
YAAAYYYY
YEAH, HE REALLY GAVE ME THE COLD SHOULDER THAT FIRST DAY...
TŌGO DID IT!
WHOOP
IN THE LAST THREE GAMES HE'S MADE SEVEN GOALS. AND HE'S ONLY 18.
I WAS A ROOKIE, BUT THEY STILL EXPECTED GREAT THINGS FROM ME. I KNEW I COULDN'T DISAPPOINT THEM.
GOOD JOB, TŌGO!
FOR A NEWBIE, YOU'RE GREAT.
TAP TAP TAP
HEY, TŌGO.

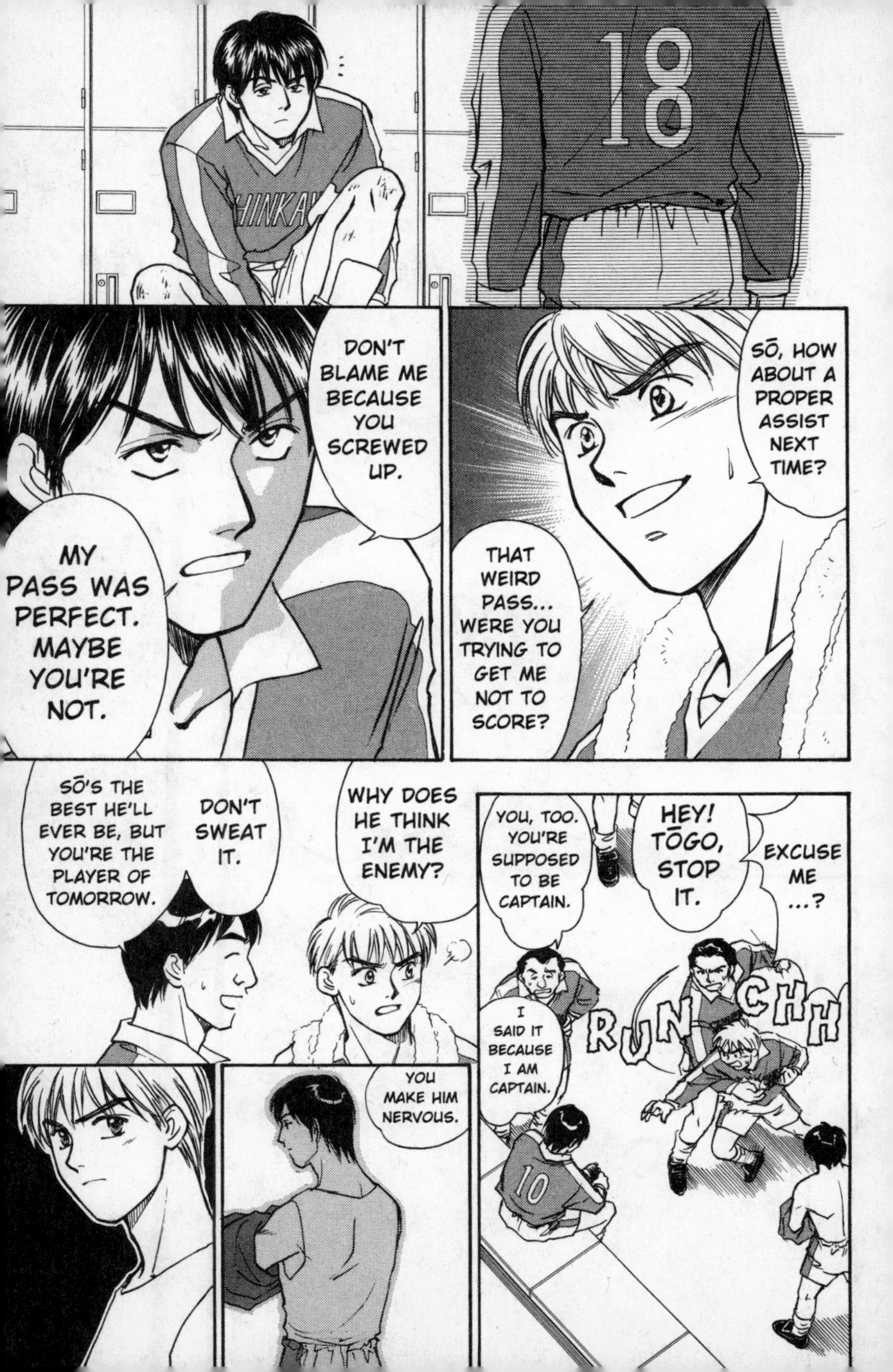

SŌ, HOW ABOUT A PROPER ASSIST NEXT TIME?
THAT WEIRD PASS... WERE YOU TRYING TO GET ME NOT TO SCORE?
DON'T BLAME ME BECAUSE YOU SCREWED UP.
MY PASS WAS PERFECT. MAYBE YOU'RE NOT.
EXCUSE ME ...?
HEY! TŌGO, STOP IT.
YOU, TOO. YOU'RE SUPPOSED TO BE CAPTAIN.
RUNCHH
I SAID IT BECAUSE I AM CAPTAIN.
WHY DOES HE THINK I'M THE ENEMY?
DON'T SWEAT IT.
SŌ'S THE BEST HE'LL EVER BE, BUT YOU'RE THE PLAYER OF TOMORROW.
YOU MAKE HIM NERVOUS.

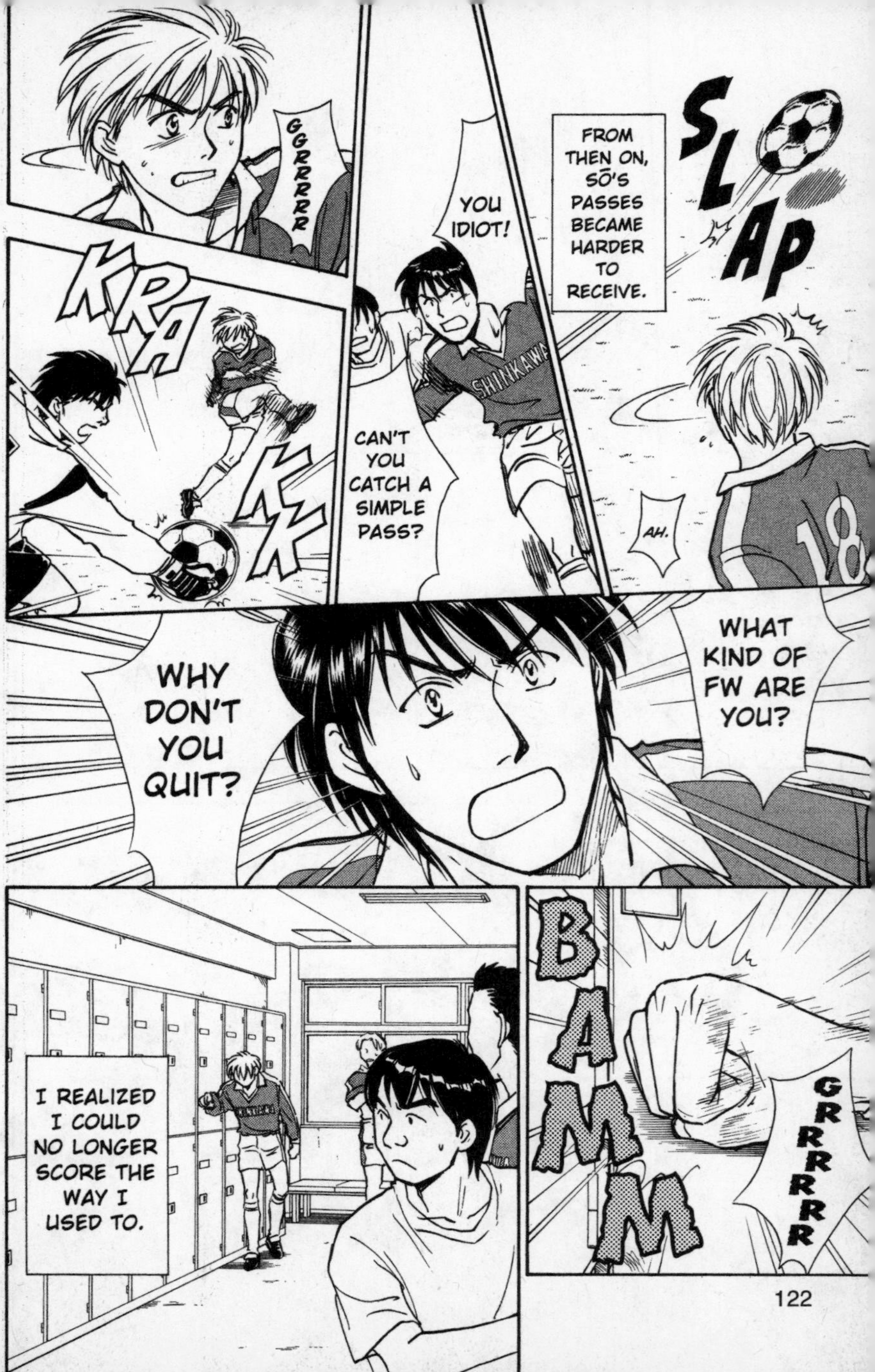
SLAP
FROM THEN ON, SŌ'S PASSES BECAME HARDER TO RECEIVE.
AH.
YOU IDIOT!
CAN'T YOU CATCH A SIMPLE PASS?
GGRRRRRR
KRA
KK
WHAT KIND OF FW ARE YOU?
WHY DON'T YOU QUIT?
BAMM
GRRRRRR
I REALIZED I COULD NO LONGER SCORE THE WAY I USED TO.

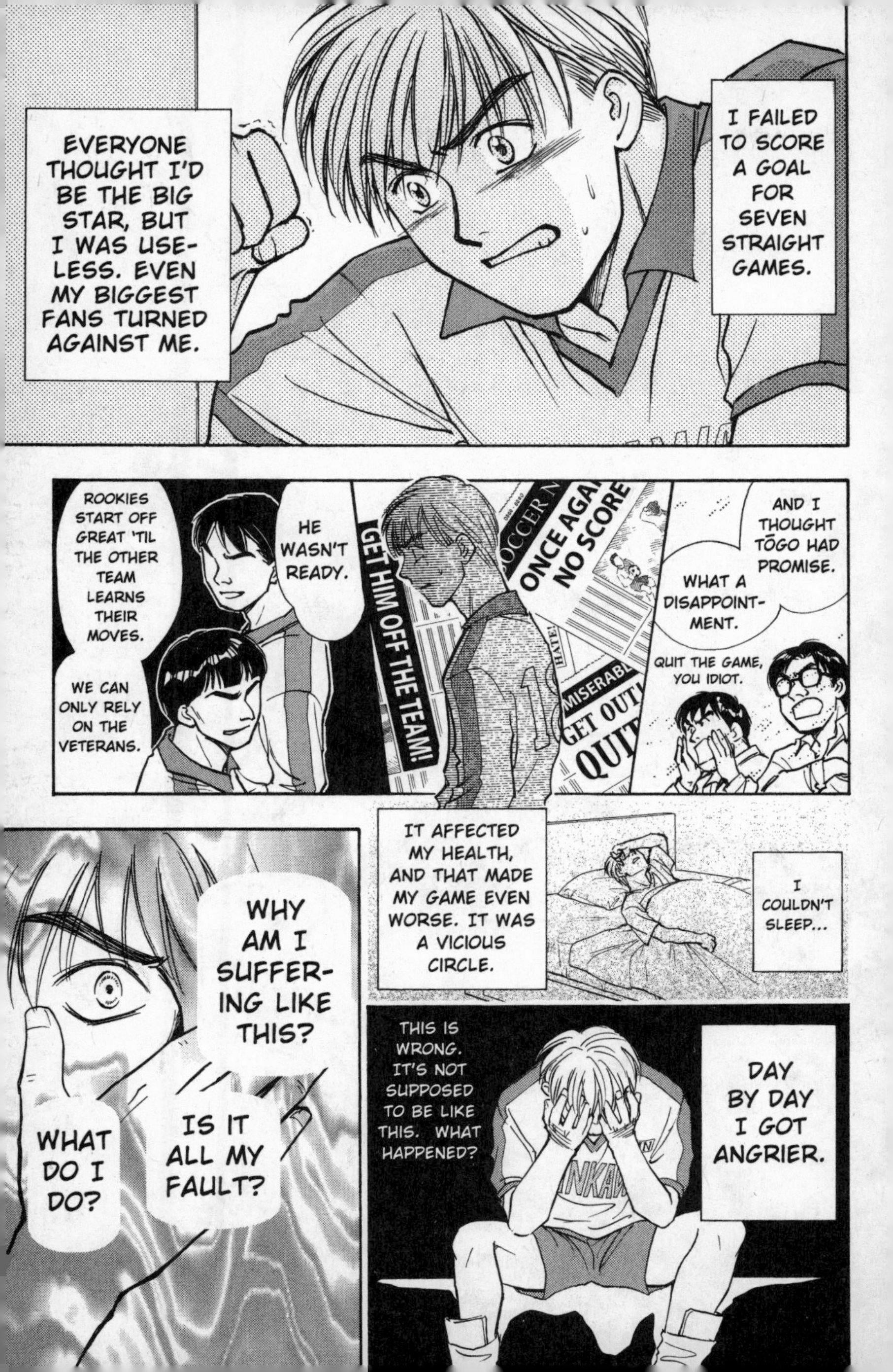
I FAILED TO SCORE A GOAL FOR SEVEN STRAIGHT GAMES.
EVERYONE THOUGHT I'D BE THE BIG STAR, BUT I WAS USE-LESS. EVEN MY BIGGEST FANS TURNED AGAINST ME.
AND I THOUGHT TŌGO HAD PROMISE.
WHAT A DISAPPOINT-MENT.
QUIT THE GAME, YOU IDIOT.
NO SCORE
HATE!
GET OUT
QUIT
GET HIM OFF THE TEAM!
HE WASN'T READY.
ROOKIES START OFF GREAT 'TIL THE OTHER TEAM LEARNS THEIR MOVES.
WE CAN ONLY RELY ON THE VETERANS.
I COULDN'T SLEEP...
IT AFFECTED MY HEALTH, AND THAT MADE MY GAME EVEN WORSE. IT WAS A VICIOUS CIRCLE.
DAY BY DAY I GOT ANGRIER.
THIS IS WRONG. IT'S NOT SUPPOSED TO BE LIKE THIS. WHAT HAPPENED?
WHY AM I SUFFER-ING LIKE THIS?
IS IT ALL MY FAULT?
WHAT DO I DO?

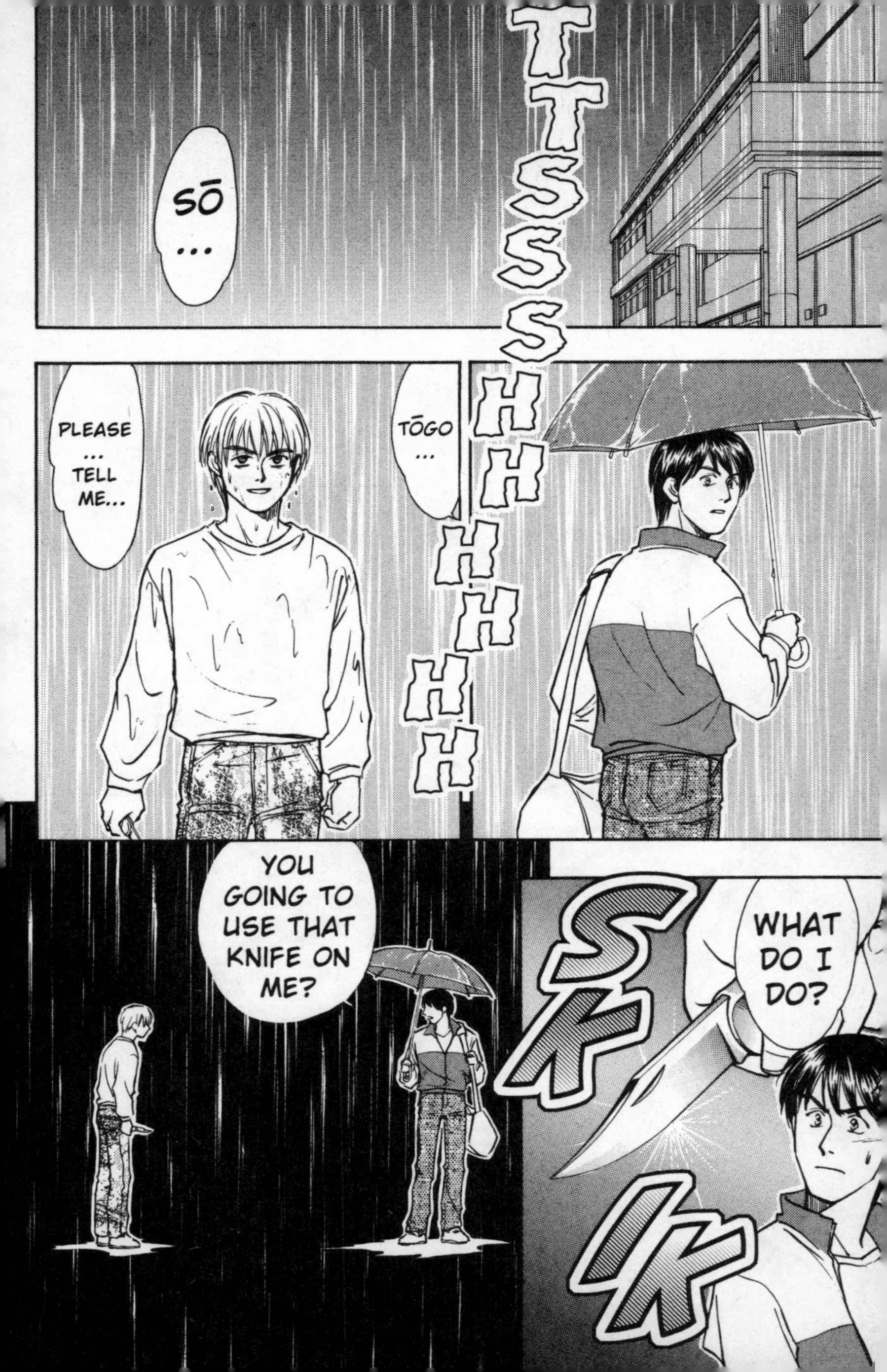
SŌ ...
TTSSSHHHHHHH
TŌGO ...
PLEASE ... TELL ME...
SKIK
WHAT DO I DO?
YOU GOING TO USE THAT KNIFE ON ME?

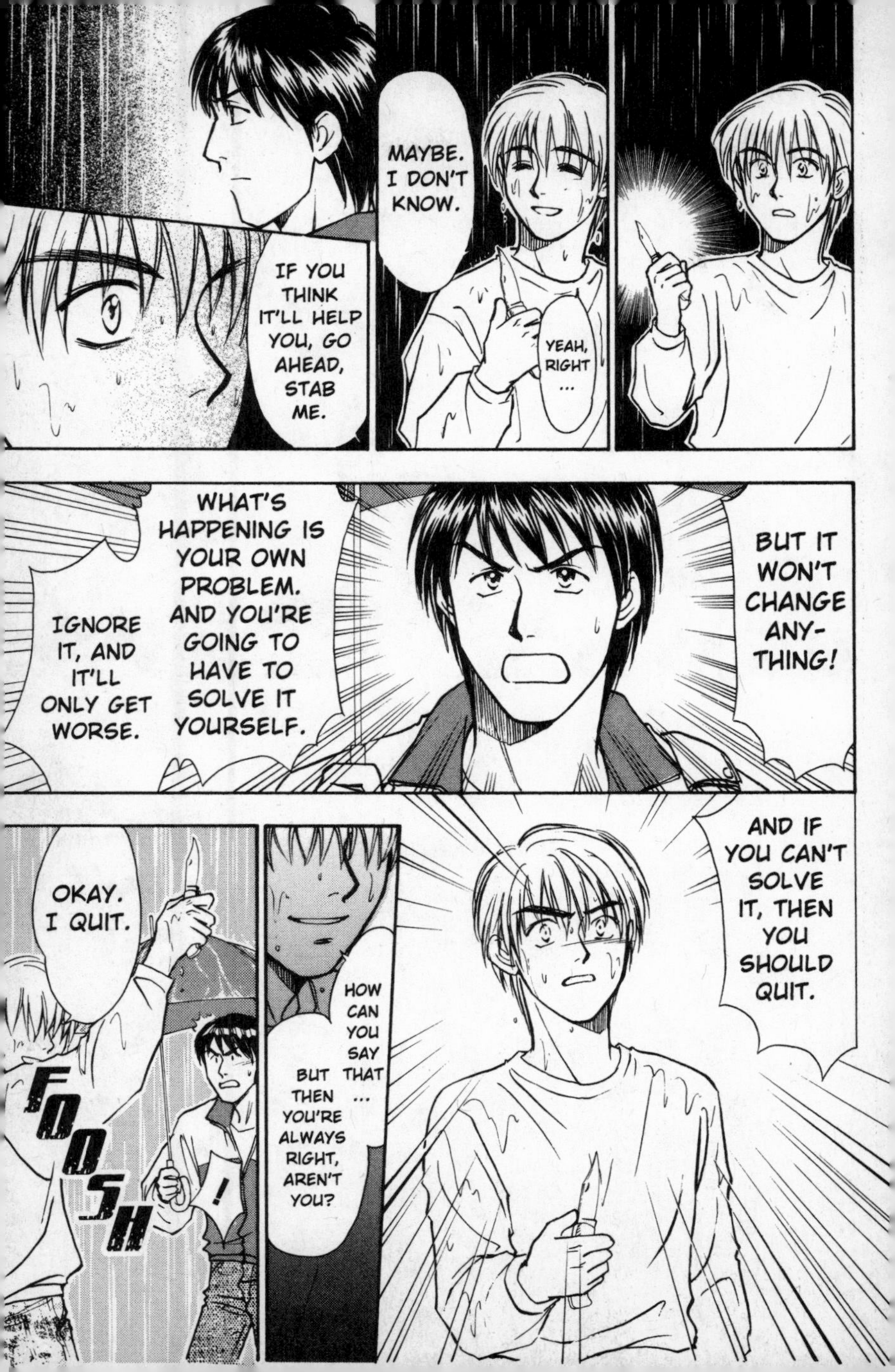
MAYBE. I DON'T KNOW.
YEAH, RIGHT ...
IF YOU THINK IT'LL HELP YOU, GO AHEAD, STAB ME.
BUT IT WON'T CHANGE ANY-THING!
WHAT'S HAPPENING IS YOUR OWN PROBLEM. AND YOU'RE GOING TO HAVE TO SOLVE IT YOURSELF.
IGNORE IT, AND IT'LL ONLY GET WORSE.
AND IF YOU CAN'T SOLVE IT, THEN YOU SHOULD QUIT.
HOW CAN YOU SAY THAT ...
BUT THEN YOU'RE ALWAYS RIGHT, AREN'T YOU?
OKAY. I QUIT.
!
FOOSH

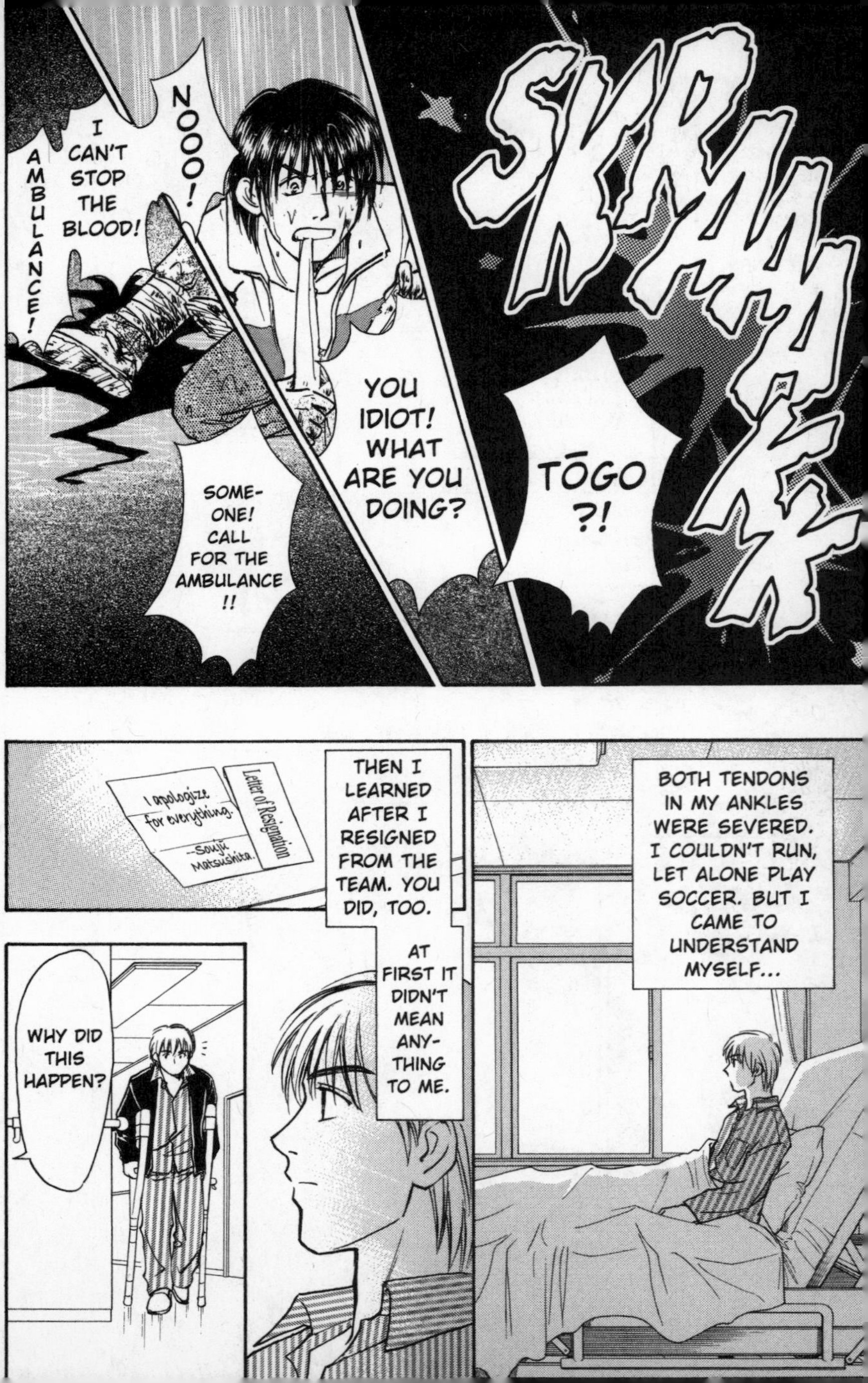
SKRAAK
TŌGO ?!
YOU IDIOT! WHAT ARE YOU DOING?
NOOO!
I CAN'T STOP THE BLOOD!
AMBULANCE!
SOME-ONE! CALL FOR THE AMBULANCE !!
BOTH TENDONS IN MY ANKLES WERE SEVERED. I COULDN'T RUN, LET ALONE PLAY SOCCER. BUT I CAME TO UNDERSTAND MYSELF...
THEN I LEARNED AFTER I RESIGNED FROM THE TEAM. YOU DID, TOO.
Letter of Resignation
I apologize for everything.
--Souji Matsushita.
AT FIRST IT DIDN'T MEAN ANY-THING TO ME.
WHY DID THIS HAPPEN?

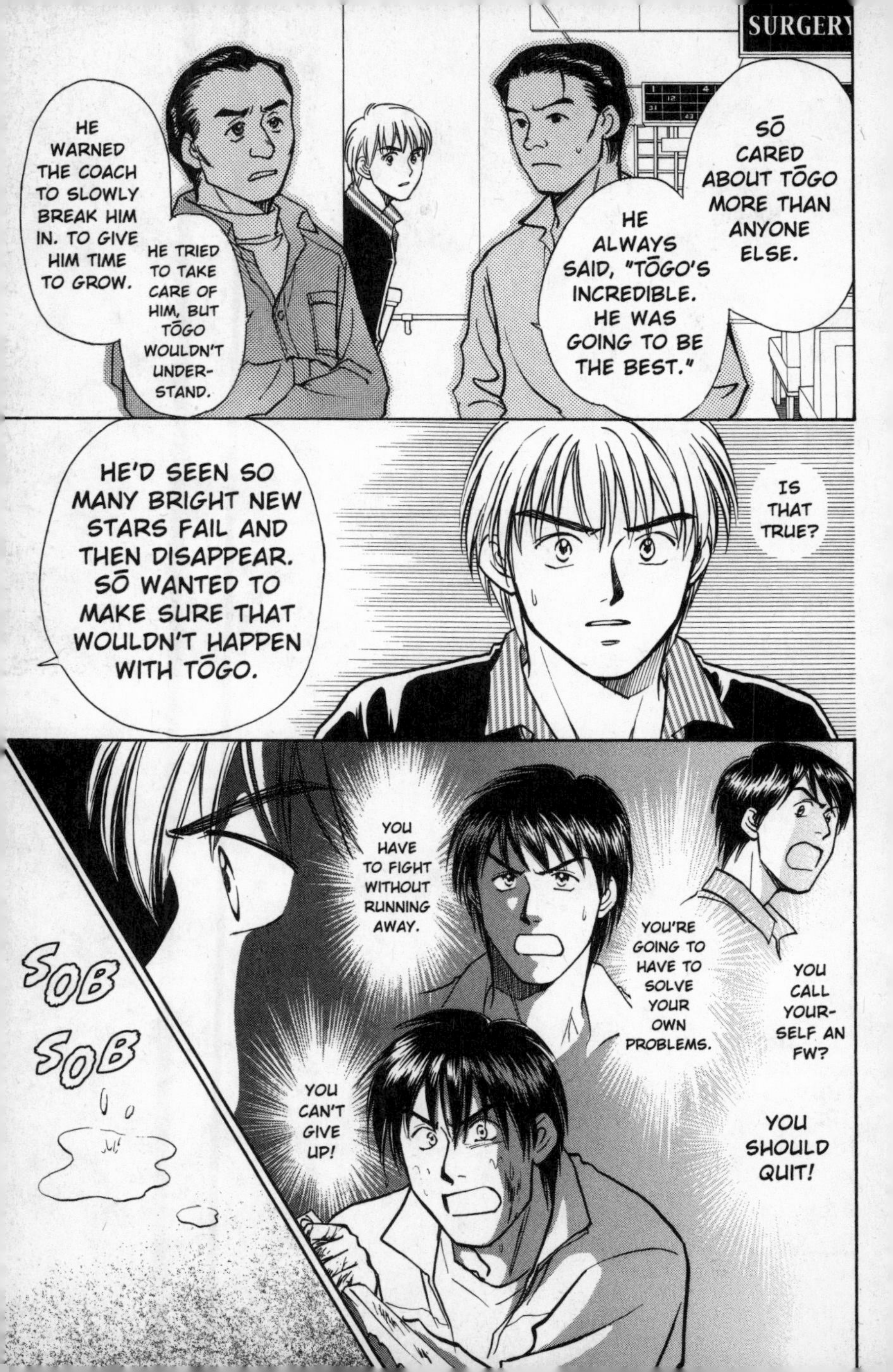
SURGERY
SŌ CARED ABOUT TŌGO MORE THAN ANYONE ELSE.
HE ALWAYS SAID, "TŌGO'S INCREDIBLE. HE WAS GOING TO BE THE BEST."
HE WARNED THE COACH TO SLOWLY BREAK HIM IN. TO GIVE HIM TIME TO GROW.
HE TRIED TO TAKE CARE OF HIM, BUT TŌGO WOULDN'T UNDER-STAND.
HE'D SEEN SO MANY BRIGHT NEW STARS FAIL AND THEN DISAPPEAR. SŌ WANTED TO MAKE SURE THAT WOULDN'T HAPPEN WITH TŌGO.
IS THAT TRUE?
YOU CALL YOUR-SELF AN FW?
YOU SHOULD QUIT!
YOU'RE GOING TO HAVE TO SOLVE YOUR OWN PROBLEMS.
YOU HAVE TO FIGHT WITHOUT RUNNING AWAY.
YOU CAN'T GIVE UP!
SOB SOB

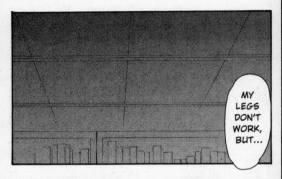

MY LEGS DON'T WORK, BUT...

SŌ...

...ONCE I BECAME A COACH, I UNDERSTOOD...

...

HOW...

...YOU MUST HAVE FELT.

I...

YOU WERE HARSH TO MAKE ME WORK HARDER. YOU CARED ABOUT ME...

BUT I WAS CONCEITED AND DIDN'T UNDERSTAND. ALL I CARED ABOUT WAS MYSELF.

I DESTROYED MYSELF, BUT I ALSO DESTROYED YOU.

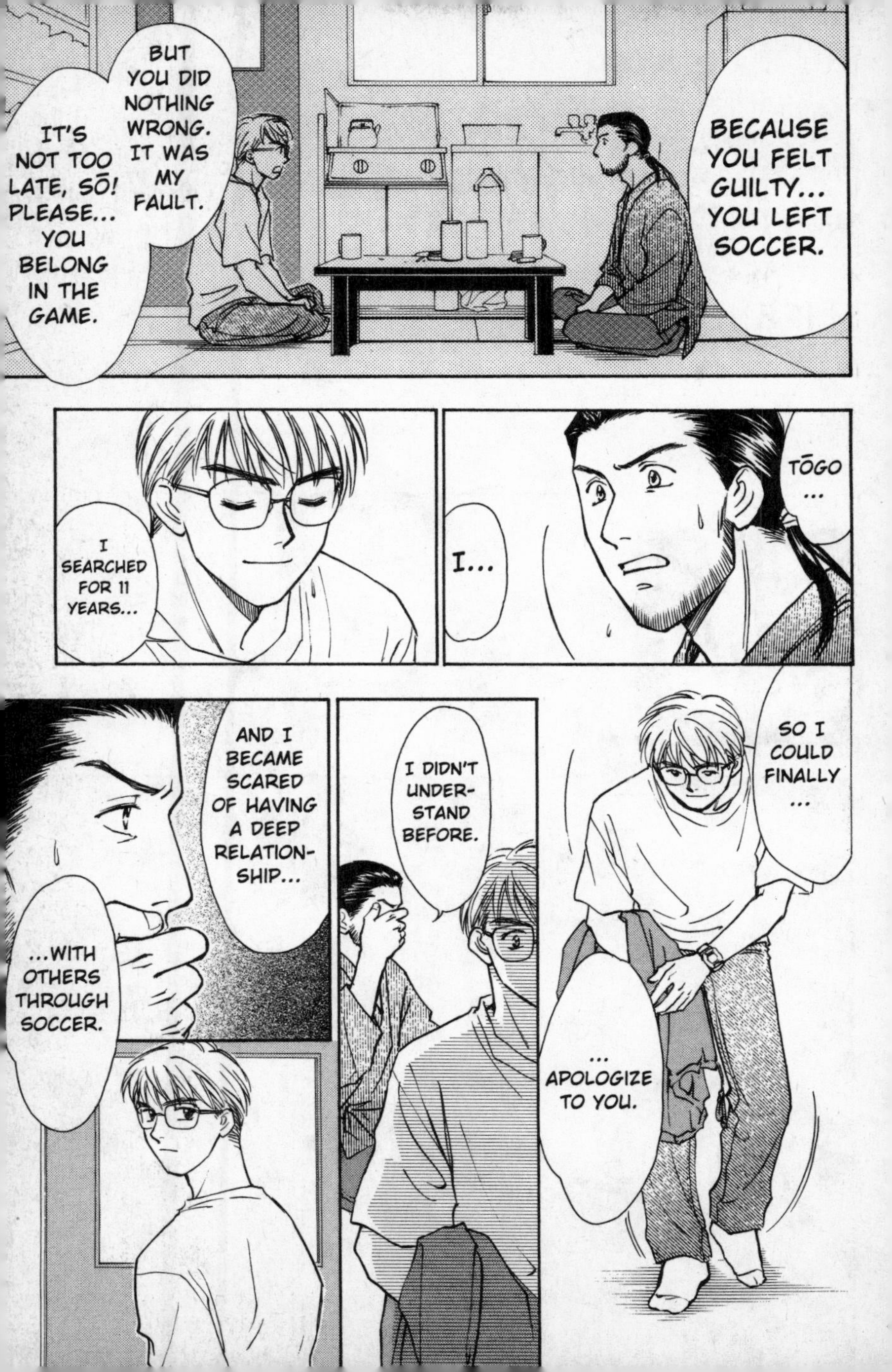
BECAUSE YOU FELT GUILTY... YOU LEFT SOCCER.
BUT YOU DID NOTHING WRONG. IT WAS MY FAULT.
IT'S NOT TOO LATE, SŌ! PLEASE... YOU BELONG IN THE GAME.
TŌGO ...
I...
I SEARCHED FOR 11 YEARS...
SO I COULD FINALLY ...
... APOLOGIZE TO YOU.
I DIDN'T UNDER-STAND BEFORE.
AND I BECAME SCARED OF HAVING A DEEP RELATION-SHIP...
...WITH OTHERS THROUGH SOCCER.

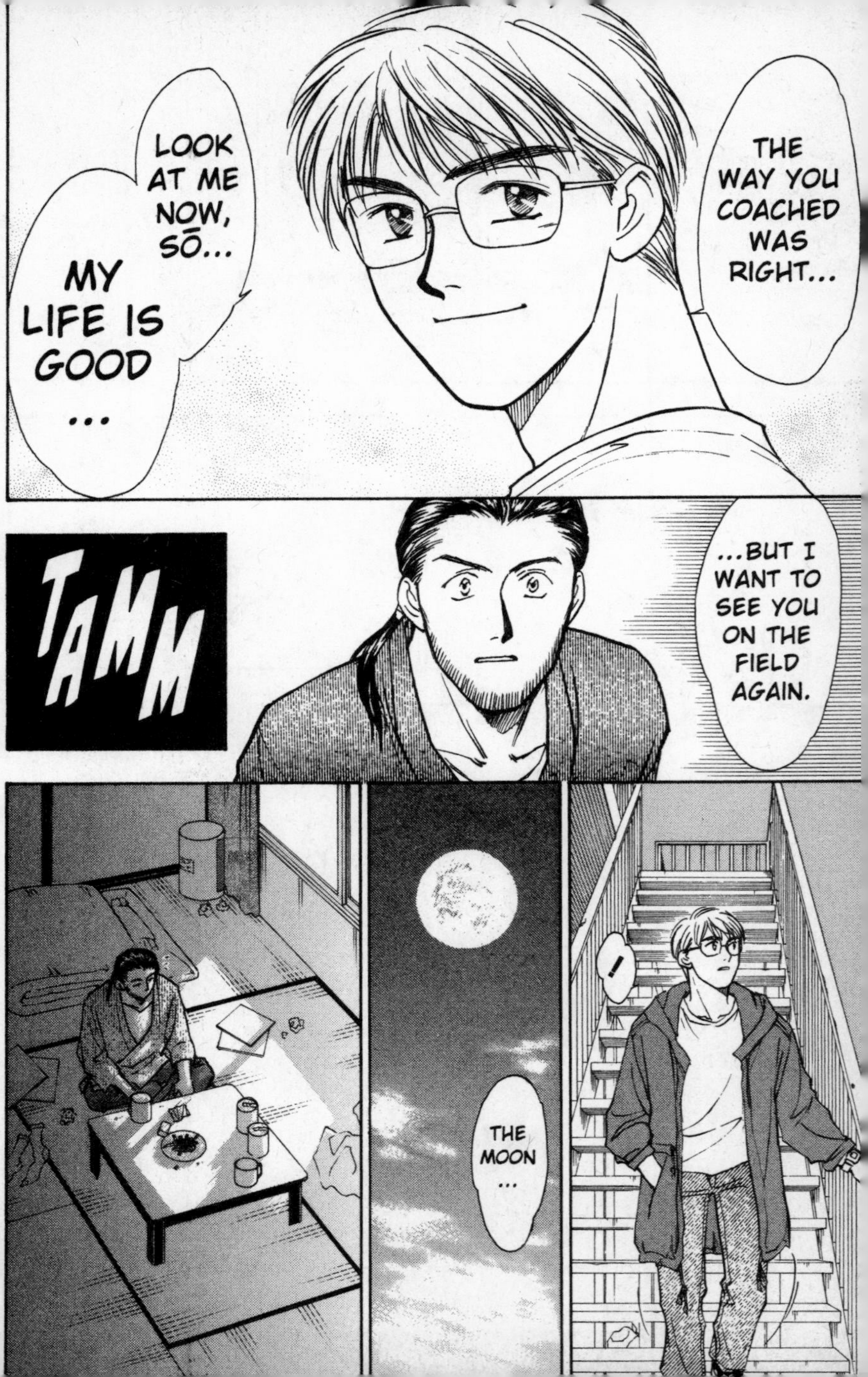
THE WAY YOU COACHED WAS RIGHT...
LOOK AT ME NOW, SŌ...
MY LIFE IS GOOD ...
...BUT I WANT TO SEE YOU ON THE FIELD AGAIN.
TAMM
!
THE MOON ...

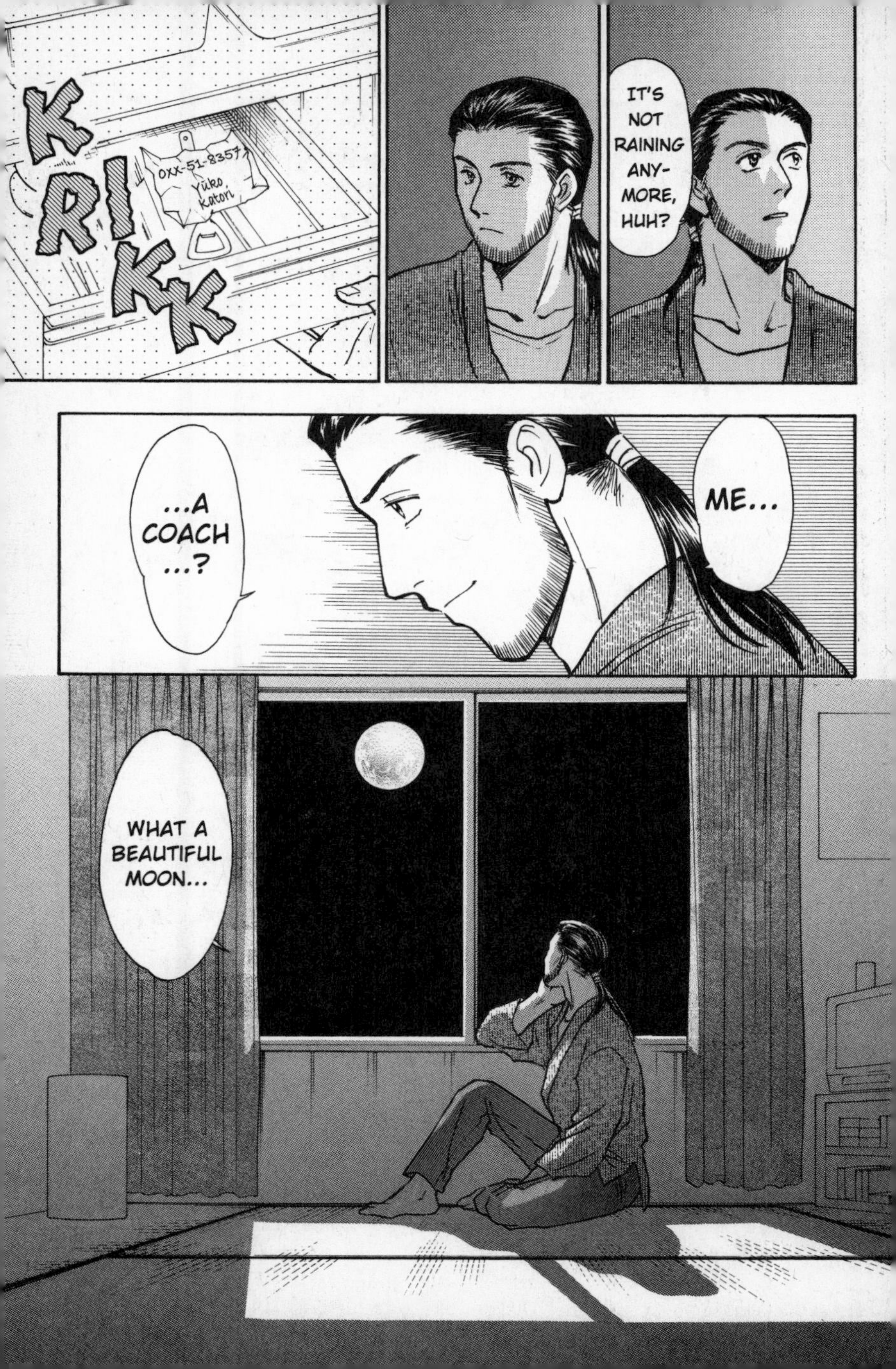
IT'S NOT RAINING ANY-MORE, HUH?
KRIKK
0XX-51-8357
Yūko Katori
ME...
...A COACH ...?
WHAT A BEAUTIFUL MOON...

# ● PRIOR TO J-LEAGUE

In 1986, a year after Japan lost the opportunity to participate in the Mexico World Cup, Yasuhiko Okudera, who played successfully as a professional in the German Bundes League, returned to Japan. The year after that, it became permissible for teams and players to freely sign contracts between themselves, which further promoted the professionalism of soccer in Japan.

However, the number of spectators did not increase. It averaged around 5,000 viewers per game. Although the players were professionals, the clubs were managed by amateurs. Realizing the problem, the Japan Soccer Association passed a resolution to establish a professional league equivalent in caliber to the ones in Europe and South America. The result was the establishment of the "Pro League Investigation Committee."

In 1990, Kazu Miura returned from Brazil and joined Yomiuri Club. He was selected as the Japan representative along with Ramos, who became a naturalized citizen of Japan. This further promoted soccer in Japan.

In addition, in 1992, Hans Ooft became the first foreigner to take a coach's position for Japan's representative team. The aim was to strengthen the team so as to participate in USA World Cup.

In other words, the start of professionalism, the opening of the J-League, was the beginning of the history of Japanese soccer and its new challenge.

# --TATSUYA WATANABE (WINNING RUN)

# STAGE.33 Trial!

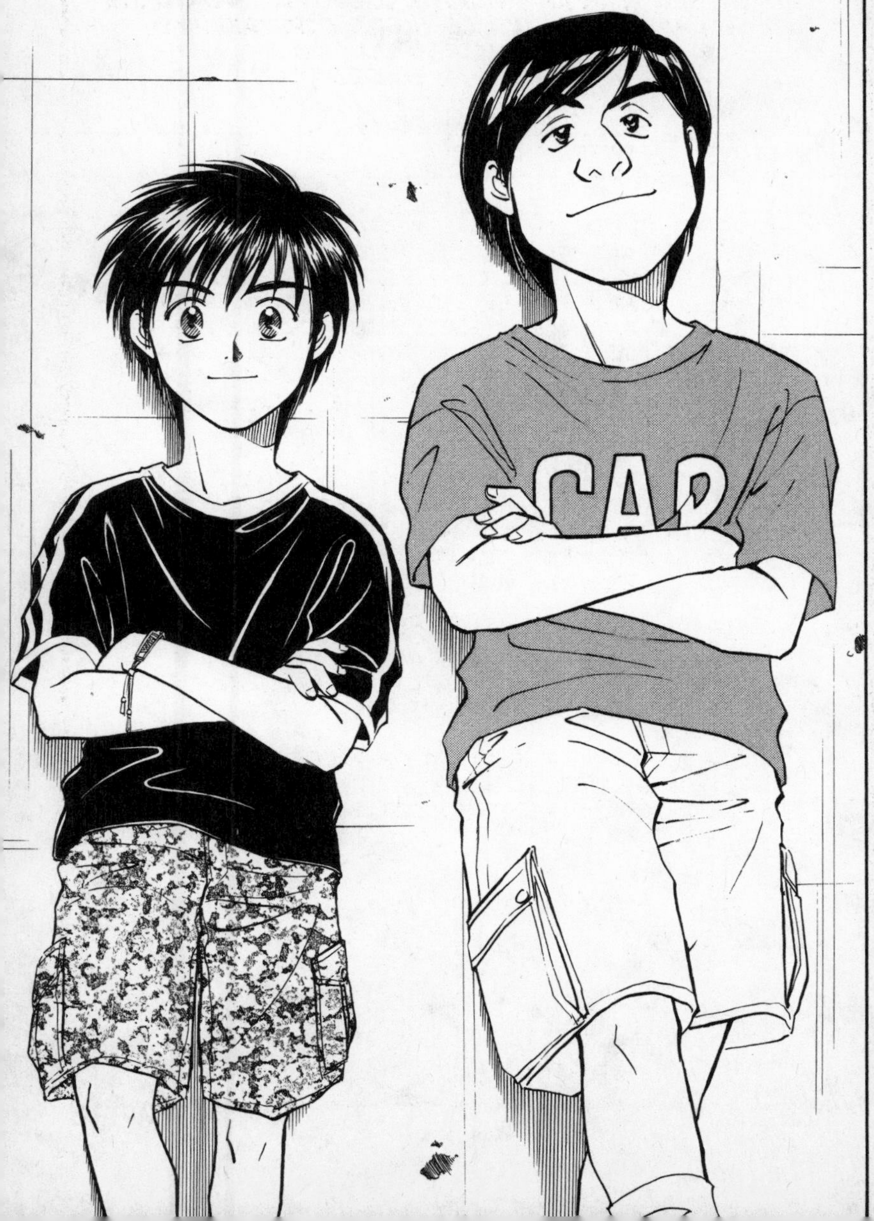

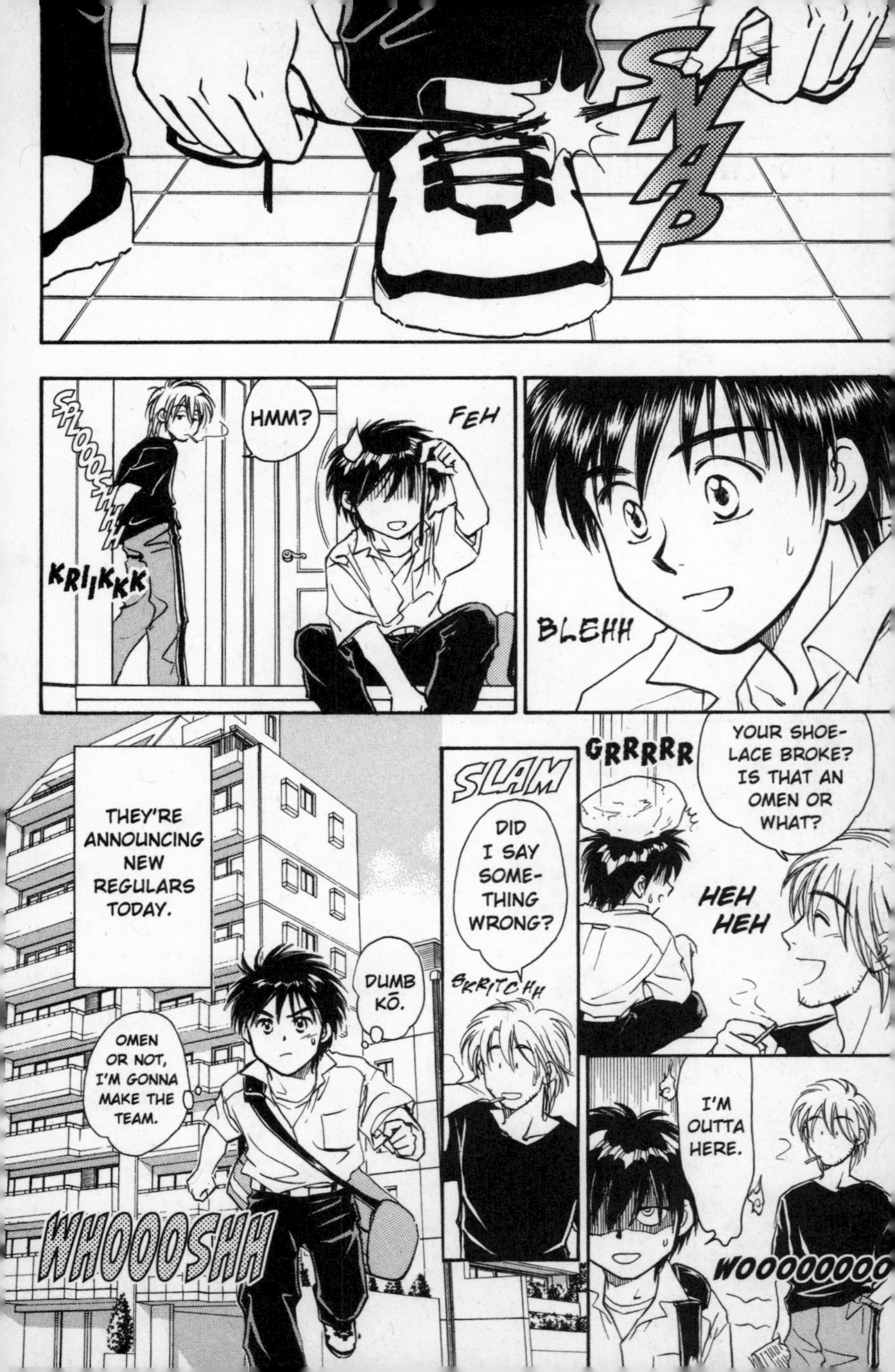
SNAP
BLEHH
FEH
HMM?
SPLOOOSHH
KRIIKKK
YOUR SHOE-LACE BROKE? IS THAT AN OMEN OR WHAT?
GRRRRRR
HEH HEH
I'M OUTTA HERE.
WOOOOOOOO
SLAM
DID I SAY SOME-THING WRONG?
SKRITCHH
THEY'RE ANNOUNCING NEW REGULARS TODAY.
DUMB KŌ.
OMEN OR NOT, I'M GONNA MAKE THE TEAM.
WHOOOSHH

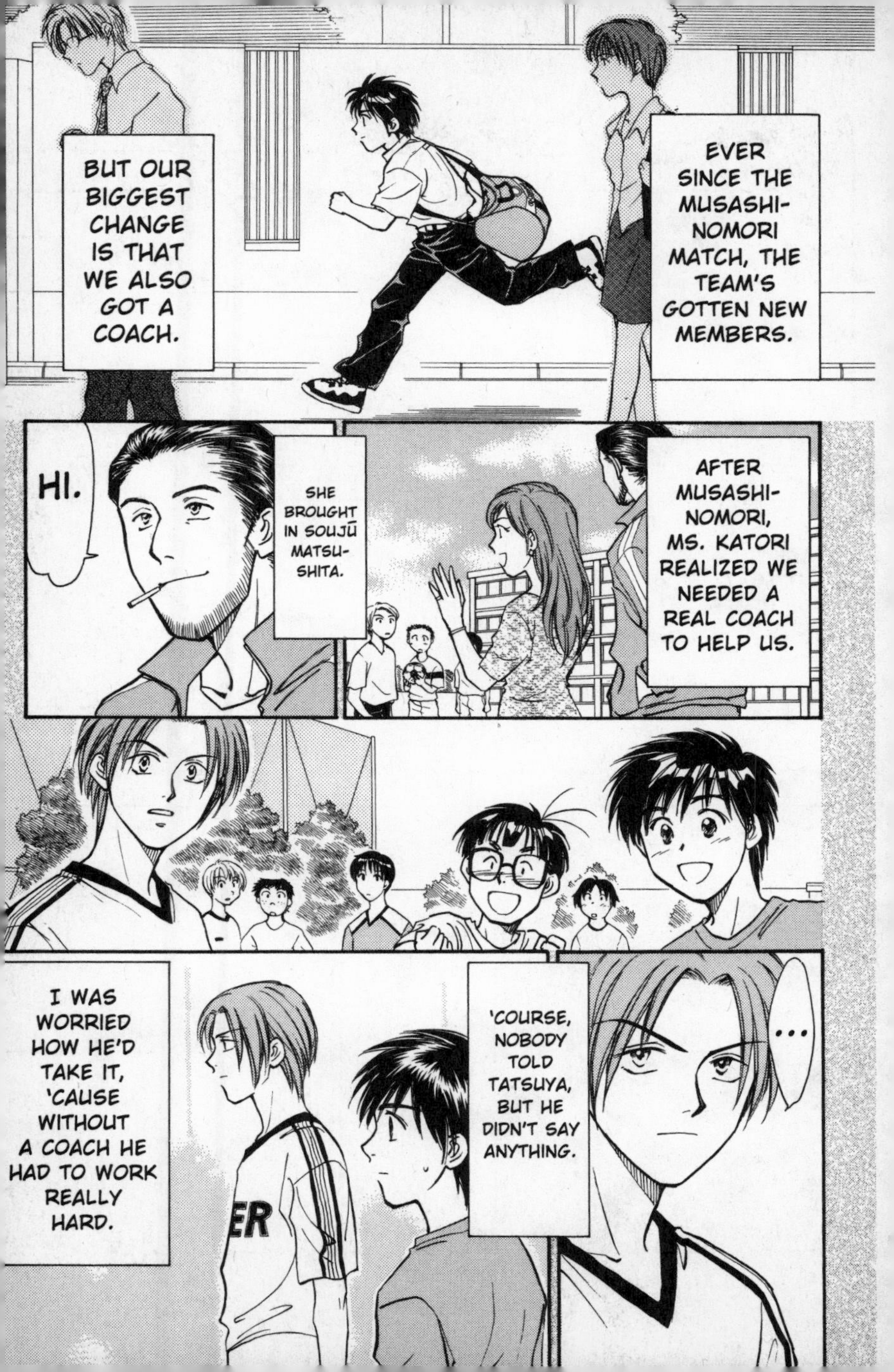
EVER SINCE THE MUSASHI-NOMORI MATCH, THE TEAM'S GOTTEN NEW MEMBERS.
BUT OUR BIGGEST CHANGE IS THAT WE ALSO GOT A COACH.
AFTER MUSASHI-NOMORI, MS. KATORI REALIZED WE NEEDED A REAL COACH TO HELP US.
SHE BROUGHT IN SOUJŪ MATSUSHITA.
HI.
...
'COURSE, NOBODY TOLD TATSUYA, BUT HE DIDN'T SAY ANYTHING.
I WAS WORRIED HOW HE'D TAKE IT, 'CAUSE WITHOUT A COACH HE HAD TO WORK REALLY HARD.

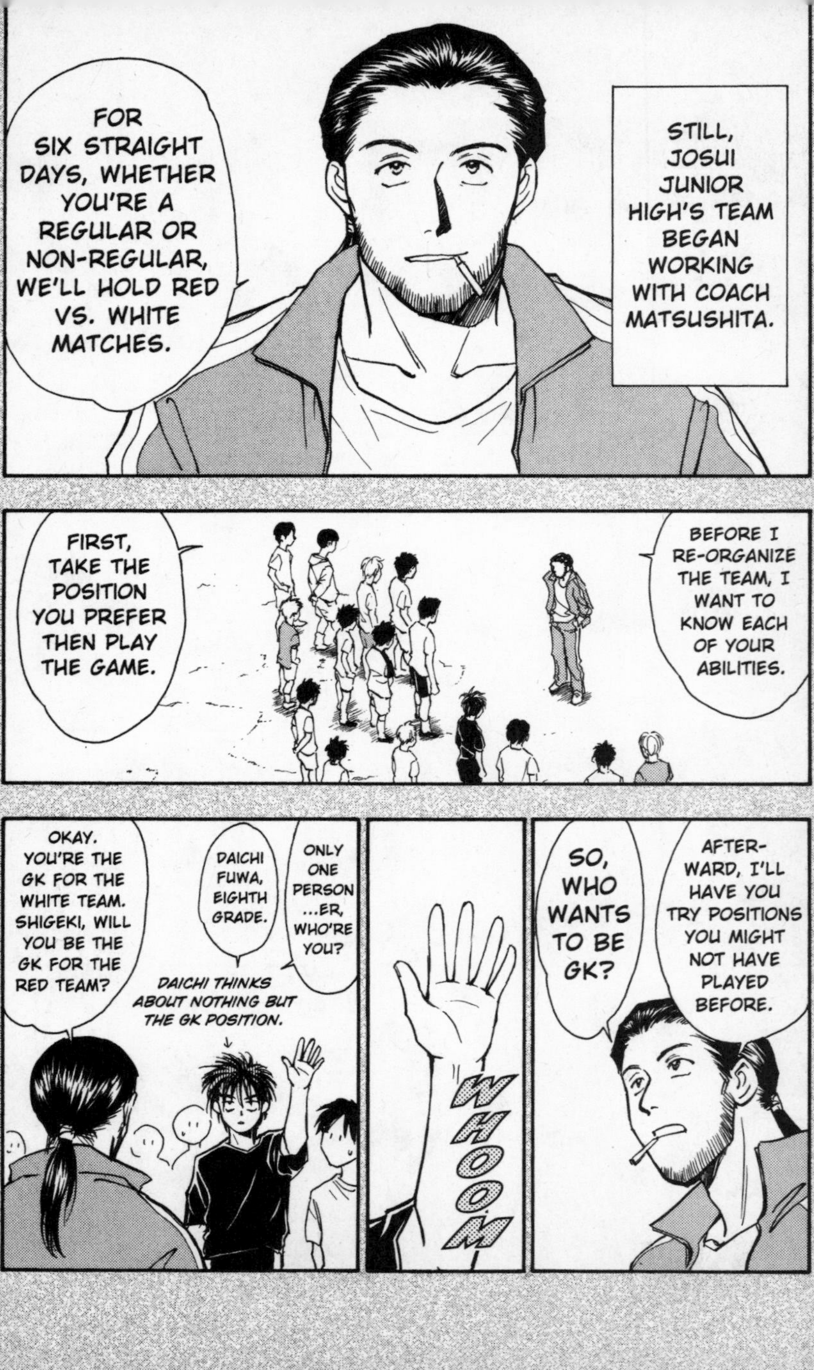
STILL, JOSUI JUNIOR HIGH'S TEAM BEGAN WORKING WITH COACH MATSUSHITA.
FOR SIX STRAIGHT DAYS, WHETHER YOU'RE A REGULAR OR NON-REGULAR, WE'LL HOLD RED VS. WHITE MATCHES.
BEFORE I RE-ORGANIZE THE TEAM, I WANT TO KNOW EACH OF YOUR ABILITIES.
FIRST, TAKE THE POSITION YOU PREFER THEN PLAY THE GAME.
AFTER-WARD, I'LL HAVE YOU TRY POSITIONS YOU MIGHT NOT HAVE PLAYED BEFORE.
SO, WHO WANTS TO BE GK?
WHOOOM
ONLY ONE PERSON ...ER, WHO'RE YOU?
DAICHI FUWA, EIGHTH GRADE.
OKAY. YOU'RE THE GK FOR THE WHITE TEAM. SHIGEKI, WILL YOU BE THE GK FOR THE RED TEAM?
DAICHI THINKS ABOUT NOTHING BUT THE GK POSITION.

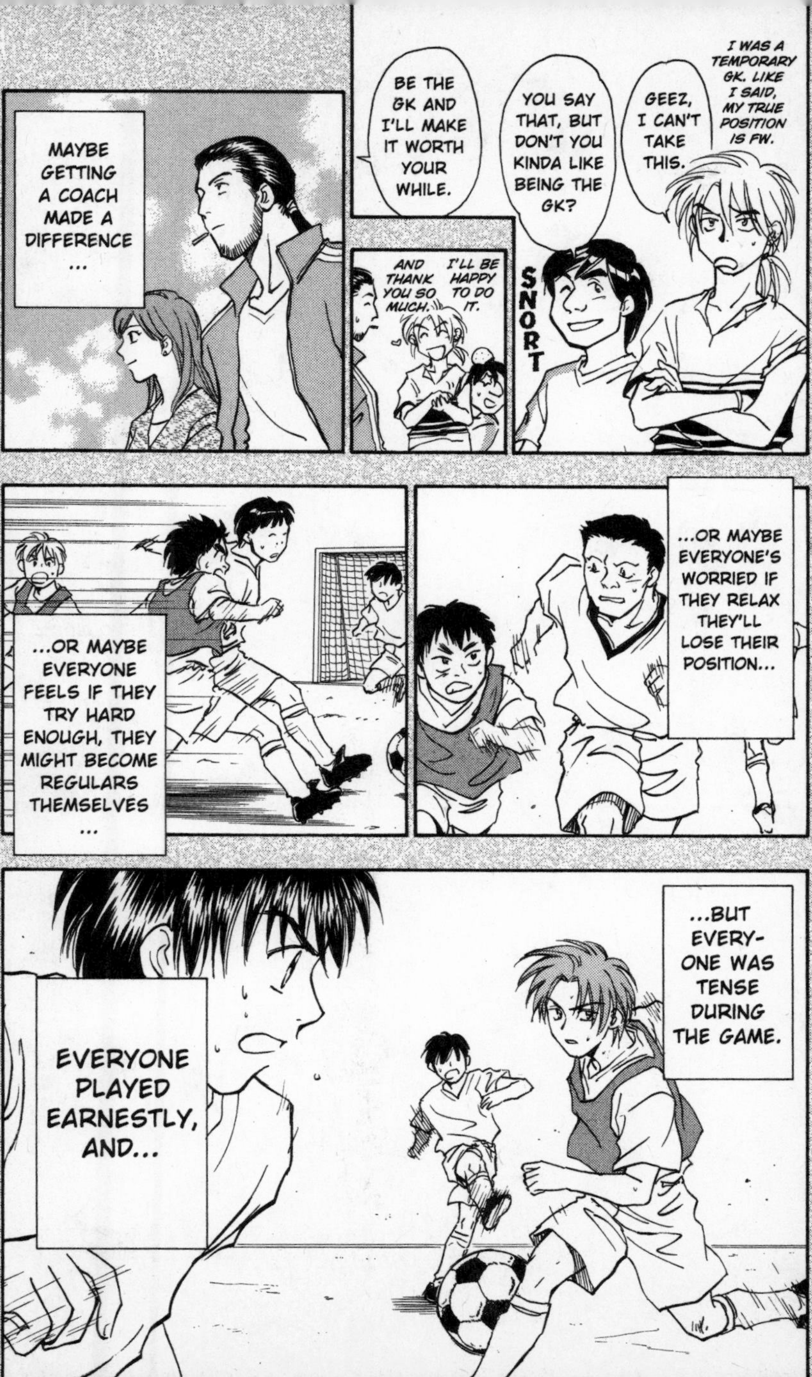

I WAS A TEMPORARY GK. LIKE I SAID, MY TRUE POSITION IS FW.
GEEZ, I CAN'T TAKE THIS.
YOU SAY THAT, BUT DON'T YOU KINDA LIKE BEING THE GK?
SNORT
BE THE GK AND I'LL MAKE IT WORTH YOUR WHILE.
I'LL BE HAPPY TO DO IT.
AND THANK YOU SO MUCH.
MAYBE GETTING A COACH MADE A DIFFERENCE ...
...OR MAYBE EVERYONE'S WORRIED IF THEY RELAX THEY'LL LOSE THEIR POSITION...
...OR MAYBE EVERYONE FEELS IF THEY TRY HARD ENOUGH, THEY MIGHT BECOME REGULARS THEMSELVES ...
...BUT EVERY-ONE WAS TENSE DURING THE GAME.
EVERYONE PLAYED EARNESTLY, AND...

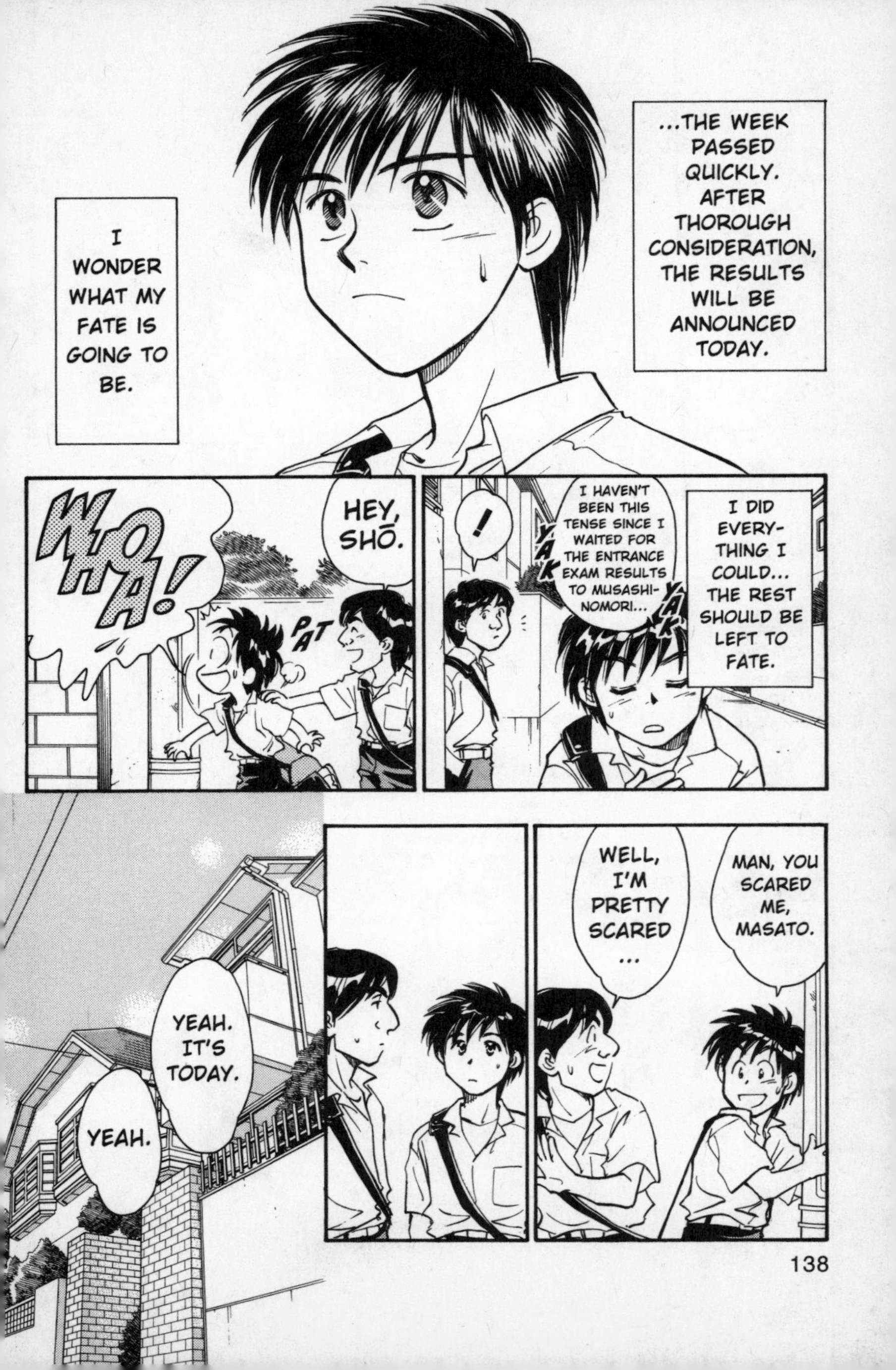
...THE WEEK PASSED QUICKLY. AFTER THOROUGH CONSIDERATION, THE RESULTS WILL BE ANNOUNCED TODAY.
I WONDER WHAT MY FATE IS GOING TO BE.
I DID EVERYTHING I COULD... THE REST SHOULD BE LEFT TO FATE.
I HAVEN'T BEEN THIS TENSE SINCE I WAITED FOR THE ENTRANCE EXAM RESULTS TO MUSASHINOMORI...
YAK
YAK
!
HEY, SHŌ.
PAT
WHOA!
MAN, YOU SCARED ME, MASATO.
WELL, I'M PRETTY SCARED ...
YEAH. IT'S TODAY.
YEAH.

READ THIS WAY

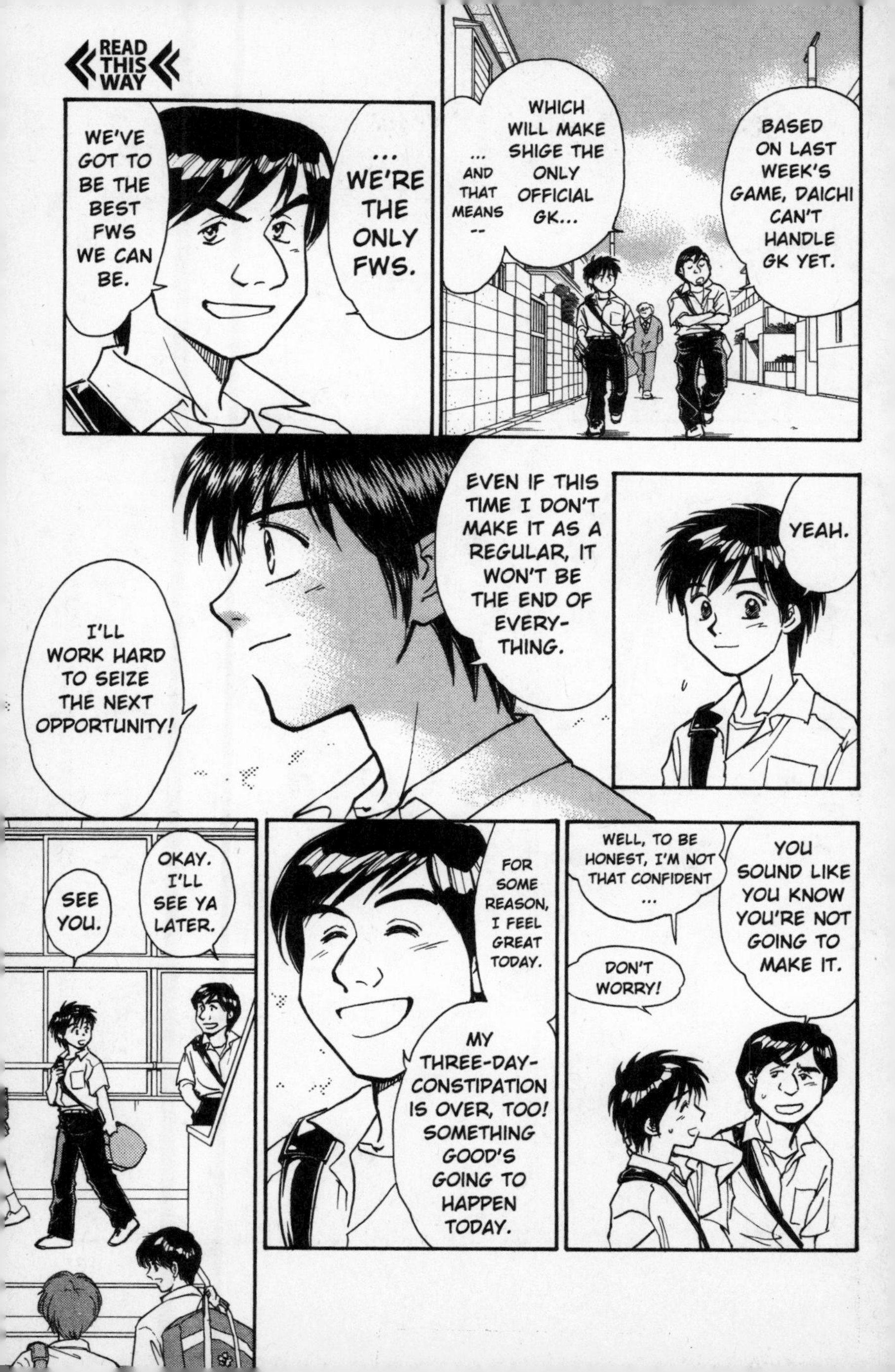
BASED ON LAST WEEK'S GAME, DAICHI CAN'T HANDLE GK YET.
WHICH WILL MAKE SHIGE THE ONLY OFFICIAL GK...
... AND THAT MEANS --
... WE'RE THE ONLY FWS.
WE'VE GOT TO BE THE BEST FWS WE CAN BE.
YEAH.
EVEN IF THIS TIME I DON'T MAKE IT AS A REGULAR, IT WON'T BE THE END OF EVERY-THING.
I'LL WORK HARD TO SEIZE THE NEXT OPPORTUNITY!
YOU SOUND LIKE YOU KNOW YOU'RE NOT GOING TO MAKE IT.
WELL, TO BE HONEST, I'M NOT THAT CONFIDENT ...
DON'T WORRY!
FOR SOME REASON, I FEEL GREAT TODAY.
MY THREE-DAY-CONSTIPATION IS OVER, TOO! SOMETHING GOOD'S GOING TO HAPPEN TODAY.
OKAY. I'LL SEE YA LATER.
SEE YOU.

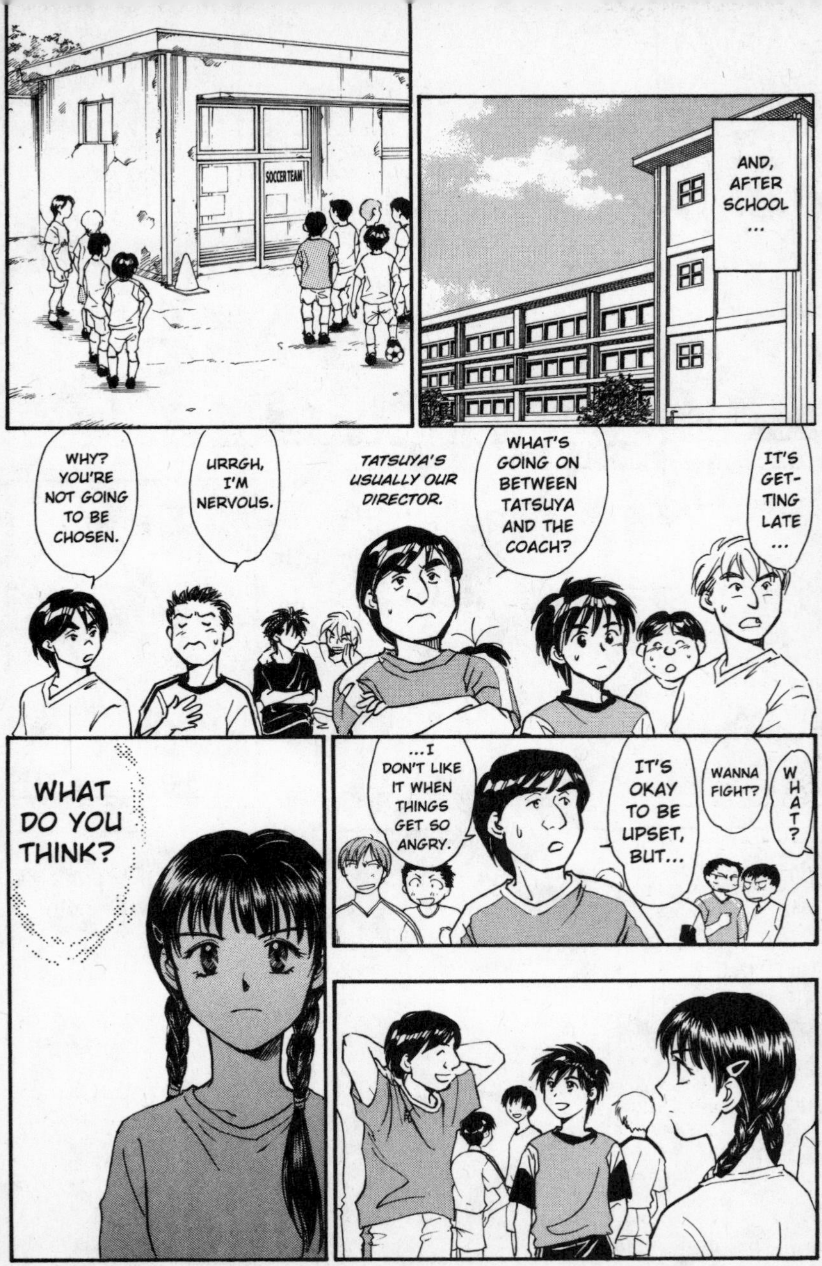
AND, AFTER SCHOOL ...
SOCCER TEAM
IT'S GET-TING LATE ...
WHAT'S GOING ON BETWEEN TATSUYA AND THE COACH?
TATSUYA'S USUALLY OUR DIRECTOR.
URRGH, I'M NERVOUS.
WHY? YOU'RE NOT GOING TO BE CHOSEN.
WHAT?
WANNA FIGHT?
IT'S OKAY TO BE UPSET, BUT...
...I DON'T LIKE IT WHEN THINGS GET SO ANGRY.
WHAT DO YOU THINK?

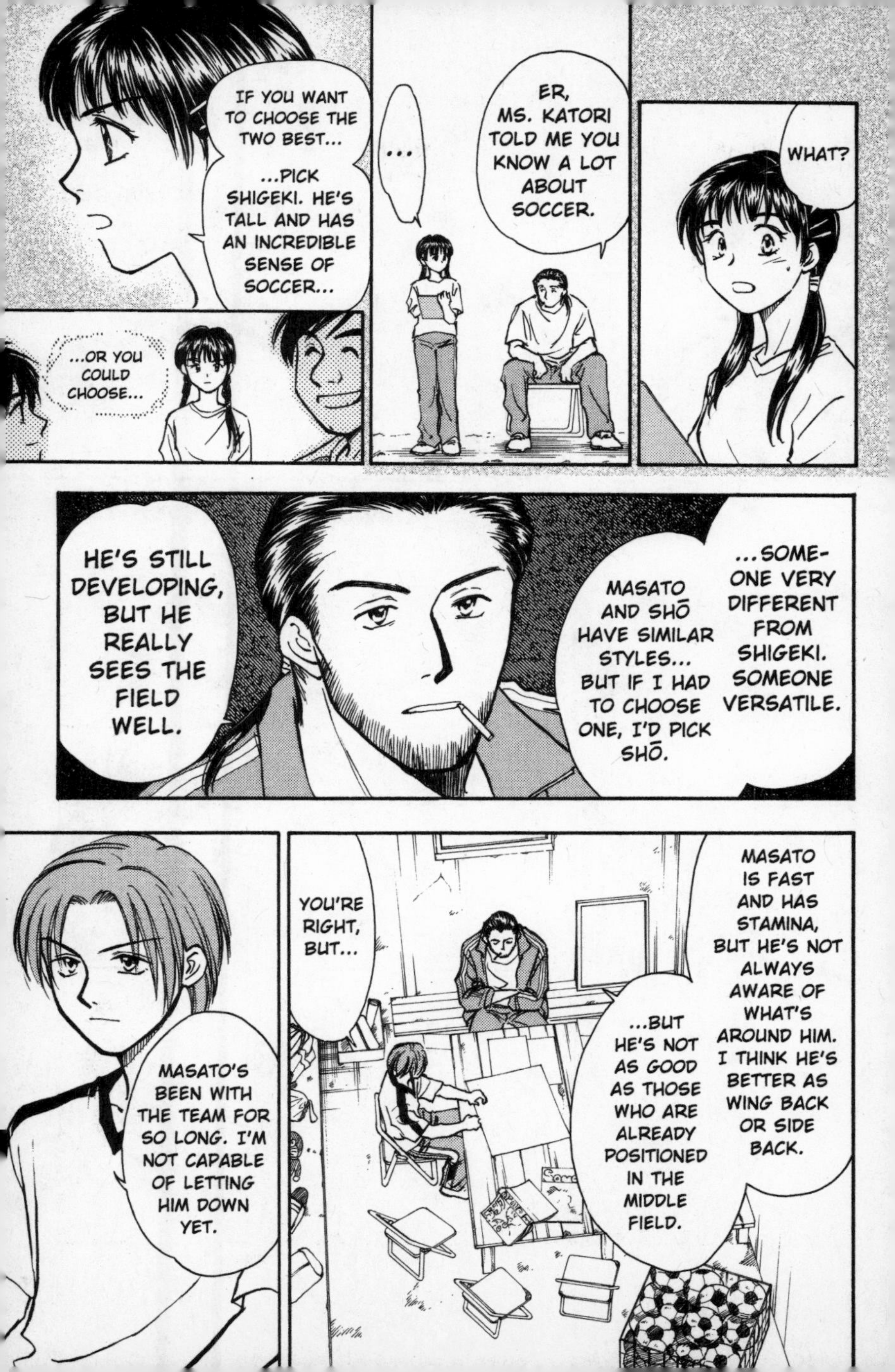
WHAT?
ER, MS. KATORI TOLD ME YOU KNOW A LOT ABOUT SOCCER.
...
IF YOU WANT TO CHOOSE THE TWO BEST...
...PICK SHIGEKI. HE'S TALL AND HAS AN INCREDIBLE SENSE OF SOCCER...
...OR YOU COULD CHOOSE...
...SOME-ONE VERY DIFFERENT FROM SHIGEKI. SOMEONE VERSATILE.
MASATO AND SHŌ HAVE SIMILAR STYLES... BUT IF I HAD TO CHOOSE ONE, I'D PICK SHŌ.
HE'S STILL DEVELOPING, BUT HE REALLY SEES THE FIELD WELL.
MASATO IS FAST AND HAS STAMINA, BUT HE'S NOT ALWAYS AWARE OF WHAT'S AROUND HIM. I THINK HE'S BETTER AS WING BACK OR SIDE BACK.
...BUT HE'S NOT AS GOOD AS THOSE WHO ARE ALREADY POSITIONED IN THE MIDDLE FIELD.
YOU'RE RIGHT, BUT...
MASATO'S BEEN WITH THE TEAM FOR SO LONG. I'M NOT CAPABLE OF LETTING HIM DOWN YET.

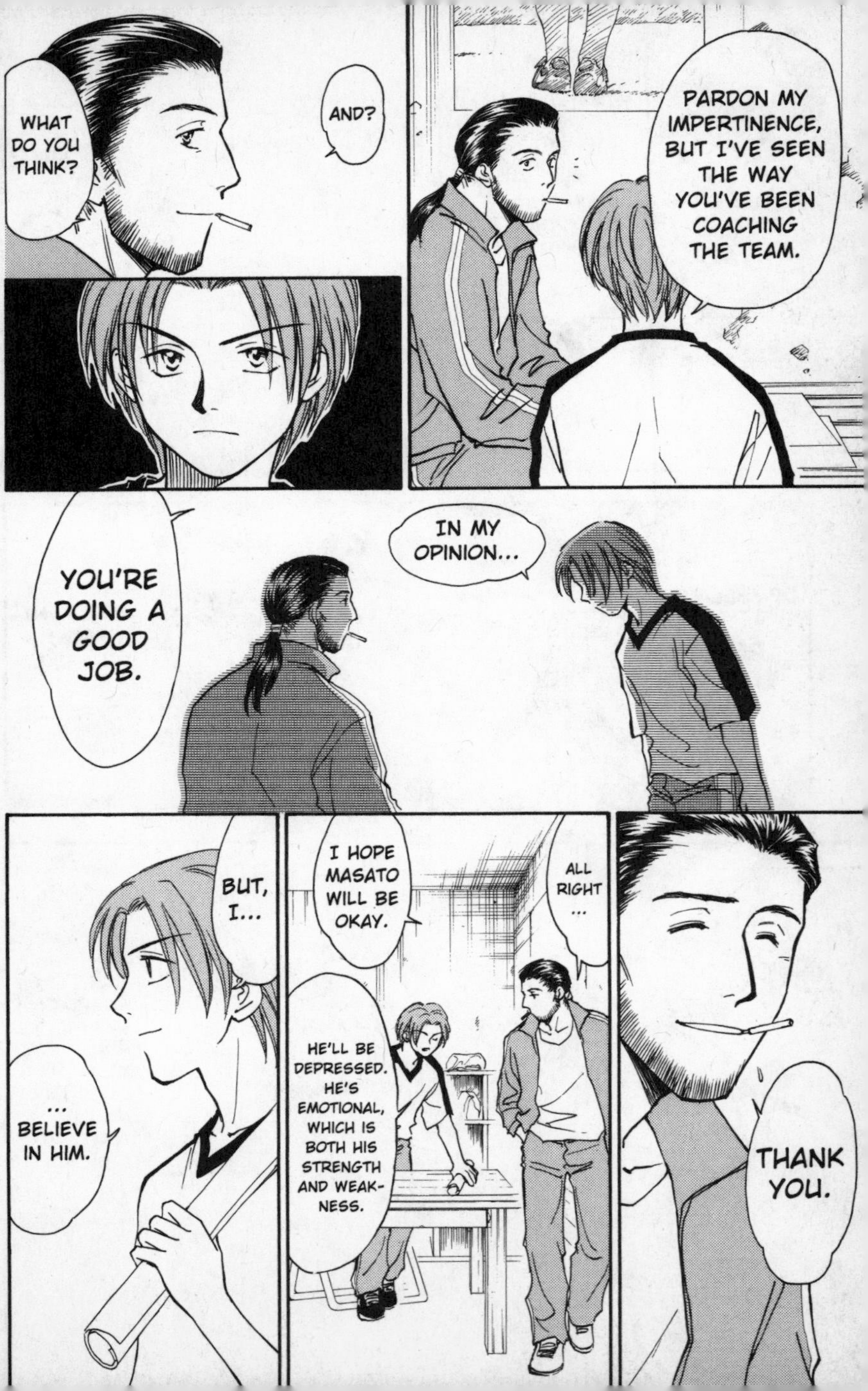
PARDON MY IMPERTINENCE, BUT I'VE SEEN THE WAY YOU'VE BEEN COACHING THE TEAM.
AND?
WHAT DO YOU THINK?
IN MY OPINION...
YOU'RE DOING A GOOD JOB.
THANK YOU.
ALL RIGHT ...
I HOPE MASATO WILL BE OKAY.
HE'LL BE DEPRESSED. HE'S EMOTIONAL, WHICH IS BOTH HIS STRENGTH AND WEAK-NESS.
BUT, I...
... BELIEVE IN HIM.

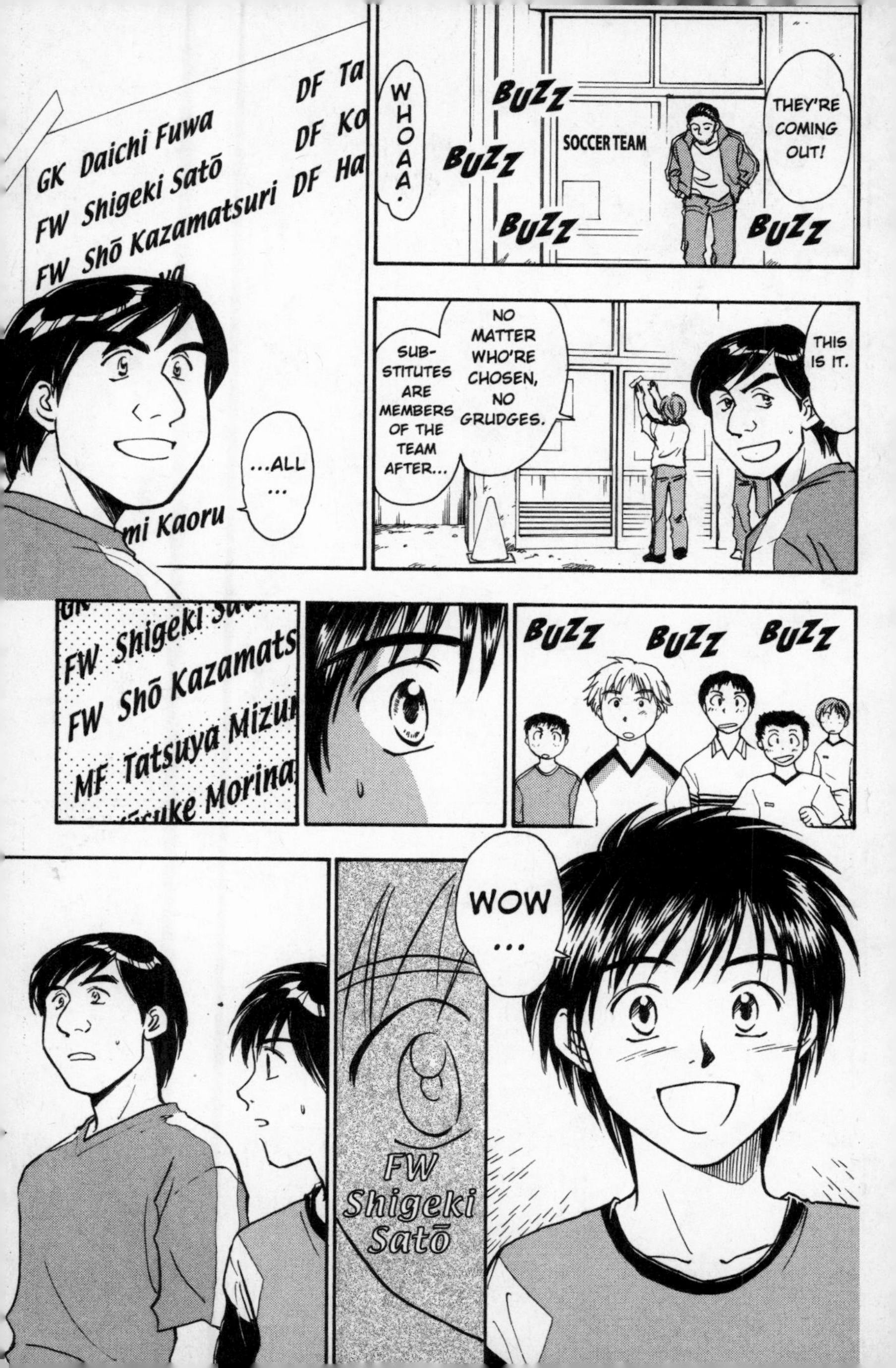
THEY'RE COMING OUT!
BUZZ
WHOAA.
BUZZ
SOCCER TEAM
BUZZ
BUZZ
THIS IS IT.
NO MATTER WHO'RE CHOSEN, NO GRUDGES.
SUB-STITUTES ARE MEMBERS OF THE TEAM AFTER...
DF Ta
GK Daichi Fuwa
DF Ko
FW Shigeki Satō
DF Ha
FW Shō Kazamatsuri
...ALL ...
mi Kaoru
BUZZ BUZZ BUZZ
FW Shigeki Sa
FW Shō Kazamats
MF Tatsuya Mizu
uke Morina
WOW ...
FW Shigeki Satō

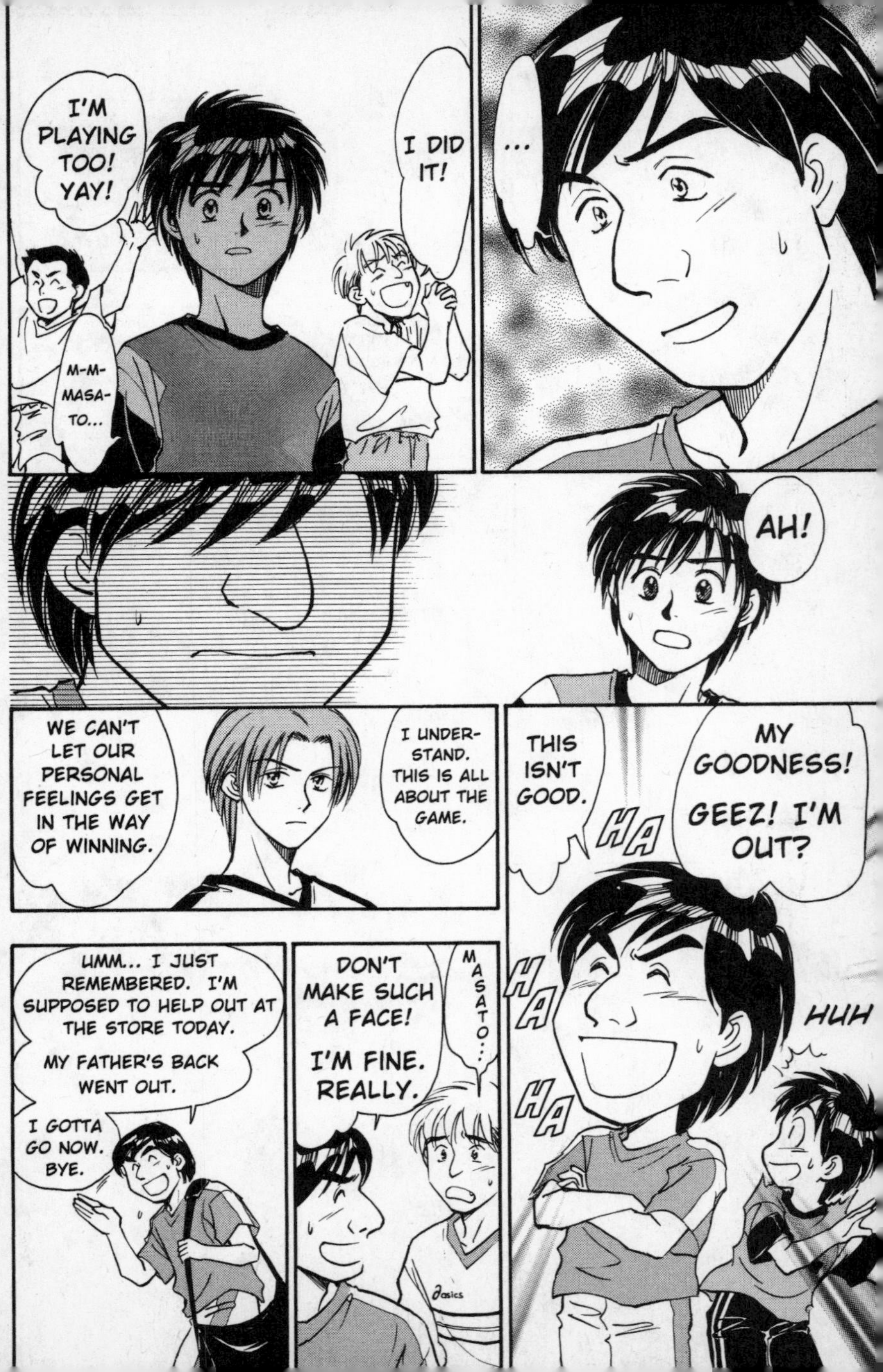
...
I DID IT!
I'M PLAYING TOO! YAY!
M-M-MASATO...
AH!
MY GOODNESS!
GEEZ! I'M OUT?
THIS ISN'T GOOD.
HA
HA
HA
HA
HUH
I UNDER-STAND. THIS IS ALL ABOUT THE GAME.
WE CAN'T LET OUR PERSONAL FEELINGS GET IN THE WAY OF WINNING.
MASATO...
DON'T MAKE SUCH A FACE!
I'M FINE. REALLY.
UMM... I JUST REMEMBERED. I'M SUPPOSED TO HELP OUT AT THE STORE TODAY.
MY FATHER'S BACK WENT OUT.
I GOTTA GO NOW. BYE.

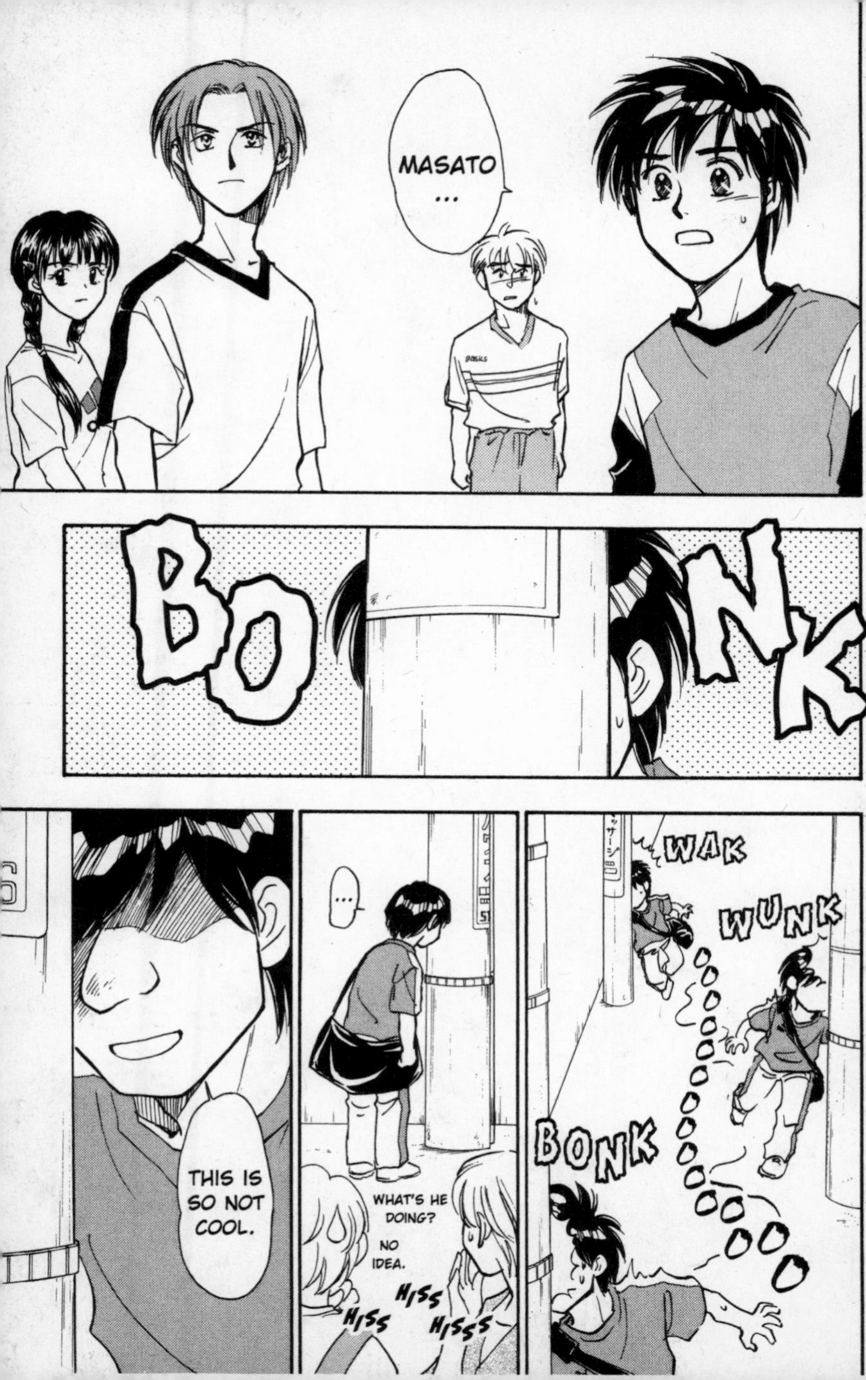
MASATO ...
BONK
WAK
WUNK
BONK
...
WHAT'S HE DOING?
NO IDEA.
HISS
HISS
HISSS
THIS IS SO NOT COOL.

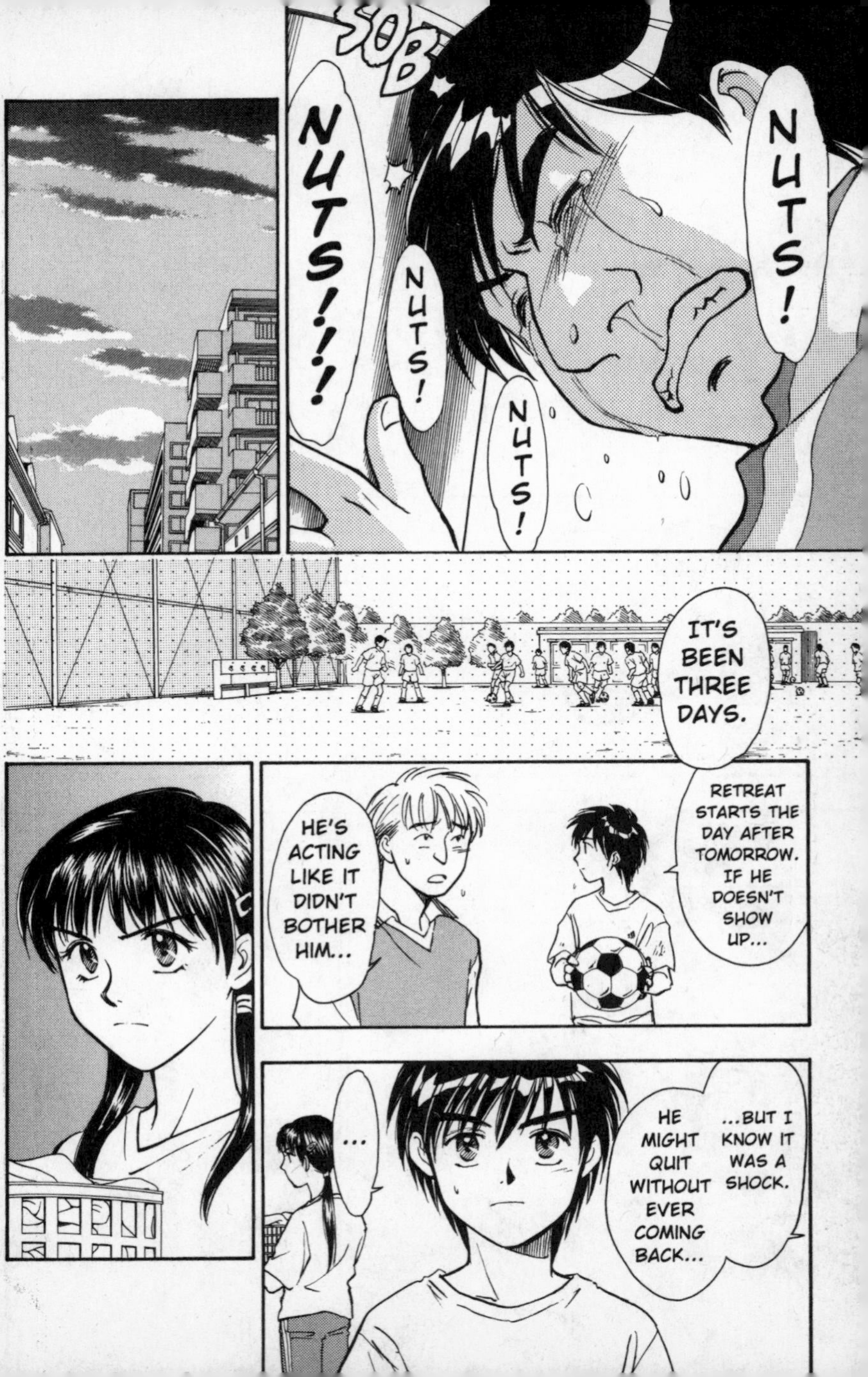
SOB
NUTS!
NUTS!!!!
NUTS!
NUTS!
IT'S BEEN THREE DAYS.
RETREAT STARTS THE DAY AFTER TOMORROW. IF HE DOESN'T SHOW UP...
HE'S ACTING LIKE IT DIDN'T BOTHER HIM...
...BUT I KNOW IT WAS A SHOCK.
HE MIGHT QUIT WITHOUT EVER COMING BACK...
...

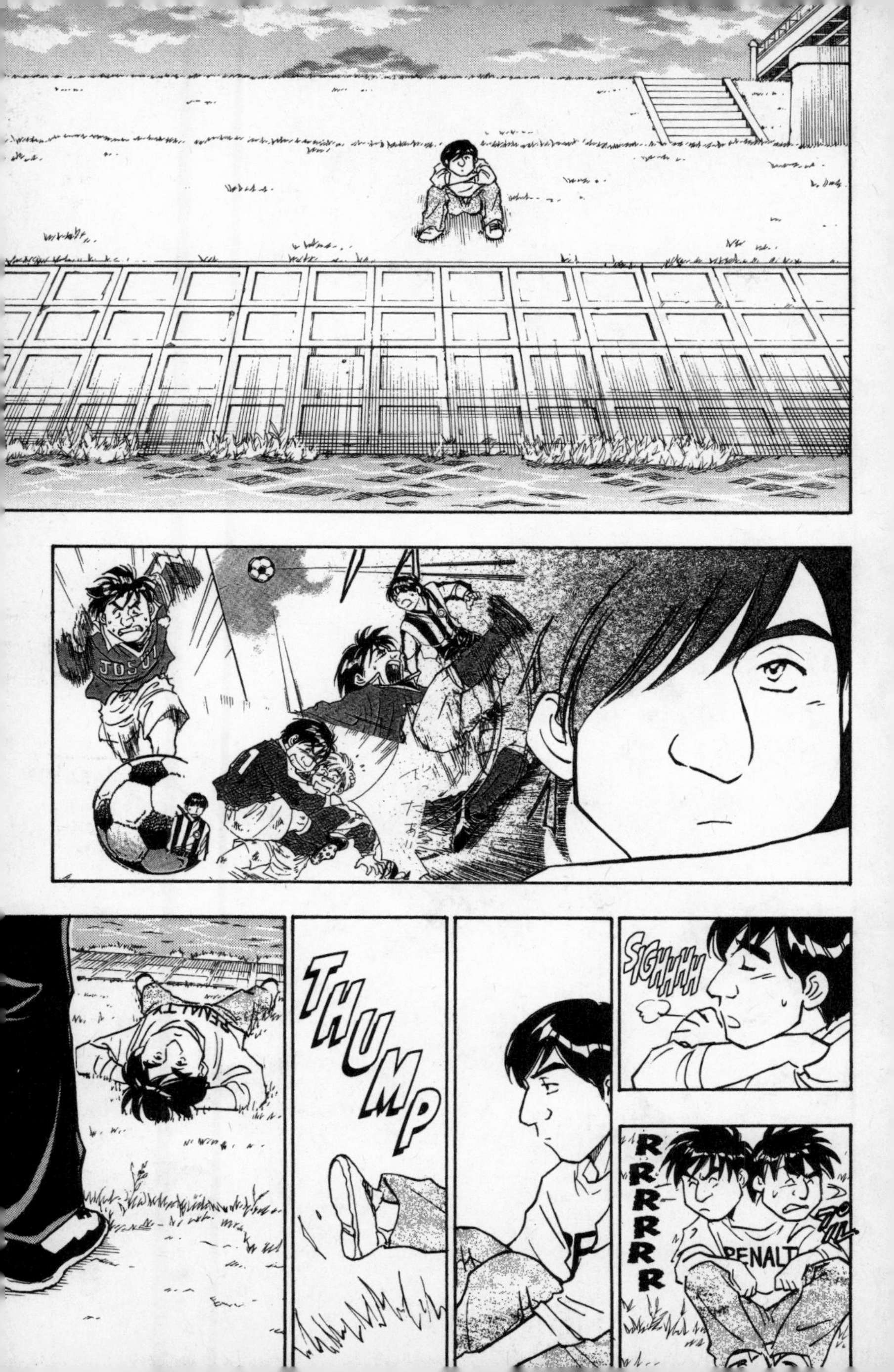
JOSUI
SIGHHHH
RRRRR
PENALT
THUMP

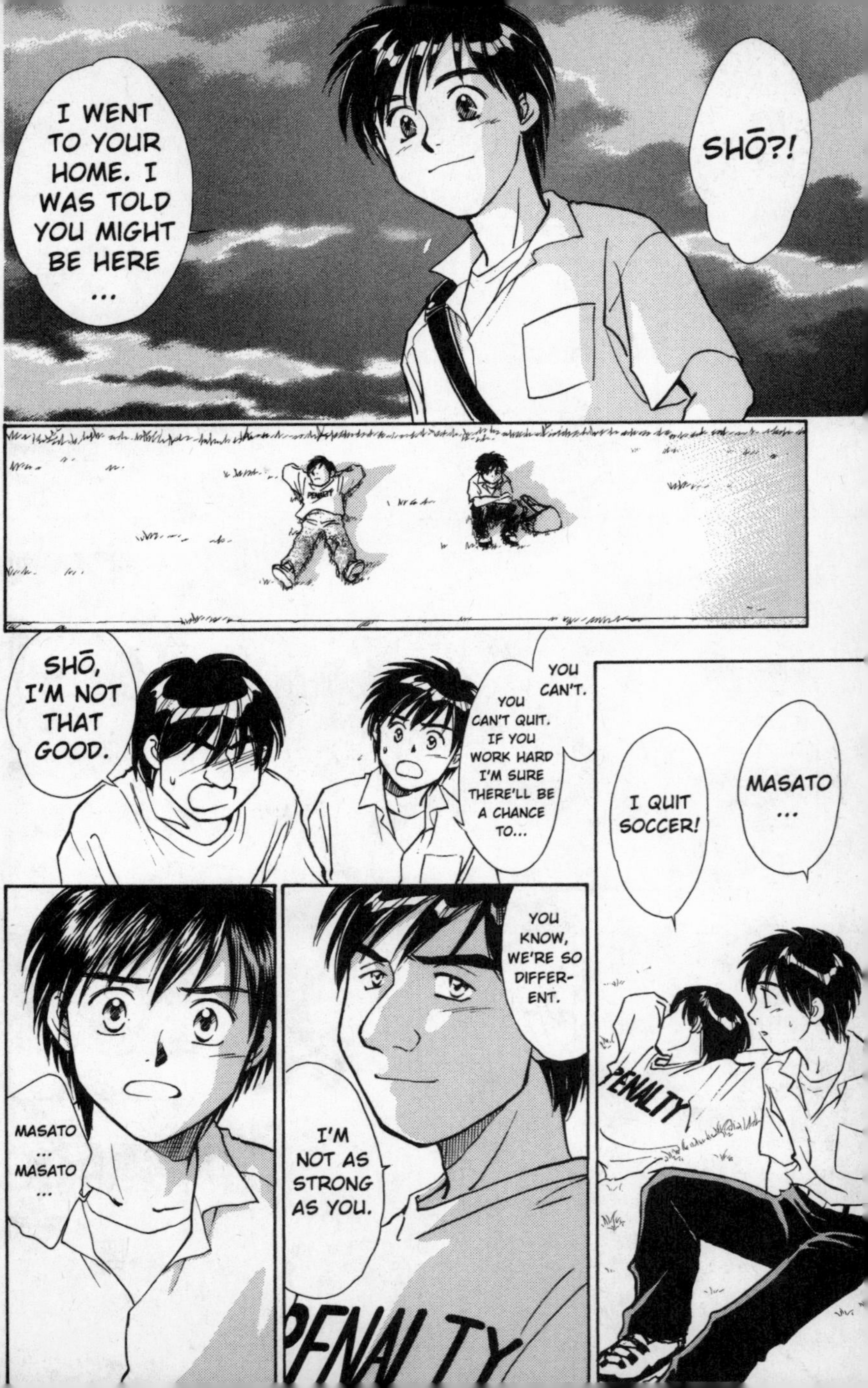
SHŌ?!
I WENT TO YOUR HOME. I WAS TOLD YOU MIGHT BE HERE ...
MASATO ...
I QUIT SOCCER!
YOU CAN'T. YOU CAN'T QUIT. IF YOU WORK HARD I'M SURE THERE'LL BE A CHANCE TO...
SHŌ, I'M NOT THAT GOOD.
YOU KNOW, WE'RE SO DIFFER- ENT.
I'M NOT AS STRONG AS YOU.
MASATO ... MASATO ...

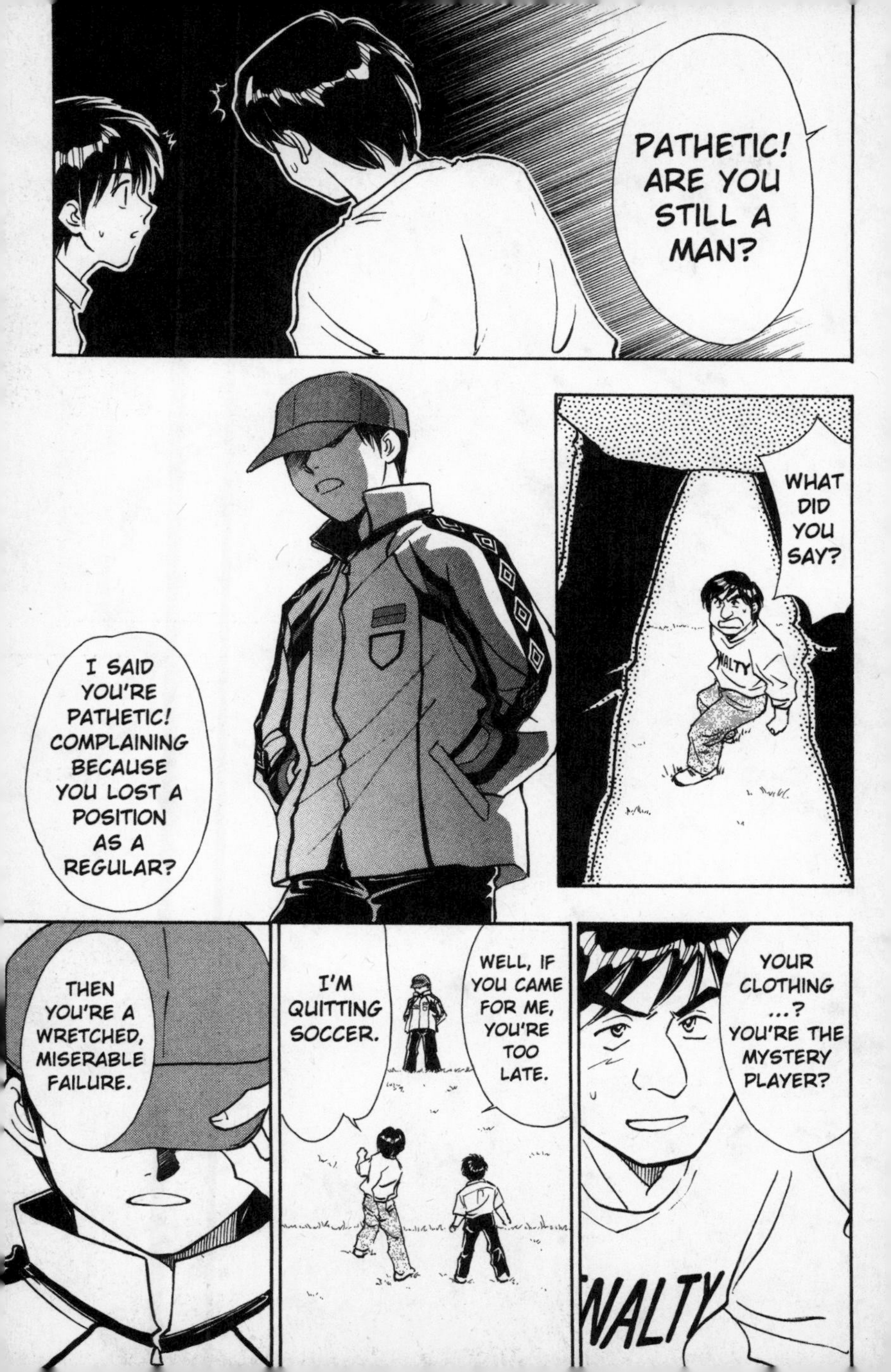
PATHETIC! ARE YOU STILL A MAN?
WHAT DID YOU SAY?
I SAID YOU'RE PATHETIC! COMPLAINING BECAUSE YOU LOST A POSITION AS A REGULAR?
YOUR CLOTHING ...? YOU'RE THE MYSTERY PLAYER?
WELL, IF YOU CAME FOR ME, YOU'RE TOO LATE.
I'M QUITTING SOCCER.
THEN YOU'RE A WRETCHED, MISERABLE FAILURE.

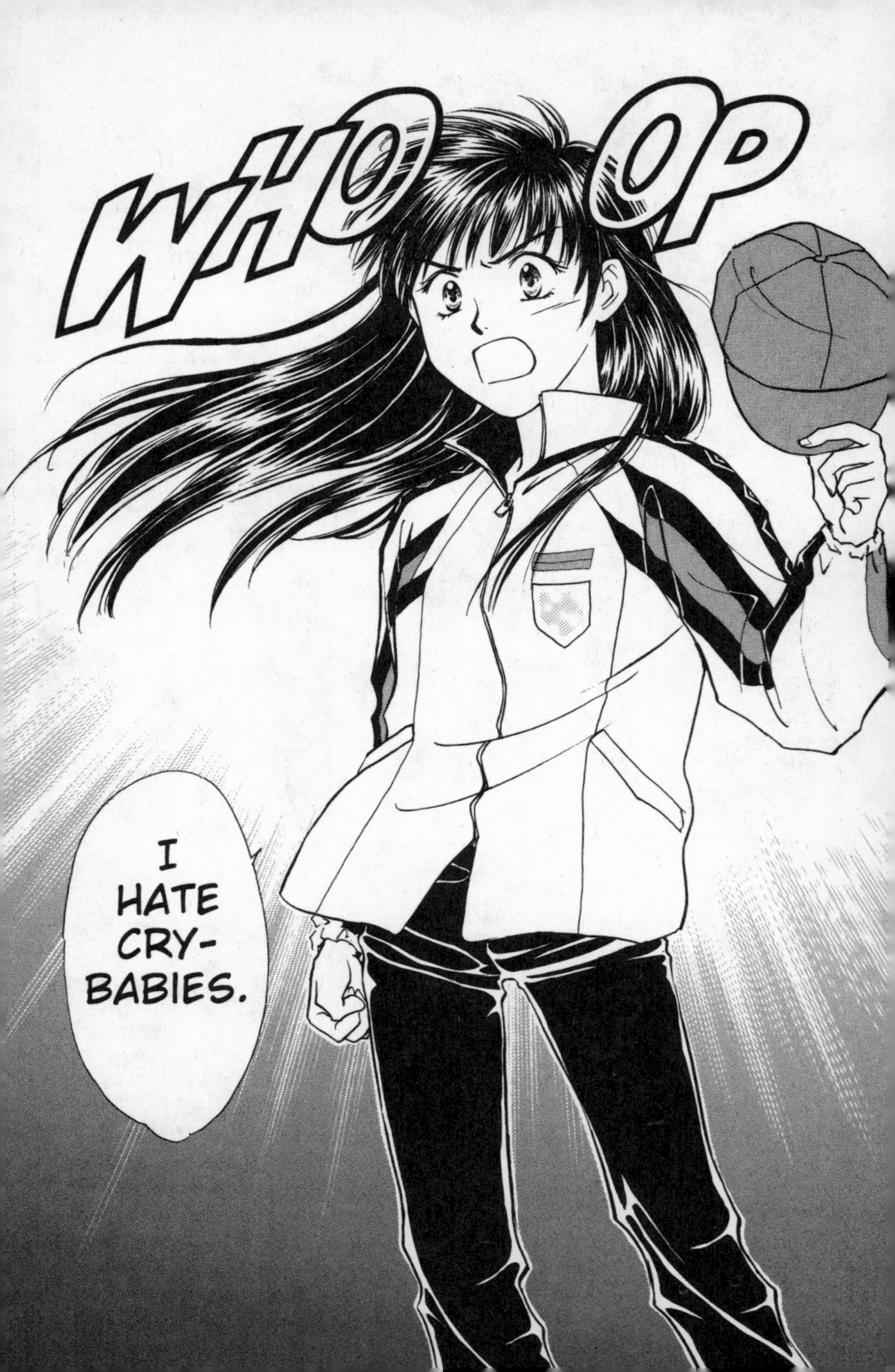
WHOOP
I HATE CRY-BABIES.

READ THIS WAY

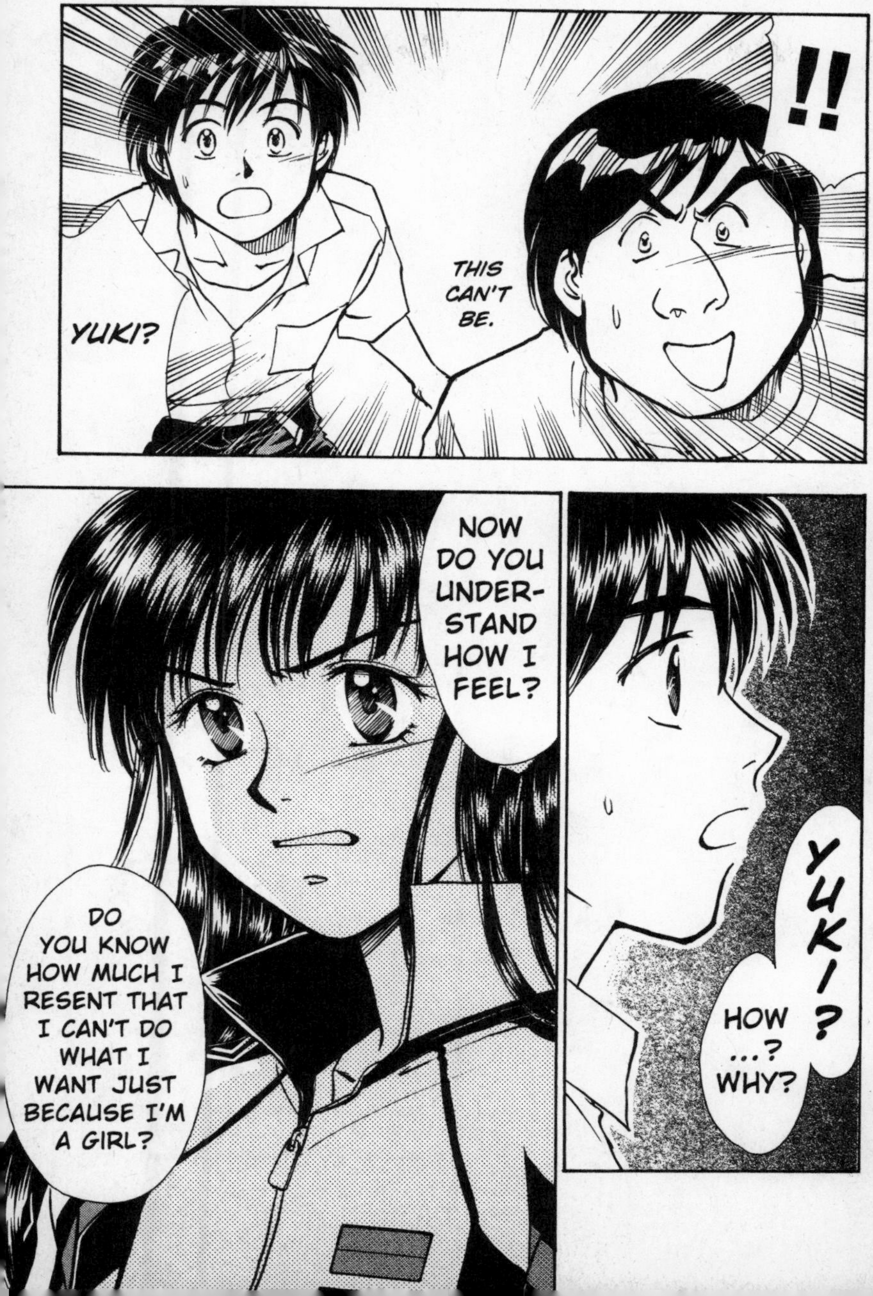
!!
THIS CAN'T BE.
YUKI?
YUKI?
HOW ...? WHY?
NOW DO YOU UNDER-STAND HOW I FEEL?
DO YOU KNOW HOW MUCH I RESENT THAT I CAN'T DO WHAT I WANT JUST BECAUSE I'M A GIRL?

IN FRONT KICK

It's a kick that sends out a high and long pass. It is perfect for adding variations like spin/curve, and therefore, it is often used for centering, corner kick as well as free kick.

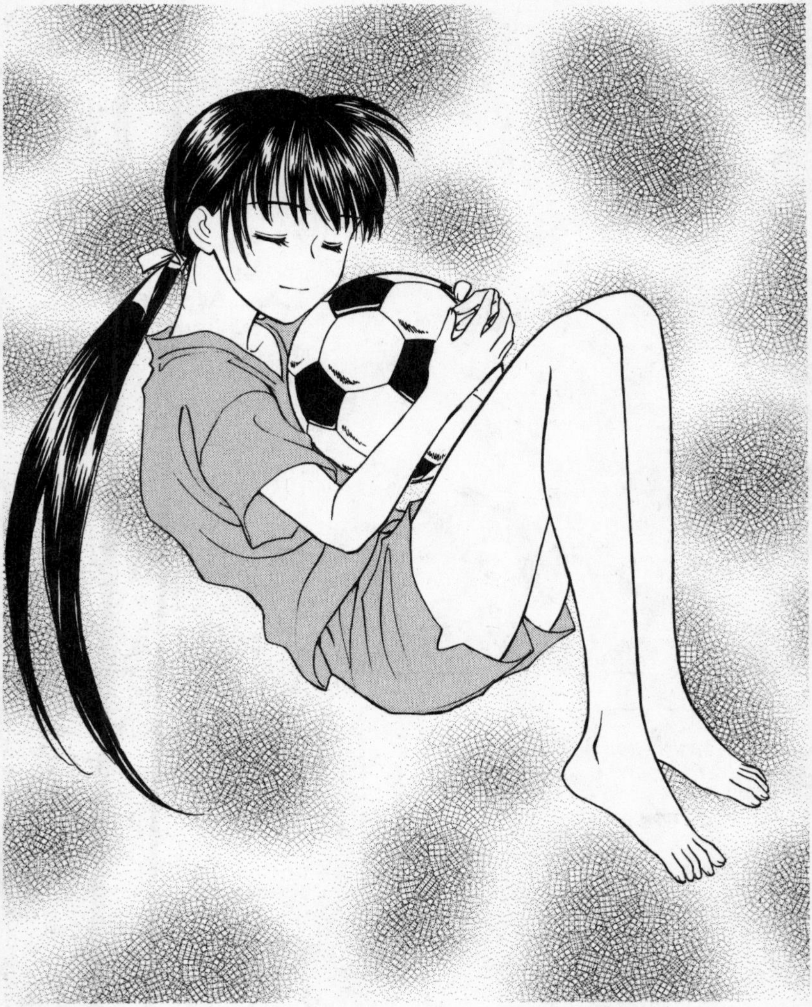

## STAGE.34

# Be True To Yourself

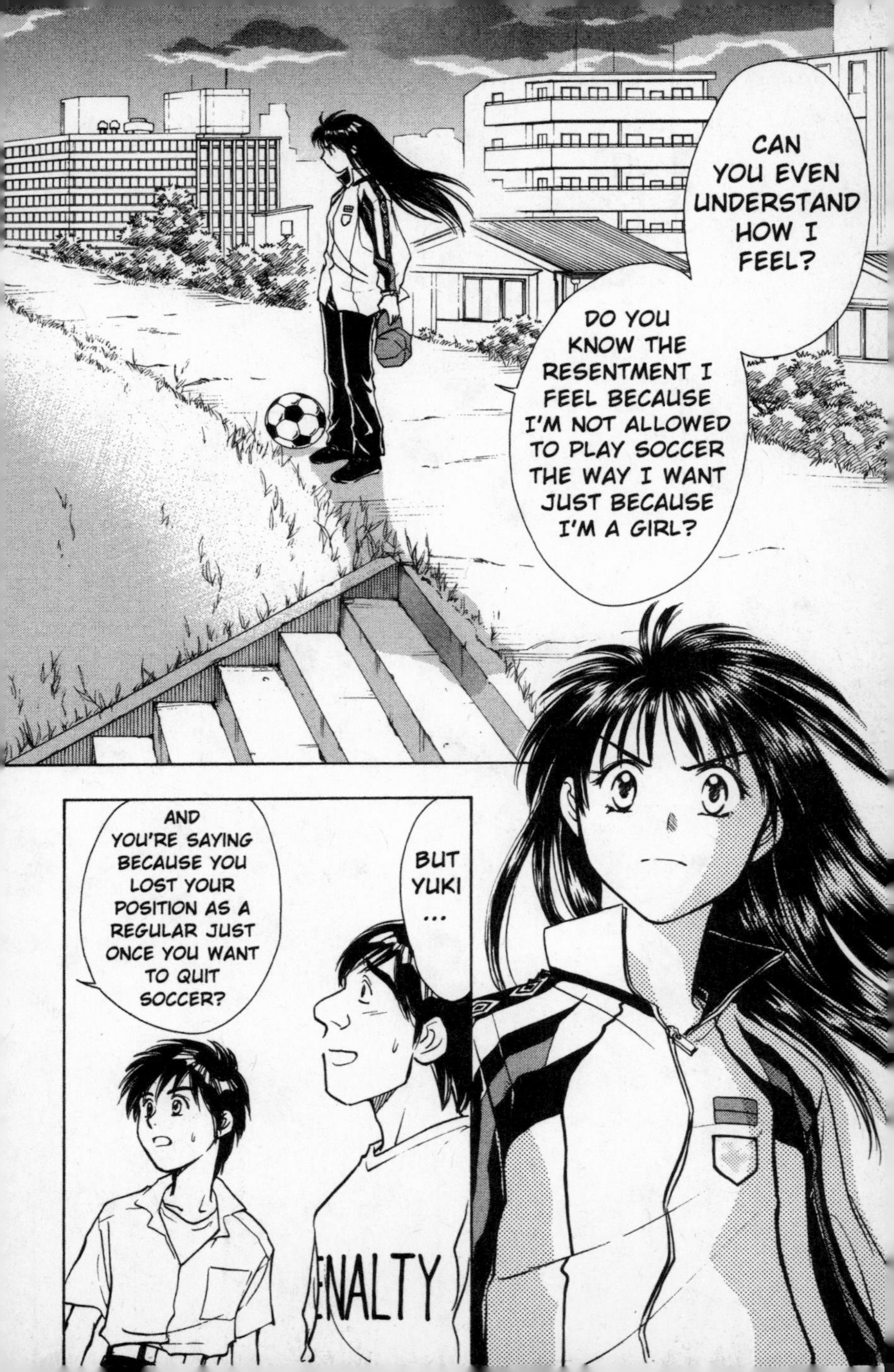
CAN YOU EVEN UNDERSTAND HOW I FEEL?
DO YOU KNOW THE RESENTMENT I FEEL BECAUSE I'M NOT ALLOWED TO PLAY SOCCER THE WAY I WANT JUST BECAUSE I'M A GIRL?
BUT YUKI ...
AND YOU'RE SAYING BECAUSE YOU LOST YOUR POSITION AS A REGULAR JUST ONCE YOU WANT TO QUIT SOCCER?

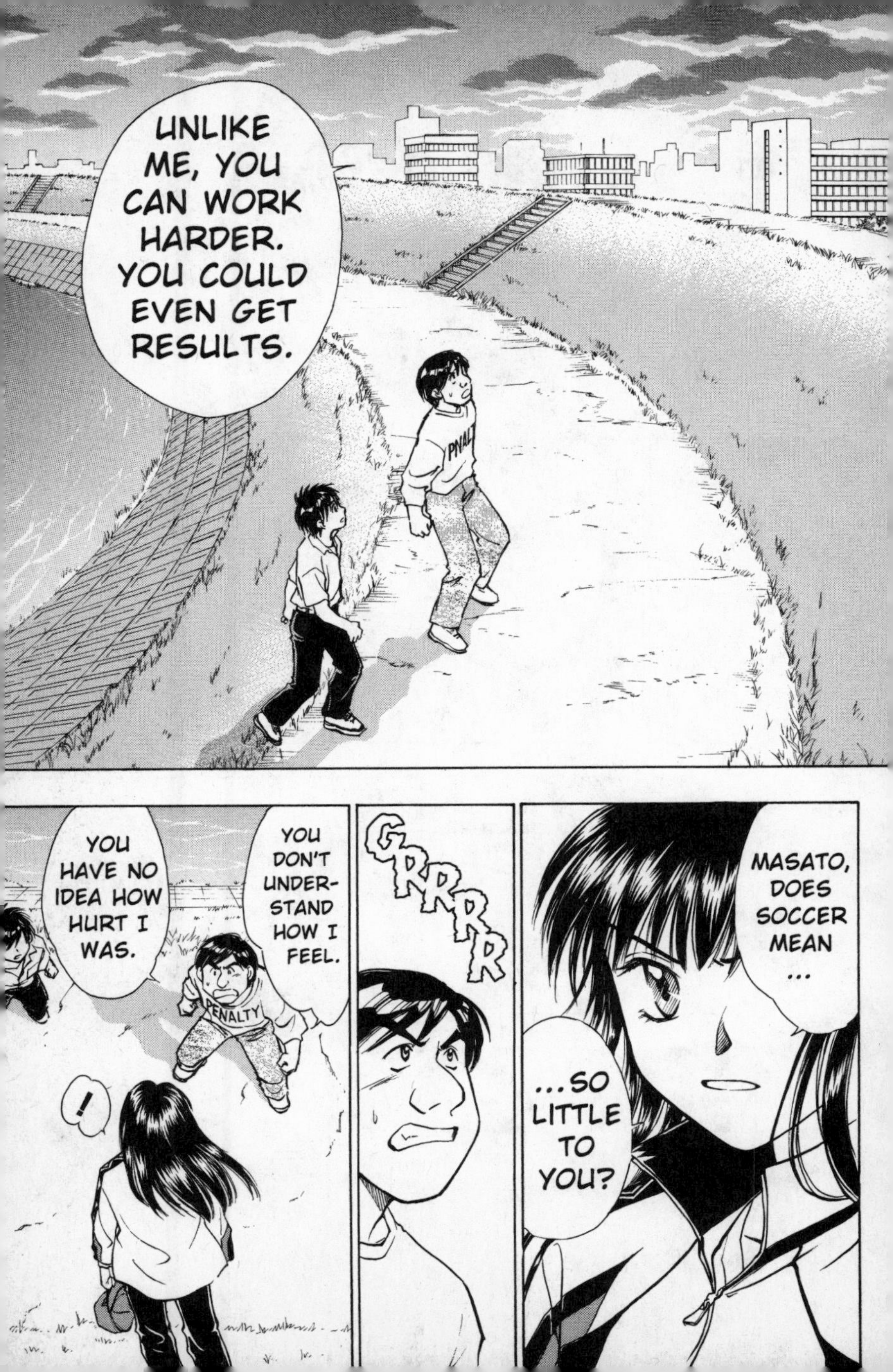
UNLIKE ME, YOU CAN WORK HARDER. YOU COULD EVEN GET RESULTS.
PNALT
MASATO, DOES SOCCER MEAN ...
...SO LITTLE TO YOU?
GRRRR
YOU DON'T UNDER-STAND HOW I FEEL.
YOU HAVE NO IDEA HOW HURT I WAS.
PENALTY
!

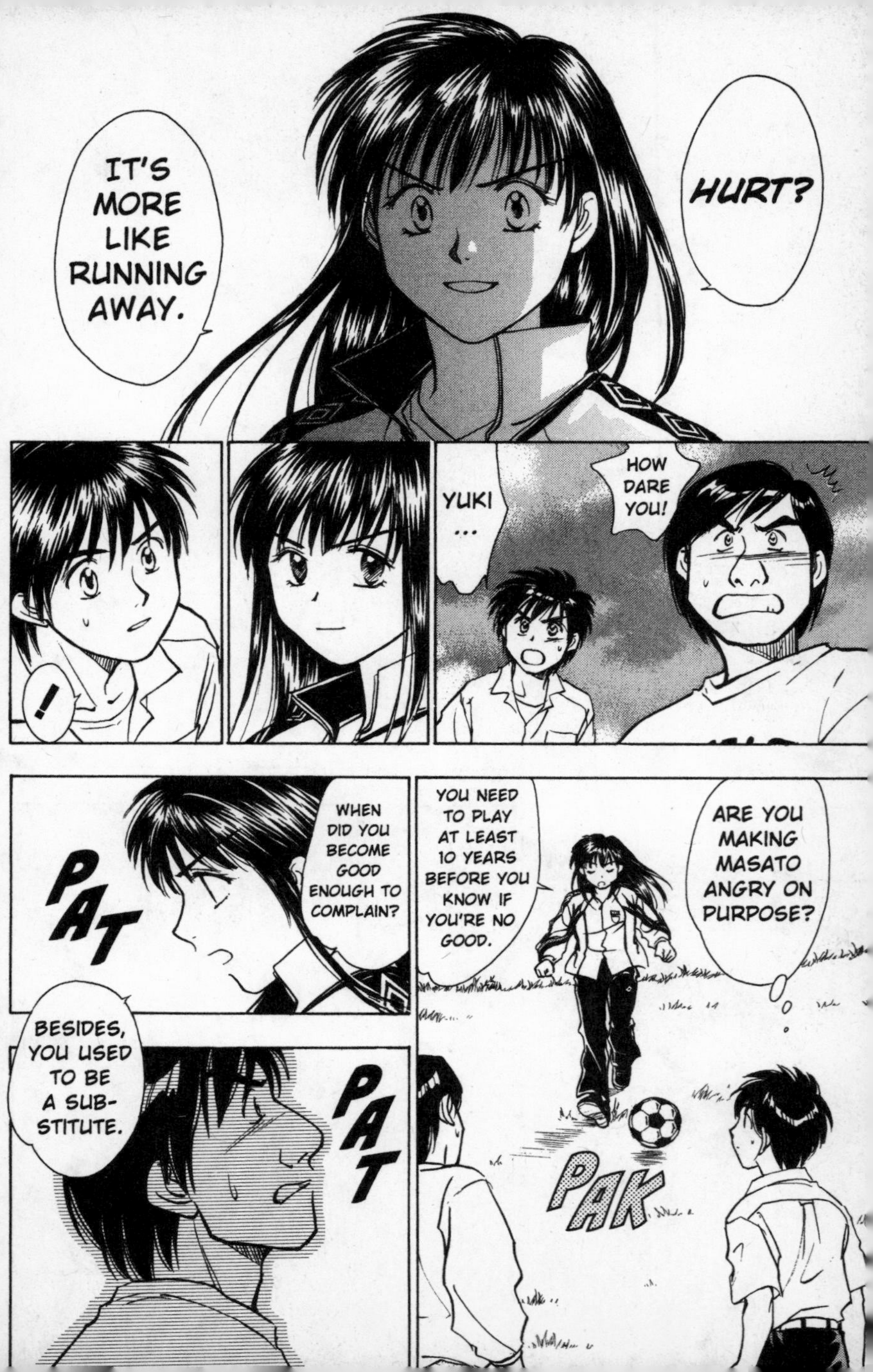
HURT?
IT'S MORE LIKE RUNNING AWAY.
HOW DARE YOU!
YUKI ...
!
ARE YOU MAKING MASATO ANGRY ON PURPOSE?
YOU NEED TO PLAY AT LEAST 10 YEARS BEFORE YOU KNOW IF YOU'RE NO GOOD.
PAK
WHEN DID YOU BECOME GOOD ENOUGH TO COMPLAIN?
PAT
BESIDES, YOU USED TO BE A SUB-STITUTE.
PAT

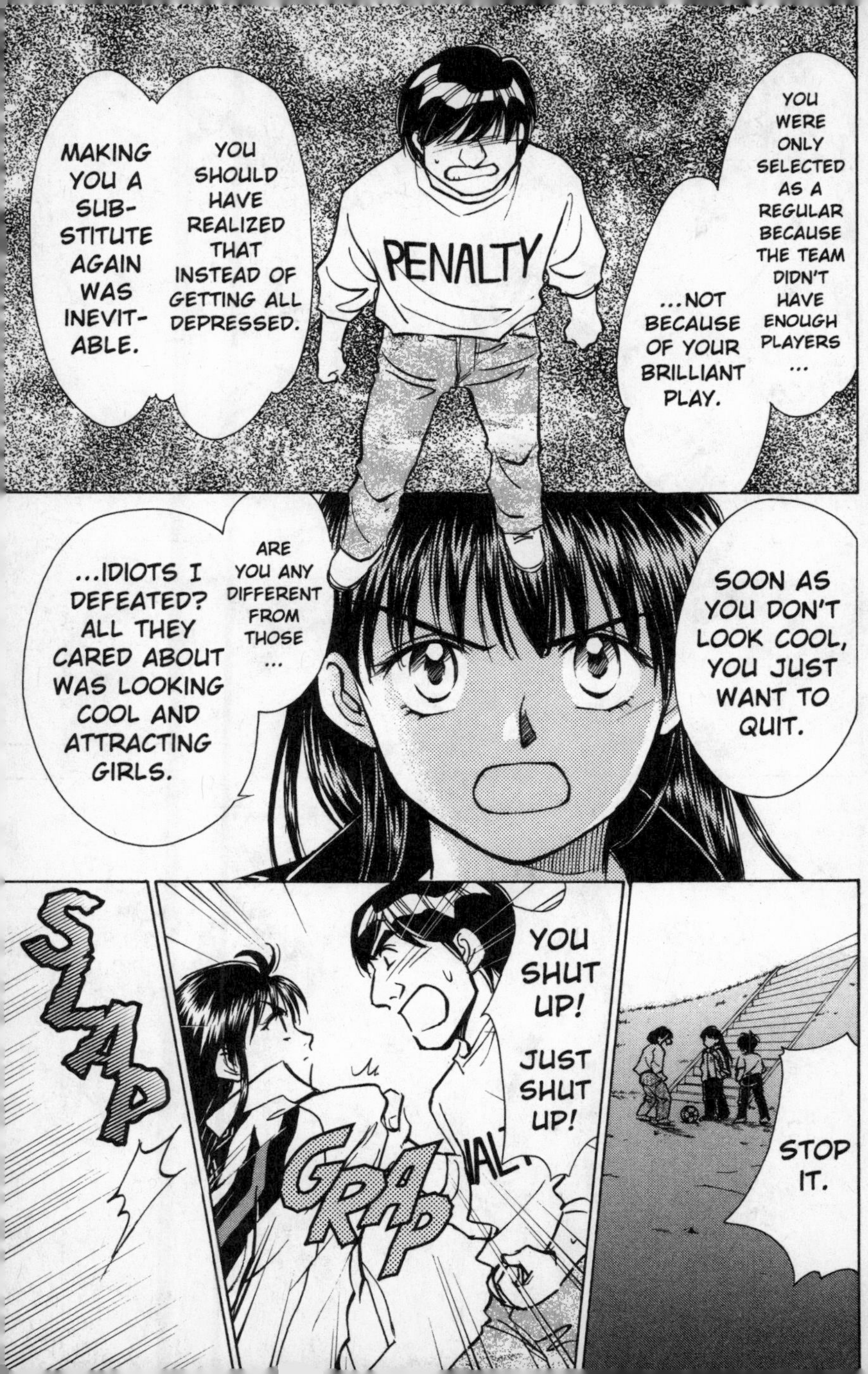
YOU WERE ONLY SELECTED AS A REGULAR BECAUSE THE TEAM DIDN'T HAVE ENOUGH PLAYERS ...
...NOT BECAUSE OF YOUR BRILLIANT PLAY.
PENALTY
YOU SHOULD HAVE REALIZED THAT INSTEAD OF GETTING ALL DEPRESSED.
MAKING YOU A SUB-STITUTE AGAIN WAS INEVIT-ABLE.
SOON AS YOU DON'T LOOK COOL, YOU JUST WANT TO QUIT.
ARE YOU ANY DIFFERENT FROM THOSE ...
...IDIOTS I DEFEATED? ALL THEY CARED ABOUT WAS LOOKING COOL AND ATTRACTING GIRLS.
STOP IT.
YOU SHUT UP!
JUST SHUT UP!
GRAB
SLAP

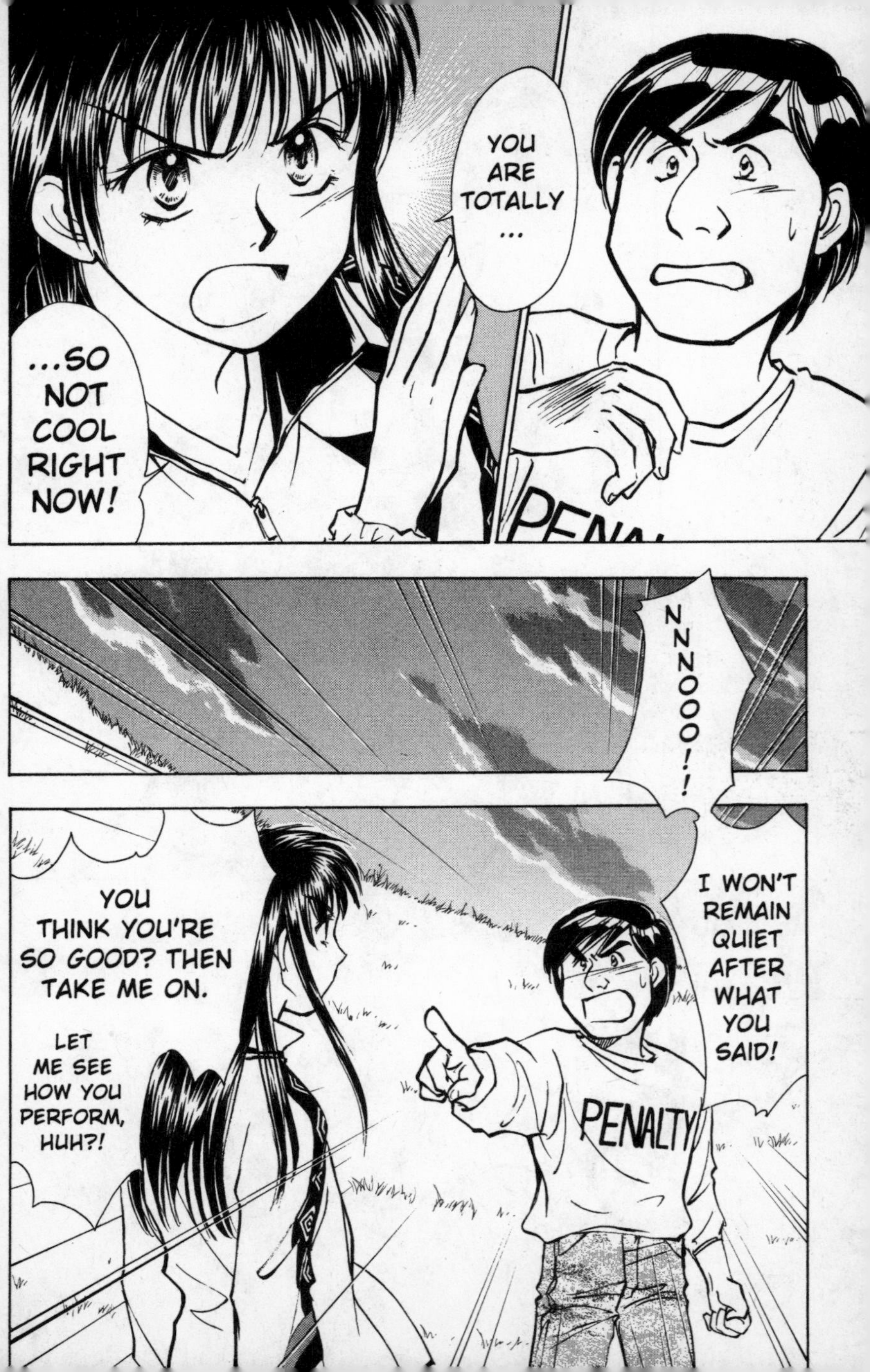
YOU ARE TOTALLY ...
...SO NOT COOL RIGHT NOW!
NNNOOO!!
I WON'T REMAIN QUIET AFTER WHAT YOU SAID!
PENALTY
YOU THINK YOU'RE SO GOOD? THEN TAKE ME ON.
LET ME SEE HOW YOU PERFORM, HUH?!

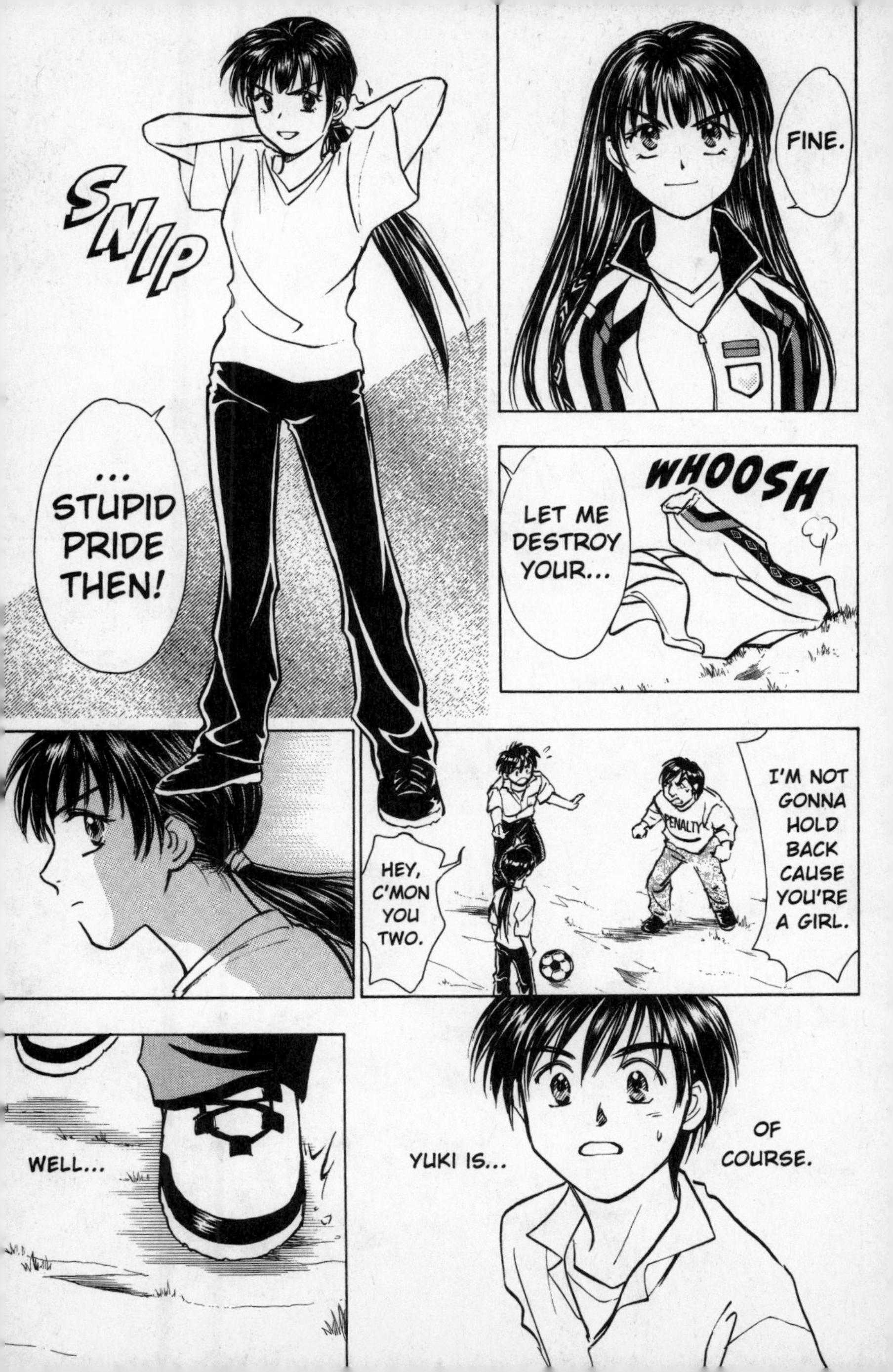
FINE.
WHOOSH
LET ME DESTROY YOUR...
SNIP
... STUPID PRIDE THEN!
I'M NOT GONNA HOLD BACK CAUSE YOU'RE A GIRL.
PENALTY
HEY, C'MON YOU TWO.
OF COURSE.
YUKI IS...
WELL...

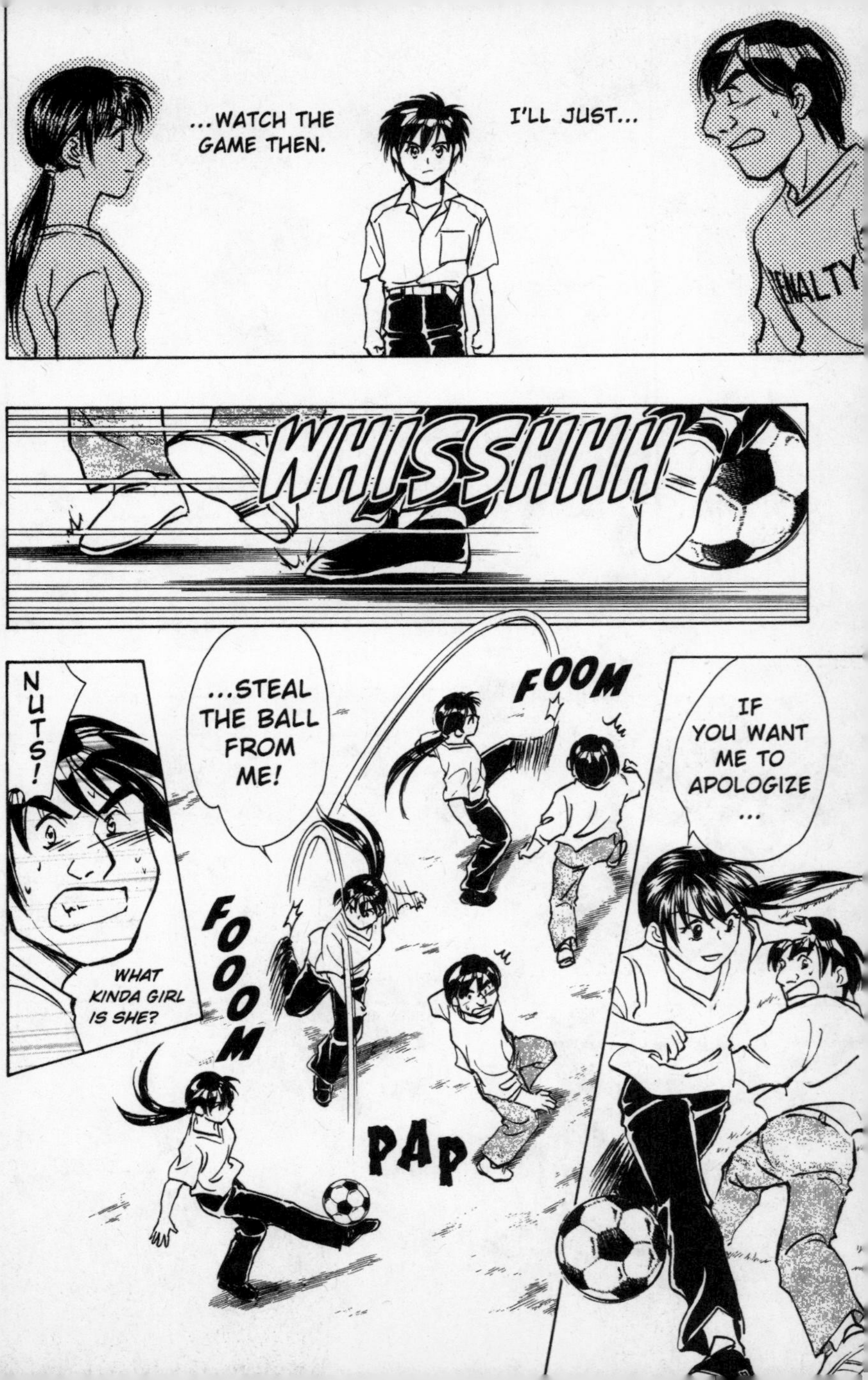
I'LL JUST...
...WATCH THE GAME THEN.
WHISSHHH
IF YOU WANT ME TO APOLOGIZE ...
FOOM
...STEAL THE BALL FROM ME!
FOOOM
PAP
NUTS!
WHAT KINDA GIRL IS SHE?

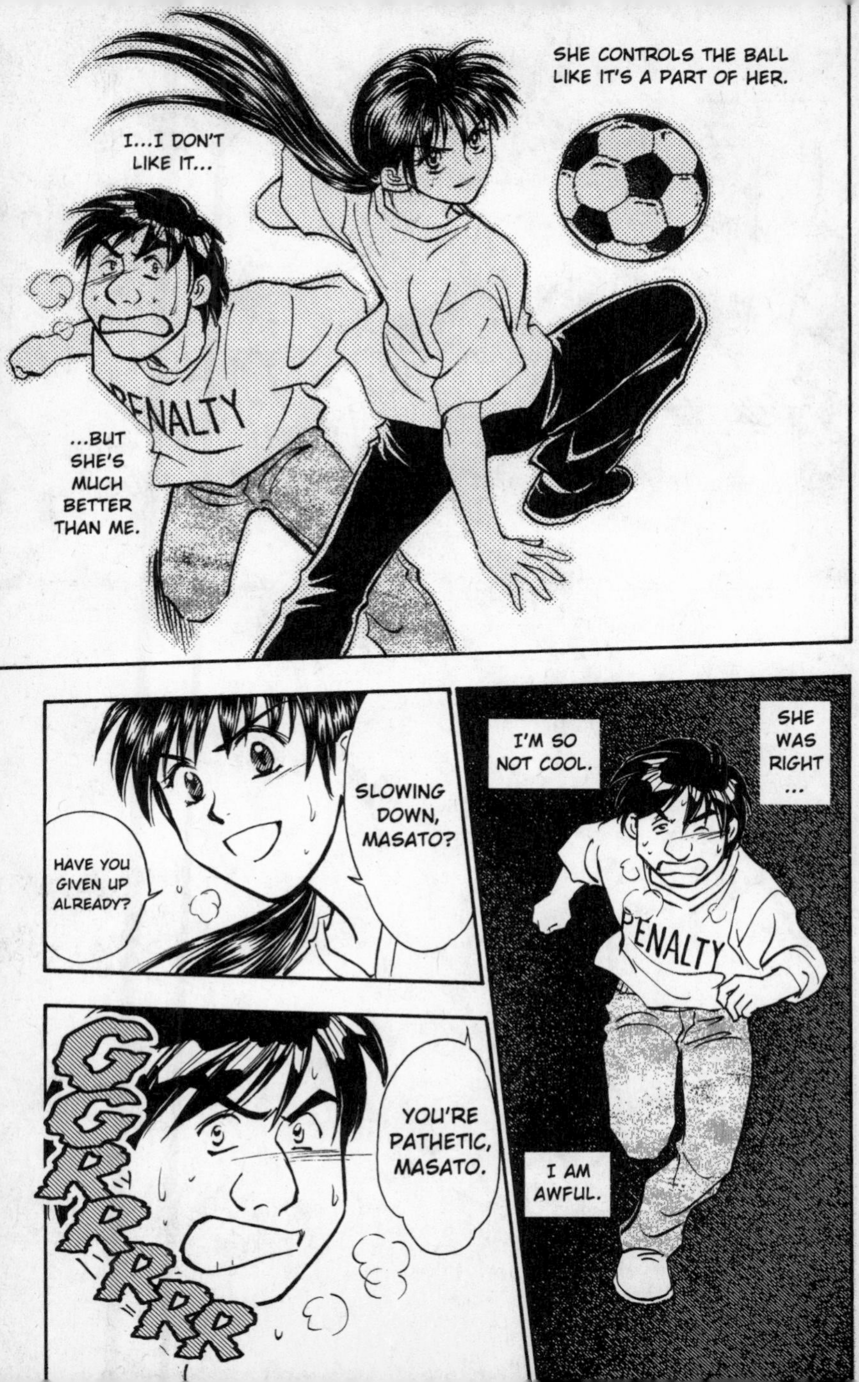
SHE CONTROLS THE BALL LIKE IT'S A PART OF HER.
I...I DON'T LIKE IT...
PENALTY
...BUT SHE'S MUCH BETTER THAN ME.
SHE WAS RIGHT...
I'M SO NOT COOL.
PENALTY
I AM AWFUL.
SLOWING DOWN, MASATO?
HAVE YOU GIVEN UP ALREADY?
YOU'RE PATHETIC, MASATO.
GGRRRRR

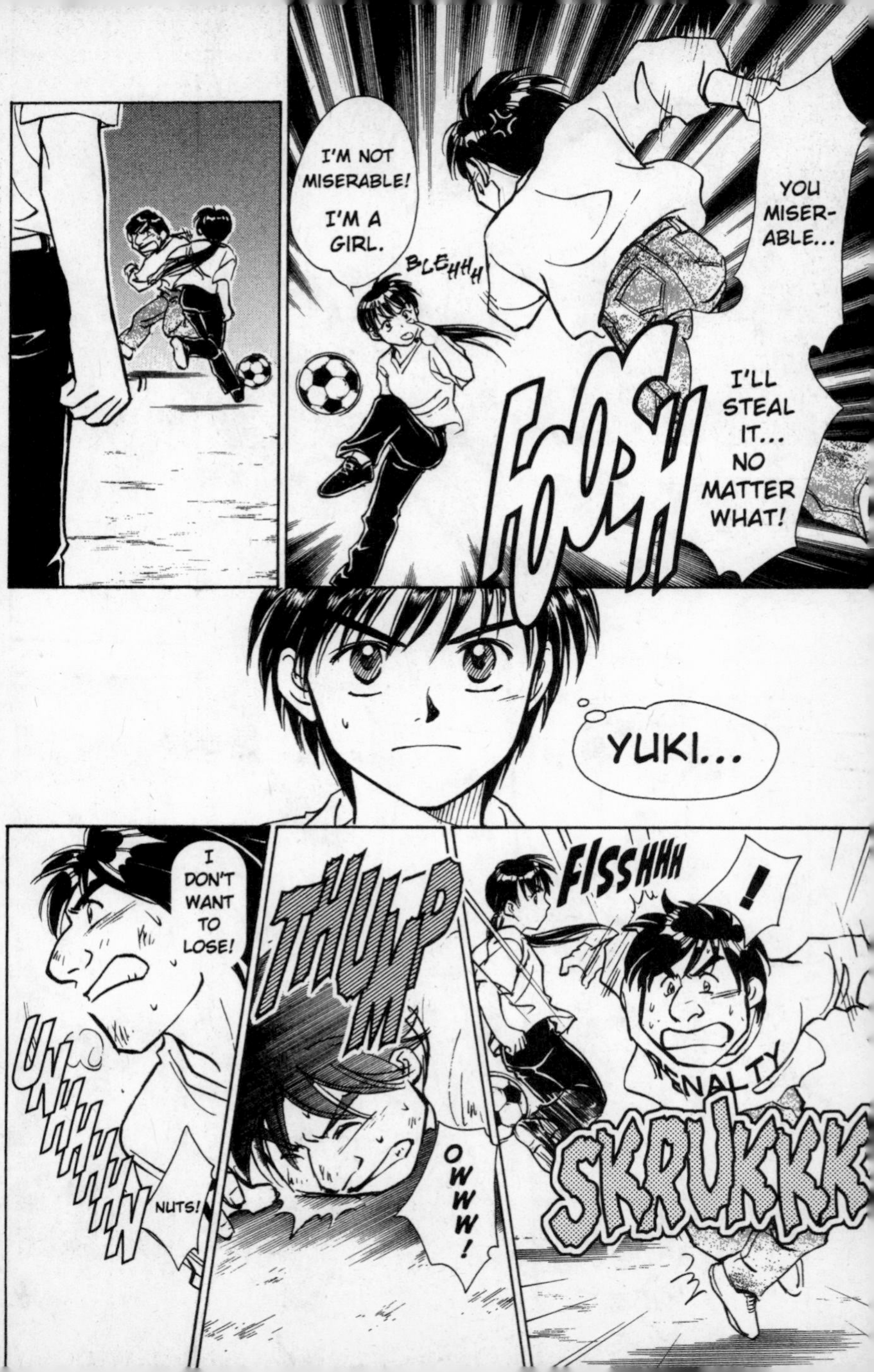
YOU MISER-ABLE...
I'LL STEAL IT... NO MATTER WHAT!
I'M NOT MISERABLE!
I'M A GIRL.
BLEHHH
YUKI...
FISSHHH
!
SKRUKKK
THUMP
OWWW!
I DON'T WANT TO LOSE!
NUTS!

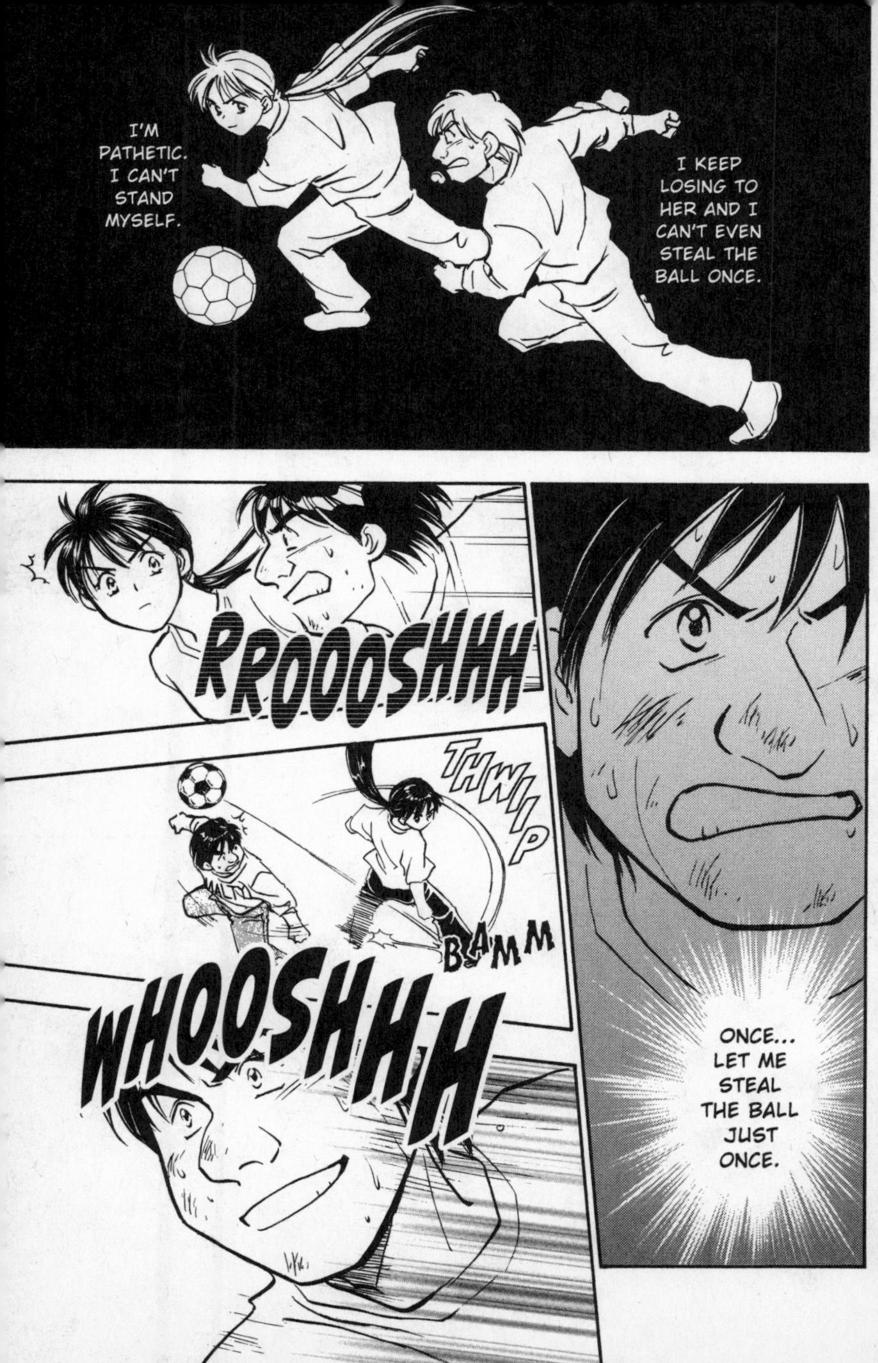
I KEEP LOSING TO HER AND I CAN'T EVEN STEAL THE BALL ONCE.
I'M PATHETIC. I CAN'T STAND MYSELF.
ONCE... LET ME STEAL THE BALL JUST ONCE.
RROOOSHHH
THWIIP
BAMM
WHOOSHHH

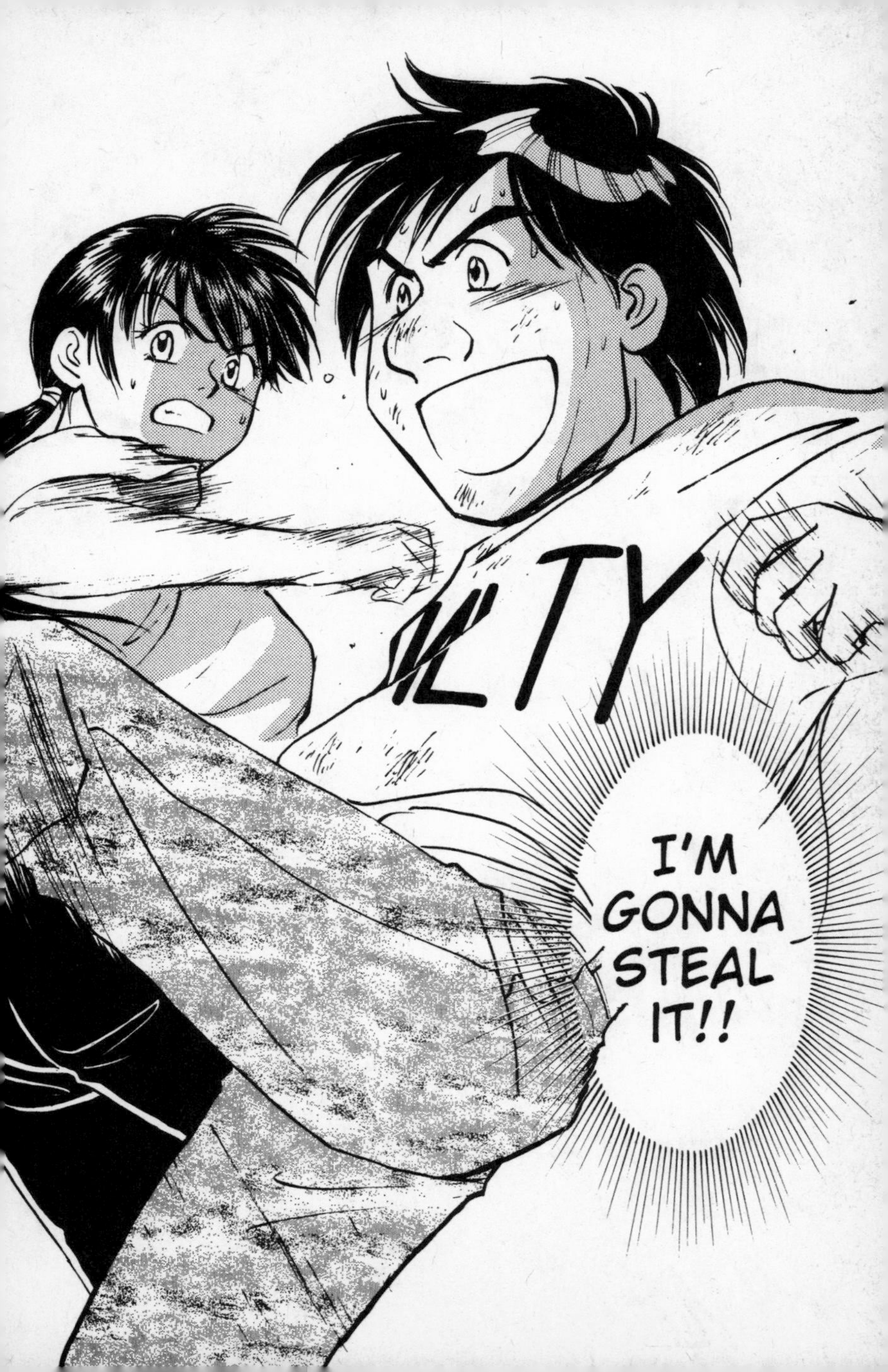
I'M GONNA STEAL IT!!

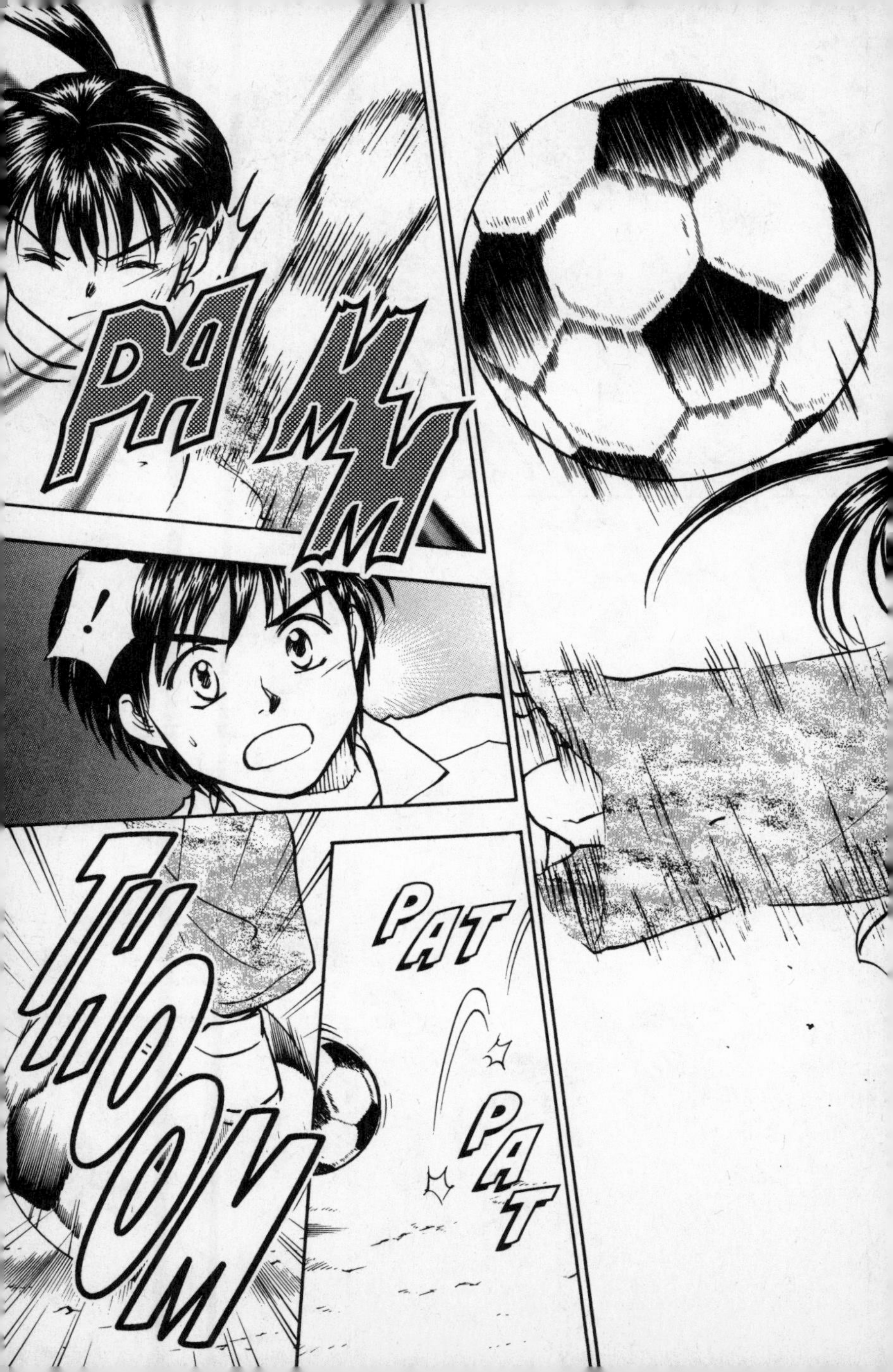
PAMM
!
PAT
PAT
PAT
THOOOM

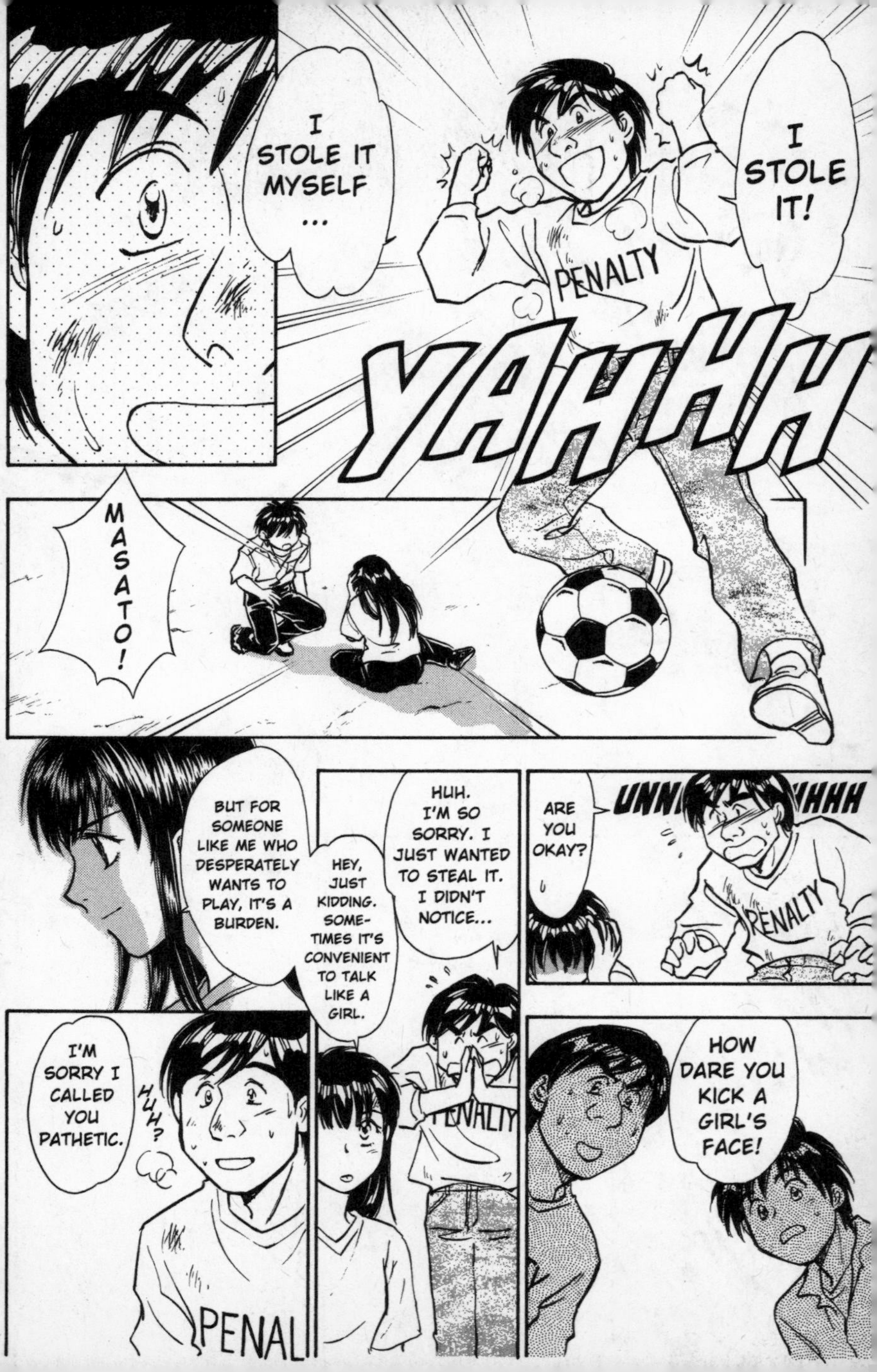
I STOLE IT!
YAHHH
I STOLE IT MYSELF ...
PENALTY
MASATO!
UNN
HHHH
ARE YOU OKAY?
PENALTY
HOW DARE YOU KICK A GIRL'S FACE!
HUH. I'M SO SORRY. I JUST WANTED TO STEAL IT. I DIDN'T NOTICE...
HEY, JUST KIDDING. SOME- TIMES IT'S CONVENIENT TO TALK LIKE A GIRL.
PENALTY
BUT FOR SOMEONE LIKE ME WHO DESPERATELY WANTS TO PLAY, IT'S A BURDEN.
I'M SORRY I CALLED YOU PATHETIC.
HUH?
PENAL

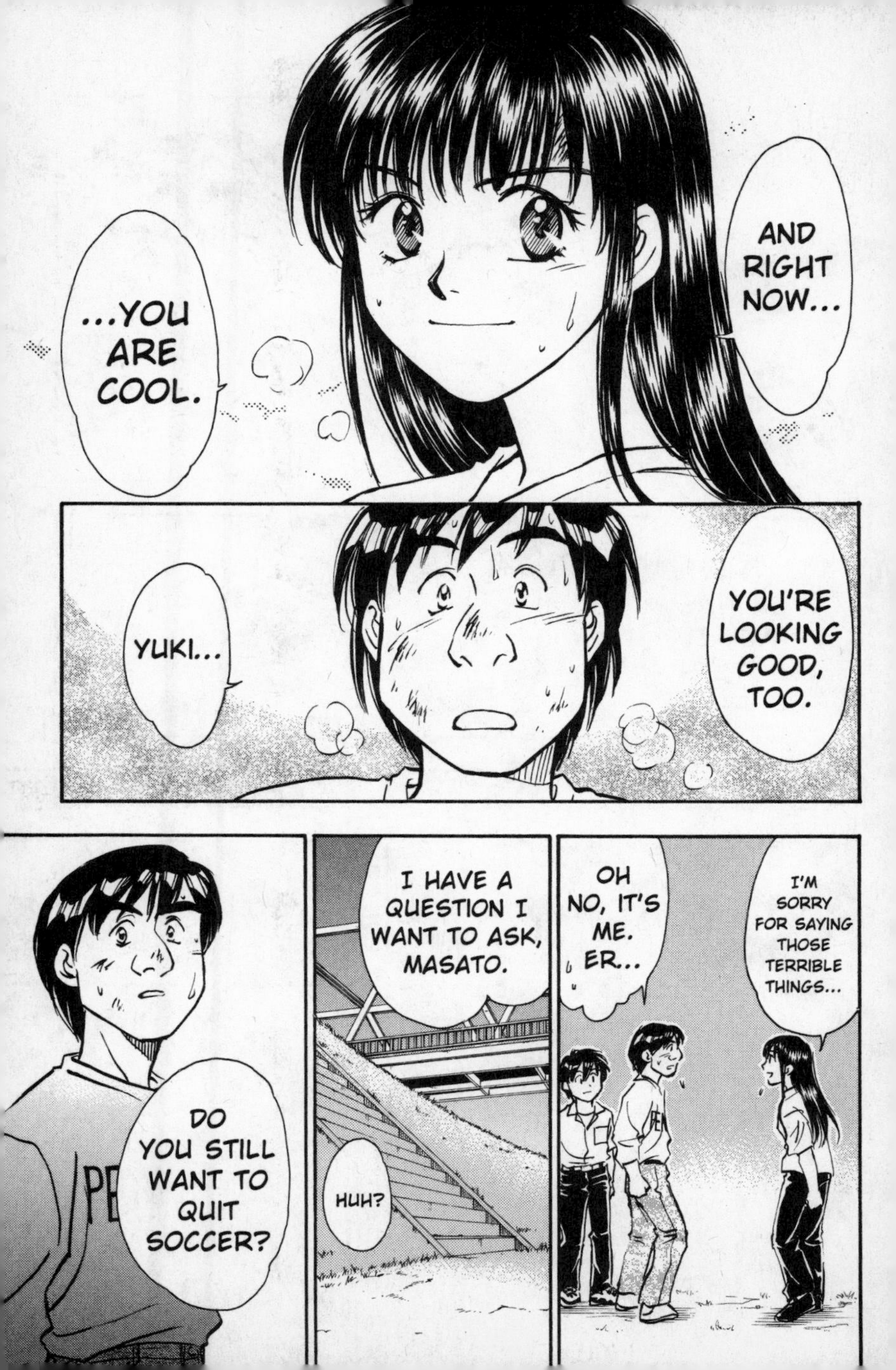
AND RIGHT NOW...
...YOU ARE COOL.
YOU'RE LOOKING GOOD, TOO.
YUKI...
I'M SORRY FOR SAYING THOSE TERRIBLE THINGS...
OH NO, IT'S ME. ER...
I HAVE A QUESTION I WANT TO ASK, MASATO.
HUH?
DO YOU STILL WANT TO QUIT SOCCER?

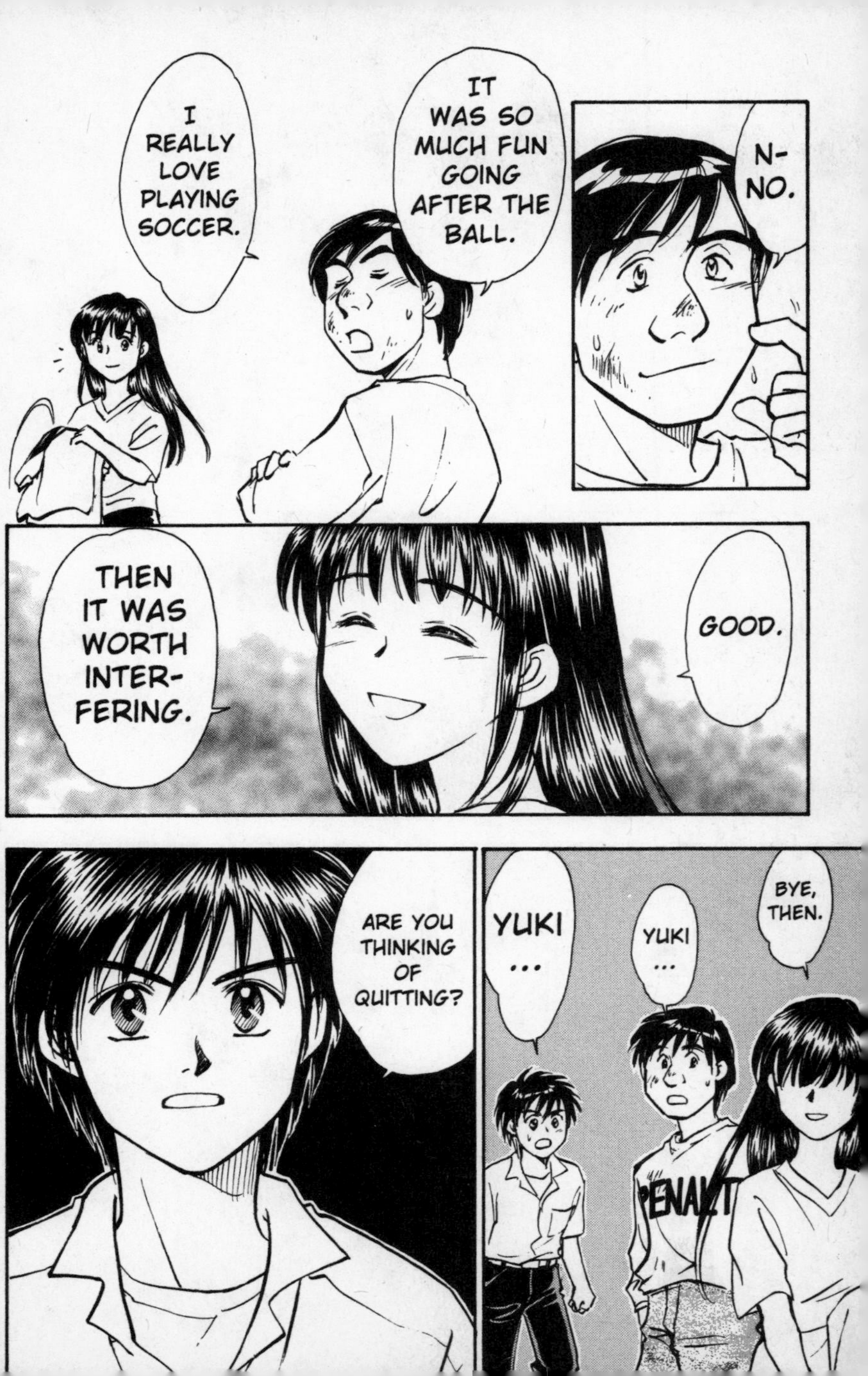
N-NO.
IT WAS SO MUCH FUN GOING AFTER THE BALL.
I REALLY LOVE PLAYING SOCCER.
GOOD.
THEN IT WAS WORTH INTER-FERING.
BYE, THEN.
YUKI ...
YUKI ...
ARE YOU THINKING OF QUITTING?

READ THIS WAY

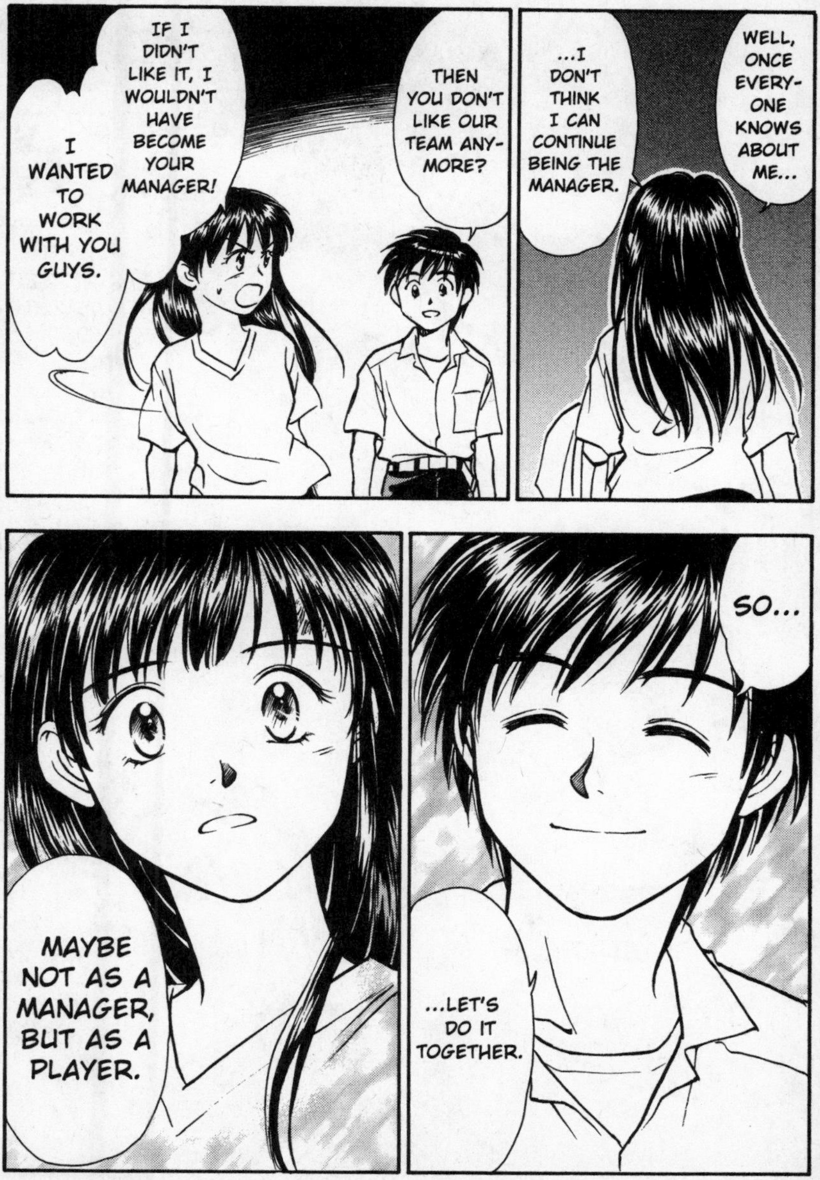
WELL, ONCE EVERY-ONE KNOWS ABOUT ME...
...I DON'T THINK I CAN CONTINUE BEING THE MANAGER.
THEN YOU DON'T LIKE OUR TEAM ANY-MORE?
IF I DIDN'T LIKE IT, I WOULDN'T HAVE BECOME YOUR MANAGER!
I WANTED TO WORK WITH YOU GUYS.
SO...
...LET'S DO IT TOGETHER.
MAYBE NOT AS A MANAGER, BUT AS A PLAYER.

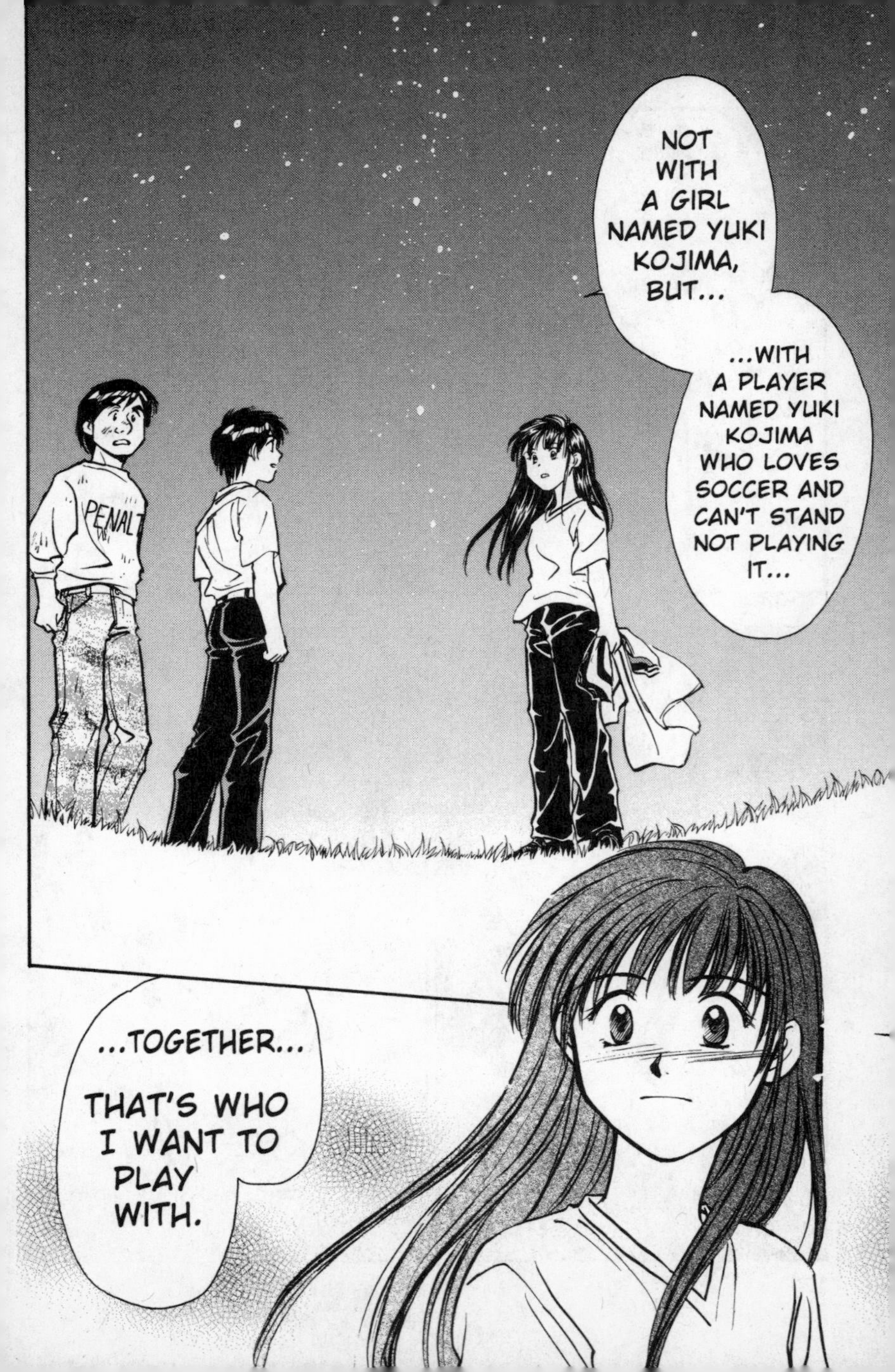
NOT WITH A GIRL NAMED YUKI KOJIMA, BUT...
...WITH A PLAYER NAMED YUKI KOJIMA WHO LOVES SOCCER AND CAN'T STAND NOT PLAYING IT...
PENALT
...TOGETHER...
THAT'S WHO I WANT TO PLAY WITH.

READ THIS WAY

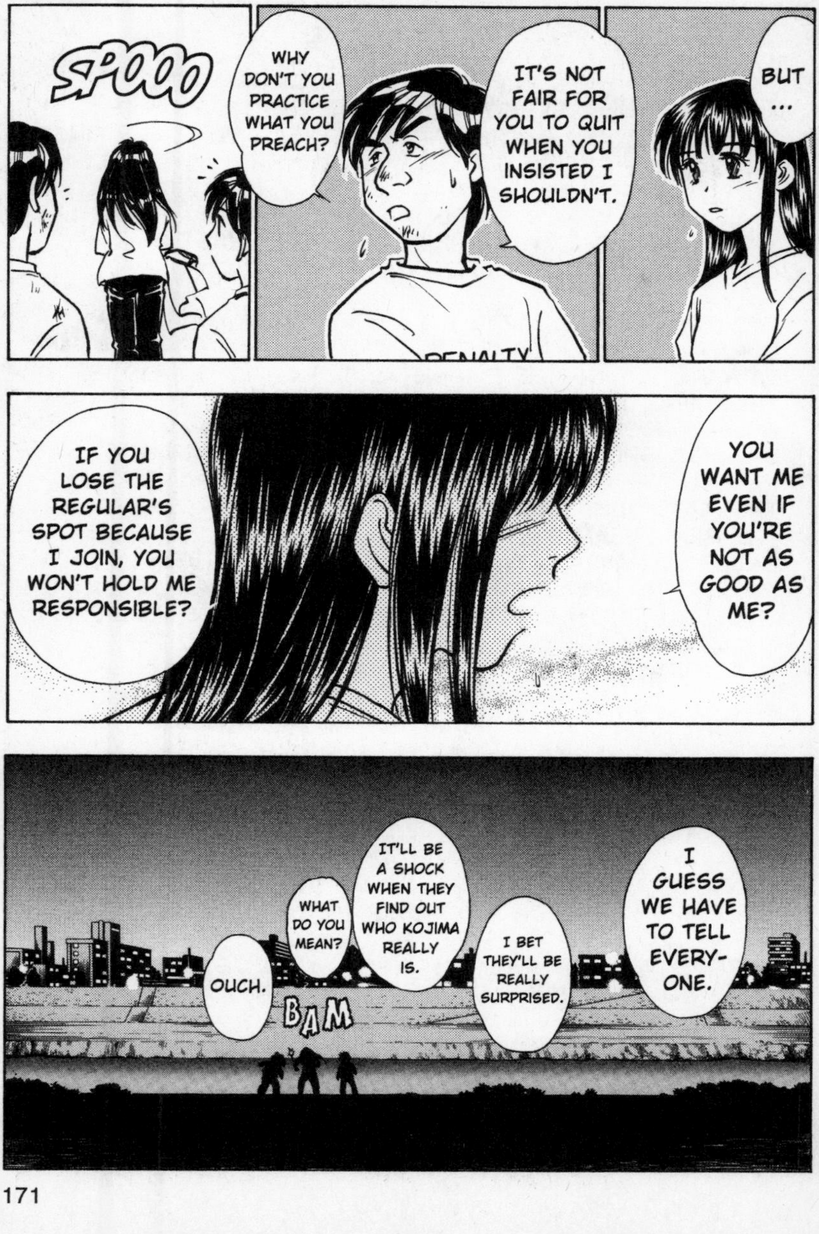
BUT ...
IT'S NOT FAIR FOR YOU TO QUIT WHEN YOU INSISTED I SHOULDN'T.
WHY DON'T YOU PRACTICE WHAT YOU PREACH?
SPOOO
YOU WANT ME EVEN IF YOU'RE NOT AS GOOD AS ME?
IF YOU LOSE THE REGULAR'S SPOT BECAUSE I JOIN, YOU WON'T HOLD ME RESPONSIBLE?
I GUESS WE HAVE TO TELL EVERY-ONE.
I BET THEY'LL BE REALLY SURPRISED.
IT'LL BE A SHOCK WHEN THEY FIND OUT WHO KOJIMA REALLY IS.
WHAT DO YOU MEAN?
BAM
OUCH.

# ● WOMEN'S SOCCER

THE HISTORY OF WOMEN'S SOCCER IS VERY SHORT.
IT WAS 1979 WHEN THE SOCCER ASSOCIATION OFFICIALLY
ACCEPTED THEIR REGISTRATION. ONLY 52 TEAMS
REGISTERED, AND IN THE FOLLOWING YEAR, 1980, THE FIRST
ALL JAPAN WOMEN'S SOCCER CHAMPIONSHIP WAS HELD.

LATER ON, IN 1989, JAPAN WOMEN'S LEAGUE (L-LEAGUE)
WAS ESTABLISHED WITH SIX TEAMS. THIS WAS THE
COUNTERPART TO THE MEN'S JAPAN LEAGUE.

FURTHERMORE, JAPAN THE REPRESENTATIVE TEAM WAS
FORMED, AND IT BECAME THE THIRD BEST, AFTER CHINA AND
TAIWAN. DURING THE BEIJING ASIA CHAMPIONSHIP IN 1990,
THE JAPAN TEAM DEFEATED TAIWAN AND BECAME THE
SECOND BEST IN ASIA. IN 1991, THE FIRST WORLD
CHAMPIONSHIP WAS HELD IN CHINA, AND THE JAPAN TEAM
PASSED THE ASIA PRIMARY, THUS SUCCESSFULLY SEIZING
THE OPPORTUNITY TO PLAY IN THE WORLD'S ARENA BEFORE
THE MEN'S TEAM DID. ALTHOUGH THE TEAM DID NOT WIN
ONCE AND HAD TO RETIRE FROM THE PRIMARY LEAGUE
DURING THE WORLD CHAMPIONSHIP, FOUR YEARS LATER,
THE JAPAN TEAM DEFEATED BRAZIL DURING THE SECOND
CHAMPIONSHIP HELD IN SWEDEN AND MADE IT TO THE
BEST EIGHT.

CURRENTLY, THERE ARE MORE THAN A THOUSAND
REGISTERED TEAMS AND MORE THAN 20,000 REGISTERED
PLAYERS. THE WOMEN'S SOCCER POPULATION IS CLEARLY
INCREASING. HOWEVER, THERE AREN'T ENOUGH
SPECTATORS FOR THEIR GAMES, AND COUPLED WITH
JAPAN'S TERRIBLE ECONOMIC CONDITIONS, MANY OF THE
L-LEAGUE TEAMS ARE DISBANDING. DESPITE THAT, IN 1999,
THE THIRD WORLD CHAMPIONSHIP WILL BE HELD IN THE
U.S.A., AND IN 2000, THE SYDNEY OLYMPICS WILL BE HELD.
JAPAN'S REPRESENTATIVE TEAM OF WOMEN'S SOCCER IS
STILL WORKING HARD, AIMING FOR HIGHER GOALS THAN
THE MEN'S.

--TATSUYA WATANABE (WINNING RUN)

# STAGE.35 Training Camp For Each!

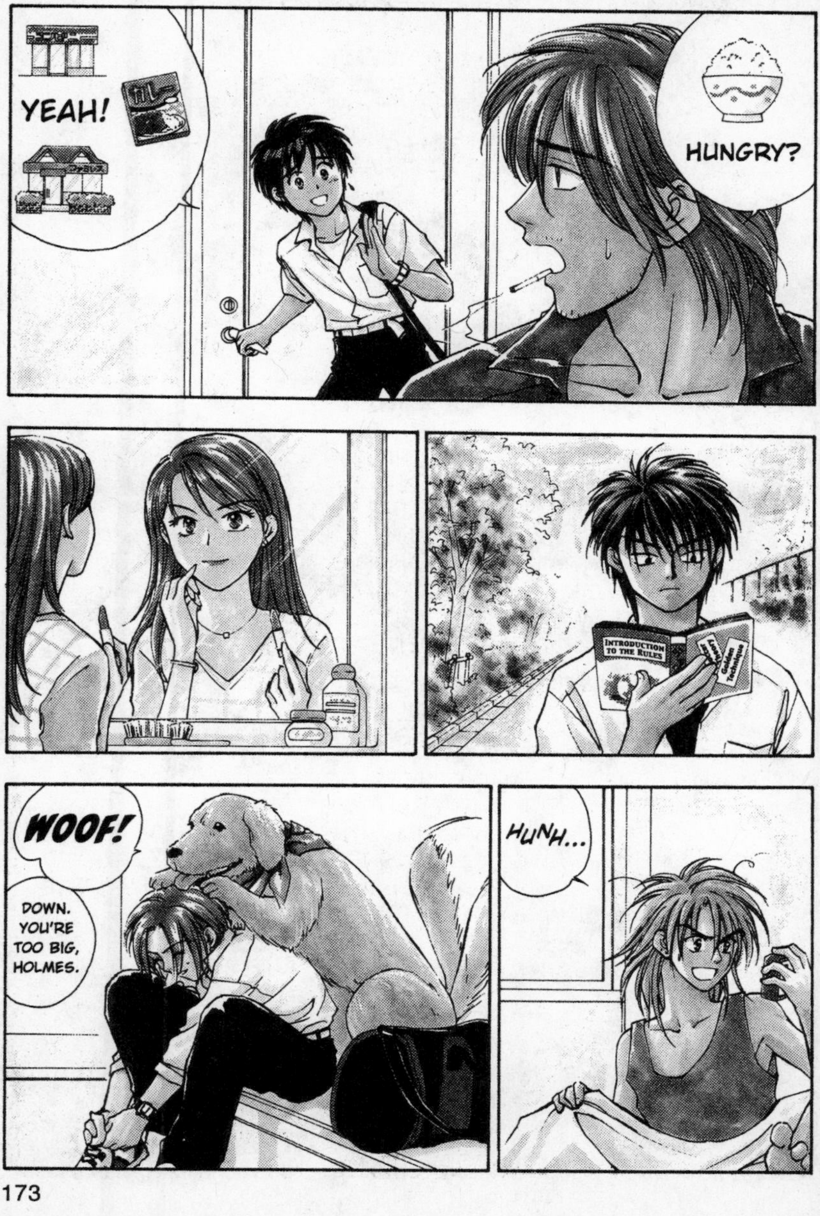
HUNGRY?
YEAH!
INTRODUCTION TO THE RULES
Golden Technique
HUNH...
WOOF!
DOWN. YOU'RE TOO BIG, HOLMES.

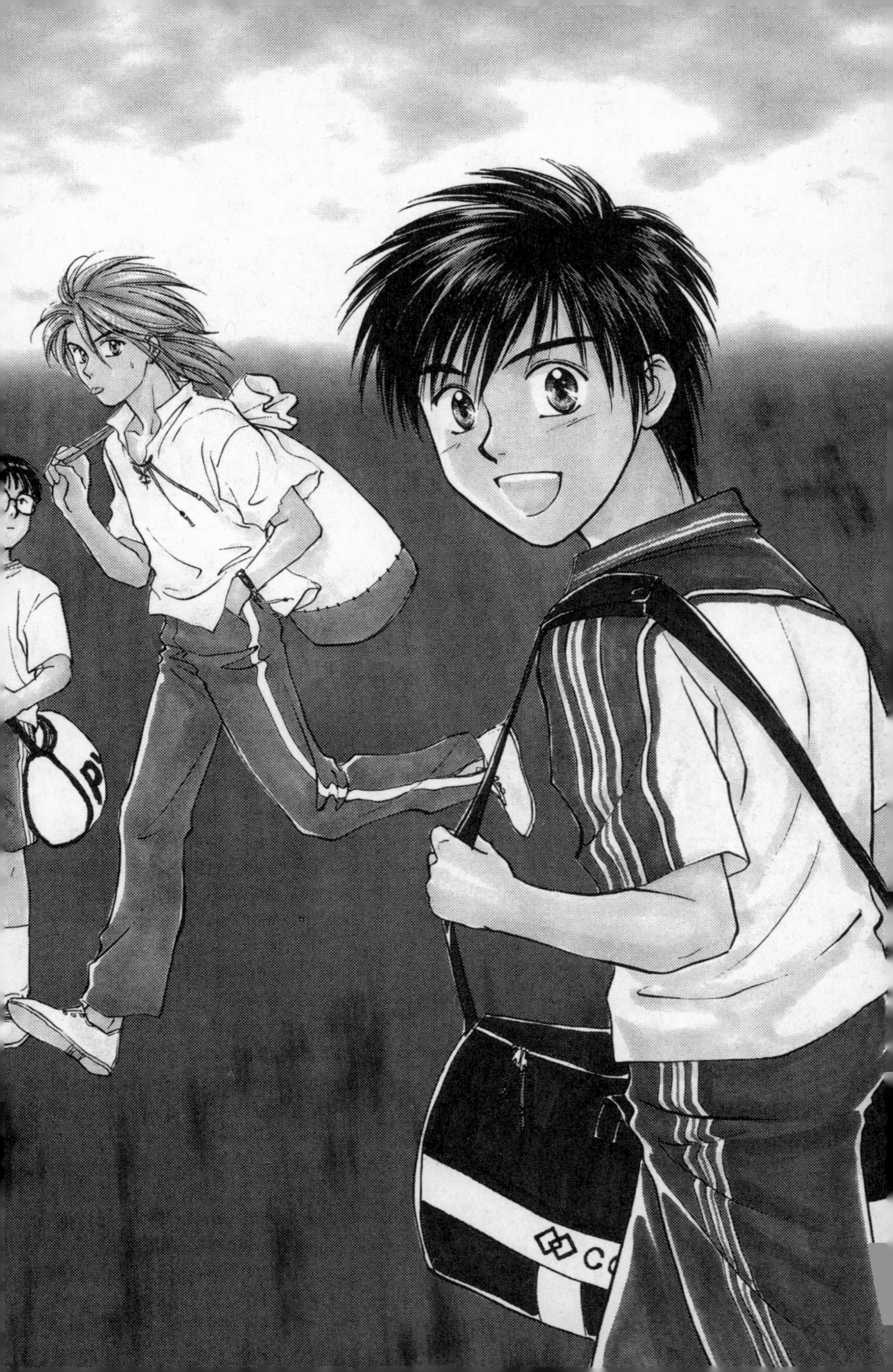

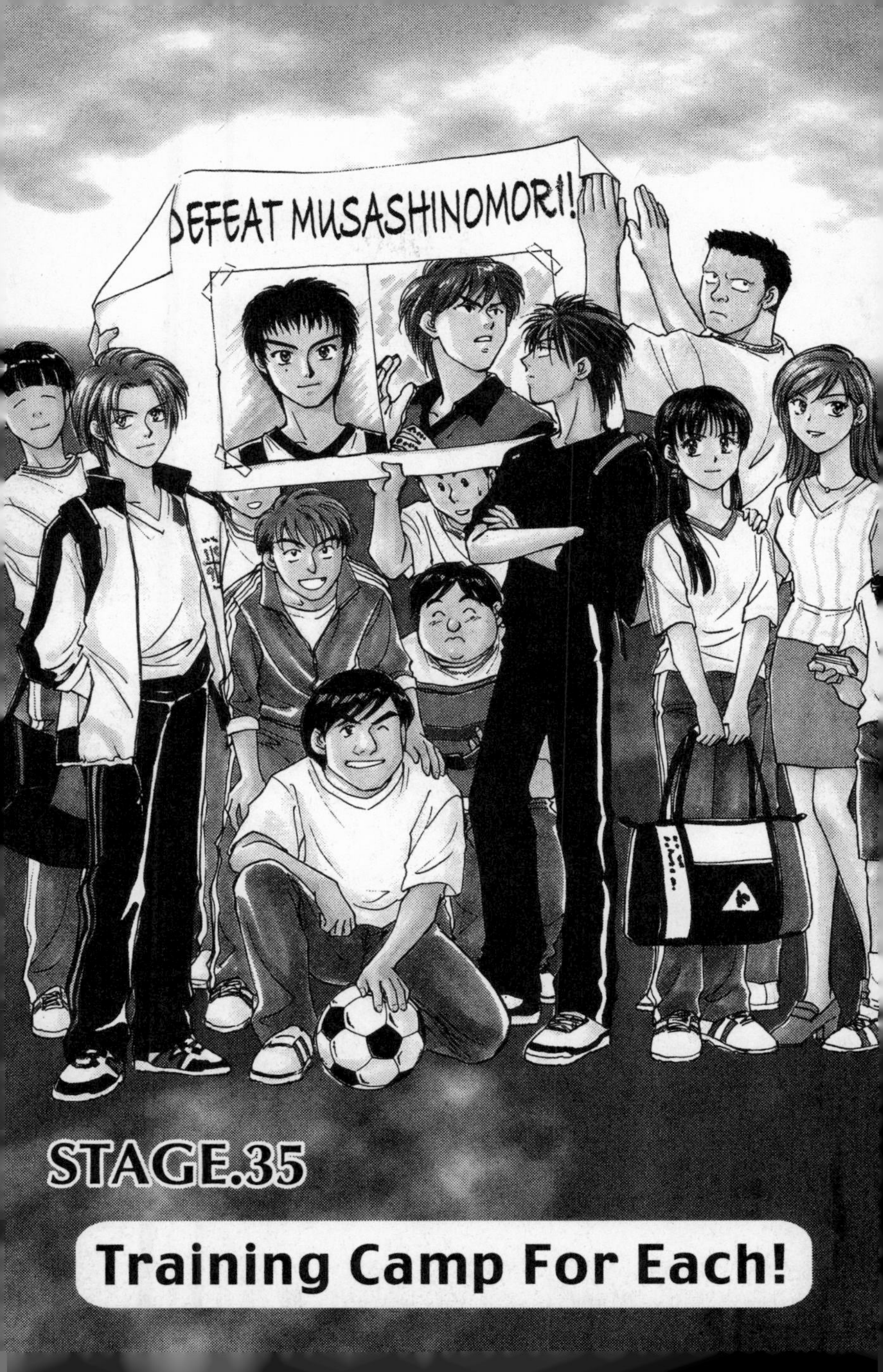
DEFEAT MUSASHINOMORI!!

# STAGE.35

## Training Camp For Each!

WHISKK

READ THIS WAY

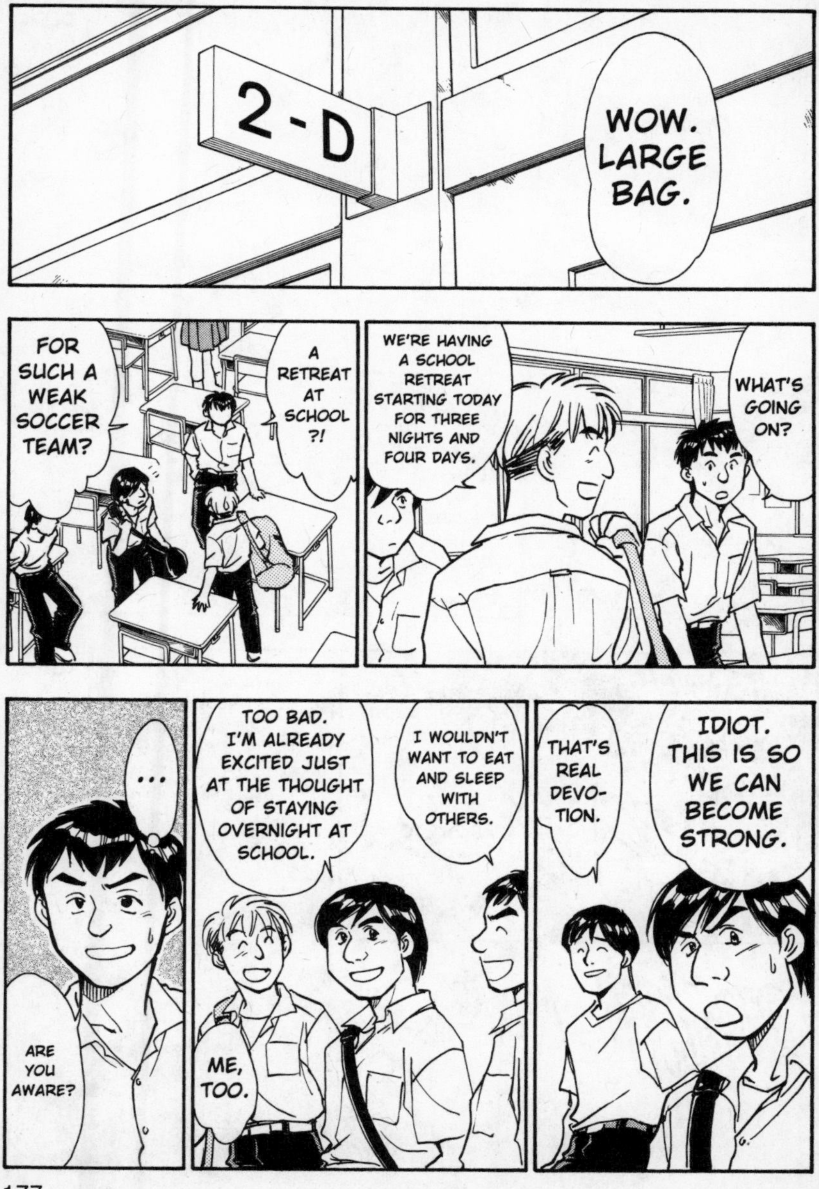
2-D
WOW. LARGE BAG.
WHAT'S GOING ON?
WE'RE HAVING A SCHOOL RETREAT STARTING TODAY FOR THREE NIGHTS AND FOUR DAYS.
A RETREAT AT SCHOOL ?!
FOR SUCH A WEAK SOCCER TEAM?
IDIOT. THIS IS SO WE CAN BECOME STRONG.
THAT'S REAL DEVO-TION.
I WOULDN'T WANT TO EAT AND SLEEP WITH OTHERS.
TOO BAD. I'M ALREADY EXCITED JUST AT THE THOUGHT OF STAYING OVERNIGHT AT SCHOOL.
ME, TOO.
...
ARE YOU AWARE?

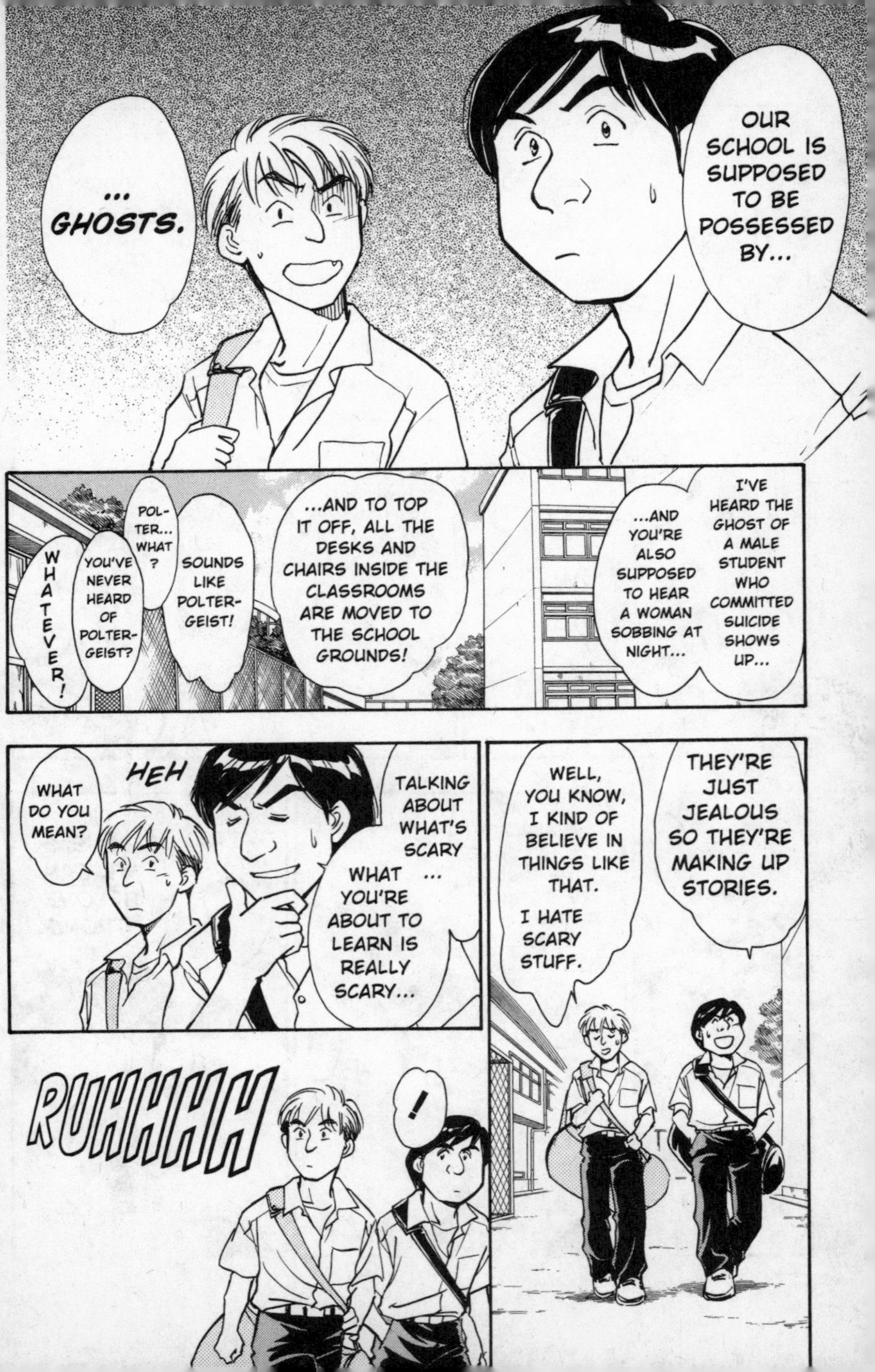
OUR SCHOOL IS SUPPOSED TO BE POSSESSED BY...
... GHOSTS.
I'VE HEARD THE GHOST OF A MALE STUDENT WHO COMMITTED SUICIDE SHOWS UP...
...AND YOU'RE ALSO SUPPOSED TO HEAR A WOMAN SOBBING AT NIGHT...
...AND TO TOP IT OFF, ALL THE DESKS AND CHAIRS INSIDE THE CLASSROOMS ARE MOVED TO THE SCHOOL GROUNDS!
SOUNDS LIKE POLTER-GEIST!
POL-TER... WHAT?
YOU'VE NEVER HEARD OF POLTER-GEIST?
WHATEVER!
THEY'RE JUST JEALOUS SO THEY'RE MAKING UP STORIES.
WELL, YOU KNOW, I KIND OF BELIEVE IN THINGS LIKE THAT.
I HATE SCARY STUFF.
TALKING ABOUT WHAT'S SCARY ...
WHAT YOU'RE ABOUT TO LEARN IS REALLY SCARY...
HEH
WHAT DO YOU MEAN?
!
RUHHHH

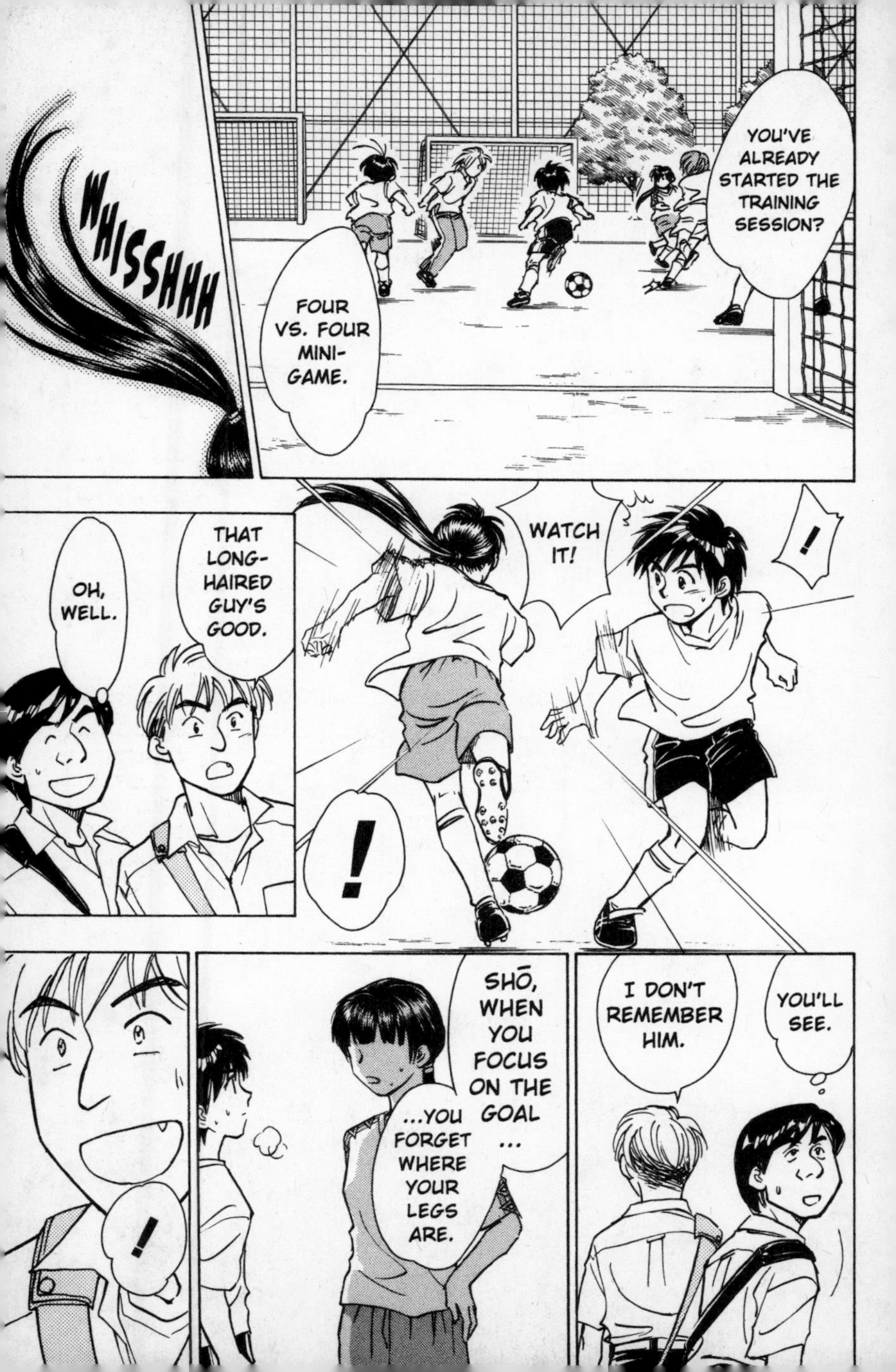
YOU'VE ALREADY STARTED THE TRAINING SESSION?
FOUR VS. FOUR MINI-GAME.
WHISSHHH
!
WATCH IT!
!
THAT LONG-HAIRED GUY'S GOOD.
OH, WELL.
YOU'LL SEE.
I DON'T REMEMBER HIM.
SHŌ, WHEN YOU FOCUS ON THE GOAL ...
...YOU FORGET WHERE YOUR LEGS ARE.
!

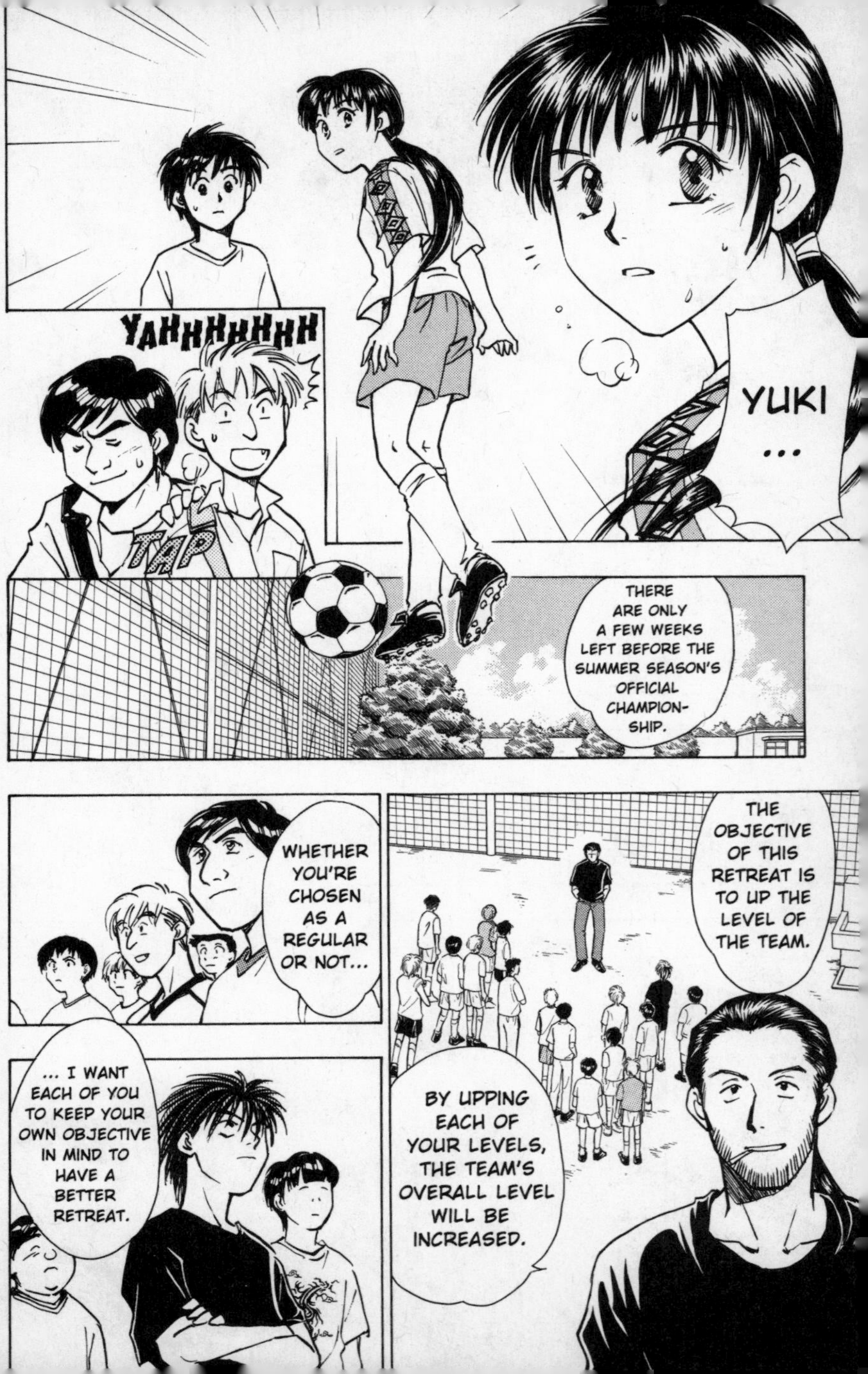

YUKI ...
YAHHHHHHHH
TAP
THERE ARE ONLY A FEW WEEKS LEFT BEFORE THE SUMMER SEASON'S OFFICIAL CHAMPIONSHIP.
THE OBJECTIVE OF THIS RETREAT IS TO UP THE LEVEL OF THE TEAM.
BY UPPING EACH OF YOUR LEVELS, THE TEAM'S OVERALL LEVEL WILL BE INCREASED.
WHETHER YOU'RE CHOSEN AS A REGULAR OR NOT...
... I WANT EACH OF YOU TO KEEP YOUR OWN OBJECTIVE IN MIND TO HAVE A BETTER RETREAT.

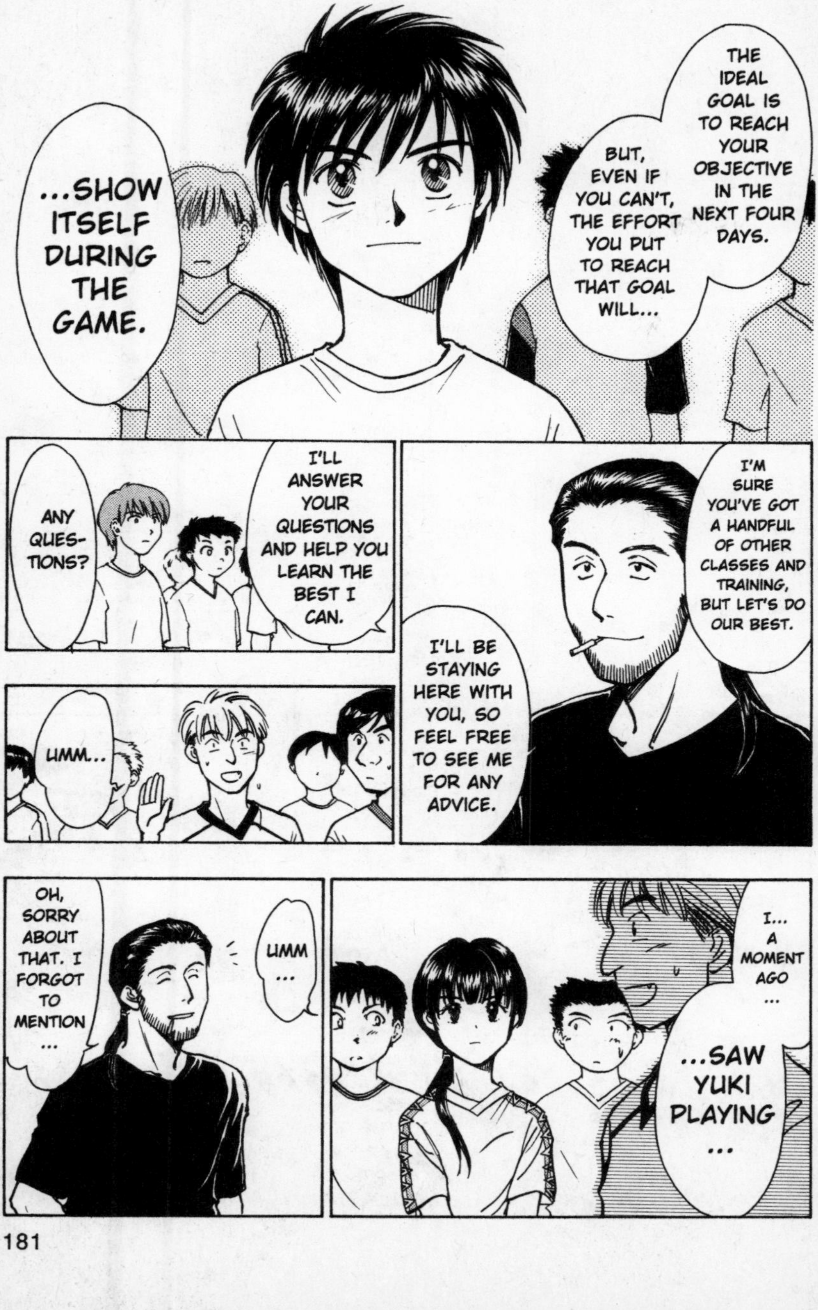
THE IDEAL GOAL IS TO REACH YOUR OBJECTIVE IN THE NEXT FOUR DAYS.
BUT, EVEN IF YOU CAN'T, THE EFFORT YOU PUT TO REACH THAT GOAL WILL...
...SHOW ITSELF DURING THE GAME.
I'M SURE YOU'VE GOT A HANDFUL OF OTHER CLASSES AND TRAINING, BUT LET'S DO OUR BEST.
I'LL BE STAYING HERE WITH YOU, SO FEEL FREE TO SEE ME FOR ANY ADVICE.
I'LL ANSWER YOUR QUESTIONS AND HELP YOU LEARN THE BEST I CAN.
ANY QUES-TIONS?
UMM...
I... A MOMENT AGO ...
...SAW YUKI PLAYING ...
UMM ...
OH, SORRY ABOUT THAT. I FORGOT TO MENTION ...

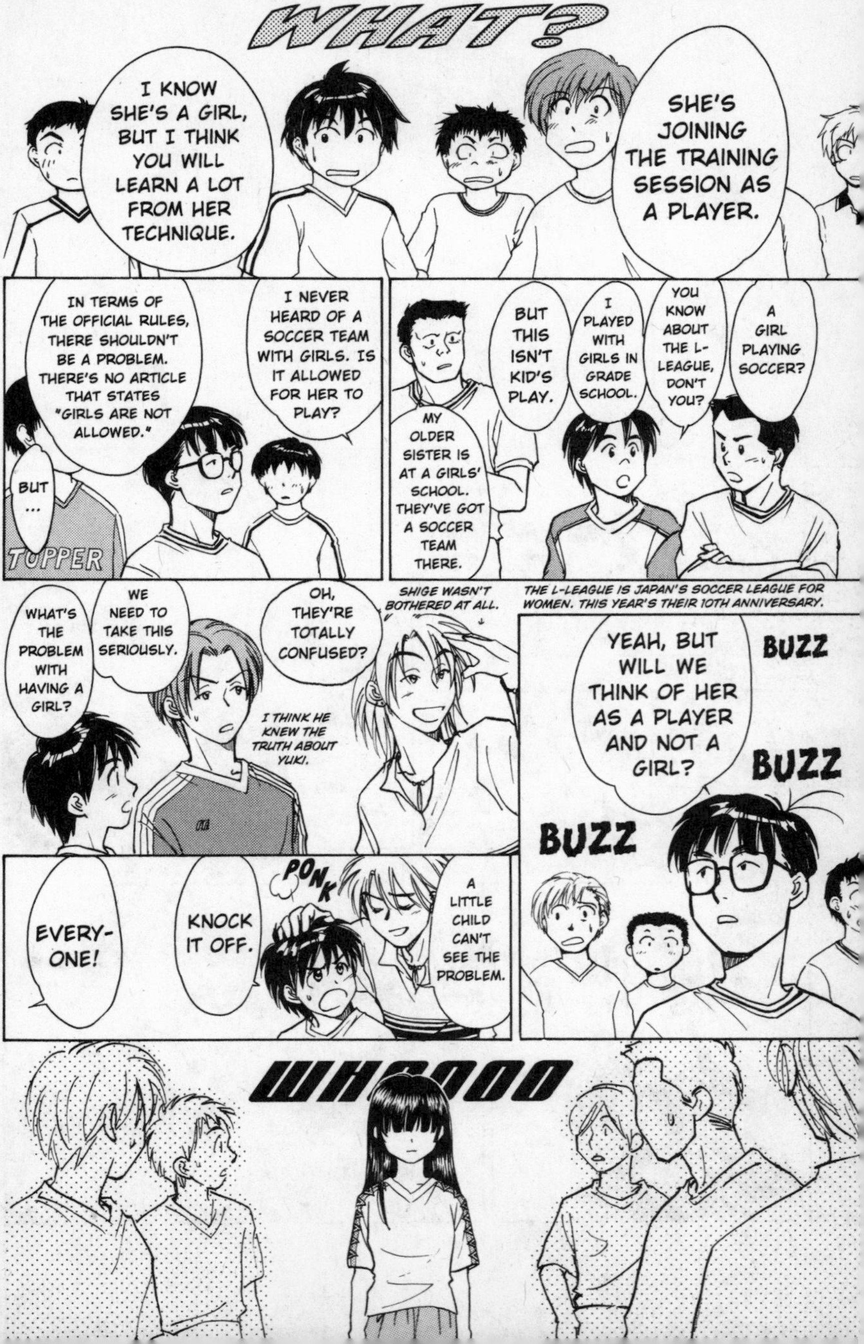
WHAT?
SHE'S JOINING THE TRAINING SESSION AS A PLAYER.
I KNOW SHE'S A GIRL, BUT I THINK YOU WILL LEARN A LOT FROM HER TECHNIQUE.
A GIRL PLAYING SOCCER?
YOU KNOW ABOUT THE L-LEAGUE, DON'T YOU?
I PLAYED WITH GIRLS IN GRADE SCHOOL.
BUT THIS ISN'T KID'S PLAY.
MY OLDER SISTER IS AT A GIRLS' SCHOOL. THEY'VE GOT A SOCCER TEAM THERE.
I NEVER HEARD OF A SOCCER TEAM WITH GIRLS. IS IT ALLOWED FOR HER TO PLAY?
IN TERMS OF THE OFFICIAL RULES, THERE SHOULDN'T BE A PROBLEM. THERE'S NO ARTICLE THAT STATES "GIRLS ARE NOT ALLOWED."
BUT ...
TOPPER
THE L-LEAGUE IS JAPAN'S SOCCER LEAGUE FOR WOMEN. THIS YEAR'S THEIR 10TH ANNIVERSARY.
YEAH, BUT WILL WE THINK OF HER AS A PLAYER AND NOT A GIRL?
BUZZ
BUZZ
BUZZ
SHIGE WASN'T BOTHERED AT ALL.
OH, THEY'RE TOTALLY CONFUSED?
I THINK HE KNEW THE TRUTH ABOUT YUKI.
WE NEED TO TAKE THIS SERIOUSLY.
WHAT'S THE PROBLEM WITH HAVING A GIRL?
A LITTLE CHILD CAN'T SEE THE PROBLEM.
PONK
KNOCK IT OFF.
EVERY-ONE!
WHOOOO

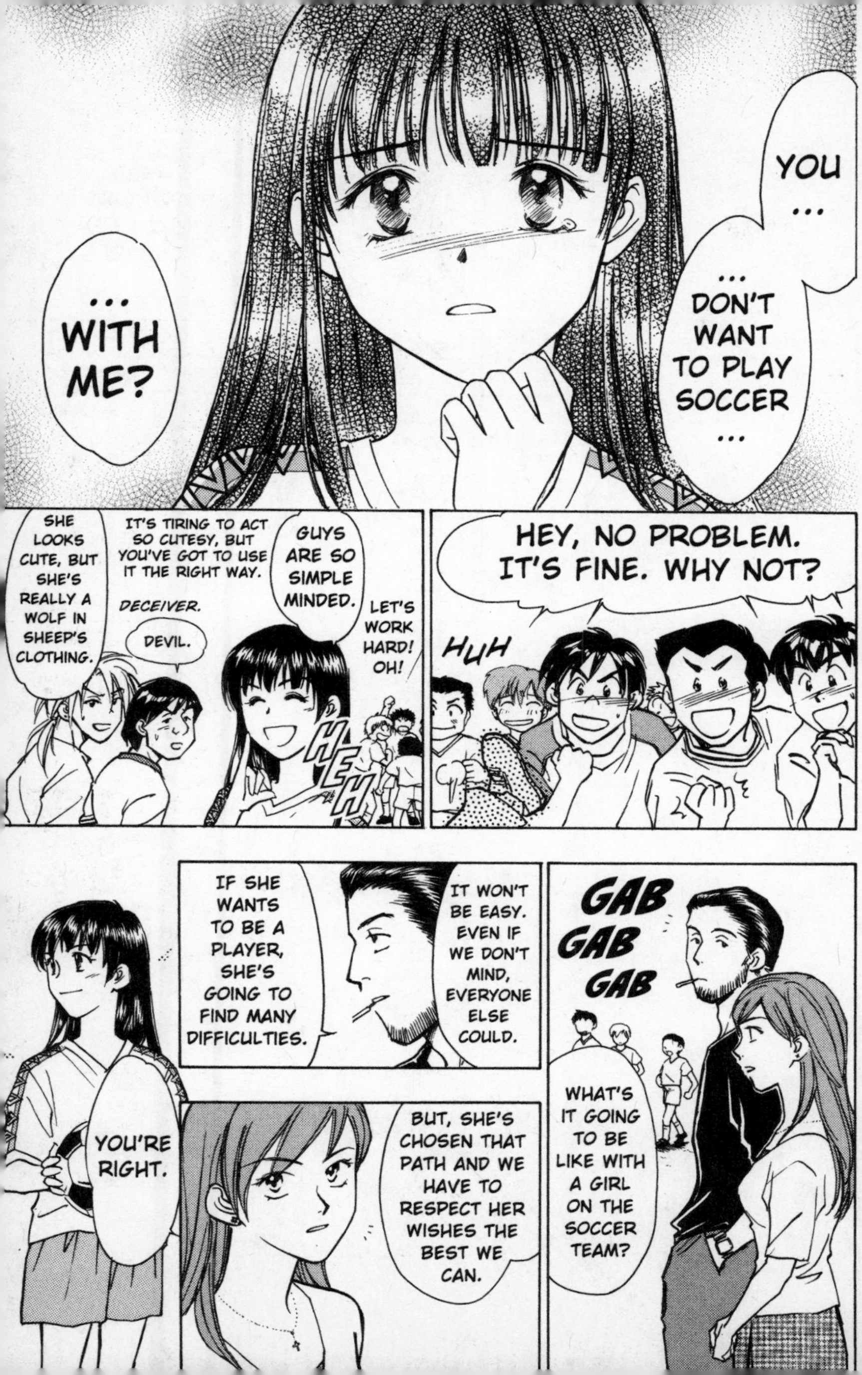

YOU ...
... DON'T WANT TO PLAY SOCCER ...
... WITH ME?
HEY, NO PROBLEM. IT'S FINE. WHY NOT?
HUH
LET'S WORK HARD! OH!
GUYS ARE SO SIMPLE MINDED.
HEH
IT'S TIRING TO ACT SO CUTESY, BUT YOU'VE GOT TO USE IT THE RIGHT WAY.
DECEIVER.
DEVIL.
SHE LOOKS CUTE, BUT SHE'S REALLY A WOLF IN SHEEP'S CLOTHING.
GAB GAB GAB
WHAT'S IT GOING TO BE LIKE WITH A GIRL ON THE SOCCER TEAM?
IT WON'T BE EASY. EVEN IF WE DON'T MIND, EVERYONE ELSE COULD.
IF SHE WANTS TO BE A PLAYER, SHE'S GOING TO FIND MANY DIFFICULTIES.
BUT, SHE'S CHOSEN THAT PATH AND WE HAVE TO RESPECT HER WISHES THE BEST WE CAN.
YOU'RE RIGHT.

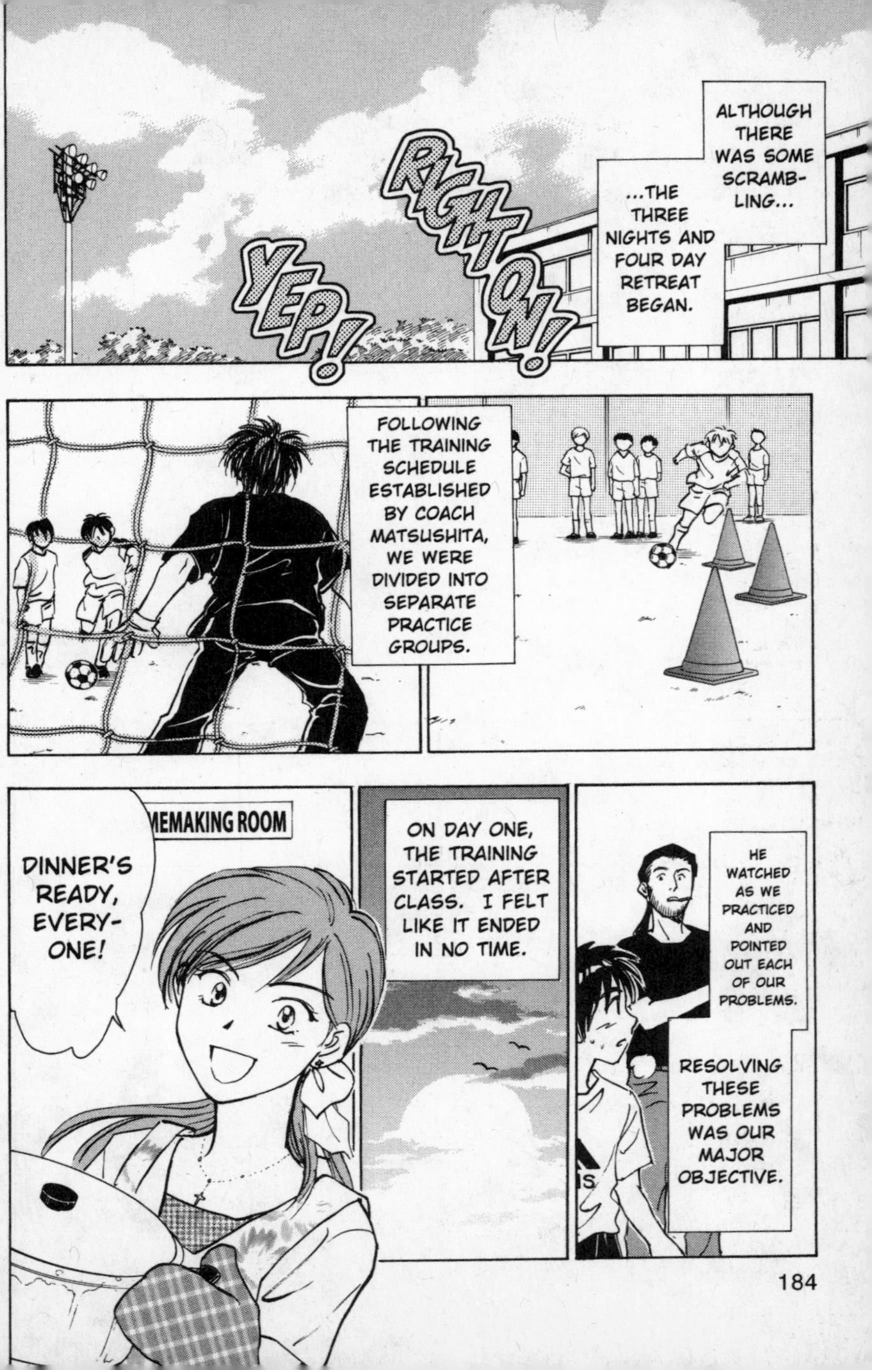

ALTHOUGH THERE WAS SOME SCRAMB- LING...
...THE THREE NIGHTS AND FOUR DAY RETREAT BEGAN.
RIGHT ON!
YEP!
FOLLOWING THE TRAINING SCHEDULE ESTABLISHED BY COACH MATSUSHITA, WE WERE DIVIDED INTO SEPARATE PRACTICE GROUPS.
HE WATCHED AS WE PRACTICED AND POINTED OUT EACH OF OUR PROBLEMS.
RESOLVING THESE PROBLEMS WAS OUR MAJOR OBJECTIVE.
ON DAY ONE, THE TRAINING STARTED AFTER CLASS. I FELT LIKE IT ENDED IN NO TIME.
MEMAKING ROOM
DINNER'S READY, EVERY- ONE!

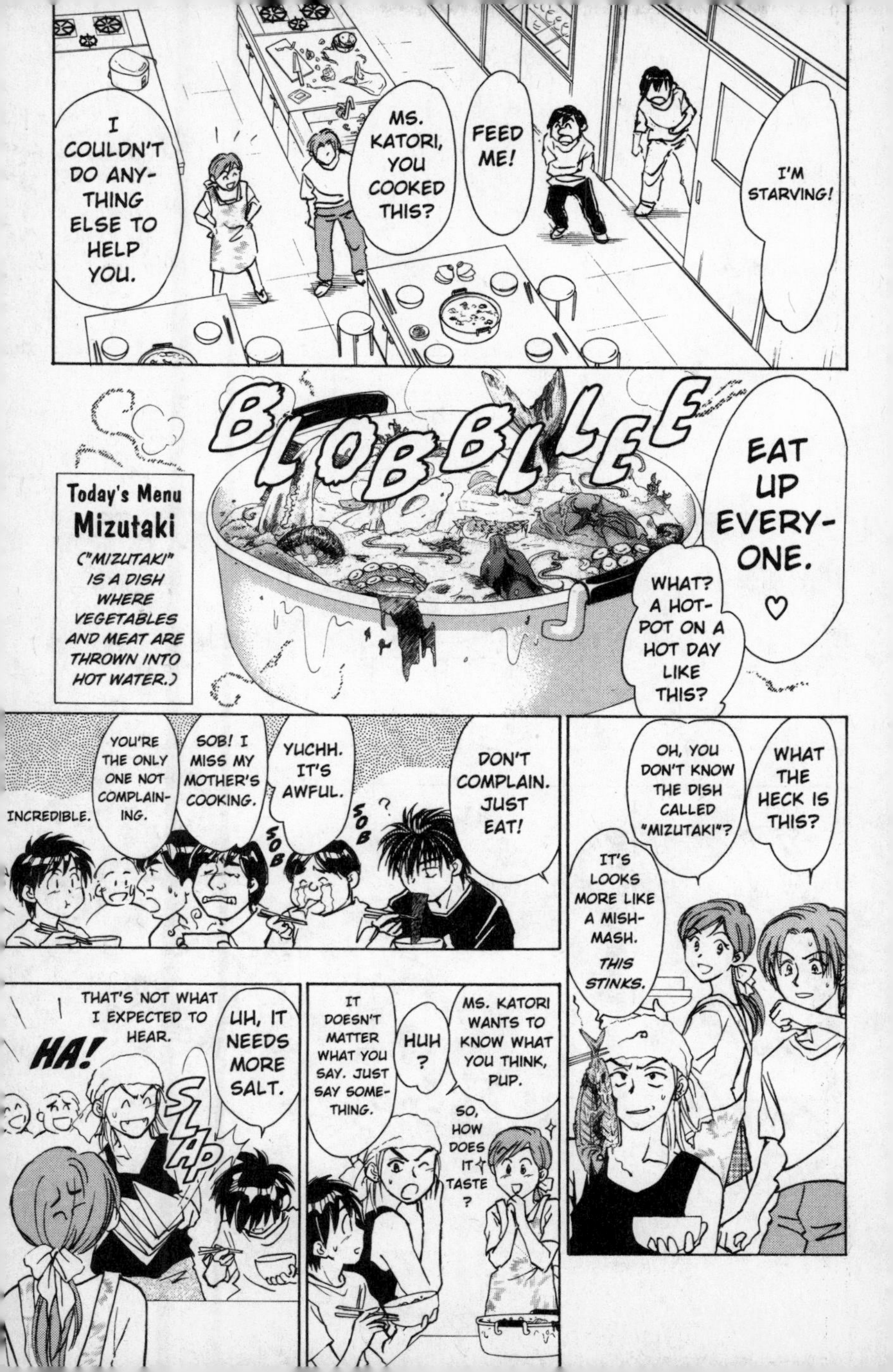
I'M STARVING!
FEED ME!
MS. KATORI, YOU COOKED THIS?
I COULDN'T DO ANY-THING ELSE TO HELP YOU.
EAT UP EVERY-ONE. ♡
WHAT? A HOT-POT ON A HOT DAY LIKE THIS?
BLOBBLLEE
Today's Menu
Mizutaki
("MIZUTAKI" IS A DISH WHERE VEGETABLES AND MEAT ARE THROWN INTO HOT WATER.)
WHAT THE HECK IS THIS?
OH, YOU DON'T KNOW THE DISH CALLED "MIZUTAKI"?
IT'S LOOKS MORE LIKE A MISH-MASH.
THIS STINKS.
DON'T COMPLAIN. JUST EAT!
SOB SOB
?
YUCHH. IT'S AWFUL.
SOB! I MISS MY MOTHER'S COOKING.
YOU'RE THE ONLY ONE NOT COMPLAIN-ING.
INCREDIBLE.
MS. KATORI WANTS TO KNOW WHAT YOU THINK, PUP.
HUH?
IT DOESN'T MATTER WHAT YOU SAY. JUST SAY SOME-THING.
SO, HOW DOES IT TASTE?
UH, IT NEEDS MORE SALT.
THAT'S NOT WHAT I EXPECTED TO HEAR.
HA!
SLAP

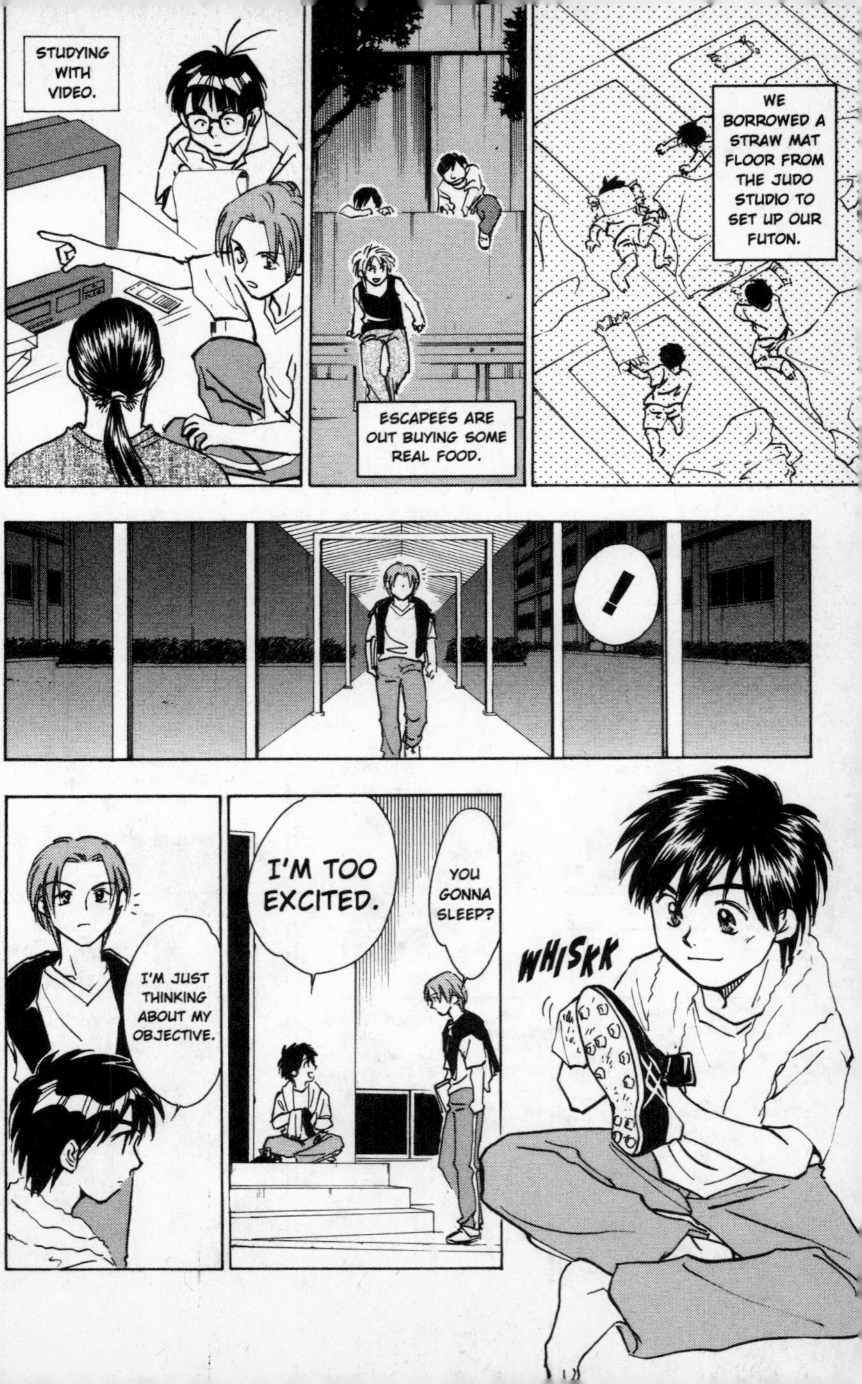
WE BORROWED A STRAW MAT FLOOR FROM THE JUDO STUDIO TO SET UP OUR FUTON.
ESCAPEES ARE OUT BUYING SOME REAL FOOD.
STUDYING WITH VIDEO.
!
WHISKK
YOU GONNA SLEEP?
I'M TOO EXCITED.
I'M JUST THINKING ABOUT MY OBJECTIVE.

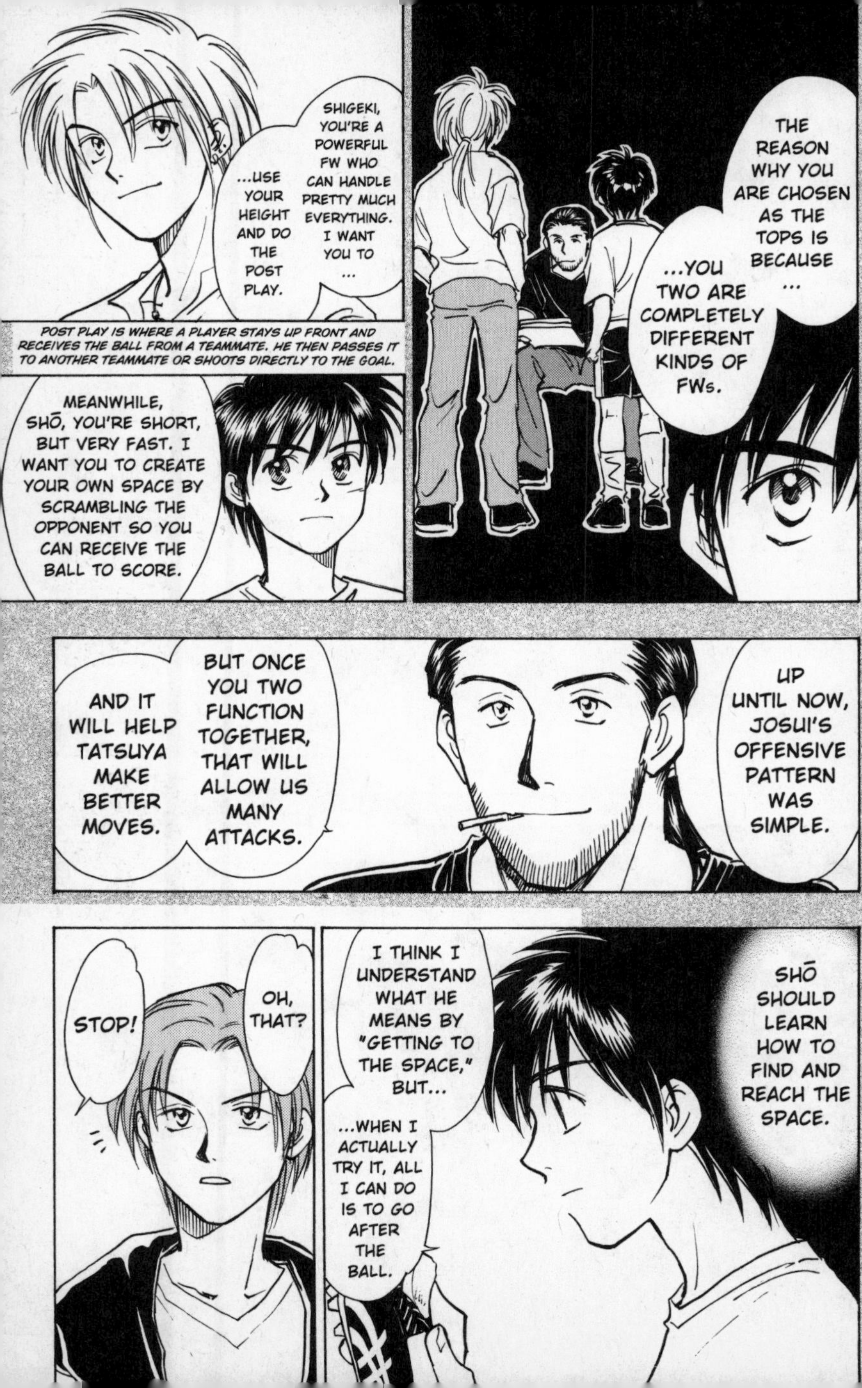
THE REASON WHY YOU ARE CHOSEN AS THE TOPS IS BECAUSE ...
...YOU TWO ARE COMPLETELY DIFFERENT KINDS OF FWs.
SHIGEKI, YOU'RE A POWERFUL FW WHO CAN HANDLE PRETTY MUCH EVERYTHING. I WANT YOU TO ...
...USE YOUR HEIGHT AND DO THE POST PLAY.
POST PLAY IS WHERE A PLAYER STAYS UP FRONT AND RECEIVES THE BALL FROM A TEAMMATE. HE THEN PASSES IT TO ANOTHER TEAMMATE OR SHOOTS DIRECTLY TO THE GOAL.
MEANWHILE, SHŌ, YOU'RE SHORT, BUT VERY FAST. I WANT YOU TO CREATE YOUR OWN SPACE BY SCRAMBLING THE OPPONENT SO YOU CAN RECEIVE THE BALL TO SCORE.
UP UNTIL NOW, JOSUI'S OFFENSIVE PATTERN WAS SIMPLE.
BUT ONCE YOU TWO FUNCTION TOGETHER, THAT WILL ALLOW US MANY ATTACKS.
AND IT WILL HELP TATSUYA MAKE BETTER MOVES.
SHŌ SHOULD LEARN HOW TO FIND AND REACH THE SPACE.
I THINK I UNDERSTAND WHAT HE MEANS BY "GETTING TO THE SPACE," BUT...
...WHEN I ACTUALLY TRY IT, ALL I CAN DO IS TO GO AFTER THE BALL.
OH, THAT?
STOP!

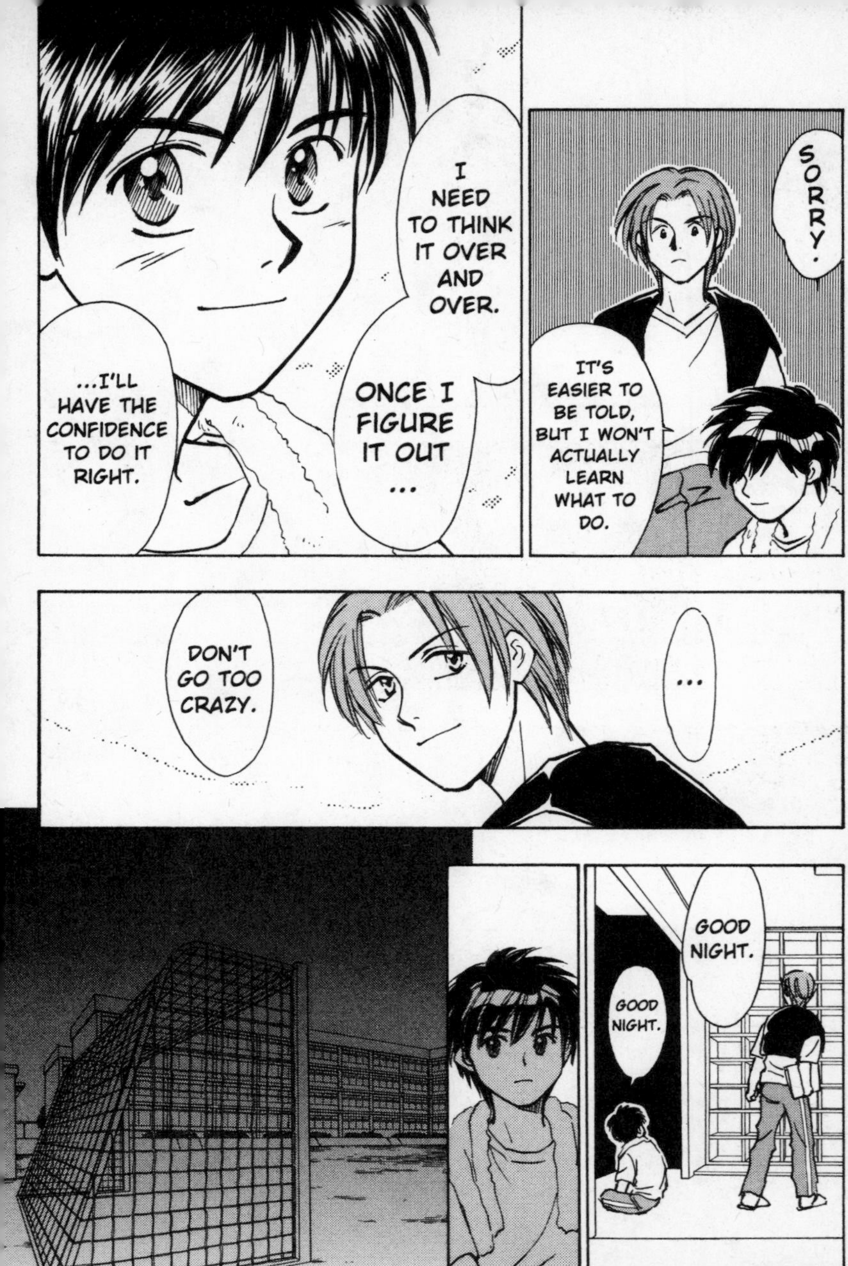
SORRY.
IT'S EASIER TO BE TOLD, BUT I WON'T ACTUALLY LEARN WHAT TO DO.
I NEED TO THINK IT OVER AND OVER.
ONCE I FIGURE IT OUT ...
...I'LL HAVE THE CONFIDENCE TO DO IT RIGHT.
...
DON'T GO TOO CRAZY.
GOOD NIGHT.
GOOD NIGHT.

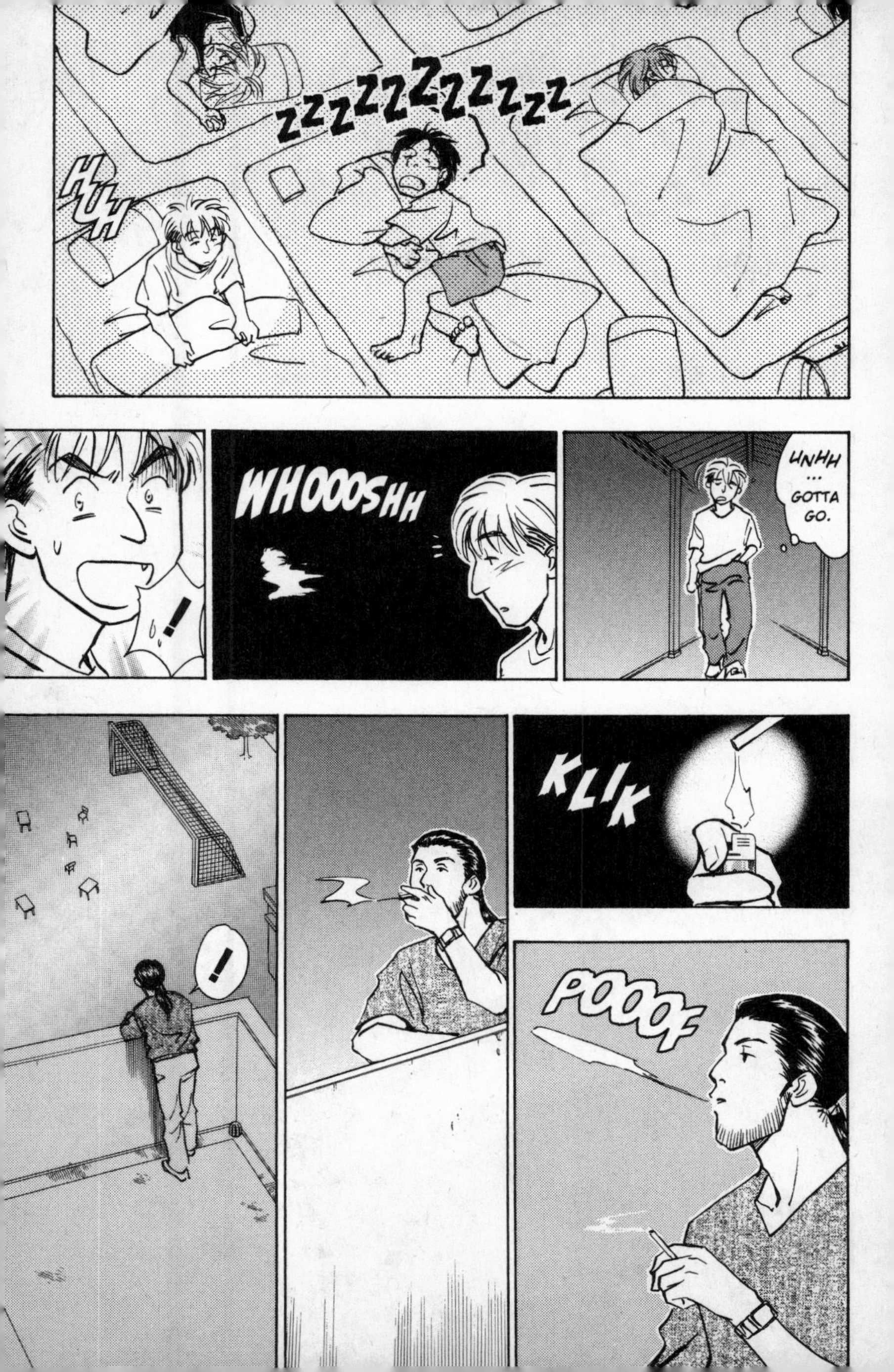
ZZZZZZZZZZZZ
HUH
UNHH ... GOTTA GO.
WHOOOSHH
!
KLIK
POOOF
!

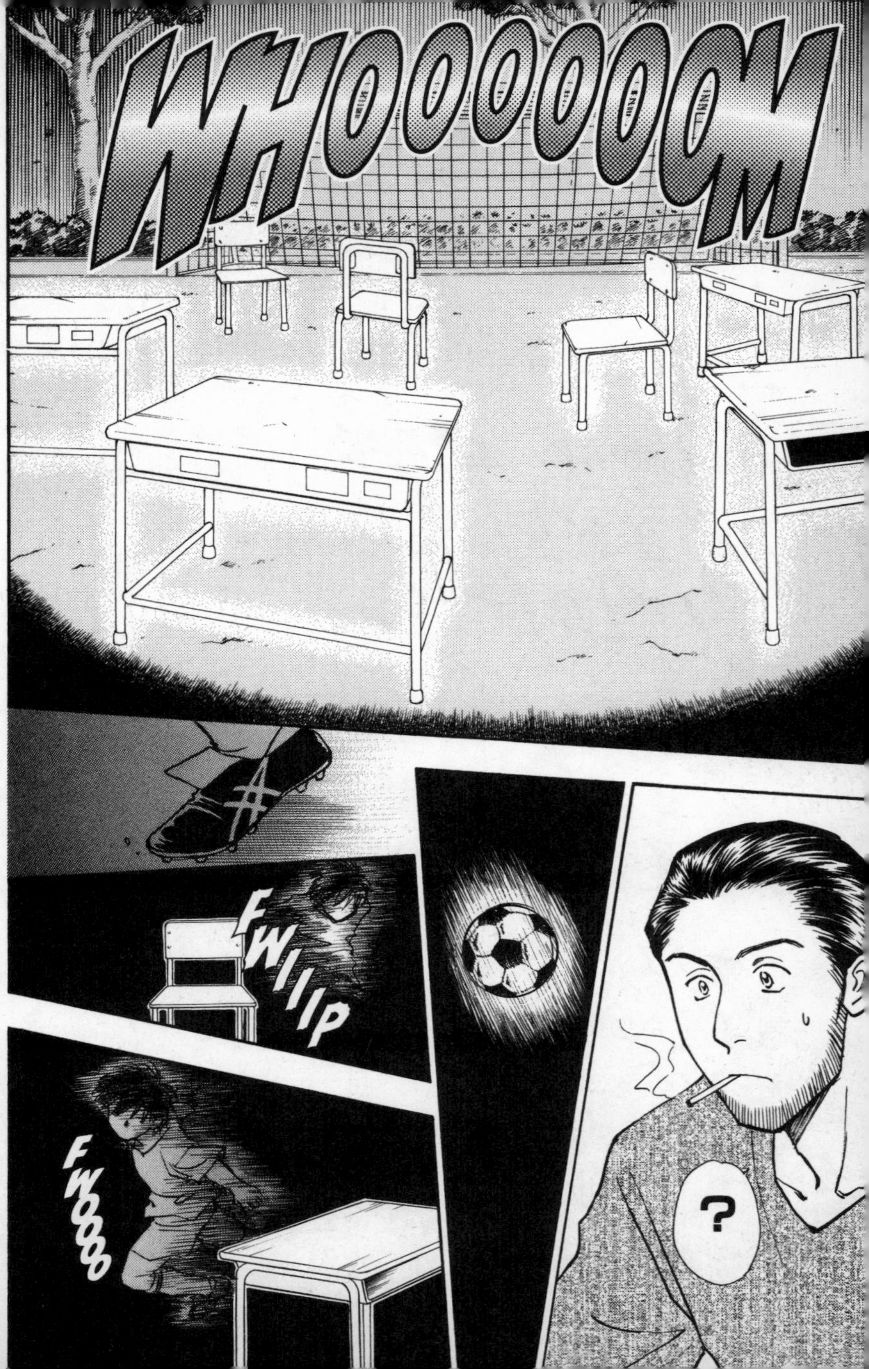
WHOOOOOOM
?
FWIIIP
FWOOOO

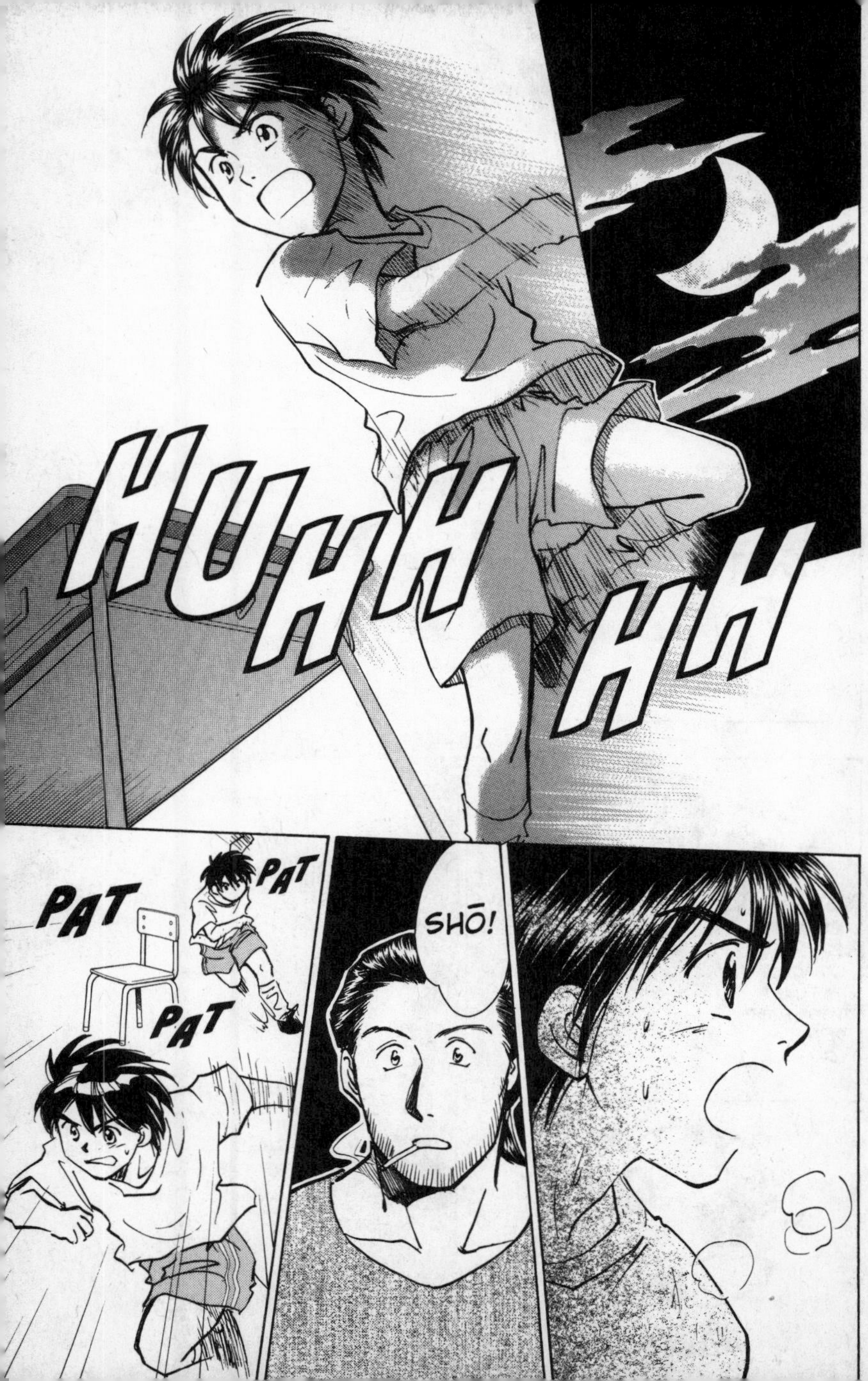
HUHH
HH
SHŌ!
PAT
PAT
PAT

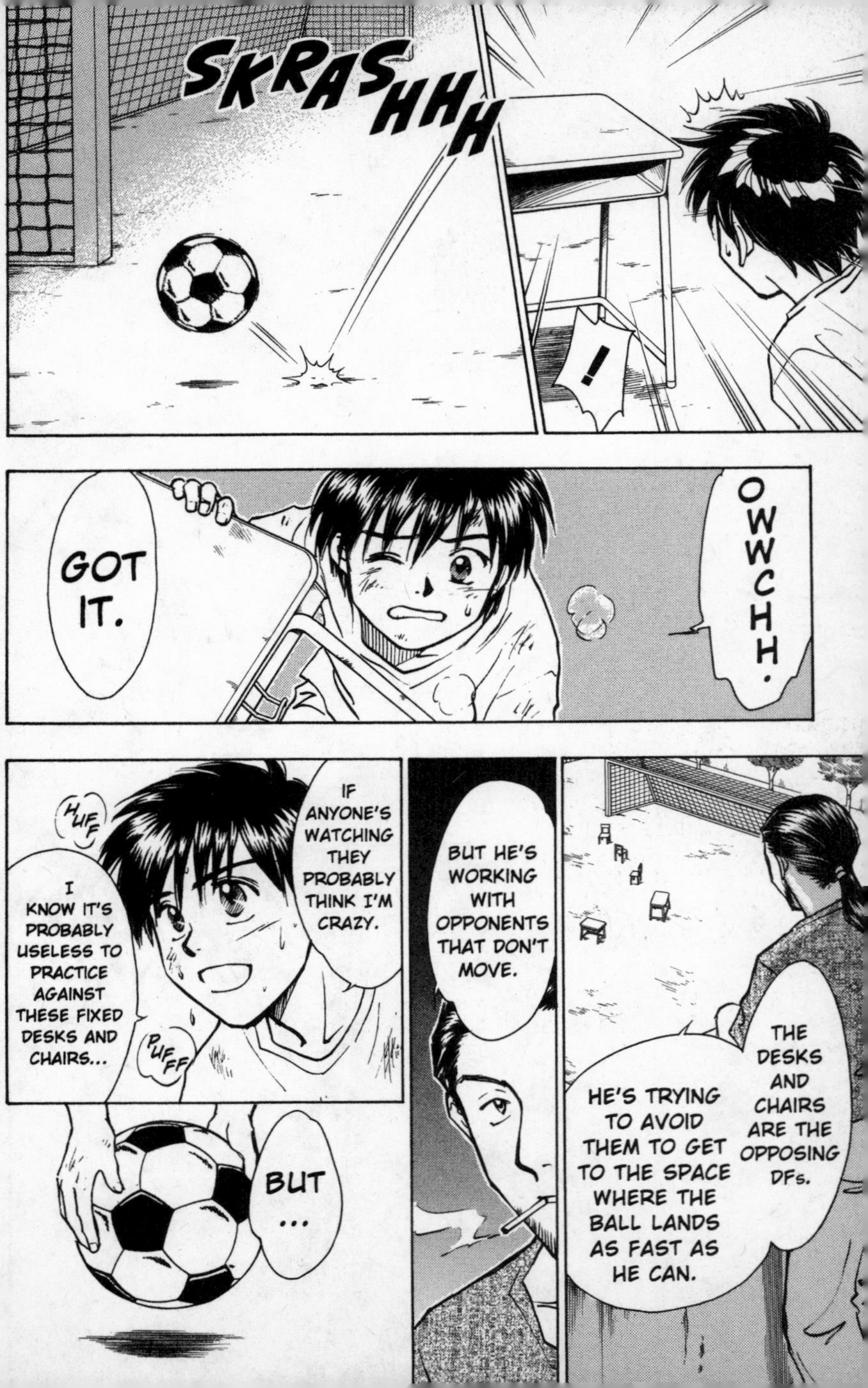
!
SKRASHHH
OWWCH.
GOT IT.
THE DESKS AND CHAIRS ARE THE OPPOSING DFs.
HE'S TRYING TO AVOID THEM TO GET TO THE SPACE WHERE THE BALL LANDS AS FAST AS HE CAN.
BUT HE'S WORKING WITH OPPONENTS THAT DON'T MOVE.
IF ANYONE'S WATCHING THEY PROBABLY THINK I'M CRAZY.
HUFF
I KNOW IT'S PROBABLY USELESS TO PRACTICE AGAINST THESE FIXED DESKS AND CHAIRS...
PUFFF
BUT ...

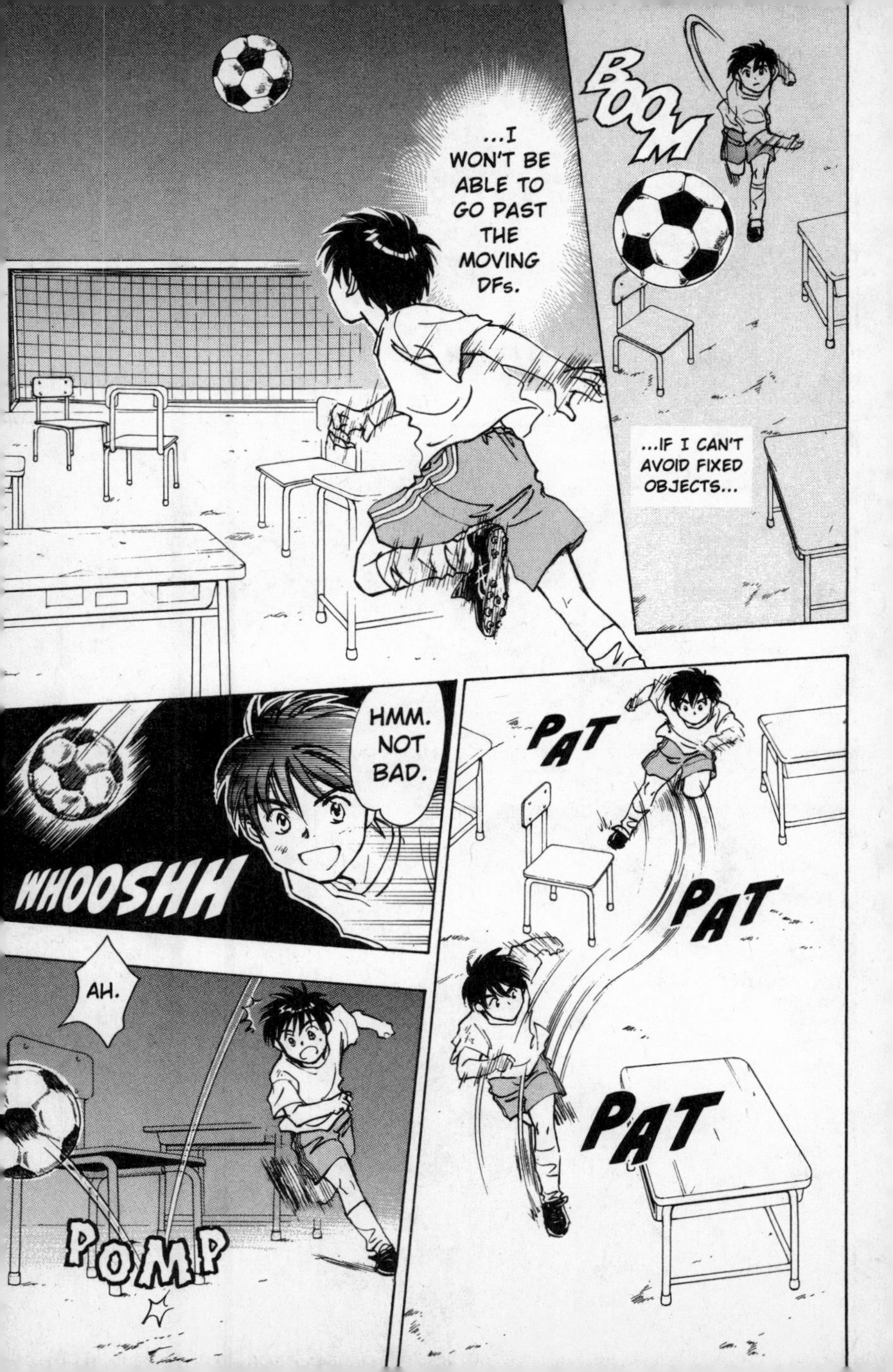
BOOM
...IF I CAN'T AVOID FIXED OBJECTS...
...I WON'T BE ABLE TO GO PAST THE MOVING DFs.
PAT
PAT
PAT
HMM. NOT BAD.
WHOOSHH
AH.
POMP

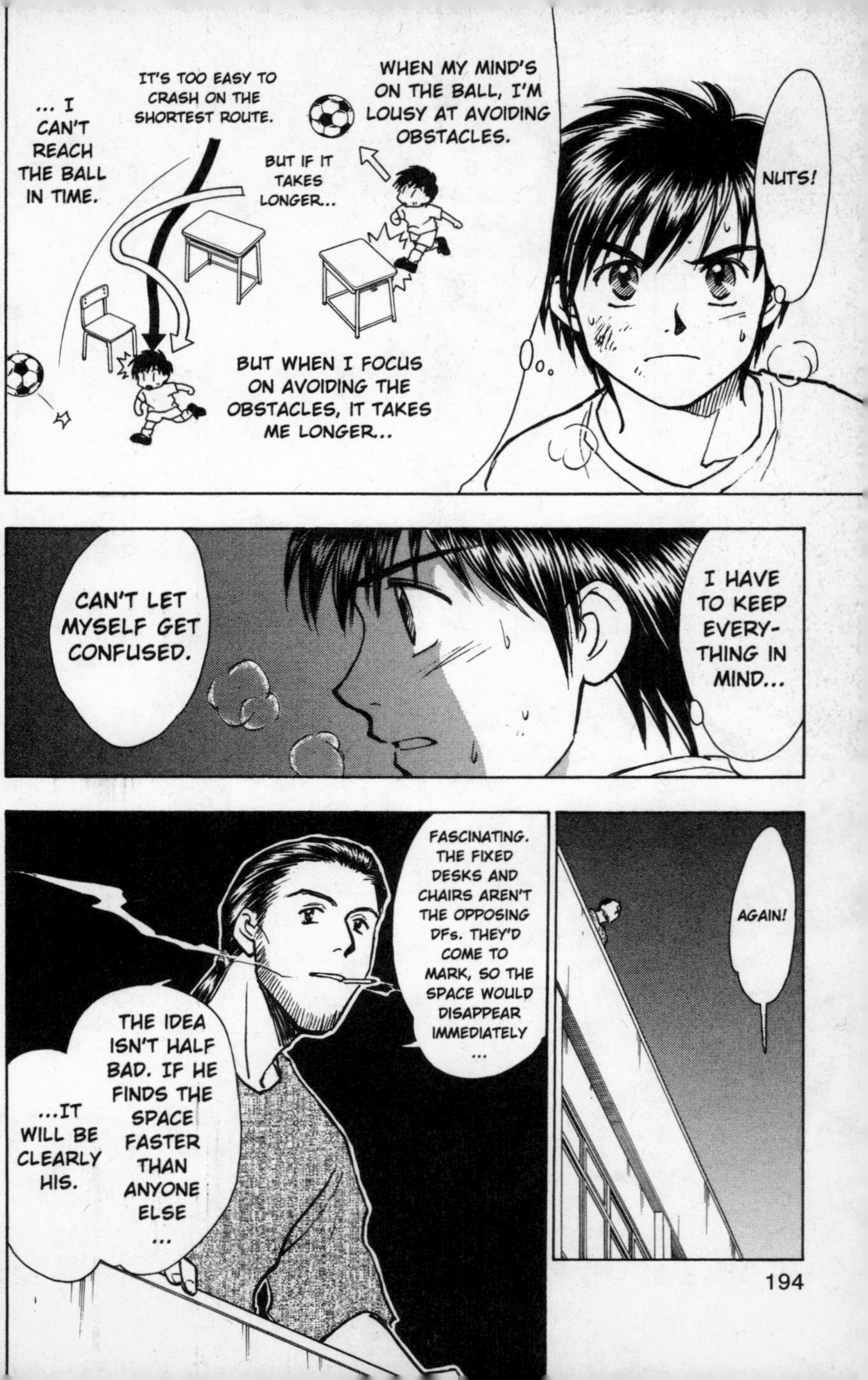
NUTS!
WHEN MY MIND'S ON THE BALL, I'M LOUSY AT AVOIDING OBSTACLES.
IT'S TOO EASY TO CRASH ON THE SHORTEST ROUTE.
BUT WHEN I FOCUS ON AVOIDING THE OBSTACLES, IT TAKES ME LONGER...
BUT IF IT TAKES LONGER...
... I CAN'T REACH THE BALL IN TIME.
I HAVE TO KEEP EVERY-THING IN MIND...
CAN'T LET MYSELF GET CONFUSED.
AGAIN!
FASCINATING. THE FIXED DESKS AND CHAIRS AREN'T THE OPPOSING DFs. THEY'D COME TO MARK, SO THE SPACE WOULD DISAPPEAR IMMEDIATELY ...
THE IDEA ISN'T HALF BAD. IF HE FINDS THE SPACE FASTER THAN ANYONE ELSE ...
...IT WILL BE CLEARLY HIS.

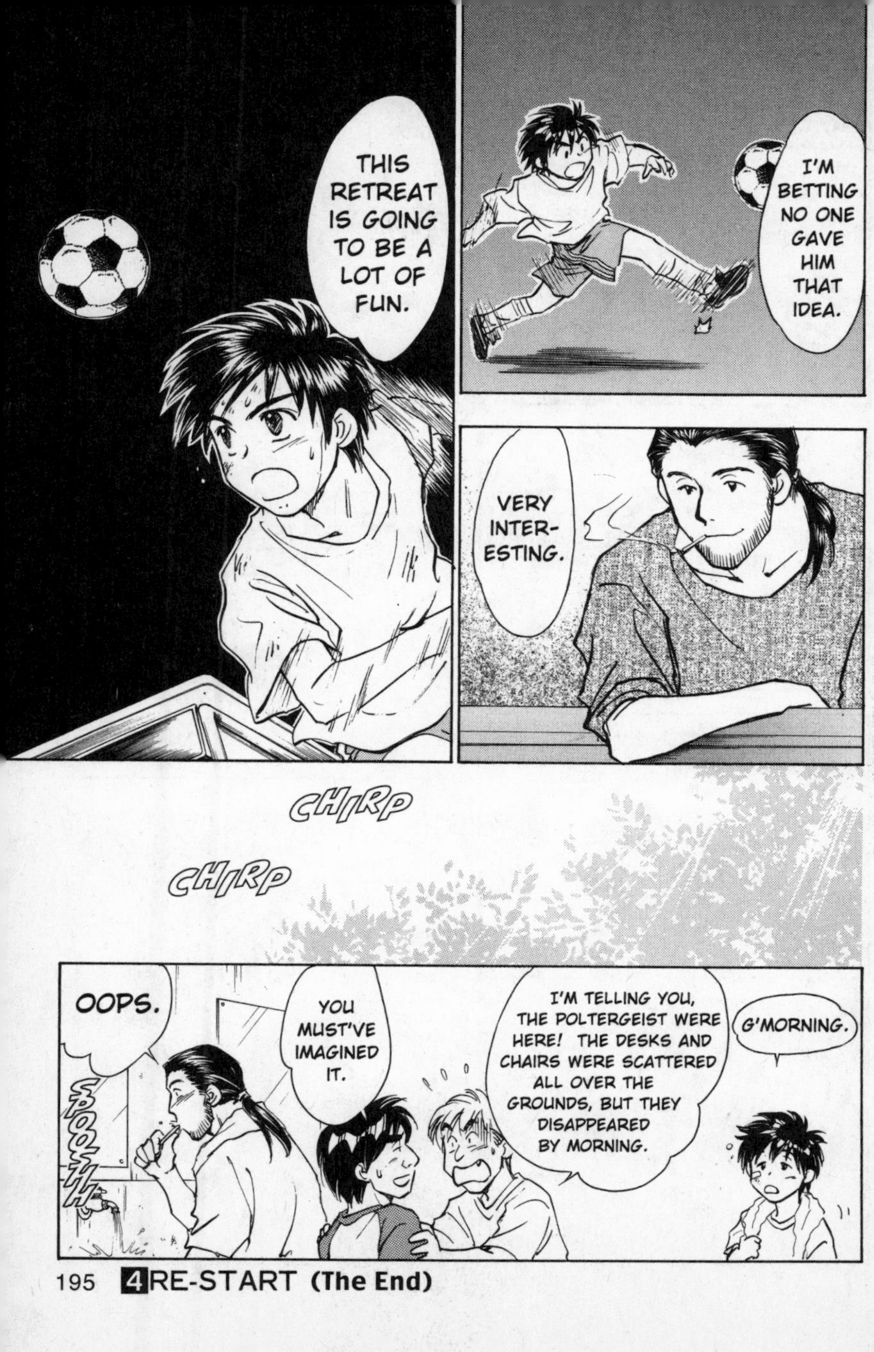
I'M BETTING NO ONE GAVE HIM THAT IDEA.
VERY INTER-ESTING.
THIS RETREAT IS GOING TO BE A LOT OF FUN.
CHIRP
CHIRP
G'MORNING.
I'M TELLING YOU, THE POLTERGEIST WERE HERE! THE DESKS AND CHAIRS WERE SCATTERED ALL OVER THE GROUNDS, BUT THEY DISAPPEARED BY MORNING.
YOU MUST'VE IMAGINED IT.
OOPS.
SPOOSHH

# SMALL WHISTLE! THEATRE!!

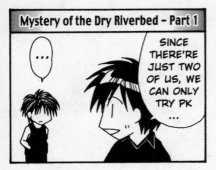

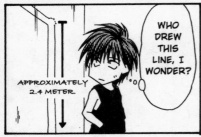

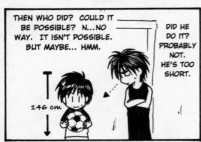

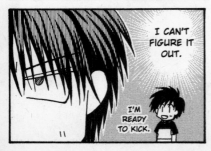

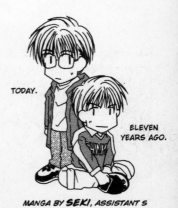

ELEVEN YEARS AGO.
TODAY.

MANGA BY **SEKI**, ASSISTANT S

## Mystery of the Dry Riverbed – Part 1

SINCE THERE'RE JUST TWO OF US, WE CAN ONLY TRY PK ...
...
WHO DREW THIS LINE, I WONDER?
APPROXIMATELY 2.4 METER.
DID HE DO IT? PROBABLY NOT. HE'S TOO SHORT.
THEN WHO DID? COULD IT BE POSSIBLE? N...NO WAY. IT ISN'T POSSIBLE. BUT MAYBE... HMM.
146 cm
I CAN'T FIGURE IT OUT.
I'M READY TO KICK.

## Mysterious Man

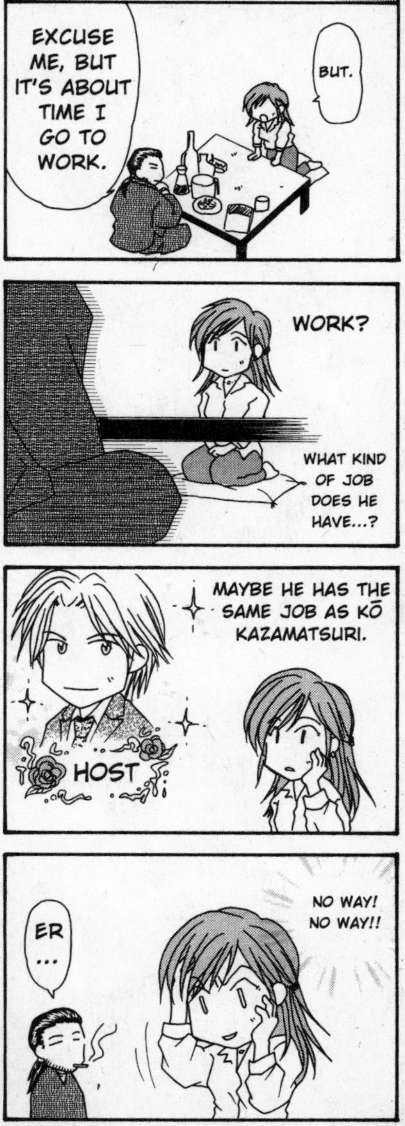
BUT.
EXCUSE ME, BUT IT'S ABOUT TIME I GO TO WORK.
WORK?
WHAT KIND OF JOB DOES HE HAVE...?
MAYBE HE HAS THE SAME JOB AS KŌ KAZAMATSURI.
HOST
NO WAY! NO WAY!!
ER ...

## Mystery of the Dry Riverbed - Part 2

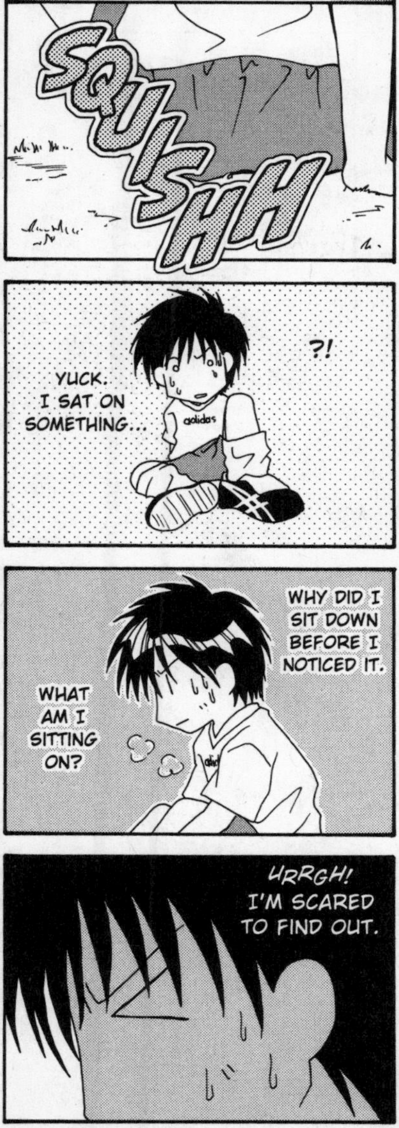
SQUISHH
?!
YUCK: I SAT ON SOMETHING...
WHY DID I SIT DOWN BEFORE I NOTICED IT.
WHAT AM I SITTING ON?
URRGH! I'M SCARED TO FIND OUT.

# DAISUKE NOTE

DAICHI
FUWA

| PERSONAL DATA | |
|---|---|
| BIRTHDAY: | DEC. 31, 1984 |
| SIZE: | 174 cm   60 kg |
| BLOOD TYPE: | AB |
| FAVORITE FOOD: | DOESN'T KNOW |
| WHAT HE DISLIKES: | ANYTHING THAT CANNOT BE EXPLAINED SCIENTIFICALLY |
| HOBBY AND SPECIAL SKILLS: | ACTIVITY OF DESTRUCTION |

YUKI
KOJIMA

| PERSONAL DATA | |
|---|---|
| BIRTHDAY: | APRIL 1st, 1985 |
| SIZE: | 155 cm   41 kg |
| BLOOD TYPE: | B |
| FAVORITE FOOD: | SHRIMP |
| WHAT SHE DISLIKES: | SILLY BRAIN-DEAD GIRLS |
| HOBBY AND SPECIAL SKILLS: | SOCCER, DRIBBLE |

| PERSONAL DATA | |
|---|---|
| BIRTHDAY: | OCT. 24th, 1961 |
| SIZE: | 182 cm 73 kg |
| BLOOD TYPE: | O |
| FAVORITE FOOD: | SOY MILK, ODEN |
| WHAT HE DISLIKES: | BUTTERFLIES |
| HOBBY AND SPECIAL SKILLS: | CROSSWORD PUZZLES, BEING SARCASTIC |

SOUJŪ MATSUSHITA

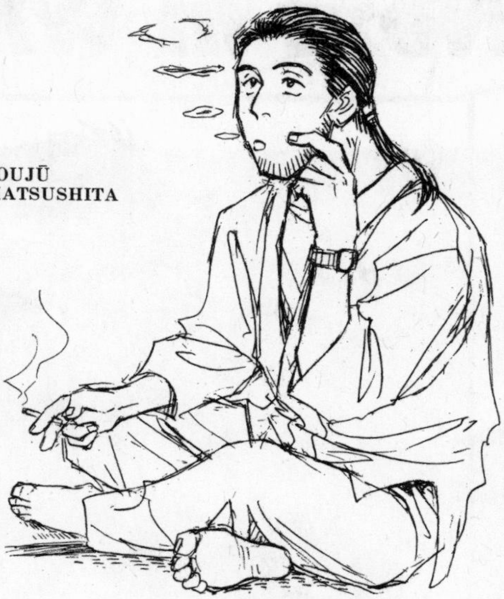

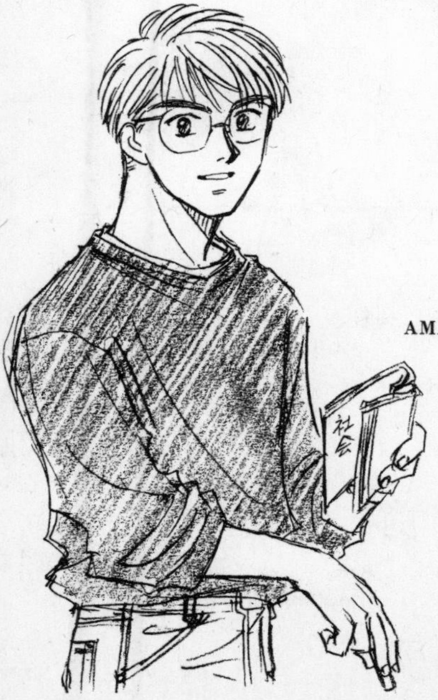
社会

TŌGO AMAMIYA

| PERSONAL DATA | |
|---|---|
| BIRTHDAY: | NOV. 7, 1969 |
| SIZE: | 177 cm 69 kg |
| BLOOD TYPE: | AB |
| FAVORITE FOOD: | KINPIRA RICE BURGER AT MOSS BURGER |
| WHAT HE DISLIKES: | EEL |
| HOBBY AND SPECIAL SKILLS: | KARAOKE, MAKING A DELICIOUS CUP OF COFFEE |

# PURE SOUL

Soccer is a team sport and that means Shô must work twice as hard to be the best teammate he can be. No matter how hard (and long) he practices, he still needs the support of 10 other players to score a single goal.

One player, however, has vowed to single-handedly crush the upstarts at Josui Junior High. His name is Ryoichi Tenjo and he is easily the best soccer player Shô has ever seen. Nobody has been able to stop Ryoichi in the past. Now, it's up to Team Josui to teach the hotheaded harrier a lesson in humility.

## *Available Now!*